CONSUMER EXPENDITURES

· CONSUMER ·

EXPENDITURES

NEW MEASURES
& OLD MOTIVES

Stanley Lebergott

PRINCETON UNIVERSITY PRESS

· PRINCETON, NEW JERSEY ·

Copyright © 1996 by Princeton University Press
Published by Princeton University Press, 41 William Street,
Princeton, New Jersey 08540
In the United Kingdom: Princeton University Press, Chichester, West Sussex

Library of Congress Cataloging-in-Publication Data

Lebergott, Stanley.
Consumer expenditures : new measures and old motives / Stanley
Lebergott.
p.   cm.
Includes bibliographical references and index.
ISBN 0-691-04321-3 (cloth : alk. paper)
1. Consumption (Economics)—United States—History—20th century.
I. Title.
HC110.C6L392   1996
339.4'7'0973–dc20   95-2852

This book has been composed in Palatino typeface

Princeton University Press books are printed on acid-free paper
and meet the guidelines for permanence and durability of the
Committee on Production Guidelines for Book Longevity of the
Council on Library Resources

Printed in the United States of America by Princeton Academic Press

1 3 5 7 9 10 8 6 4 2

For R.W.L.

"Whose love indulg'd my labours past,
Matures my present, and shall bound my last!"
—Alexander Pope

I do not wish for fortune more than sufficient
for my wants—my natural wants, and the
artificial ones which habit has rendered
nearly as importunate as the other.
—JANE WELSH CARLYLE

Our people, abundantly schooled and newspapered,
abundantly housed, fed, clothed, salaried and taxed.
—HENRY JAMES

· C O N T E N T S ·

· LIST OF TABLES ·

· P R E F A C E ·

SANTAYANA wryly noted a "want of rationality and measure in the human will, that has not learned to prize small betterments and finite but real goods."[1] This study reports on American consumption of such goods and services since 1900. Some were life-saving, of course. Others were essential. But most were, indeed, "small betterments and finite but real goods."

Chapters 1–8 grew out of reflections on the extensive new data developed in Appendixes A and B.

Chapter 1 contrasts the use of consumption rather than income to assess economic well-being. Hundreds of laws and thousands of articles do rely on money income as a measure. But most Americans dimension their economic well-being by their consumption, not their income. After all, how much "well-being" do they derive from money income handed to the tax collector? (Often via withheld taxes, without even seeing the income taken away.) The briefest review of the world since the income tax was put in place reveals how American millionaires (first), and trade union members and domestics (somewhat later), learned how to collect nontaxable consumption rather than taxable income.

Leaders of communist nations made that same discovery. It is consumption, not income, that reflects the flow of services humans seek from goods they buy. (Chapter 5 compares the ratio to average family consumption—for American millionaires with that for leaders of the Soviet Union.) The difference may help explain some of the speed, and bitterness, with which the Soviet system collapsed.

Chapters 2, 3, and 4 utilize the new data to assess mass consumption this century, to reassess some widely held views on the 1920s and 1930s. Was prosperity in the 1920s doomed because of a "flawed" consumer spending base, as leading historians seem to agree? Was the precipitous 1929–30 fall in consumption as decisive in creating the lengthy Depression of the 1930s as leading economists have held?

Chapter 6 examines the doubtful meaning of "the consumption function," so ubiquitous in modern economics.

Chapter 7 proposes a wider view of the forces shaping consumption than econometric studies commonly achieve. For those studies have been constrained by the limitations of consumer budget surveys (discussed in Chapter 9). Few factors beyond price and income appear in most empirically oriented models of the complex world of consumer expenditure. We propose a way to add some forces now hidden in that black box, "consumer tastes." Chapter 8 offers some initial views based on our new data by state.

Part C derives several hundred new series for PCE components annually 1900–1929. These are directly comparable with the official BEA series as revised in 1993, in both current and constant prices. Similarly detailed, and new, series by state are also estimated for key dates 1900–1982. Both sets appear in the Appendixes. Chapters 9 and 10 outline how the new series were estimated. Chapter 11 reviews the validity of existing time series and budget survey data.

The basic U.S. estimates were completed in 1980 with grants SOC-7726362 and BNS-7622943 from the National Science Foundation, herewith gratefully acknowledged. After that preliminary set was submitted to NSF, several years of support by Wesleyan University facilitated their revision, adjustment to successively revised BEA benchmarks, and development of the state estimates in Appendix B.

Revising more than 25,000 estimates over a decade, repeatedly adjusting them to new BEA benchmarks and index bases, as well as editing them by extensive computer regressions, was a long task. It benefited from sterling work by a succession of students whom it is a delight to recall—Diana Farrell, Rose Gower, Suhwon Hwang, Mark Kiefer, Karen Kilby, Andrew Leighton, Alan Mairson, Cheng Ong, David Rubin, Aaron Siskind, Leslie Sundt, Jeffrey Young, and Nadja Zalokar. Opportunities handsomely provided by the Center for Advanced Study in the Behavioral Sciences made possible a draft of the initial chapters.

From Edward Denison, Charles Schwarz, and George Jaszi to Gerald Donahoe and Greg Key the skilled staff of the Bureau of Economic Analysis has been unfailingly helpful. Joan Halberg surely established a world record of competence and good cheer when creating draft after draft, including immense tables, in the era before personal computers and printers. Fran Warren held to that same high standard when preparing the final draft. Joan Jurale, Chief Reference Librarian of Wesleyan, and Steven Lebergott, head of Inter Library Loan, helped locate a sequence of indispensable references. Together these many creative people made this book a more than ordinarily cooperative product. Lastly, the text has benefited by suggestions from Professors Stanley Engerman, Richard Grossman, and David Selover.

· P A R T   O N E ·

· C H A P T E R   1 ·

MEASURES OF WELL-BEING: INCOME
VERSUS CONSUMPTION

Pleasure in the course of evolution has become
throned among grosser subject energies.
— F. Y. Edgeworth, *Mathematical Psychics*

WHO KNOWS how large an income Louis XIV enjoyed? Or Midas? Or
Montezuma? Or any dominant figure before capitalism arrived?
Who knew Gorbachev's income? Deng's? Castro's? Or any domi-
nant figure under communism?

The exceptional role of money income developed in recent centuries. That change accompanied an economic advance in capitalist
markets, at a political price. Communist and authoritarian regimes,
however, minimized that price, skillfully and shrewdly.

I

Among its singular triumphs finance capitalism may well count the
widespread acceptance of two propositions. One, that money income measures "economic welfare"—exactly. Two, that money defines how much "well-being" any job yields. Even astute and sensi-
tive scholars evaluate Economic Inequality simply in terms of
"income rewards."[1] Legislators and the media (have been persuaded)
that money income, even before taxes, measures economic "well-being." (It is the only measure used in a trio of technically adroit papers
by leading economists at a recent AEA session on "How the Rich Have
Fared, 1973–87," on "Deficit Reduction and Income Redistribution,"
and on "Inequality . . . in Ten Modern Nations . . . ")[2]

Nonmonetary income characterized precapitalist modes of production. Feudal lords exacted services and goods in kind. So did
slave owners. Peasant incomes also came in kind—food, housing,
scraps of clothing. Churchmen and monks lived on tithes and gifts
of food and services. So did artists, and peripatetic philosophers.

Capitalism, however, monetized incomes. Consumption ceased to be decided by one's heritage, noble or slave. Because income now came in monetary form it could be more readily spent in many ways. These permitted multiple choices. Workers and peasants began to range through markets, buying goods and services once restricted to blue bloods or Brahmins. (Indeed, the speed with which the lower middle classes adopted High Fashion troubled critics as early as Moliere, as recent as Hirsch.)

This all afforded new freedoms to workers, and advanced their real income. But it created a distinct threat. All participants could now be labeled by a single, simple number—their money income. There is, however, an "uncompromising objectivity" about a dollar sum (in Simmel's words).[3] Its objectivity seems to permit simple comparison between the "welfare" of individuals. Those opposed to capitalism saw that money income figures readily demonstrated how rich the capitalists were, and how poor the workers. Money income became a succinct measure of potential "well-being," even of "happiness."

"The rich" have long been widely disliked. Not because they consumed much of the national output. If anything, the prudent and charitable rich (e.g., J. D. Rockefeller) were disliked even more than "Coal Oil Johnnies" who lit cigars with $100 bills. The simple fact of riches was central. Money income figures demonstrated, and dimensioned, such riches.

II

Two significant changes flowed from that dislike. First, the role of nonmonetary income expanded. And second, the usefulness of relying on money income distributions then eroded.

The changes developed differently in capitalist than noncapitalist nations. In capitalist nations dislike of the rich helped bring the income tax. U.S. income tax rates were initially low—so low that La Follette, the leading Senate radical, shocked his colleagues when he proposed a 10% marginal tax rate (on incomes over $100,000). His proposal collected only a handful of votes.[4] Time marched on. Under the New Deal the top rate was moved to 90%. When the Republicans swept into office in 1953, after two decades out of power, they triumphantly cut the 90% rate to 89%. (Only a quarter of a century later, when farmers and truck drivers discovered that they also were paying "high" marginal rates, was the top rate really cut.)

Not surprisingly, the rich reacted to decades of such rates. They substituted away from money income—to capital gains, stock options, and deferred compensation; to the company automobile, dining room, and fishing camp. Uniformed butlers served water to advertising executives on silver trays. A high official might even have a single peeled orange delivered to him daily, costing his firm $80,000 a year.[5] But matters did not end with such oddities, nor with the very rich.

Lower-income people too discovered how their income increases went to taxes. They too began to convert money to nonmonetary income. As Jimmy Hoffa remarked in 1963, his teamsters were "going home with $200 a week in their pockets, and it might be better to put most of an increase we negotiate into fringes instead of wages."[6] (For such fringes were not taxed.)

Fringe benefits to workers were not even 2% of wages by 1931. By 1979 they had reached 20%.[7] As tax rates rose fringes rose. An increasing share of national output then began to flow to middle-income families in nontaxable form. It came as medical insurance, life insurance, in-plant cafeterias, sales meetings and business trips (to vacation spots in the U.S. and Europe), company bowling teams, cars for personal use, etc. Salaried employees became part-time insurance salesmen—charging off the family car as a business expense. Impecunious college teachers imitated pecunious lawyers. They pursued professional endeavors in fascinating places to which the less intellectual could also resort, but not with equal tax advantage. Serious students could gather in Newark or Gary. But how much more enticing to meet in New York or San Francisco.

The income tax created a lively industry devoted to tax avoidance. That is well known. Less well known is how it distorted the pattern of real income receipt. Direct consumption expanded at the expense of money income receipt. That outcome has been largely ignored by most of those who invoke Gini coefficients to measure "inequality."

III

Yet consumption is what counts for most people, not income. Pretax incomes may once have created joyous money illusions. But no more. How many aesthetes such as Charles Chaplin and Ingmar Bergman emigrated to nations with income taxes lower than the country where they made their money?[8] Leading singers, just as tax lawyers, understand how consumption differs from money income "before taxes."

Leading entertainers understood as well as tax lawyers how direct consumption can be superior to money income before tax. One got Paramount to pay for "$600,000 or so in the salaries and living expenses of a half dozen relatives and cronies, a valet, a personal trainer, a 24-hour limousine and driver and a luxury motor home and driver, not to mention . . . a $253 tab at McDonald's." All while producing one movie.[9] One spectacular New York Yankees star had a contract that required that $100,000 a year—not part of his taxable income—be paid by the team management to the David M. Winfield Foundation.[10]

Managers of New York's Port Authority relied on its own helicopter, and two pilots, to ferry them from JFK airport to Manhattan. At $979 an hour, plus the cost of standby time for the pilots, each trip cost over forty times what private charter firms charged for the same trip. Such trips were business expenses, not included in income before (or after) taxes, by the usual studies of income distribution.[11]

What about the poor? The BLS reports that those with incomes below $5,000 in 1984 consumed six times as much as their reported income permits. Their miserably low "income" only averaged one-fourth as much as that for the $5,000–$10,000 income group. Yet they somehow spent more on food. And clothing. And, alcohol, transportation, entertainment, insurance, and pensions.[12]

How did they manage to do so? Not by drawing down their assets. For low-income families had a mere $513 in financial assets (bank account, savings bonds, etc.).[13]

Income as reported by "the poor" fails to include the value of food stamps, medicare, housing subsidies, or illegal income. Official U.S. income and expenditure surveys assume everyone is completely law abiding. They therefore omit the billions earned from marijuana, heroin, and crack, as well as chop shops, prostitution, and other illegal activities. Nor do they allow for mere understatement. Reports for spending on goods and services, even by the lowest tenth, provide a more realistic view of their economic well-being than do their reported "incomes." To contrast the well-being of different groups requires study of their consumption rather more than the money income they report to federal agencies.

IV

Dislike of large, and measurable, money incomes brought its most spectacular result in noncapitalist nations. Leaders of such nations learned a basic survival lesson, which served them well for decades: what counts politically is money income. Not what is consumed in unobtrusive ways. Their leaders therefore took modest salaries. They collected the fruits of power and position in nonmonetized form, via what Amartya Sen calls "entitlement relations."[14] Workers and peasants were nonetheless plucked to benefit the elite.

Expenditures that flowed to leaders without their receiving money income, or at bargain rates, were richly varied. "Mr. Andrew" flew from Madison Avenue to Zaire "every two weeks for the last eight years . . . to cut the hair of President Mobutu Sese Seko."[15] In most Communist nations one significant perquisite was access to state controlled housing. Their housing tended to be superior in quality, lower in price, or both. As long ago as 1928 the Smolensk Party Committee mentioned housing to characterize the workers' mood: "You [Communists] can live well off. You have apartments but we live under bad conditions. Give us such apartments, or one like Maksim Gorky's."[16]

Data on Communist nations are hard to come by, but one Hungarian survey is suggestive. It reported that the proportion of high bureaucrats and professionals with high incomes was four times as great as that for unskilled workers. Nonetheless, 48% of the bureaucrats were given first-class state housing by the state, compared to 23% for unskilled workers. High-income bureaucrats often acquired other housing for less than unskilled workers.[17]

Describing what she saw of China after the Cultural Revolution, Nien Cheng wrote: "Though the salary of a member of the Politburo was no more than eight or ten times that of an industrial worker, the perks available to him without charge were comparable to those enjoyed by kings and presidents of other lands. And the privileges were extended to his family, including his grandchildren, even after his death."[18]

As a member of the elite Federation of Women she had access to an "internal shop" of the Shanghai Revolutionary Committee. Visiting it with a young friend, each staggered away with four loaded shopping bags. These included not expensive rarities, but items "from cashmere coat material to steel saucepans." Friends also asked her to "bring special food home from the restaurant," associated with another "internal shop."[19]

Consumption remains the simple goal of production in most nations, as Smith, Fisher, and Keynes declared. But noncapitalist elites consumed more efficiently than capitalists. For they largely cut out the intermediate stage of making money income. These Socialist classes had not turned to self-denial. Instead they created an Aladdin's lamp economy—at least for themselves. By not collecting high incomes they muted the dangerous malaise produced by the vision of high incomes. That single, brilliant, advance helped insulate them for decades from the ever-increasing dislike and envy that high money incomes create in capitalist nations. As late as 1992, an American academic could emphasize that inequality of (income distribution) was less in China than most of the world's nations.[20] Thus, even after the events of 1989, the widely reported desire for socialism "with a human face" and "true equality" still reflected a strong desire for income equality. Communism's elegant simplification of the effort-income-consumption sequence may still forecast the future economy.

· C H A P T E R   2 ·

WAS THE GREAT DEPRESSION
DRIVEN BY CONSUMPTION?

THE UNPRECEDENTED SEVERITY of the Great Depression has generated a host of explanations, many of which emphasize consumption. Some point vaguely to the "exhaustion of consumer purchasing power" in the 1920s, to a mechanism that drove savings up and wages down (cf. chapter 3). Among the newer analyses, Temin emphasizes the greater decline of aggregate consumption in 1929–30 than 1920–21.[1] His thoughtful "spending hypothesis" provides an opportunity to reconsider the role of consumption.

Instead of looking merely at the single aggregate for total consumption we have developed data for approximately one hundred separate components of total consumer expenditure. And rather than merely comparing the 1929–30 decline with 1920–21 we contrast it with experience in the twentieth century's prior six recessions. That comparison removes the puzzle of the unusual severity of the 1929–30 decline, but displaces it to another year.

Prior studies of the Great Depression have emphasized the severity of consumption decline, but ignored its breadth. Both, of course, should be considered. A given change in total consumption is consistent with vastly different changes in its components. If many items change, rather than a few, however, the macro consequences will differ. The wider the decline across consumer goods industries, the wider the havoc wreaked in those industries that supply investment goods, and materials inputs.

I

What helped make the depression great were four interrelated changes in consumer expenditure. They converted a garden-variety market crash into The Great Depression. Only the first of these has received much attention so far.

1. Aggregate consumption declined. Items that accounted for 91%

of 1929 PCE declined by 1930.[2] The fall in the aggregate was not, as Temin asserts, about as severe as the decline in 1921. It was in fact milder: 10%, rather than 17%. (Our numbers differ chiefly because we utilize our new, detailed data for thirty-nine service items, rather than the usual two, and for dozens of detailed goods series rather than only three subtotals.)[3]

2. About as many individual sectors had declined by 4% or more (in real terms) 1929–30 as 1920–21: twenty-six categories versus twenty-four. (Table 2.5).[4] Massive declines of 20% or more were actually fewer in 1929–30 than 1921–22 (4 versus 8).

3. What decisively contrasts 1929–30 with earlier twentieth-century recessions, however, is that so few sectors gained. During every prior twentieth-century recession at least twenty-three sectors gained. In 1929–30 only seven did so (table 2.1). In every previous (twentieth-century) recession, sectors such as electricity, telephones, gas and oil, domestic service, private education, cleaning materials, and foreign travel all increased. Yet none of them rose in 1929–30.

Food gained by $2 billion 1926–27. In 1929–30 it fell by $900 million. Housing, which had risen by $1.9 billion 1926–27, fell by $470 million. Automobile sales had risen in three earlier recessions (1907–8, 1914–15, 1923–24). Clothing rose in 1907–8 and 1926–27. Both fell markedly in 1929–30.

4. At least as important in creating a decade of desolation was the

TABLE 2.1
Recession Years
Number of Consumption Sectors
Declining and Rising

	(Current Prices)		(Constant Prices)	
	Decline ≥ 4%	Rise	Decline ≥ 4%	Rise
1907–8	17	30	15	27
1913–14	15	38	12	24
1920–21	35	23	23	20
1923–24	9	44	7	36
1926–27	10	41	5	39
1929–30	39	7	26	12
1937–38	23	14	19	16
1948–49	13	33	8	28
1953–54	8	42	6	33
1957–58	8	46	6	29
1973–74	5	52	13	23

Source: Tables 2.4, 2.5.

TABLE 2.2
Post-Recession Years
Number of Sectors Declining and Rising

	(Current Prices)		(Constant Prices)	
	Decline	Rise	Decline	Rise
	≥ 4%		≥ 4%	
1908–9	0	51	0	45
1914–15	10	39	12	27
1921–22	6	51	3	42
1924–25	3	54	4	37
1927–28	4	46	2	40
1930–31	48	3	22	16
1938–39	3	53	3	44
1949–50	2	55	2	40
1954–55	2	53	3	40
1958–59	18	36	4	42
1974–75	4	55	6	27

Source: Tables 2.4, 2.5.

failure of consumption to recover in the immediate post-recession year, 1930–31. Table 2.2 shows that spending on forty-eight PCE items declined 1930–31. In earlier recessions, however, fewer than ten items declined during the first post-recession year. (And no more than eighteen in recessions between 1938 and 1974.) This extraordinary contrast appears in the constant dollar data as well.

The Great Depression was no stock market drama in October 1929 followed by a production collapse in 1929–30. Indeed, the 1929–30 fall in prices, production, and employment differed surprisingly little from the fall in 1920–21, or prior twentieth-century recessions. A major difference was that the decline continued into 1930–31. Recovery in earlier recessions had occurred, sector after sector, in the year following the break. In 1930 the economy waited for Godot, who failed to appear.

II

In sum, the 1929–30 decline in total consumer spending, though severe, does not stand out among twentieth-century recessions. Two other phenomena do.

One was the paucity of expenditure categories that rose amid the overall decline.

The other, perhaps even more important, was the width of the continuing decline the year after the crash. The contrast with past and prior recessions is indeed, extraordinary: forty-eight categories fell compared to ten (or fewer) in earlier recessions.

Why the unprecedented lack of strong categories in 1929–30? And why the even greater number of declines 1930–31? Such pervasive results had to have had a pervasive cause, or causes. It will not suffice to point to one or two expenditure categories, as usually done. The overbuilding of apartment houses, the speculative boom in Florida real estate have been emphasized—which did slow imputed rents. The UK's naval mutiny and its departure from the gold standard, did affect foreign travel. Overproduction on Malaysian rubber estates and Brazilian plantations did reduce spending on auto tires and coffee by reducing prices. But these are mere examples, at best powerful local forces.

We suggest three broad factors, two demand and one supply, at work.

1. One demand factor was a consequence of the speed at which consumers raised their standard of living during the 1920s. Table 2.3 shows how unprecedented were worker (and therefore, consumer) real income gains during that decade.[5]

Between 1920 and 1929 real incomes rose far more swiftly than consumers had been accustomed to over the prior decades. Spending patterns had not become firmly oriented to such unprecedented increases in real income. Many relatively new goods had not yet become inelastic "needs." When incomes dropped in 1929–30 consumers therefore cut back spending on such new items more readily than in earlier recessions. Habit persistence had once buoyed real expenditure for item after item in the face of rising unemployment. In 1929–30 the situation differed: habits suited to the new high levels of income were not rigidly in place.

For it was the bulk of the population, not the unemployed, who created the spending collapse. Had the unemployed spent nothing at all in 1930, aggregate consumption would have fallen by a mere 6%. However, spending for many items—autos, tires, furniture,

TABLE 2.3
Annual Increase in
Earnings per Employee
(1914 dollars)

1900–09	$ 98
1910–19	102
1920–29	174

shoes, clothing, tobacco, china, wheel goods, etc.—fell far more than 6%. Over 90% of the total 1929–30 PCE decline represented spending cuts by families of employed workers. Many, if not most, had suffered no cut in real income. (Hours reduction for many was offset by retail price declines.) However, automobiles were still a luxury, as were radios. Central heating and electricity were either a novelty or a luxury for many. After all, two-thirds of the population had neither of these household conveniences two decades earlier.

The expenditure decline therefore reflected a downward adjustment from a spending level to which even employed consumers had not yet become habituated. It has long been recognized that excess demand for housing disappeared once the housing stock had reached its 1926 level. It has not been equally recognized that the stock of consumer habits as emphasized in, say, the Houthakker-Taylor state adjustment model, affected many other consumption items as well.[6] The habit stock obsolesced quickly in the face of the widespread catastrophe of 1929–30.

2. A second demand factor stemmed from the destruction of consumer assets in 1929–30. The immense and widespread failure of banks was without precedent. One of the major political parties had happily assured the nation in 1913 that the FRB would keep things right; deposit insurance was unnecessary.[7] But more than a thousand banks failed from 1929 to 1930. And two thousand more between 1930 and 1931.[8]

Thousands of depositors thus lost a substantial portion of their wealth. Half of America's families also saw the value of their homes plummet. Others lost in stock values as well. Unprecedented wealth effects were at work throughout the nation because (a) a larger proportion of families had financial assets and homes in 1929 than in earlier recessions, and (b) wealth per family had also been greater. Such wealth effects cut consumption, even by those who remained employed.

3. The destruction of so many banks further cut consumer spending by reducing the supply of new products offered to consumers. Entrepreneurs who wished to finance nascent industry—new automobile parts, better radio tubes, more varied electrical appliances—found bankers far less venturesome. So did those who wished to finance novel products within established industries (e.g., food products, phonograph records, electric hair curlers). Hence fewer decisively novel attractions appeared to stimulate spending by the 90% of the work force who remained employed.

Consumers who bought new products in 1908 helped end the 1907 recession. They were certainly no richer than their successors

TABLE 2.4
Personal Consumption Expenditures:
(current prices)

	Number of Items												
	Declining by								Rising by				
	Over 30%	30.0–20.0	19.9–10.0	9.9–7.0	6.9–4.0	3.9–1.0	Under 1%	0	Under 1%	1.0–3.9	4.0–6.9	7.0–9.9	10+
Recession Year													
1907–8	2	4	5	1	5	5	3	3	4	10	8	2	10
1913–14	0	2	6	3	4	5	3	1	0	12	13	8	5
1920–21	9	9	10	4	3	1	1	1	0	4	6	2	11
1923–24	0	0	3	3	3	1	2	0	5	16	6	12	10
1926–27	0	1	4	3	2	5	1	2	2	12	9	13	7
1929–30	2	3	17	7	10	7	2	2	2	4	1	2	0
1937–38	1	1	7	6	8	3	4	3	2	10	3	0	1
1948–49	0	1	3	2	4	8	4	1	3	6	7	7	13
1953–54	0	0	0	2	6	4	1	0	4	11	15	10	6
1957–58	0	0	1	1	2	3	4	0	2	10	18	14	4
1973–74	0	0	2	1	2	0	1	0	1	2	9	13	28
Post-Recession Year													
1908–9	0	0	0	0	0	0	3	2	1	13	10	11	27
1914–15	3	0	1	3	3	7	2	2	1	12	11	6	11
1921–22	0	1	2	1	2	1	2	1	0	9	13	11	18
1924–25	0	1	1	1	0	2	0	1	1	8	11	17	18
1927–28	0	1	0	2	1	4	2	0	4	7	9	11	19
1930–31	4	6	20	9	9	3	1	3	0	2	1	0	0
1938–39	0	0	2	1	0	2	1	3	0	2	16	8	13
1949–50	0	0	0	1	1	0	1	0	1	10	10	13	22
1954–55	0	0	1	0	0	0	2	0	2	9	5	22	17
1958–59	0	0	3	6	9	4	0	0	1	4	6	14	12
1974–75	0	1	1	0	2	0	0	0	0	4	7	16	28

TABLE 2.5

Personal Consumption Expenditures:
(constant dollars)

Number of Items

	Declining by								Rising by				
	Over 30%	30.0– 20.0	19.9– 10.0	9.9– 7.0	6.9– 4.0	3.9– 1.0	Under 1%	0	Under 1%	1.0– 3.9	4.0– 6.9	7.0– 9.9	10+
Recession Year													
1907–8	1	2	8	3	1	4	1	1	1	11	5	3	8
1913–14	0	3	4	2	3	7	1	1	4	8	7	2	7
1920–21	5	3	7	4	4	4	0	0	2	6	3	6	5
1923–24	0	0	3	1	3	1	2	0	1	8	14	4	10
1926–27	0	1	1	1	2	8	2	0	1	11	11	6	11
1929–30	1	3	9	7	6	6	2	0	4	4	4	2	2
1937–38	1	1	2	6	9	6	3	1	5	8	4	1	2
1948–49	0	0	4	1	3	3	3	2	5	8	8	4	8
1953–54	1	0	0	2	3	3	2	0	2	16	7	5	5
1957–58	0	0	1	0	5	10	1	1	2	14	11	3	1
1973–74	0	2	4	2	5	8	4	0	1	10	8	2	3
Post-Recession Year													
1908–9	0	0	0	0	0	0	1	1	1	10	7	9	19
1914–15	2	0	1	3	6	6	2	2	1	10	2	4	11
1921–22	0	1	2	0	0	3	0	0	1	5	8	4	25
1924–25	0	0	1	1	2	4	0	0	2	6	12	6	13
1927–28	0	0	0	0	2	1	2	2	3	10	8	6	16
1930–31	1	3	7	6	5	7	1	1	2	7	5	1	3
1938–39	0	0	2	0	1	1	0	0	1	12	12	3	17
1949–50	0	0	0	2	0	3	0	0	2	12	7	8	13
1954–55	1	0	0	2	0	3	0	0	2	8	12	8	12
1958–59	0	0	1	1	2	2	0	0	0	13	15	5	9
1974–75	0	1	0	1	4	10	0	0	3	13	6	4	4

TABLE 2.6
Recession and Recovery: 1920–1931

	Construction			Passenger Car Sales	Machinery and Equipment Production		
	Residential	Public Utility	Industrial		Industrial	Electrical	Farm
Recession Year							
1920–21	+1.4	−.2	−.7	−4	−299	−59	−39
1923–24	+3.0	+.4	−.2	−4	+594	+37	+301
1926–27	−1.1	+.2	−.04	−8	+71	−7	−14
1929–30	−4.7	+.1	−1.1	−17	−218	−135	−40
Post-Recession Year							
1921–22	+6.4	+.8	−.3	+8	+154	+22	+30
1924–25	+3.3	−.1	+.2	+5	+94	+12	+42
1927–28	−2.9	−.3	+.3	+9	+77	+49	+18
1930–31	−5.0	−1.4	−1.0	−8	−738	−108	−163

Sources: Construction and car sales—Census, *Historical Statistics . . . to 1970.*
Production—William H. Shaw, *Value of Product Since 1869* (1947).

Notes: Construction: Billions of 1957–59 dollars. Machinery and Equipment: Millions of 1913 dollars. Cars: Hundreds of thousands of cars.

in 1930. Nor were those whose spending helped end the recessions of 1914 and 1921. The failure by employed workers to purchase innovations in 1930 reflected the reduced supply of bank lending officers willing to venture on novelty, not merely reduced consumer wealth and forebodings of income declines.

4. The unprecedented across-the-board decline of consumer spending in 1929–31 in turn squeezed virtually every capital good and material supplying industry. For example, office and store furniture sales fell 20%. Machinery production was cut by 30%[9] (table 2.6). Both had suffered only small declines in 1919–20 and 1923–24. Indeed, their output actually rose in 1926–27. In those earlier recessions consumer spending had declined nowhere near as widely, and their investment sequelae were also milder.

In turn, production of inputs for the investment industries fell. Slackened consumer demand for housing and autos meant that orders for refrigerator motors and sheet steel plummeted, and steel production then collapsed. In prior twentieth-century recessions steel fell no more than 15%. It now fell 28%.[10] The unprecedented breadth of continued decline in consumer expenditure and its failure to rise in as many sectors as in prior recessions forced the unprecedented decline of investment. Together they define the Great Depression.

· C H A P T E R   3 ·

DID UNDERCONSUMPTION END THE
BOOM OF THE 1920s?

I

Leading historians agree that "flawed prosperity" in the 1920s, which portended the Great Depression, stemmed from inadequate consumption:

> "Insofar as one accepts the theory that underconsumption explains the Depression, and I do, then the Presidents of the 1920s are to blame for operating a . . . government responsive mainly to large business corporations. This led, among other unfortunate consequences, to the failure to maintain an adequate level of purchasing power on the part of workers and farmers, which left the economy with inadequate underpinnings."[1]

> Foster and Catchings had in some respects the most striking insights of any American economists of the decade. Contrary to . . . orthodox economic theory the flow of money to the consumer could not keep pace with the flow of consumers' goods. . . . Both corporations and individuals had to save; yet every dollar saved . . . inevitably (worsened) the shortage of consumer demand."[2]

> "Why did the United States economy fail to overcome the drag of weak sectors (in the 1920s)?

> > Consumption expenditures . . . dropped a full 40% between 1929 and 1933 . . . another explanation for the drop in consumption was the increasingly skewed distribution of wealth . . . in the 1920s. . . . Labor received only partial compensation for the increases in its productivity. . . . The value of that extra output flowed (to) employers and investors as profits and dividends. The inequitable distribution of wealth was particularly harmful in an economy so focused upon consumer spending. The relative shortage of disposable income in the hands of salaried and wage work-

ers caused the country to suffer from the malady of "undercon-sumption." Too few buyers had the money to purchase all the goods that the bountiful farms and scientifically managed factories could produce. A wealthy American who collected the profits from labor's increasing productivity could hardly be expected to buy thousands of toothbrushes, hundreds of radios, or dozens of cars.

Consumer spending could never keep pace with production as long as the distribution of wealth remained so inequitable. Few contemporary Americans recognized the significance of undercon-sumption in causing and prolonging the Depression."[3]

"The most serious (problem) was the failure of consumer demand to keep pace with industrial output . . . (that) failure . . . partially re-flected the increased inequality that developed in the nation's income distribution during . . . the 1920s. The relative concentration of income in the hands of the rich tended to encourage savings relative to consump-tion. . . . (That created) the basic problem of underconsumption."[4]

"Even in the industries that were prosperous during the twenties there were elements tending to undermine the economic structure. Most im-portant . . . there was an increase in the proportion of total income going to profits. . . and a decrease in the relative proportion going to wages and salaries . . . the obvious result was the tendency to pile up wealth where it would be used chiefly for the further expansion of in-dustrial units rather than . . . in the hands of those who would use it to purchase manufactured commodities."[5]

"As the 1920s stretched on, the prolonged investment boom was sow-ing the seeds of its own demise, through its contributions to increasing productivity and inadequate purchasing power . . . consumer demand could not seem to keep pace . . . "Gains in productivity caused . . . ca-pacity to rise faster than wages . . . leading to inadequate consumer demand."[6]

II

A central chapter in the book of capitalism has long described the death of individual firms amid ceaseless, albeit "creative, destruc-tion." But when does this all accumulate into depression? Analyses such as those quoted imply a simple sequence:

1. The income distribution becomes "distorted." Too little goes into wages and salaries, too much to profits and dividends.

2. Savings intensify the shortage of consumer demand.

3. The wealthy fail to use their greater profits to buy more tooth-

brushes—or radios and cars. Instead they buy more factories—though the landscape is littered with bankrupt factories.

4. "Too little" consumption then brings on the depression.

However, the central assumption in all this has no foundation. For the proportion of total income going to wages and salaries did not decline during the 1920s. Kuznets's authoritative studies show it actually rose, from 57.8% in 1919 to 59.9% in 1929.[7] (None of these scholars has made, or cited, alternative estimates.) But, of course, the numbers are secondary. For even myopic millionaires who spend their money "to expand industrial units," were chiefly hiring and paying workers who made cement, bricks, glass, and steel, or put up buildings for expansion. Why would such workers buy cars, toothbrushes, and radios less regularly than other workers?

III

What about the immediate trigger—"too little consumption?"[8] Was consumption unusually weak in the 1920s? We need not rely on implications from indirect testimony on the flow to profits and dividends—even had that shown any "excess"—to imply a shortfall in consumption. We can now directly examine whether most, or even many, consumption sectors were unusually "weak" during the '20s.

Per capita total consumption did not in fact decline during the late 1920s. It continued to rise along its 1900–20 growth path (table 3.1).

TABLE 3.1
Personal Consumption
(per capita, 1987 dollars)

1900	3268
1905	3736
1910	3882
1915	3771
1920	3653
1921	3418
1922	3702
1923	3981
1924	3994
1925	4171
1926	4289
1927	4300
1928	4411
1929	4551

IV

Even though the underconsumption view lacks real analytic or empirical basis, one can ask what sectors might have "underconsumed" in the 1920s? For a systematic answer, we turn to a simple model of the real flow of consumption in each of the twelve major sectors. Consumption is taken as a function of (*a*) its level in the prior year and (*b*) the change in the unemployment rate from that year.[9] Table 3.2 reports the residuals from that overall model. It suggests that consumer expenditure was no weaker in the 1920s than earlier decades, nor more widespread. The Appendix reports data for twelve major consumption categories during the eight years between the post-war collapse of 1921 and 1929. Of ninety-six possible year-to-year declines only three of note actually took place—clothing in 1924, transportation (e.g., autos), and household operation in 1927.

Irregularities are endemic in most economies, and certainly in capitalist ones. But the recessions of 1908, 1915, 1921, 1924, and 1927 were short. And the economy recovered within a year. An upturn followed each of the thirty business cycle declines since 1854–57.[10] And upturns appeared as swiftly in the 1920s as in prior decades, if not more so.

TABLE 3.2
Consumption Shortfalls
1900–1929*

	$\bar{R}^2$	Number of Years with Negative Residuals		
		1900–9	1910–19	1920–29
Total	.93	4	6	2
Food & Tobacco	.76	2	4	5
Clothing	.86	6	6	4
Personal Care	.99	2	8	4
Housing	.98	4	4	3
Household Op.	.86	4	7	4
Medical Care	.94	4	6	5
Personal Bus.	.95	7	6	5
Transportation	.95	7	5	2
Recreation	.99	3	6	5
Education	.95	5	6	5
Religion & Welfare	.56	2	7	8
Foreign Travel	.69	1	5	6
Memorandum:				
Sum of 12 Sectors		47	70	56

Computed from: $PC_1 = f[(PC_{1_{t-1}}), (Unemp_t - Unemp_{t-1})]$.

The historic record, then, does not reveal the U.S. economy in 1929 poised for the deepest plunge in history because of any trend to "underconsumption." Nor does it show consumption being choked by "fundamental weaknesses" in income distribution, or the flow of wages relative to profits. To understand why the Great Depression originated, or why it continued so endlessly, requires more than simple hypotheses of underconsumption and inequality. More plausible explanations are to be sought in behavior during 1929–39, not 1920–29. Some of these elements were canvassed in chapter 2.

· C H A P T E R 4 ·

MASS CONSUMPTION AND
"AMERICANIZATION"

I

Histories of many nations have been dominated by the activity of tiny groups—the nobility, the clergy, the intellectuals. But, even before De Toqueville, travelers saw the new United States as a different land, and the American as "this new man" (in Emerson's phrase). One reason they did so was that behavior and consumption patterns across U.S. economic and social classes seemed so homogenized as compared to Europe. Indeed, when mass production began producing those results in Europe, well over a century later, the acute Ortega y Gasset called it the Revolution of the Masses.

America set that pattern much earlier because so immense a variety of consumption items became available at prices the masses could afford. And their price and quality made them acceptable to persons much further up the social scale. In part "mass production" was responsible. But in no mean measure it was also mass, cheap, transportation of goods by the railroad. When the automobile came along it intensified the trend toward mass production, mass distribution—and thereby homogenization. Movies, advertising, and radio further reduced consumption differences while concurrently reducing differences between the perspectives of those who consumed.

As recently as the Roosevelt era the South was largely a separate world from that of the North. But the election of Truman, Johnson, Carter, and Clinton marked the changed meaning of geographic differences in the U.S. The supermarket or discount store shopper found the same mass consumption washing machine, radio, blue jeans, and wheaties in Atlanta and Portland, Maine, as San Francisco or New York City. (Bewildering variety in specialized items did not conceal the fact that a host of standard products were available across the nation, and were consumed across income and class lines.)

II

What major factors made table 4.1's income-expenditure coefficients of determination by state wither away?

1. Markets expanded in low-income states, as did capital supply. Together they drove per capita income levels in low-income states up from 1929 levels. The coefficient of variation for state per capita incomes inevitably fell, between 1929 and 1970, from 36% to 15%. And by 1970 consumers in what were once lower-income states followed their tastes for item after item almost heedless of any "income constraint."

2. Production sources multiplied. So did distribution sources. Together their expansion drove down the cost of transporting food from producer to consumer. Ever more automobiles dotted the streets of hamlets and villages. Their use forced retailers to compete ever more fiercely. Competition between retailers and producers also intensified.

Together such dramatic increases in competition drove down the price disadvantage of states that had once imported most of their manufactured goods. Georgians, Nebraskans, and Vermonters no longer paid so much more for cigarettes and furniture than North Carolinians or than Michiganders (for cars) or New Yorkers (for clothing). The price constraint on their behavior had weakened.

3. Complementary social and economic forces helped create a standard American style for all states, whatever their income. (a) Advertising was one such factor—newspapers, point of sale, catalogs, radio. (b) The foreign born died off (decreasing from 16% of the U.S. population to 5% between 1920 and 1970). So did the habits and traditions they had perpetuated from "the old country." (c) Isolated farms once permitted more or less deviant lives—Silas Marner's and Ethan Frome's, deviant in religion, language, choice of food, and lifestyle. But Americans living on farms fell from 28% to 5% of the population between 1920 and 1970. Farm families could not long maintain religious habits, formal polite speech, or parental discipline once they began frequent trading and living in alien villages and towns. Pressures toward conformity in expenditure style became overwhelming.

4. Children have long carried novelty home, bringing knowledge of the habits and styles in their friends' families. Beginning in the 1890s children in the open country went to consolidated schools. Children in cities began attending large high schools. Group norms could more readily be imposed on children in such schools than was possible in isolated, one-room country schools, where each child had only a few peers.

TABLE 4.1
Per Capita Income and Specified Expenditures by State
Coefficients of Determination

	1929	1970	1977
Total	.953	.825	.550
Food & Tobacco	.777	.388	.457
Clothing, Accessories & Jewelry	.109	.737	.604
Personal Care	.626	.406	.326
Housing	.877	.720	.206
Household Operation	.913	.554	.271
Medical Care	.847	.749	.676
Personal Business	.829	.650	.583
Transporation	.436	.348	.100
Recreation	.882	.508	.154
I.			
Purchased Food	.644	.267	.367
Food Furnished	.686	− .016	.036
Farm Food	.330	.316	.194
Food less Alcohol	—	—	—
Alcohol	—	—	.063
Tobacco	.455	.492	.063
II.			
Shoe & Shoe Repair	.817	.618	—
Clothing (inc. military)	.035	.752	.651
Jewelry	.516	.417	.124
Clothing Service	.613	.357	.455
III.			
Toilet Articles	.208	.334	.118
Barber & Beauty	.885	.363	.422
IV.			
Non-farm Owned & Tenant	.879	.689	.466
Farm Housing	.036	.262	.014
Other Housing	.323	.021	.024
V.			
Furniture	.655	.454	.184
Clean & Polish	.105	.117	.087
Electricity & Oil	.724	.007	.008
Water & Sanitary	.142	.121	.044
Fuel & Ice	.589	.053	− .005
Telephone	.783	.779	.673
Domestic Service	.709	.016	.036
Other	.619	.357	.332

Continued on next page

TABLE 4.1—*Continued*

	1929	1970	1977
VI.			
Drugs	.467	.167	.300
Physicians, Dentists & Orthod.	.695	.628	.433
Hospitals	.839	.399	.396
VII.			
Brokerage & Finance	.517	.507	.402
Life Insurance	.726	.629	.555
Legal Services	.496	.533	.429
Funerals	.365	− .018	− .021
Employment Agencies	.584	—	—
Union Dues	.064	—	—
VIII.			
Transportation	.436	.348	.100
IX.			
Books & Maps	.447	.407	.209
Magazines	.476	.414	.213
Toys	.626	.673	.420
Musical Instruments	—	—	—
Plants, Seeds	.819	.076	.096
X.			
Private Education	.244	.493	.423
Higher Education	.271	.394	.062
Other Education	.687	.261	.252
XI.			
Religion	.699	—	—
Welfare	.659	—	—
XII.			
Travel	.633	.609	− .021

These powerful forces combined to increase uniformity in expenditure patterns. They thereby severed the once close link between income and the choice of individual goods.

III

In 1936 Keynes forecast "Economic Possibilities for our Grandchildren." He foresaw the pall of economic necessity lasting through his generation, and the next. It might then lift. Yet within a decade urgent economic necessity ceased to typify the American economy.

The economic forces constraining the consumer began to loosen. That break is evident in the contrasting columns of table 4.1.[1]

These show the link between personal income and separate expenditure items, by state, for three dates. In 1929 income still dominated state consumption patterns: the median coefficient (R^2) relating income to the typical item in the long list of consumer goods was .60. State differences in spending were thus readily attributed to differences in income, whether the item was electricity, commercial amusements, domestic service, jewelry, tobacco, etc. All this changed by 1970, however. The median correlation plummeted— from .60 to .06. This age-old compelling income constraint had been loosened.

IV

Our consumption data should reveal something of these forces. To the extent that immigrants became assimilated, and homogenized to an average American pattern, the differences between states should have diminished. States with the great immigrant ports of arrival— New York, Massachusetts, Louisiana, California—should stand out from the median more in 1900 than later. As transport improved, price differences between states should have diminished. High returns to capital (and labor) in some states should have diminished as capital (and labor) flowed in from other states. The outcome of these processes should have reduced differences in per capita expenditure among the states.

V

Table 4.2 shows one dimension of this homogenization process. The coefficient of variation (cv) for per capita spending on a wide range of goods and services falls throughout the century. For many consumer items it falls in every period. The most extreme declines, however, occur from 1900 to 1929, when the annual inflow of over a million immigrants a year was cut by two-thirds. Tobacco consumption represents an extreme in successive declines. Its cv in 1982 is only one-sixth that for 1900. The popularity of the telephone did not spread quite as completely, but its cv fell to one-fourth of that in 1900 by 1982.

What are the significant exceptions?[2] Farm food consumption and home rental values both reflect the increased marginalization of farming, and its specialization in fewer states. Theater expenditures reflect a similar specialization, as regional theaters from New Haven to St. Louis closed. These forces were somewhat offset only in recent years by the willingness of foundations and governments to

TABLE 4.2
Coefficient of Variation for Specified PCE Items
(per capita, 1987 prices)
1900–1982

	1900	1929	1970	1977	1982
Total	.336	.352	.269	.149	.146
Food, Alc, Tob	.242	.257	.266	.124	.109
Food Furnished	.941	.634	.651	.424	.271
Food on Farms	.409	.580	.783	.759	.802
Tobacco	1.046	.480	.280	.219	.158
Alcohol	1.059			.361	.310
Total Clothing and Acc.	.215	.410	.283	.143	.171
Clothing—Women's		.462	.287	.158	.167
Clothing—Men's		.370	.256	.121	.163
Shoes	.782	.478	.252	.119	.161
Jewelry	.547	.537	.376	.252	.271
Cloth.-Acc.	.649	.587	.622	.535	.740
Laundry		.474	.416	.237	.274
Personal Care	.63	.446	.235	.162	.191
Toilet Articles	.593	.479	.228	.168	.225
Barber	.707	.546	.646	.231	.266
Total Housing	.570	.484	.378	.256	.213
Owner	.713	.581	.415	.242	.235
Tenant		.605	.446	.326	.344
Other Rental	.886	.646	1.097	1.044	.902
Farm	.488	.578	.583	.752	.779
Furniture	.338	.462	.175	.175	.180
China, Glass	.571	.571	.216	.204	.168
Other Dur.	.590	.590	.187	.138	.155
Other Semi-dur.	.415	.415	.137	.134	.155
Cleaning	.222	.777	.181	.265	.210
Gas		.955	.427	.454	.477
Electric	.251	.392	.257	.264	.207
Water	1.479	.490	.412	.336	.340
Fuel	.254	.775	.852	.924	.997
Telephone & Telegraph	.945	.626	.131	.89	.217
Domestic	.363	.640	.252	.404	.412
Other Houshold Op.	.955	.690	.363	.273	.318
Drugs	.485	.245	.224	.120	.152
Ophthalmic		.889	.228	.386	.332
Physicians	.434	.338	.216	.176	.169
Dentists		.456	.253	.277	.274
Other Professionals		.639	.246	.362	.328
Hospitals	.903	.684	.243	.310	.326
Brokerage Charges		1.228	.561	.422	1.495

Continued on next page

Table 4.2—*Continued*

	1900	1929	1970	1977	1982
Life Insurance	.654	.463	.164	.141	.142
Legal	.558	.443	.291	.318	.372
Funeral	.780	.516	.205	.252	.236
Motor Vehicle		.324	.121	.314	.160
Tires		.366	.173	.195	.173
Auto Repair		.344	.594	.192	.226
Gas		.327	.198	.206	.184
Tolls			1.084	1.11	.895
Auto Insurance		.287	.187	.224	.425
Local Transportation		.856	.830	.837	
Intercity Travel		.496	.295	.429	
Recreation	.681	.552	.311	.592	.439
Books	1.040	.802	.528	.348	.356
Magazines	.800	.910	.363	.355	.896
Toys—Non-dur.	.810	.442	.632	.524	.248
Toys—Durable		.751	.331	.271	.367
Music/TV/Radio	.610	.492	.251	.174	.420
Flowers	1.140	.616	.380	.125	.153
Spectator Amuse.		.648	.488	.738	.562
Movies		.609	.356	.280	.301
Theater		.988	1.836	1.549	1.853
Spectator Sports		2.472	1.156	.952	.822

subsidize theaters and opera houses from Manhattan to Hartford and Seattle.

Water charges and automobile tolls are chiefly fixed in markets made by governments. (Private water companies were few in 1900 and in later years.) Government prices inevitably respond to different forces from those dominated by direct factor cost competition and multiple consumer choices.

Other expenditure categories include products that differed enormously over the decades. Thus "radio, TV" includes "musical instruments, radio, records, TV, VCRs." That its cv declines so frequently is more of a marvel than that it increases in the last period—when VCRs and cable TV inundated the "music" markets.

· C H A P T E R   5 ·

THE ELITE'S SHARE OF CONSUMPTION:
U.S. VERSUS USSR

THE LEADERS of Communist nations long emphasized how "obscene" the money differentials under capitalism were. They knew that what mattered was consumption, not income. They determined their own well-being by fixing their consumption entitlements, not by the modest money incomes for their positions.

How great a consumption gap separates the elite from the average family in the U.S. compared with that gap in the Soviet Union? That question is at least as meaningful as money income comparisons. For a rough answer we estimate consumption in 1984–85 by the upper 1.5% of the Soviet Union—its "Nomenklatura."[1] That group included heads of the Communist Party, government agencies, the KGB, as well as heads of enterprises, technical institutes, etc. For the U.S. we focus on the top 1.6% of the tax filing population in 1985, that is, those with adjusted gross incomes of $100,000 or more.[2] What were the consumption shares of each, and how were they achieved?

I

The typical salary of the head of a Central Committee Desk in the USSR was 5,400 rubles a year in 1985, plus another month's pay as a "rest-cure allowance."[3] From that he deducted 11% for income tax.[4]

The income of the top 1.6% in the U.S. during the same period averaged $213,000. From that they deducted 39% in taxes—$66,000 for Federal taxes plus $18,000 for state and local taxes.[5]

II

Members of the U.S. elite deducted an average of $9,100 for contributions to charity.[6] Some did so because of noblesse oblige; others, because of the pressures of their position. The USSR, however, was

officially dedicated to welfare and communism. Nomenklatura
members, therefore, felt no need to make charitable contributions.
Indeed, "since charity [was defined as] unnecessary in the Soviet
Union it is not permitted. No church may give alms to the poor; no
private groups of concerned citizens may organize to dispense aid."[7]

III

In his extraordinary 1989 campaign rallies Boris Yeltsin urged "aboli-
tion of stores, clinics, and other facilities reserved for senior officials."[8] What did these provide the Nomenklaturists?

Six major subsidy programs can be noted: food, housing, medical
care, transport, education, vacations. The value of these subsidies is,
of course, omitted from their money income. They did not need to
spend a single ruble to enjoy them.

1. Most notorious was the Kremliovka food subsidy. Its coupons
entitled the holder to "medical nutrition." "The holders are not sick,
they are the high Nomenklaturists. There are three coupons per day:
'breakfast,' 'lunch,' and 'dinner.' Almost all Kremliovka holders prefer to receive their meals as a food basket full of luxuries that are
normally unobtainable in Moscow, let alone the provinces. These
are distributed at the Kremlin canteen . . . and the 'House of the
Government'. . . . The American journalist Hedrick Smith draws a
very accurate picture of the Nomenklaturists and their wives arriv-
ing at the Kremlin canteen and quickly disappearing behind an ordi-
nary-looking glass door surmounted by a panel with the words 'Pass
Office.' Later they are to be seen emerging laden with big brown-
paper parcels and taking their seats in the limousines that have been
waiting for them. Smith does not mention . . . the drivers and domestic servants who go there to fetch the multilayered aluminum
Kremlin lunch containers. Helpings are so ample that a single portion is enough to feed a whole family."[9]

"The Central Committee building in Moscow, possesses at least
three dining rooms, on different floors. These evidently serve different categories of officials, and the most select room has a militia man
at the door. The range and quality of food seems to be comparable
to that in very good restaurants outside but the prices are considerably lower."[10]

Moreover, Nomenklatura members and wives were spared hours
each week waiting in line at stores and restaurants. The increasing
number of ordinary citizens prepared to "wait in line" (and collect
high fees for doing so), further testified to the importance of that
advantage.[11]

. . .

Transactions in collective markets help to value this combination of higher quality and access. The Soviet Union stipulated that prices in these markets "may not exceed prices of similar products in state stores . . . more than threefold."[12] Soviet consumers pay for quality as well as access. Between 1965 and 1980 farm deliveries of milk rose by only 25%. But state sales of milk and cheese increased by 116%.[13] (Well water, of course, has been added to milk for centuries by canny, if unscrupulous, private entrepreneurs.) Starch and water were also pumped into state produced meat to achieve production quotas.[14]

Soviet consumers in 1989 valued quality by paying more—for example, collective stores charged 3.5 times the price of beef in state stores.[15] For clothes, foreign currency stores charged 20 to 25% of official Soviet ruble prices.[16]

Waiting time was also priced: "Long lines snake into the street for such ordinary items as sausage, rice, coffee and candy."[17] People who work at night, or are retired, can legally spend hours waiting in such lines. The fee charged to keep one's place in line measured the value of access to the scarce goods. "Roughly speaking we can assume a [usual] profiteer's markup . . . of 40 to 100 percent of the state price of the commodity. . . . Sometimes profiteers sell their place in line. . . . It is somewhat cheaper to buy a place in line than to buy the commodity from the profiteer."[18] Since it was only "somewhat cheaper to buy a place in the line" most of the 40–100% markup measures the value of waiting in line.

In 1989 *Pravda* reported officials in one central USSR region consumed over 50% of all high-quality food in their region—though they represented .04% of the population." The *Moscow News* "published similar data about Leningrad."[19]

We assume that the official 3 to 1 price ratio for collective markets measures the advantage to the Nomenklatura in both access and quality differences for expenditures on meat, dairy products and fruit, and apparel and consumer durables.[20] (It probably understates the Nomenklatura's margin of advantage for auto fuel, parts, repairs, and housing maintenance.

2. The housing subsidy was a second major item not included in money income.[21] The average family benefitted from a subsidy too. But the subsidy to the Nomenklaturists was substantially greater.

The advantage of their high-quality, well-located housing was measured by the black market. "To get an acceptable flat it is common practice to pay an extra amount to the appropriate official."[22] Law cases specify the transaction values involved. In one, an official took 20,000 to 40,000 rubles in bribes for housing and cars. In another, "pretending to act as an unofficial housing agent, he took 100,000 rubles; in a third, "bribery in assigning housing," 100,000 rubles.[23] (In Poland "a three-room flat with a ten-year waiting list is resold at ten times its selling price.")[24]

Many Russian families live in a single room. Twenty percent of urban families (and at least 30% of Moscow families) share their kitchen and bathroom with another family.[25] Nomenklaturists, however, as Voslensky notes, have "large homes." Some have "as many as eight rooms, others being allotted a whole floor, consisting of two adjoining flats turned into one. . . . Particularly favored by law, presumably because many work at home, are writers, composers . . . academics. They may have 20 square meters above the norm."

The Soviet Census reports 9 square meters of housing space per capita in the cities, 11.3 in Moscow.[26] If one-quarter of Moscow's families were Nomenklaturists, and the remainder were squeezed to the national urban average, the Nomenklaturists would have 18 meters. Or twice the figure for the rest of the city. Voslensky adds that housing "for the Nomenklatura is built under special supervision and is not standardized or jerry-built. Good, solid, buildings contain spacious apartments, quiet elevators, wide and comfortable staircases." They also have preferred locations within the city.

Voslensky's description of space and facilities suggests something considerably grander for the Nomenklatura. However, we use the relatively modest figure Katsinelinboigen reports: in Moscow a one-room separate apartment "with all amenities [gas, electricity, running water, bathroom], located near a subway station," rents for approximately 600 rubles. (A single room "in an apartment with all the amenities occupied by the family renting a room, near a subway station, will cost approximately 350 rubles.")[27] We contrast that 600-ruble value with a rental of say 125 rubles a year for the average (i.e., urban and rural) family. (Rent and utilities for the average industrial worker's family ran about 135 rubles in 1974.)[28]

A blunt measure of the value of otherwise unattainable housing, not necessarily up to the average quality of the Nomenklatura, is given by the bribes paid. In distant Dushanbe 3,000 rubles were paid for a one-room apartment. In Moscow, more recently, the charge was 2,500 per room.[29] At least a fivefold advantage for the Nomenklatura over the average Russian in housing expenditure appears to be a moderate estimate.[30]

3. The Nomenklatura rely on their own restricted access, nationwide network of medical clinics.

Shipler reports a "widespread conviction among Russians that medical care you don't pay for is just about worthless." Hence fee-charging polyclinics were even established in some cities. "Russians think [these] were less crowded and of higher quality." Side payments were generally required for medical visits, choice of surgeons, pharmaceuticals, even ordinary nursing.[31] ("An American tourist who broke her hip in Moscow, not realizing that she had to bribe, spent four days lying in her own excrement, grossly mistreated and abused" the [U.S.] embassy doctor said.") Even such standard prescription medicines as insulin were regularly available only in clinics for the Nomenklatura.[32] As Morrison asks, "How to estimate the benefit to parents of a seriously ill child of access to a special hospital where he can obtain treatment unavailable in ordinary hospitals?"[33]

We approximate a value for such access, and for the superior medical care of the Nomenklatura, as follows. "Valery Rutgaizer, the head of the State Planning Commission's social welfare department complained in the newspaper *Sovietskya Kultura* that the quality of care is two to three times higher in the special clinics [for the Nomenklatura]. 'This is the heart of social injustice,' he said."[34]

Beyond the quality difference, the Nomenklatura also received more care. Their office visits to physicians were not ended after a few minutes, as for the typical worker. They were also referred to specialists more often, and given more laboratory tests. They thus received more accurate diagnosis and treatment, and could remain in the hospital long enough for full recovery. By contrast, average workers went to ordinary hospitals, where patient beds lined hallways, storage rooms, etc. The Nomenklatura could also count on readier, more regular, access to medicines (even such old standards as insulin) than ordinary Russians could.

The expansion of the cooperative sector in the Gorbachev era surfaced the story of a Moscow dentist who charged four times the regular rates, yet had an endless waiting list, because he used high-speed Czechoslovak drills, Japanese disposable needles, etc.[35] (The U.S. rich, who also demand high-quality care, spend about seven times as much as the typical American family.)[36] A fourfold margin of advantage for Nomenklatura medical care would seem to be a moderate estimate, allowing for both quality and quantity.

4. Few members of the Nomenklatura had an entire fleet of top of the line cars, as the Secretary General did. (Brezhnev had a Cadillac, Rolls Royce, Lancia, Lincoln, Mercedes, Monte Carlo, etc.)[37] "For many high posts a car [with chauffeur] is apparently a fringe benefit."[38] Kruschev's adviser, Fedor Burlatsky, writes that "officially more than half a million cars were held for the use of individuals, with one or two drivers per car."[39]

In addition, permission to buy a car at official (i.e., below market) prices was available to most of the Nomenklatura. They achieved this through a web of political connections, if not directly. Selling prices of old and battered vehicles were so far above official prices that any such privilege was worth a considerable sum. A Zhiguli, equivalent to a Ford Maverick, was officially priced at 5,500 rubles.[40] (Getting one required a three- to ten-year wait as of 1984,[41] and seven years in 1989.[42] Official users paid an average of only 860 rubles, and had far shorter waits.)[43] Given their readier access to official cars, repairs, gas, and chauffeurs, the ratio of the Nomenklatura's advantage over ordinary citizens in transport could have readily reached ten to one.

5. Children of the Nomenklatura were given priority access to the better schools and colleges, at no charge.[44] The American rich, however, pay a sevenfold to one premium to enroll their children in such schools: in 1984, about $12,000 compared to $1,700 for all colleges. Since the select USSR universities also provided unique access to better official jobs, the ratio of advantage could well be more than seven to one.

6. A member of the Nomenklatura also received "his vacation cost-free, for he stays free of charge for a month at a Central Committee or Council of Ministers rest home. His wife stays at the same establishment for a very small fee, and his children are sent to a first-class pioneer camp."[45] By contrast, average Russians paid up to 1,000 rubles to rent a comfortable summer dacha in 1977; or 200 for a mere room in a dacha (with access to an outhouse).[46]

The Nomenklatura also benefitted from items available in the restricted network of "closed" stores. "The best analogy would be if the American government set up a set of elegant stores [say, Tiffany's] which were set aside exclusively for members of the Republican National Committee and no one else. Without access . . . most of the goods in such stores [could not] be purchased legally, regardless of price. . . . Moreover, most sales are not limited to jewelry and ordinary luxuries, but . . . basic foods such as meat, fruits, and vegetables. To the ordinary Soviet shopper, they are luxuries, and more often than not, unavailable most of the year. As the famous Soviet comedian Arkady Raikin put it, "We have everything, of course, but not for everyone."[47]

Admissions to the ballet, the opera, etc. were also differentially available to the top group. Occasional opportunities to travel abroad, even to Iron Curtain countries, were restricted to them. How much was it worth to the Soviet Elite to get rare items at discount rather than pay black market prices? Plus the ability to travel abroad?

For the U.S. rich, by contrast, prices are not lower in real estate offices, clothing stores, furniture stores, but are typically marked up. However, we omit this element, thereby further understating the Nomenklatura's consumption advantage.

IV

How can this staggering set of advantages be summed?

Morrison notes that "due to recent events, information on this system" for Poland's top 1 1/2% became public in 1980–81. A mid-level official's salary of 10,000 zlotys "when all the usual advantages are taken into consideration can be estimated at 30,000 to 40,000 zlotys. The reports on these practices concur with reports [for] the U.S.S.R."[48]

A similar three or four to one entitlement ratio appeared for many USSR items reviewed above: food, apparel, and durables.[49] For medical care, transport, education, and travel significantly greater ratios were indicated. We therefore adopt a ratio of four as a plausible, very moderate, estimate of the extent to which the Nomenklatura's consumption of all goods and services exceeded the average family's expenditure for goods and services.[50]

V

The American rich do not, of course, spend all their before-tax income. Capitalism, as Keynes remarked, awards income to the very rich on condition they not use it all. "The capitalist classes were allowed to call the best part of the cake theirs . . . on the tacit condition that they consumed very little of it in practice."[51] America's richest saved about 20% of their income.[52] The Nomenklatura, on the other hand, saved far less. Significant property inheritance was not permitted, and savings deposits paid a mere 2.2%.[53] Survey data indicate 8% and 6% saving rates for USSR managers and professionals.[54] We estimate the Nomenklatura saved no more than 10%.

VI

Table 5.1 uses the preceding estimates to compare consumption by the American rich (top 1.6%) with that by the Soviet Nomenklatura's top 1.5%. The American elite family consumed about 3.8 times as much as the average U.S. family.[55] The Nomenklatura likewise consumed about 3.8 times as much as the average Soviet family (3.5 times that of the factory or office worker, but considerably more

TABLE 5.1
The Ruling Classes
circa 1985

U.S. Rich (Top 1.6%)			USSR Nomenklatura (Top 1.5%)	
I. Average gross income:		$211,000	Average Urban Salary (Rubles)	5,400
Income Tax			Income Tax 593	
Federal	$65,000			
State and Local	$17,000			
			+ Rest Cure 450	
Net Income		$129,000	Net Income	5,257
II. Charitable contributions		$9,100		
III. Superior entitlements				21,600
			Kremliovka	
			Housing	
			Health	
			Education	
			Transport	
			Vacations	
			Durable Goods	
			Imported Items	
			cigarettes	
			liquor	
			Admissions (Ballet, Opera)	
			Travel option	
IV. Saving		$42,120		540
V. Consumption expenditure per member of elite		$77,780		26,317
VI. Elite consumption as ratio to average urban		3.8		3.5
Elite consumption as ratio to average in nation		3.8		3.8

than that for the great rural population). Given our intentional understatement of the Nomenklatura's advantage, the Soviet ratio
might well have exceeded 3.8.[56] Nien Heng surmises the Nomenklatura in China consumed at 8 times the national average.[57] Consumption comparisons, in sum, tell a far different story about "inequality" in the USSR than the usual comparisons of money income,
particularly money income before tax.

· PART TWO ·

· C H A P T E R 6 ·

BEYOND THE CONSUMPTION FUNCTION

THE CONSUMPTION FUNCTION

In 1936 Keynes first reported his "normal psychological law"—that consumption rises when real income does, "but not so fast."[1] It proved to be one of those psychological tendencies on which he erected the foundations of modern macroeconomics.[2] But his "propensity to consume" was merely stipulated. It was "a statement of statistically observable fact which Keynes raised to the rank of an assumption. "Nothing is gained (by that statement) except a spurious dignity," said Schumpeter.[3]

Why was that "psychological law" supposed to prevail? Because every component of consumption was income inelastic? Surely not. Yet if even one component were elastic it would be necessary for (1) the quantity of at least one other to rise less than real income, or for (2) the sum of quantity rises to be neatly cancelled by price rises. Which of these assumptions was premised? And what analytic basis could it possess? Keynes had invoked a complex implicit theory with respect to these bewildering alternatives.[4]

Western micro data have long since revealed that individual consumer incomes in any given period need not limit spending. Keynes's "fundamental law" never applied to families described in U.S. expenditure surveys. For they typically reported both dissavers and zero savers in years of rising income. Would, however, the law apply at a macro level to individual consumption items?

The "consumption function" homogenized the immensely varied behavior that actually shapes expenditure on individual items. What was gained by doing so? Consider how it changed in the bland year from 1922 to 1923 (tables 6.1, 6.2). Both were relatively stable, non-war, small-government years. The PCE deflator rose by 2%. That figure is, of course, simply the weighted average of price changes in quite different groups of industries: (1) those with marked productivity gains—gasoline, automobiles, tires, and tobacco (whose prices fell); (2) industries whose prices changed irregularly during a com-

TABLE 6.1
Percent Change in Price
1922–23

Productivity Pricing		Conventional Pricing		Regulatory or Cartel Pricing	
gas and oil	−13%	MD's	−5%	electricity	+6%
auto	−7%	personal business	−3%	brokerage	+6%
tires	−5%	shoes	0	gas	−2%
tobacco	−2%	cloth service	0	tolls and insurance	−3%
		barbers	0	phone	0
		hospital	−5%	purch. trans.	0
		auto repair	−2%		
		nondurable toys	+9%		
		cycles	−9%		
		musical inst.	+21%		
		foreign travel	−3%		
		recreation serv.	0		
		flowers	−1%		
		religion & welfare	+2%		
		cleaning material	+1%		

TABLE 6.2
Percent Change in Quantity
1922–23
(all items: +9.39%)

Negative Elasticity		Inelastic		Unit Elasticity		Elastic	
ice	−7	tobacco	7	toilet articles	10	auto repair	61
welfare	−2	ophthalmology	6	books	9	auto	52
jewelry	−1	recreation serv.	6	phone	9	tolls	44
		housing	6	hh operation	8	tires	29
		gas	6	cleaning	8	stationery	28
		religion	6	recreation	8	toys, cycles	24
		MD	5½	medical care	8	electricity	24
		domestic	5	barber	8	flowers	20
		purch. trans.	5	water	8	hh furnishing	18
		food	5	business	8	gas and oil	17
		education	3			hospital	17
		musical inst.	2			shoes & clothes	13
		cloth serv.	½			toys (nd)	12
						brokerage	11
						foreign travel	11

plex regulatory process; and (3) "conventional pricing" industries, whose (reported) prices changed little.

A decline in the overall PCE deflator 1922–23—which did keep money PCE from rising as much as income—was therefore partly fixed by consumer choice between products made by these three groups of industries. The "consumption function," relating income and consumption changes 1922–23, reflected both many declines and marked increases (of 8% to 10%) for at least ten components. What "psychological propensity" could have predicted declines for ice and jewelry, a rise for toys and foreign travel, and a great surge for four automotive items? Or their net outcome?

When families allocate their income do they really give priority to, say, a consumption total (which includes furs, jewelry, and overseas trips), rather than to a saving total that includes home mortgages and life insurance? Contrariwise, do rising cash balances and increased stock ownership take priority over PCE inclusive of payment of hospital charges? If not, what analytic justification is there for a "psychological propensity" that determines the aggregate "consumption function" or "saving function?"

Aggregate "consumption functions" usually mask a considerable variety of changes in quantity and price. It is the elasticities for individual items that determine cyclical changes in consumption, rather than the mere ratio of expenditure aggregate to income aggregate. And an economy with assets that can quickly be monetized, with financial institutions that offer many kinds of credit, is not one in which a grand aggregation to total consumption is necessarily very instructive.

THE BUDGET CONSTRAINT

Income is typically included in consumer demand studies, attaining considerable statistical significance. But what analytic basis is there for including that variable? It is assumed to measure one phenomenon—which it does not. It attains statistical significance (usually)—because it proxies for another. Granted, the rich do differ from the poor. One group generally prefers Chateau wines and ballet tickets; the other, beer and bowling. Becker and Stigler have emphasized how such differences in tastes can depend on income. But if tastes and income both interact and are collinear, an identification problem precludes simply using income to measure some fixed "budget constraint."

In most demand functions, income marks a limit on consumer behavior: "The consumer wishes to maximize this utility function subject to the budget constraint $Z = P_iQ_i = m$ where m is total expenditure."[5] Or, "The consumer has a positive sum, called income, of say u monetary units, at his disposal for purchases during the budget period."[6]

But financial markets work to prevent "the budget constraint" from being a real limitation. Since the Phoenicians and Pharaohs they have enabled families to buy houses and cars despite the budget constraint of their income. And those who shun credit can draw on past savings.

When this century began, the Commissioner of Labor Statistics found 16% of American families dissaving.[7] Still others expanded current consumption by borrowing. By 1941 a third of those surveyed had a net deficit on current account.[8] (Even in that end-of-depression year 25% of the families borrowed to buy furniture or household equipment, 9% to buy an automobile, while 13% had mortgages on their home.)[9]

Annual surveys by the Survey Research Center for the Federal Reserve Board during 1946–57 repeatedly showed a significant percentage of families dissaving. And in the 1982–83 BLS survey low-income families reported spending three times as much as their annual average "income" of $2,515.[10]

Income constitutes an even more dubious measure of how the "budget constrains" specific expenditure items. The BLS reported that the lowest-income families averaged $385 for "education" in 1987—over twice as much as those with incomes of $15,000–$20,000. Nor did their very low incomes preclude their spending more than those with incomes of $5,000 and over for entertainment, alcohol, and new cars.[11]

· · ·

Income constrains how much consumers could spend for an item—if they devoted their entire income to it. It does not fix how much they will spend. At any income level consumers could decide to spend nothing for beef, books, or refrigerators. The income coefficient in demand studies only reports how much a family decided to spend for (1) a given item as against (2) all other items of expenditure plus saving.

Income does indeed achieve statistical significance in most models of consumer demand, whether demand for food or perfume, autos or laundry soap. But income is collinear with consumer "tastes." Both derive from a common set of forces. Both are shaped by reli-

TABLE 6.3
Percent of 1929 Income Recipients in Same Income
Interval in 1933, or One Lower

1929 Income	
$1–249	79.1%
250–499	71.4
500–749	62.4
750–999	47.6
1,000–1,499	47.0
1,500–1,999	53.4
2,000–2,999	51.8
3,000–4,499	56.4
4,500–7,499	53.9
7,500 and over	60.0

gion, education, parental income, family size, parental education, and race. When cross-section studies of expenditure patterns classify families by income they implicitly attribute to income effects that derive from tastes, or some combination of the two.

Families do tend to remain at the same relative position in the income distribution for years at a time. Inflation and deflation change current income flows without shifting the decile position for most families. They were there last year and probably will be there next year. Table 6.3 suggests how stable was the percent remaining in the same income interval (or one lower) even during the massive economic upheaval of 1929–33.[12] (Over the longer time interval, 1971–78, a third or more of those in an income quintile remained there [table 6.4].) Most people remain within any (relative) income group. They become a reference spending group for those

TABLE 6.4
Percent of 1971 Family Income
Recipients in Same Quintile in 1978

Lowest	56%
Fourth	34
Third	31
Second	32
Highest	49

Source: Computed from Greg J. Duncan,
Years of Poverty, Years of Plenty (Ann Arbor,
1984), p. 13.

who move in—from below or above. And their spending patterns
will dominate that group's patterns. In consequence, the income of
each such resident group will appear to be the major determinant of
expenditure in cross section.

But the correlation of income with "tastes" should preclude its
frequent use to measure "the budget constraint," or the exact nu-
merical importance of income elasticity in shaping demand for items
or groups.

· CHAPTER 7 ·

TASTES—AND OTHER DETERMINANTS
OF CONSUMPTION

This is fine, for me, at least at present.
— Abbe de Saint-Pierre

I

Leading approaches to modeling consumer behavior offer little guidance in explaining long-run differences in consumption. An alternative involves that "black box," consumer tastes.

One leading theory views the household as seeking to maximize "its total lifetime utility . . . influenced by its expectations concerning the future behavior of prices and rates of return."[1] Of such perspectives Arrow has remarked: "For any set of excess demand functions there is a choice of preference maps and of initial endowments, one for each individual . . . whose maximization implies the given aggregate excess demand functions." Thus, "the hypothesis of rational behavior has in general no implications."[2] Let consumers give up high-button shoes, or *Gone With the Wind*, and the theory provides no guidance on how the household then maximizes.

An alternative, preferred by many critics of economics, emphasizes irrationality. It has never been described with more gusto than by Keynes, who saw consumers as driven by "enjoyment, short-sightedness, generosity, miscalculation, ostentation and extravagance."[3] That pack of motives, however pejorative, explains investment in housing quite as well as consumption of, for example, furniture, automobiles, and jewelry. (Blenheim, the Breakers, the Carnegie mansion, or even "Bide-a-wee" are obvious examples in the housing category.) The motives apply, indeed, to government expenditures as well. Why did the White House policemen need operetta-style uniforms? Why did "prestige" require that the U.S. be the first nation "to put a man on the moon," or send a mission to Mars? Spending for such programs burgeoned at the very time that

"America discovered poverty." Nor had useful research on cancer and heart disease then reached its limit. The Keynesian analysis of motives, then, as the simplest versions of "rational consumer behavior," yields "in general no implications."

. . .

Thoughtful analyses of consumption do agree in emphasizing the past as prologue.

1. Houtthakker and Taylor long ago emphasized state dependence, in which a stock of goods or habits shapes present consumption.[4]

2. Becker and Stigler declare that tastes are invariant, but see "l'appetit vient en mangent." Consumption, accumulating over time, creates a capital stock (of habits) that induce more consumption—of good music, heroin, etc.[5]

3. Fisher sees the household's "objective function [strictly, functional] . . . changing as a result of past consumption activities."[6]

4. Cyert and De Groot argue "that when utility is a weighted average of several variables . . . the particular weights used in the utility function are subject to change as a result of experiencing particular values of the variables." Hence they propose "an adaptive utility function in which the utility . . . received by the individual . . . will change as a result of learning through experience."[7]

Emphasizing the past, however, only remands the determinants of consumption to some earlier period. The autoregressive approach may indeed help in getting high empirical coefficients. But it does little toward the specifics of a causal model.

. . .

Granted, present consumption is path dependent. But what follows? In this regress past consumption usually lacks an explanation. It is, however, possible to specify the relevant elements that shape past consumption—and thereby, present consumption. And do so by reference to empirically observable variables, no less objective than prices, incomes, and more so than cost.[8]

What are these new variables? Surely not the black box of "tastes." Most economists would be dubious, or downright suspicious, of any invocation of tastes. Few doubt their impact on consumer demand. But measuring tastes is surely a task for another discipline—any other. (Moreover, sotto voce, "they wouldn't know how to do the job anyway.") Without challenging that view it is worth reconsidering what demand analyses actually require.

· · ·

Demand at the micro level is plausibly a function of one's past and one's peers as well as prices and incomes. The most accurate forecast of any family's housing expenditure in a given interval may indeed be given by its housing expenditure in the prior interval. What it spends for vegetables, medical care, or circuses in a given period correlates well with what it spent in the prior period.

But that indefinite regress eventually discovers that prior period choices are shaped by definite factors, cultural and demographic— parental education, income, race, geographic location, size of city, ethnic background. As well as the consumers' own education, gender, work experience, etc. There is no need to enter the elysian or murky gardens of other social sciences to locate variables that shape tastes—and income. If reduced form demand functions ever specified a set of tastes, or a "lifestyle," they would nonetheless depend in turn on such antecedent variables. Consumption analysis, therefore, need not rely on any amorphous, reduced form, of taste or lifestyle. It can reach back to objectively measurable determinants.

Tastes have causes, explained by other variables. Tastes are hammered out of life experience. Economists are acquainted with many powerful variables that shape such experience. Using these independent factors as explanatory variables makes it possible to reckon with tastes—yet omit them from the model. Tastes then prove to be only an intervening variable in the system of interest.

· · ·

Family background produces the first great sorting. Children raised by Seventh Day Adventists buy few parimutuel tickets as adults. Those from laborer's families buy few opera tickets. School experience further sorts out the stream of experience. Savings and expenditure behavior differ between those who finish high school or college and those who do not.

Such background forces help create the (unmeasured) "tastes" in individuals, and the accumulated "experience" that Houthakker-Taylor, Becker-Stigler, Fisher, and Cyert-DeGroot agree shapes expenditure preferences.

How far do the antecedent, and objectively measured, elements of family background, schooling, etc. explain differences in consumption choices? From Sir John Sinclair's consumption studies in the eighteenth century, Le Play's in the nineteenth, to the Bureau of Labor Statistics' in the twentieth century, survey data have been classified by a few variables. These often included marital status and size of family. (Among others, Deaton and Muellbauer; Lewbel, Pollak, and Wales; and Barnes and Gillingham have called attention to "demographic variables in demand analysis.")[9] It is a long-overdue task to consider what wider range of factors shape consumption, via tastes. No list could be exhaustive. Nor is one requisite. The variables need not be measured more precisely than, say, the price figures commonly used. (Price series, after all, always omit discounts, speed of delivery, regularity in ordering, and provision of credit. And retail or wholesale price indexes miss major quality changes, even product changes, by the linking process.) How much is lost by omitting some aspects is an empirical question. But absent any direct measure of tastes there is no reason to remain in the empirical desert, and continue relying on little but price and income to explain consumer demand for most items.[10]

II

For detailed models of consumer behavior a common triad of factors has been invoked: income, prices, and tastes. Only the first two have been used for applied work. Some difficulties in their use, however, must be confronted. The income variable may work empirically primarily because it proxies typical family preferences in the respective income interval. Such preferences change slowly. Family relative income also changes slowly (cf. chapter 6, part 2, *supra*). Hence differences in income come to proxy for expenditure preferences. And that is why differences of income correlate so well with differences in expenditure for most items in consumer surveys.

Income's dual role is masked in many demand studies. Coefficients from equations using detailed state estimates for different years help demonstrate that dual role in chapter 8. Income as one of the independent variables proves significant for some items in any given year, but only some. Even high correlations for a given year weaken over the decades. This is so because income may successfully proxy for group preferences at any point, but preferences inevitably shift over time.

During periods of unemployment most workers have jobs, and typically alter their expenditures very little.[11] They continue paying for houses, cars, insurance. They retain their children in parochial schools and keep their telephone service. They are likely to shift to a cheaper physician, mechanic, or beautician. (They may substitute hamburgers for steak, or delay replacing the car. But even such shifts tend to occur only after they have drawn down their savings and/or put additional family members into the labor force.)

Income and tastes go their separate ways when significant mobility occurs in the relative income structure. This was most obviously so in the transition to the Great Depression, World War II, and after. But persistence is more characteristic. Hence the meaning of the income variable in money demand analysis conflates "tastes" and "the budget constraint."

Prices

Prices play a leading part in empirical demand functions. But their role, too, is unclear. It is not the price of white bread that determines the demand for white bread. At best it is its price relative to that for the nearest alternative (e.g., whole wheat, rye, rice). The usual procedure, deflating by the general consumer price index, will not do. For over 95% of that index reflects supply and demand adjustments for other items—for furniture, rent, hospital services, and autos. Surely the average of price movements for those other items is irrelevant to the consumer choosing between white bread and wheat. If the powerful collinearity between most price movements did not exist, the usual deflation by the CPI could yield very odd demand functions indeed.

Nor does theory give any guidance as to which goods the consumer idiosyncratically chooses between at the margin. In Becker's blunt comment: "The traditional theory of consumer choice . . . has nothing to say about which products are close substitutes."[12] Folk wisdom spots the alternatives when choices are made repeatedly— for example, white bread or brown, hamburger or steak. But what is the relevant price ratio for infrequent purchases, and wider categories? The consumer who decides not to buy a new Saab may repair the old Chevrolet, make a down payment on a second home, or buy a ticket to the Far East instead. Price relatives remain essential in demand theory. But "which price relative" is a difficult theoretical question for actual econometric work.

Most demand functions in the major comprehensive study by Houthakker and Taylor do not include statistically significant price ratios. That outcome may stem from the failure of official prices to reflect quality and transaction terms adequately. Or because the expenditure data relate to a group of items (e.g., "purchased food") rather than specific commodities ("white bread"). But use of the entire CPI to mark the price of the relevant alternative may also contribute.[13]

Use of price deflators in cross-section demand analyses (as in chapter 8 below) also suffers from the quality and character of the data available.

The most authentic and widespread date provided for spatial comparisons are those of the BLS for city-to-city comparisons. We note below two of its largest constituents, food and housing, which together account for roughly half of all spending reported in the BLS expenditure surveys.

For food the most recent BLS study indicates that food prices for forty-two areas within the continent all fell within 6% of the U.S. average for 1990, and thirty-four within 5%.[14]

Allowance for between city differences of this magnitude, therefore, would change the relative size of state expenditure aggregates very little. More important, such allowance would change the relative importance of various causal factors very little.

Housing, on the other hand, is among the least portable items. We compare the BLS rent differences with those from the much larger sample of Housing Census reports (chapter 11, table 11.5). The comparison yields striking results. Cincinnati rents as reported by BLS lie within 2% of the Census estimates. But there is a 30% difference for Cleveland; 21% for Detroit; 25% for Milwaukee, etc. These discrepancies are far too great to warrant using the BLS intercity price comparisons for deflation of city data. Using them to deflate the expenditure figures in Appendix B would certainly be premature.

The law of demand has not been repealed. But the frequent lack of statistical significance for a price variable in this, and other creative demand studies, suggests that we have yet to specify what price ratios are really needed for long-run analysis. We therefore omit a price variable from the demand functions shown in chapter 8.

III

The objective factors that help shape "tastes," and thereby expenditures, underly chapter 8. We treat each American state as a laboratory of long-run behavior. For its equations we go to the factors that form "tastes," influencing consumers as they pursue their elusive optimum (or even a tolerable future). The factors include the following:

Age

Tastes vary with attitudes toward what is socially appropriate for each age, and its physical limitations. True, some church-going teenagers never go to the movies. Some oldsters go dancing on Sundays. But spending—for baby bottles, graduation gowns, dining room suites, and false teeth varies as do "the seven ages of man." Smiling auto salesmen rarely sell Cadillacs to hip twenty-five-year-olds, or power-packed sports cars to staid sixty-year-olds.[15] Persons at the same income level, and confronting the same prices, differ wildly. An older group chooses Perry Como's records, a younger, Michael Jackson's or Ice T's. One prefers operettas to rock concerts, and meat to vegetables. We treat the percentage of the population in different age groups as a straightforward proxy for experiences and attitudes widely shared within each age cohort.

Marital Status

Marital status proportions by state reflect further differences in life experience. Millions choose to marry, given the persons they have met, their attitudes toward accepting responsibility, etc. Others hesitate. Hundreds, even thousands of psychological studies agree that unmarried persons, and married ones differ, at any age. Obviously they do in their twenties, but also in their sixties. Rates for illness, mortality, attitudinal measures, all differ. What elements distinguish those who marry from those who do not is a difficult question. But clearly those elements do not yield random behavior. Nor do the set of factors that distinguish between those who divorce and those who remain married.

Such marital status ratios will also proxy for experiences that shape consumption. From 1900 to 1929 marriage implied payments to midwives and doctors, and the purchase of diapers and baby furniture. Such conventional expenditure implications have shifted notably since then. Nonetheless, two single persons at a given income level still rarely buy the same set of goods as a married couple. And the directions of divergence, as their magnitude, can be examined from state data, even if budget survey results do not so permit.

One compact measure of family relationship is the percentage of women who are single. Another, the percentage who are divorced. The percentage of families headed by women, available for 1980, is also likely to be significant. Each of these groups has constraints, goals, and values, that differ from those for married women.

Family Composition

Families achieve economies of scale in consumption. Their members also prefer certain expenditures to others. The decision to have 0, 1 . . . 10 children is usually not a random one. Families differ in their preference for more children as against more goods, or "higher-quality" children (in Becker's phrase). The "cause" of such differences may be indefinitely obscure. But parents with seven children have surely revealed different preferences from parents with only one child. They also differ in the ratio of food to housing purchases, of baby food to wine, of spending for apartments versus houses. One set of family composition variables relates to the number of children (1–3, 4 and over).[16] Depending on the age breaks available from the census we also use the percentage of families with children under 21, 18, or 10.

Color/Race

Black, Oriental, Hispanic, and White families follow different life courses. Their experiences differ, as do their value systems. Such differences are likely to mark differences in consumption choices.

Occupation Groups

Grouping people into classes is an antique, widespread, and difficult enterprise. That is so whether the classes are those noted by Smith and Marx, or cultural groups. But the task is obviously relevant. One broad measure refers to the major census occupational groups—professionals, laborers, operatives, etc. Each has a different way of life, set of attitudes, and backgrounds. Such differences affect tastes, and through them, expenditures.

Country of Birth

In a nation created by immigrants and their descendants, the process of Americanization has long been central. And its consequences will appear in consumer expenditure patterns. Those raised abroad will have different tastes than those raised in the U.S. No review of immigrant narratives or voting behavior is required to entertain that possibility.

The further distinction between those born in, say, Southern Europe, Scandinavia, or the Orient is potentially significant. Its importance is obvious in preferences for wheat versus rye, and rye versus rice. But its importance for other items has to be quarried from the empirical record. Moreover, the importance of "country of origin" may well have changed as life in those nations changed relative to the U.S. between 1900 and 1982. Significance in one era may wither away by a later one.

Citizenship

One level of difference in spending patterns is indexed by the percentage of foreign born. A further level requires distinguishing new arrivals from those who have been here for half a century. Because aliens include the newest arrivals plus those who remain more committed to "the old country" and its way of life, we create a variable for the percentage of foreign born who were aliens.[17]

Conspicuous Consumption

Veblen's dramatic, darling phrase emphasizes a point made by observers since Moses: most humans value what others have. ("Thou shalt not covet thy neighbor's house, ox . . . ") But this basic insight has not been operationalized. Has anyone asked a national sample of Americans how much they shaped their spending in accord with their neighbors' verbal opinions? Who would trust the replies if asked? Veblenians have offered shrewd canards, but little more.

The simple emulation/envy of the Veblenian model, however, can be proxied by the frequency of interpersonal contact. We use two alternative measures of the extent of visible alternative models of consumption behavior as displayed to the average person.

1. First is the percentage of population that is urban. For many decades farmers lived more isolated lives than city people. But their isolation dwindled between 1900 and 1929 as Sears Roebuck catalogues, parcel post, and rural roads spread. It fell further as the telephone, radio, and TV became ubiquitous. As the states became increasingly homogenized over the decades one would expect this variable dwindled in significance.

2. A second measure of person-to-person contacts, and point-of-sale advertising, is population density.

The two variables are related, but they are not identical. In 1970 New York had much the same urban percentage as Illinois, but its density was almost twice as great. New York's density was not even half that of New Jersey, but they were equally urbanized.

Consumers in densely settled areas may have frequent contacts with other people because they prefer to live where there are many people and stores. Or they may share similar values because they have more frequent contacts. Or both. In either case, frequency of contact and similarity of expenditure behavior are linked together via shared values.

Weather

The "objective world" into which consumers must fit is shaped by variations in heat, humidity, and wind flow. Greek legends of deities associated with the weather suggest how ancient is recognition of its importance to human existence.

Eskimos acquire clothing that completely covers the body. Denizens of Key West are less insistent on that point. The relationship of expenditure to climate is hardly simple. Since Darwin it has been notorious that the Tierra del Fuego Indians wear virtually no clothing, yet fish in ice-cold waters and survive in freezing temperatures. Anthropologists report that Bolivians of the high Andes rely on clothing to protect themselves from extremely low temperatures, but not housing. Their open shelters hold little warmth: "Indoor temperatures are not much different from ambient temperatures for most of the day."[18] (Presumably eons of evolution selected out human species that adjust to the environment without the need to adjust further by building closed houses.)

Neither economic theory, however, nor psychology, designates the most relevant measure of the physical environment. It is, then, an empirical question how consumption responds to the physical environment. We urge testing three NOAA series with the greatest market over the decades as the Federal government responded to pressures for information from farmers, its greatest constituent group. These are: inches of rain, 1:00 P.M. humidity, and number of days below 32 degrees Fahrenheit.

Region

Budget studies frequently classify consumers for example, as living in Northeast, Midwest, South, and West, or New England vs. plains states, etc. So do many econometric analyses.[19] That classification may serve marketers, government units, manufacturers, and trucking firms very well, but it lacks any analytic basis.

A dummy variable for "Region" is unhappily a crude empirical average of many supply factors (wage rates, land prices, productivity, and price differences) and at least as many demand forces (a geographic clumping of tastes, income, color, occupation, weather, industry mix, and prices of final products). These factors are all combined with unknown and unintended weights to specify 8, 10, or a dozen regions. So happenstance an average permits few inferences. Do consumers spend more for a good *because* they live in the West (Portland, Oregon), and less because they live in the East (Portland, Maine)?[20] If consumers in one region spend more is it because their incomes differed? Or their occupations? Or the prices they faced? Or their family's composition? Or the number of retail stores per inhabitant? Or the historic interaction of forty other factors?

The sole element in "region" *per se* that can function as a conceptually clear factor in shaping consumption demand is physiography. Of its many constituents, many elements have been recorded by NOAA. Some can plausibly affect human behavior and consumption. We have experimented with several. One of value has been degree days. (In fact, the correlation between degree days in each state and dummies for the nine census regions is $R^2 = .549$.[21]) A second is inches of precipitation.[22] We use both (above) as explicit weather factors.

· C H A P T E R 8 ·

WHY STATE CONSUMPTION
PATTERNS DIFFER

Two ROUTES have been followed to explain variations in what consumers spend. Economists focus on income, relative prices, and wealth. Survey and sociological analysts, however, deal with demographic variables—age, sex, and family relationship. And general social critics have tackled stereotypes and cultural groupings—"the French," "the Greeks," "the Nineteenth century," "immigrants," the bourgeoisie.

The new PCE estimates by state (Appendix B) permit joint consideration of both economic and noneconomic factors. Some variance is necessarily omitted by state averages, but much remains. We test below how key economic and noneconomic forces shape housing expenditure, food, clothing, etc. The first part focuses on such changes in 1900–82; the second, on the role of individual variables, such as ethnicity, age, etc.

I. HOUSING, 1900–1982

Weather

Surely the weather is the first fundamental factor in housing expenditure. Housing offers protection against the elements, and is driven by "objective" climatic determinants. But its impact proves to be unexpected. The colder the state, the more presumably spent for housing. Insulation against the cold must raise the cost. So too would the need to provide structures for coping with snow and ice loads.

To index that determinant we use the Weather Bureau's (NOAA) "degree days"—the number of days below freezing. Other key weather variables are apparently highly correlated with this measure. Thus seventy-one city reports for degree days correlate .90 with inches of precipitation (rain and/or snow), and .91 average daily temperature.[1]

The results are unexpected. Residents of colder states did not spend more than those in warmer ones, whether in 1900 or 1929. In fact, they spent significantly less—after allowance for other variables (table 8.1). That result becomes even more striking if one considers the higher wage rates imbedded in the cost of constructing Northern housing, and much Western. Moreover, land values in the North, and hence ground rents, were surely greater than in the South.

From 1885–1914 mill workers in North Adams, Massachusetts, Providence, Rhode Island, and Portland, Maine, lived in rickety three- and four-story tenements and ramshackle slums, whose construction was hardly superior to those in South Carolina, Georgia, or Oklahoma mill towns.

Why, then, were coefficients in 1900 and 1929 negative, and significantly so? The explanation (errors in data aside) may be related to one primary offset: lower interest rates in the North. Housing has long been a primary example of long-lived assets, in which interest rates play a major role in cost. They were distinctly lower in the

TABLE 8.1
Housing Expenditure (per capita)
(t Statistics)

	$\bar{R}^2$	Alien	Percent Foreign Born	Over 65	Percent Children 1–3	4+	Heating Degree Days
1900							
Owner + Tenant	.58	−.9	3.6	1.8	−1.2	−2.1	−2.8
1929							
Owner	.78	−1.3	9.5	6.3	4.6	0	−4.1
Tenant	.72	−.8	9.5	2.1	2.2	0.1	−3.9
(Owner + Tenant)	.79	−1.2	10.6	4.8	3.9	0	−4.5
1970							
Owner	.52	−.1	6.2	−.5	.6	−.9	−0.1
Tenant	.47	2.3	4.0	−1.4	−.7	−1.9	2.2
(Owner + Tenant)	.59	.7	6.6	−.9	.2	−1.4	0.7
1977							
Owner	.51	2.7	1.1	−3.6	−2.7	−1.4	4.5
Tenant	.73	3.4	4.8	−3.5	−2.5	−3.4	3.9
(Owner + Tenant)	.63	3.2	2.3	−4.0	−3.0	−2.2	4.8
1982							
Owner	.51	1.6	2.3	−3.0	−1.8	−2.4	3.3
Tenant	.82	1.7	9.5	−1.9	−.7	−2.4	2.8
(Owner + Tenant)	.70	2.0	4.8	−3.4	−2.0	−3.0	3.9

North in 1900.[2] The balance of these forces in 1929 again yielded a negative coefficient for days freezing.

But after World War II the forces behind the housing boom changed the housing stock, significantly. The GI bill, federal housing guarantees, selective destruction by the Federal highway program—all contributed to that change. Millions of Americans moved out of run-down farm homes and mill town tenements. Many shifted to apartments with such novel facilities as running water, flush toilets, and electricity. Others moved into single-family homes. Most of these were built in tracts, with uniform construction and architecture. Song writers from more splendid locales and with better incomes complained that these "ticky tacky houses" lacked charm. But many workers found them superior to those in which they, and their parents, had been raised.

By 1970 home owners in colder climates still did not spend significantly more than their peers in warmer ones. But they no longer spent significantly less. After 1945, they presumably made do with less expensive construction than average, in order to be able to own rather than rent.

Tenants in colder states, however, did spend more by 1970. They may have preferred different trade-offs. But that shift may have been intensified, or even created, by legislation and regulation. As well-publicized state and federal hearings on slum housing continued, building codes began to require better plumbing, heating, and lighting facilities than had characterized millions of owned homes, much less rented ones. Who paid for these improvements? Obviously, the tenants.

By 1977 the sign on the climate variable was reversed. The baby boom owners apparently had different preferences. Brick housing increasingly replaced wood, as did stone and brick veneer. New heating units were engineered in response to higher prices for oil and gas after the Arab oil embargoes of 1973 and 1980. New houses were insulated more fully than those built in prior decades. (A decision that may have been regretted when lawsuits over asbestos insulation proliferated in later years.)

Children

Family living in 1900 generally offered few economies of scale, despite the advantages that Fourier, Ripley, and Gilman imagined sprang from "associated economy." But housing proved a signal exception for most years shown in Table 8.1. States having a higher percentage of families with children spent less (per capita) on housing.

But not in 1929. Possibly because an unusually long sequence of increased real incomes from 1915 to 1929 had led both to (*a*) more marriages and children in every state, and (*b*) the purchase of more housing space and amenities. However in 1900, 1977, and 1982 the more families with children in any state the less it spent for housing per capita. Moreover, families with four or more children clearly spent less per capita on housing in 1982 (as in most prior year).

Foreign Born

The variable for "percentage of foreign born" in the state concurrently induced more uniformly statistically significant t ratios than any of the five other variables in table 8.1. Evidently the foreign born set a high value on housing, whether as owners or tenants. However, this is not because their incomes were higher, or their style of life ran above the average for natives. Moreover, large families (four or more) were more common in this group, a factor that would also have reduced their expenditures.[3]

That coefficients for foreign born nonetheless turn out to be significantly positive is therefore highly meaningful. In 1900 such coefficients appeared for Americans of Polish, Swedish, and Irish origin.

That these origins implied greater than average expenditures presumably testified to their search for stability after the disruption of moving thousands of miles from their European homes. They formed Polish and Irish neighborhoods from Boston to Chicago, and from Cleveland to San Francisco, which persisted for decades.

But no such coefficients appeared for those of Hispanic origin in 1970 and later, when that group became central in political endeavor. Perhaps the difference reflected the fact that in 1900 and 1929 those of European origin could rarely afford to visit friends and relatives in Europe. They remained, and became "Americans." By contrast, Hispanics frequently returned to Mexico on cheap bus tickets after 1929, and to Puerto Rico as air fares fell after 1945. Visits, and even longer stays, were common for both major Hispanic groups.

Alien

The percentage of the foreign born that was alien (i.e., did not yet hold citizens' papers) was also linked to greater spending on housing. Only marginally 50 in 1900 and 1929, perhaps because in those years so many arrived in high-rent ports (e.g., New York and Boston). But the relationship had become statistically significant by 1979–82.

Why so? Surely not because discrimination by builder or realtor cartels developed. For such arrangements would have been most feasible, and most effective, in the first half of the twentieth century, not the second half. The more likely explanation is that most of a newer generation of aliens held different preferences and values than earlier ones. Moreover, our data on size of family ignore the presence of roomers. The 1901 BLS expenditure survey shows, for example, that alien and foreign-born families had significant numbers of roomers and boarders. So do the 1910 Immigration Commission Reports.

Age

Finally, age. Prior to the Social Security Act of 1936 older Americans lived with their children. They typically had little alternative. After that act was passed, however, families increasingly split up. Younger people moved out, not remaining to care for their parents. The family with two and three generations ceased to be the norm. Retirees and widows lived as separate families. And they spent less than the average for housing.

II. Food

Off-Premise Food (Grocery Store)

Perhaps the most striking aspect of the food regressions is the marked decline in the $\overline{R}^2$ for off-premise food (grocery stores) after 1929 (table 8.2). The foreign born continued to buy at a greater rate than native Americans. (And, in the second set of regressions, both income and habits—PCE—continued to be significant, while the proportion of women in the labor force did not become significant.)

The temporal shift reflected three major changes. (1) Older people ate more, and better. Grocery sales were no longer smaller in states with more older people. Higher income, separate Social Security incomes, and increased pension incomes had brought that result. (2) Farmers and rural residents no longer spent significantly less than city people for food. Farm housewives increasingly produced less of their own food, and bought more from the store. (3) Rising incomes and expanded welfare programs, not least food stamps, meant that families with children no longer economized on groceries.

The vast new array of baby foods in jars followed centuries when

TABLE 8.2
t Statistics for Food (per capita)
variables

	Food—Off-Premise				Food—Meals & Bev			
	(t Statistics)							
	1929		1982		1929		1982	
Percent of Population								
Foreign Born	6.5		4.1		3.3		1.6	
Over 65	−2.2		0.9		−1.4		0.6	
Urban	1.8		0.2		2.4		2.6	
age 0–9		−4.1		−1.1		−.05		0.3
Black		−1.7		−0.4		0.6		−1.1
% of Families with 1–3 Children	−2.3		2.3		−1.7		1.9	
4 + Children		−6.0		−2.0		−0.4		−1.7
PCE per Capita		3.2		4.1		4.6		5.5
% of Women in Labor Force		0.4		−0.3		−1.1		2.6
$\bar{R}^2$	.90	.88	.20	.45	.60	.75	.40	.66

	Total Food (off-premise + meals & bev)				Off-Premise as % of total food			
	1929		1982		1929		1982	
% of population								
Foreign Born	5.1		3.0		−1.6		0.2	
Over 65	1.0		0.3		0.9		−1.1	
Urban	1.0		1.2		−1.9		−3.2	
age 0–9		−3.8		−0.8		−0.5		−0.9
Black		−1.3		−0.8		0.3		1.1
% of Families with 1–3 Children	−1.3		1.7		0.1		−1.9	
4 + Children		−0.1		−2.5		−0.1		0.3
PCE per Capita		4.4		5.6		−2.7		2.5
% of Women in Labor Force		0		0.9		1.7		2.9
$\bar{R}^2$	.71	.90	.41	.63	.29	.48	.22	.41

housewives prepared special dishes for their babies, and/or fed them part of what was cooked for the family. The equally vast array of packaged breakfast foods also reflected family willingness to spend as much for children as adults. Large families (four or more children) continued to spend less per child than per adult. Each 1%

TABLE 8.3
Food Expenditure
(t Statistics)

	$\bar{R}^2$	Income per Capita	Percent Foreign Born	Black	Women in the Labor Force	Children 1–3	Children 4+	Degree Days
						t Statistics		
1929								
Purchased Food	.92	3.3	3.9	—	−1.6	−2.3	—	—
Meals & Beverages	.79	—	5.0	—	−2.8	—	−1.8	−3.3
1982								
Purchased Food	.42	—	—	—	—	—	—	—
Meals & Beverages	.66	3.1	—	−4.9	—	2.9	−1.5	−5.1

Note: − indicates less than ≤1.5.

increase in the percent of large families reduced per capita food expenditure by about 3% in 1929, and again in 1982. (Large families did not spend less for most items other than food and housing, however.)

For off-premise food, the proportion of children aged 0 to 4 did not significantly change per capita food spending in 1929.[4] Nursing babies did consume less purchased food. So did those fed with scraps from the parental plate. But increasingly babies began to be fed from purchased jars of baby food. These cost more per pound (of applesauce, meat, and vegetables) than adult food. In 1982 the coefficient for younger children continued not to differ significantly from zero.[5]

The BLS surveys for 1982–83—closest in date to our 1982 results—apparently reach a different result. Careful studies using BLS surveys to assess the cost of children,[6] estimate that small children consumed about one-third of what either parent did in families with "oldest child under 6."[7]

However, the BLS data for these families necessarily ignore half of all children under 6[8]—those living in families with older children, or with one parent. The data may thus not provide an unbiased estimate of the cost of food for young children (or the cost of other items).

Children aged 5–14 are another matter. Their caloric needs may well be greater. And they did increase the average in 1982 (but decreased it in 1929). Which suggests more use of leftovers and cheaper snacks in 1929, before rising incomes and different parental standards increased spending for the vocal 5–14 age group.

Persons over 65 spent less than younger people on food in 1929 (t = −3.0) and 1982 (t = −1.8). They bought less food to cook at home and spent less at McDonald's and other restaurants and bars.

Meals and Beverages

Meals and beverages have always had a substantial recreational/luxury dimension. They provided a modest luxury in which the foreign born could indulge without throwing their entire budget out of whack. Not so, however, for older people, or families with children, through 1929. By 1982, however, children from families with one to three children had become primary patrons of McDonald's and similar establishments. Families with four or more children continued to draw a line at such spending. Finally, since most restaurants and fast-food establishments relied on volume sales they were concentrated in urban areas both in 1929 and in 1982.

Total Food

Restaurants partially substitute for grocery stores. Indeed, the variables reviewed above apply about as well to total spending for food as either groceries or meals. (Though the presence of older people in a state had no impact in 1929 or 1982.)

A more clear-cut measure of substitutability is the simple ratio of off-premise food expenditure to total spending for food. The most consistent significant finding for that ratio was that the income/habit variable was negative at both dates. The most obvious significant change was associated with the increased role of women in the labor force. In 1929 women added to their family income to put more groceries on the table than their husband's income permitted. By 1982, however, women workers were no longer primarily from the working class. They came from families at all status levels. In state after state they expanded restaurant and take-out purchases at the expense of supermarket purchases for food to be cooked at home.

III. Clothing, Shoes: 1900–1982

For all items, at all dates, the percentage urban has the highest and most regular sequence of significant t statistics. Where else but in cities does one see the Jones's frequently, or the Trumps at all? Where else is it easy to shop for the variety of styles, sizes, and prices? Granted, advertisements and catalogs are available in the Maine woods and the Florida Keys. But the full range, exact quality, and realistic color appears only in the selection offered by discount store counters, department store racks, and supermarket aisles. Reluctant shoppers, and those contemptuous of such worldly emphasis, may not respond. But libraries that offered, say, only The World's Twenty Best Novels would elicit an equally negative response from such critics.

Dominant and significant factors for food and housing in 1929 had lost importance by 1970, thanks to shifts in behavior and preference. Such changes were far less frequent for clothing. The percentage foreign born—highly significant in 1900, 1929, and 1970—lost significance only slightly by 1982.

In 1900 and 1929 older people commonly worked till the day they died. They therefore spent significantly more for work shoes, which were better built and therefore relatively expensive. But as work changed, and retirement began years before death, older people no longer spent more than average for shoes. (This shift took place well before teenagers and slum dwellers acquired expensive athletic shoes as commonly as exurbanites.)

Older men also spent more for clothing in 1929. But their pattern of work and conformity changed by the 1970s. Burly workmen were once photographed wearing collars and ties on the job. And their Sunday best was required as regularly for trade union marches as for church. But in time sweaters and leisure wear sufficed in most environments.

The more children a family had, the less it spent (per capita) for clothing (men's, women's, shoes, and jewelry alike)—in 1900 or 1970 or 1982. (1929 represents a puzzling exception. In that year alone, families with one to three children spent more than average per capita. Perhaps it only meant that with higher wages more marriages, more births, and more expenditure on clothing would take place in families who prudently had no more than one to three children. (For families with four or more children, negative coefficients dominated each clothing category in nearly every year.)

IV. CLOTHING: 1982

Regressions for five clothing items in 1982 yielded the t statistics in table 8.4.

Total PCE proves highly significant, proxying habits imbedded in the level of living in the separate states. More surprising are the contributions of other variables.

TABLE 8.4
Per Capita Expenditure on:

	Clothing		Jewelry	Shoes	Shoe Repair
	Women's	Men's			
PCE per cap	9.9	7.0	6.9	6.3	3.5
Degree Days	−3.6	−0.1	−6.2	−2.8	−1.6
% of pop 0–4	−1.8	−1.2	1.8	0	3.2
% of pop GT 65	−1.5	−0.9	0	−1.8	−1.8
% Spanish orig	−.02	−0.1	1.0	0.4	0.0
$\bar{R}^2$	.81	.68	.66	.61	.39

Weather

One assumes that clothing is bought primarily to protect from the weather. But if so, why did women need significantly less protection than men? The source of the negative 3.6 coefficient is suggested by the significantly negative signs for jewelry and shoes. When bundled up for cold weather few people linger on their way. Women therefore give less attention to style in colder than in warmer climates, their own style, or that of those they may encounter. They thus pay less attention to their clothing, their shoes, and their jewelry, and spend less for items that embody style. (They also spend less for shoe repairs, since their inventory of shoes is smaller.)

Age

The coefficients for the youngest age group (0–4) and the oldest (65+) reveal how different the responsiveness is to the accumulation of habits, preferences, and disabilities reflected by age. Less was spent for clothing when children were present but (oddly enough) more for jewelry. The latter, however, may reflect expenditure for wedding rings and wedding gifts. In terms of statistically significant measures, women's clothing expenditures were down when either the young or the old were present. The inference is that less was spent by older women on their clothing, and less spent for young children. Not so for men's, which were not significantly depressed. (Adult women may also have cut their spending when children arrived. However, the concurrent increase for jewelry suggests that was not likely to have been a factor.)

In other regressions the percentage black proved significant for men's clothing (−2.6). That percentage may indicate that men reduce such expenditures to help provide for the children. However, if that were so the percentage black should have a negative impact on spending for jewelry, shoes, and women's clothing and jewelry, which it does not.

V. MEDICAL: 1900–1982

In an era when medical care has become a major item on the public agenda it is difficult to remember how recent such concern is. Before antibiotics, modern appliances for surgery, and other wonders of modern medicine, medical care was infrequently considered urgent and valuable. Illness and death of course aroused concern. But that concern was not much more effectively allayed by medicine than patent drugs, or by nurses who relied on kindness and compresses.

How were state expenditures for four medical categories linked to related variables over three-quarters of a century (table 8.5)? At all dates shown, each type of medical expenditure was significantly related to total consumer spending. Those with higher incomes spent more on whatever physicians, dentists, hospitals, and other professionals, could offer. In some cases it could assist. (The longevity of John D. Rockefeller was notorious, although Baptist restraint probably contributed more than physicians.) Expenditures on drugs were also positively related at most dates. (1977 provides an odd, inexplicable, deviation.)

At one end of the age distribution are children up to the age of nine. In general, the more children in a state the less the expenditure on medical care. Most items at every date had a negative coefficient for children, though many were not statistically significant. Presumably children were healthier than the typical adult.

By 1929, however, births in higher-income states increasingly took place in hospitals. By 1970 the ubiquity of births in hospitals had canceled any positive relationship. Most lower-income states had followed the higher-income ones in relying on hospital assistance for births. The danger of death from staph, common enough in the era of Oliver Wendell Holmes and Ignaz Semmelweis, had ceased— thanks to modern antibiotics. Nor had disease strains resistant to penicillin really begun to spread. By the 1980s the nation's values had led to spending $100,000 a piece to keep alive babies born with heroin in their system. But the numbers involved were not enough to affect overall results.

What of those over sixty-five? In 1900 they died at home, without benefit of hospital expenditure. By 1929, however, the greater their share in the population the more that was spent for hospitals (and,

TABLE 8.5
Medical Expenditure (per capita)
(t Statistics)

	$\bar{R}^2$	t Intercept	Tot PCE	Pop 65 +	Pop 0 to 9
1900					
Physician	.62	.94	3.28	− .52	− .98
Hospital	.54	.24	3.30	−2.21	− .53
Dentist	.78	− .78	5.99	1.10	.03
Prof. Serv.	.73	.58	4.60	− .19	− .77
1929					
Physician	.77	1.17	5.53	− .15	− .78
Hospital	.87	− 3.80	10.84	1.99	2.86
Dentist	.78	1.55	4.50	.004	−1.92
Prof.	.54	1.95	2.76	.37	− .85
Drugs	.68	4.60	1.62	−1.85	−3.70
Funeral	.40	− 2.82	4.51	2.45	2.86
1970					
Physician	.46	2.93	4.47	−1.90	−2.76
Hospital	.27	.85	3.78	.31	− .94
Dentist	.44	.95	5.35	− .02	−1.39
Oth. Prof.	.38	− .03	4.44	2.38	− .66
Drugs	.20	.35	3.20	− .82	.52
Funeral	.40	2.55	− .94	2.97	−2.18
1977					
Physician	.43	− .36	5.54	1.54	.19
Hospital	.44	.37	3.53	1.82	−2.11
Dentist	.52	.90	5.21	− .72	−1.99
Oth. Prof.	.19	.76	2.40	− .15	−1.38
Drugs	− .06	3.17	− .58	− .39	− .49
Funeral	.27	2.58	−1.53	1.49	−2.37
1982					
Physician	.35	− .55	4.73	1.19	1.11
Hospital	.35	− .47	2.60	2.77	− .53
Dentist	.47	− .45	5.35	− .94	.47
Oth. Prof.	.37	− .96	3.40	2.70	− .09
Drugs	.40	1.28	4.31	−1.92	.40
Funeral	.31	2.05	−2.53	2.71	−1.06

of course, for funerals). Interestingly, their presence did not push up spending for physicians in any significant way.

In the first half of the twentieth century old people spent no more than average caring for their teeth, despite the small group that spent a good deal for bridges and plates. Over the past half century the spread of fluoridation, plus greater care for children's teeth, eventually meant fewer problems among the old. Without such forces at work no pattern of significant change appeared for spending on physicians and hospitals. The increased role of medicare and medicaid, of course, drives a wedge between any judgments on consumer spending and medical care.

The foreign born spent more for hospitals at all dates. But they were not, over time, a uniform group. Legislation and INS enforcement led to different nationality flows after 1900, and certainly after 1929. The newer, foreign-born group spent more for dentists and physicians in 1970 and 1977.

· PART THREE ·

· C H A P T E R   9 ·

ESTIMATING PROCEDURES: U.S.
CONSUMPTION, 1900–1929

THE METHODS used to estimate annual U.S. personal expenditures for 100+ BEA consumption items in Appendix A are described below. Those for most service expenditures have been reported previously.[1] Part I in this chapter outlines the procedure used for most goods. Part II describes the approaches for revised housing and welfare expenditure. Part III outlines how the price deflators were derived.

The present study develops data for the one hundred consumer expenditure items in the national income accounts. It relies chiefly on the Censuses of Retail Trade, Services, Housing, Government, and Population. Each Census drew on an enormous sample of knowledgeable respondents. For the most part the reports rest on detailed and original records rather than fleeting and vagrant consumer memories. Thus the 1977 Census of Retail Trade collected data from firms with over 85% of all retail sales.[2] The 1977 Census of Services relied on direct reports for about 70% of all services in scope.[3] The 1980 Census of Housing collected rent and value data from over 95% of the population.[4]

These new data are consistent with BEA data for the U.S. (in the 1993 revision), and are benchmarked to them. For selected years these totals are allocated among the fifty individual states in chapter 10.

I. GOODS

The starting point for most estimates of goods is the series William Shaw derived by adjusting and interpolating Census of Manufactures output data.[5] His estimates are refinements of those originally provided in Kuznets's *Commodity Flow and Capital Formation* (1938).[6] We increased Shaw's series, at manufacturer's level, to retail purchase levels using margin data from Barger's major study.[7] Barger derived distributive spread by kind of retail outlet as a percent of retail value.[8] He also provided a very detailed allocation of input (producer's value after transportation charges) by both wholesale and retail channel of distribution.[9] The distributive spread shown for individual types of stores—for example, 30.7% for country general stores in 1899—was applied to the percent of all clothing output sold through such stores; the 29.4% spread for department stores applied to the 7% of all clothing sold through department stores, the 24.4% spread for mail-order sales applied to the 1% of all clothing sold by mail, etc. This weighting procedure yields a distributive spread estimate (inclusive of transport, wholesale, and retail charges) for 1899 that can be added to Shaw's totals to arrive at a retail value for the type of product.[10] A similar sequence gave other decennial margin percentages.

These percentages were interpolated to give intercensal proportions, these then being applied to Shaw's annual estimates of production by type of good.[11] The resultant series were then used to extrapolate the BEA 1929 figure.

Exceptions to the above procedures are outlined below for:

> Food
> Alcoholic Beverages
> Wood
> Cleaning and Polishing Materials
> Toilet Articles and Drugs
> Magazines, Newspaper
> Stationery
> Other Fuel and Ice
> Toys
> Flowers and Seeds
> Expenditures Abroad
> Remittances in Kind

Food

Shaw's basic estimates for value of food produced were, however, not used, chiefly because of the unlikely pattern they report. His constant dollar series is shown in table 9.1.[12]

How likely is it that U.S. constant dollar food expenditures rose between 1900 and 1901 from one plateau to another, and again between 1905 and 1906? We suspect that factory output in the few sample states he used for intercensal interpolation (none of them a major food producer) was an unsatisfactory guide.

TABLE 9.1
Food Expenditures
(Shaw: constant dollars)

Year	($Billions)
1897	3.8
1898	3.8
1899	4.2
1900	4.2
1901	4.8
1902	4.7
1903	5.0
1904	5.0
1905	5.1
1906	5.8
1907	5.9
1908	5.3
1909	5.9
1910	6.1

His estimates would not, however, have been rejected had the Department of Agriculture not developed a substantial body of new data since the 1940s, when Shaw's work was concluded. Deferring details, it may be noted that the estimates made here really consist of two parts. The first utilizes the USDA data on the value of food produced in the U.S. It does not attempt, as Shaw does, to distinguish between food that went directly to consumers versus that going to factories, using factory output for the latter. Hence no problem arises of omitting food that is "manufactured" in "factories" not located by the census—for example, slaughtering, canning vegetables, bread baking in small factories below the census minimum size, and in farms or homes. To this estimate the distributive margin from farm through retail stores is added, derived from USDA data for the farmers' share of the consumer dollar. The major elements in the estimate are outlined below.

Value of food at farm level 1900–29:

A. Gross income to farmers from the production of food was derived from the Strauss and Bean USDA study.[13]

B. Exports of crude food were deducted after adjusting them from port to farm value.[14]

C. Exports of manufactured food were deducted after a similar port-farm value adjustment, and after excluding the value added by manufacturing.[15]

D. The series computed by deducting (B) and (C) above from (A) was then divided by the USDA series for the farmers' share of the consumers' food dollar for 1913–29.[16] For the years prior to 1913 the 1915 ratio was used. That ratio, reflecting the early rise in exports to Europe as a result of the war, would also be consistent with the general farm prosperity indicated by the preference of farm organizations for a 1910–14 parity base period. (Attempts to compute a ratio directly using retail and farm prices proved unsatisfactory because of the character of the underlying BLS retail price series. Since, however, the farmers' share varied by only 2 points in 1913–17, and only 3 points in 1920–29, to assume constancy during the more stable 1900–13 period seems reasonably safe.)

The procedure used above tacitly assumed that the trend in the value added in manufacturing food moved as did the value of food bought for processing by factories.[17] (This item constitutes about 20% of the value of food at retail.[18]) A review of data from the Census of Manufactures shows that the ratio of value added in food factories to the value of farm products they purchased was quite stable.[19] We therefore accept the trend computed above as an adequate basis for extrapolating the 1929 BEA figure for consumer food expenditures.

The food expenditure total includes the amounts for purchased meals and beverages. This is acceptable because the underlying production data include all food and beverage raw materials, while the markup using the USDA distributive margin provides for processing and handling at retail.[20]

FARMER'S HOME CONSUMPTION OF FOOD

Volume. The USDA has estimated the volume of farmer's home consumption of food in 1910–29.[21] To extend this back to 1900 we compute the ratio, for 1910 onward of this volume index to employment on farms—a measure of the change in adult farm population.[22] The ratio shows no change in 1910–14 and indeed very little change on through 1922 (when it is 1.99 compared to 1.98 for the prewar years). We therefore use the 1910 ratio to derive figures for earlier years. (Presumably the USDA used a constant consumption rate per person on farms or some such measure.)

Value. The index of prices received by farmers for food products, as estimated above, was multiplied by the volume index to give a series for value of food. This index was then used to extrapolate the 1929 OBE estimate for food consumed on farms.

FOOD FURNISHED GOVERNMENT AND COMMERCIAL EMPLOYEES

The number of persons in the armed forces each year plus the number of those in domestic service, was computed as a percentage of the U.S. population.[23] These percentages, applied to the estimates of food derived above for the entire U.S., gave totals for food furnished to government and commercial employees.

It was necessary to allow for the fact that wartime expenditures per soldier were higher than those for civilians. The cost of food per U.S. soldier was $121 in fiscal 1917, but $334 in fiscal 1918.[24] In fiscal 1919 the average was $224.[25]

Given the pattern of monthly expenditures by the Quartermaster-General it was concluded that in calendar years 1917 and 1919 subsistence per capita for the armed forces did not significantly exceed that for the civilian population. In calendar 1918, however, they were an estimated $334, double the civilian average.

Since there is no benchmark for this series prior to 1929 an alternative 1900 estimate was made as a check. It was arrived at by multiplying the sum of (the armed forces plus number of domestics) by the retail food price index derived above. The 1900 estimate in the resultant series was 30% of the 1929 total—virtually identical with the 29% implicit in the series derived.

Alcoholic Beverages

An 1899 benchmark is estimated in table 9.2:

TABLE 9.2
Alcoholic Beverages, 1899
(in $ millions)

1. Manufacturers' Value	$342
Distributive spread	
2. Return on capital	109
3. Wages & entrepreneurial income	256
4. Taxes	
Federal	168
State	53
Total	$928

1. The manufacturers' value of product was taken from the 1900 Census.[26]

2. The amount of capital invested in retail and wholesale liquor distribution in 1896 was $957 million, while rentals for real estate

and fixtures used in the distribution of liquor averaged 9.41% of the value of such investment.[27] Assuming the same rate of return on owned as rented capital—about half the capital was rented (57%) and half owned—gives the estimated return on capital.[28]

3. For wages and entrepreneurial income we assume that entrepreneurs and full-time equivalent employees in the industry averaged what bartenders did in 1901.[29] (The equivalence between earnings by full-time employees and entrepreneurs in most industries is, of course, assumed in estimates of the Bureau of Economic Analysis for the 1930s and Kuznets for the 1920s.)

4. The yield of the U.S. Internal Revenue tax on alcohol is reported by the Treasury Department.[30] State and local taxes were estimated at $51 million for 1896 and $55 million for 1902.[31] We interpolate to derive the 1899 figure.

How adequate is this estimate? Manufacturers' value and tax data came from the Census of Manufactures and the Census of Wealth, both of established high quality. Distributive spread is based on the Commissioner of Labor's survey of 29,258 establishments in fourteen states.[32] They imply a margin that is 39% of retail value. Barger, having reviewed many articles in the literature of the liquor trade and retail industry, estimates distributive spread for liquor stores in 1899 at 46%, and, for bars, at 55%.[33] But he does not allow for state liquor taxes, while his liquor store margin is derived from a small sample of Massachusetts stores.[34] Hence his results do not plausibly contradict the present 1899 estimate.

The 1899 dollar total derived above was extrapolated to 1900–19 by multiplying gallons of distilled spirits and malt liquor consumed in each year by their price.[35]

The national income accounts do not knowingly include illegal expenditures. The BEA data, therefore, report no expenditures on alcohol in 1920–29. (Warburton estimates $4.8 billion was spent—illegally—in 1929.)

Cleaning and Polishing Materials, Toilet Articles and Preparations, and Drug Preparation and Sundries

Shaw combines these items into one group. To provide series comparable with the separate BEA series we utilize Shaw's detailed listing (based on Census of Manufactures data) for output under each of these headings.[36] The share of total group output in each of these categories was computed at census dates, interpolated, then applied to his annual group estimates.[37] These series were then increased for distributive spread using Barger's data on sales of such products by type of store.

Magazines, Newspapers, Stationery, etc.

Shaw combines these groups. To separate out the stationery category we compute its ratio to the group total in census years from his output data. For intercensal years Shaw's stationery output series was interpolated by an index of stationery use. We assumed stationery use varied as the number of letters sent. The index was therefore computed as the product of a quantum index—the number of postage stamps—times Shaw's price index for the combined newspaper and stationery group.[38]

Shaw's group 4 series for magazines and newspapers was marked up by the margin procedure outlined in part 1, that series then used to extrapolate the BEA 1929 figure.[39]

Other Fuel and Ice

We combine items from separate Shaw groups, and add them to a series for fuel wood—a product not included in Shaw's commodity output series.

1. Fuel wood: Shaw estimates U.S. household consumption of coal (i.e., domestic sizes) at $105 million for 1900.[40] Adding transport and distributive margin to this figure gives a $202 million retail figure for coal.[41]

For wood a U.S. Forest Service survey estimated 14.2 million cords consumed in towns and cities in 1908—that is, not on farms.[42] Now the Census of Manufactures for 1910 reported 5.5 million cords consumed by factories in the prior year.[43] Therefore, allowing for both a smaller population in 1900 and wood consumption by nonfarm business, we estimate urban family consumption of 8 million cords in 1900. Even at $6 a cord adding this wood figure to the coal total estimated above gives under $250 million a year for urban family fuel. The Cost of Living Survey for 1900, however, implies fuel expenditures of $345 million.[44] In part this difference may reflect an understatement in Shaw's estimate of coal.[45] For the urban population we conclude that the Cost of Living survey provides a more adequate benchmark for expenditures on fuel than does the aggregation of (a) Shaw's coal in domestic sizes plus (b) wood consumption, the volume then marked up for distributive margin.

For the rural population the problem is somewhat simpler. The 1908 Forest Service survey estimated 70 million cords consumed by farm families.[46] We estimate 12.44 cords consumed per farm family.[47] The Census of Agriculture data for 1909 indicate $43 per farm reporting "cut (forest) products used or to be used on farms."[48] (Only 38% of all farms reported consuming such products.) If the farm consumption consisted only of cordwood this figure would imply $3.45 per cord. This figure compares favorably with the $2.61 reported by Pierson for farm and city combined. (Fence posts, rails, etc., would account for the balance of total consumption.)[49] Hence the $35 fuel figure W. C. Funk reported based on his USDA field investigation of 483 farm families in 1909 appears not unreasonable.[50] It is consistent with these census-derived figures. His estimate, for 1909, should be reduced somewhat to give a 1900 figure. We therefore conclude by using the same $32 figure for farm and nonfarm families in 1900. (Nonfarm families averaged 4.7 rooms per family.[51] Farm families would have larger houses and greater consumption. On the other hand, the distributive margin for the latter's fuel was less. We assume these influences approximately canceled each other.) The 1900 benchmark was therefore computed as $32 each for 16 million families or $512 million.

Domestic wood consumption from 1900 to 1929 was estimated by deducting wood consumed by factories from total wood consumption.[52] The 1910 census showed factories consumed 5.5 million cords. Of these the largest single consumer was the brick and tile industry, which took nearly 20%.[53] By 1919, however, the census reports that brick and tile producers relied wholly on coal, oil, and other fuels.[54] We assume that the proportion of cordwood consumed by other than households declined linearly from 5.5 (out of 76.0) in 1908 to 0 in 1919. Extrapolating the implied percentages, and applying them to the total cordwood consumed, gives consumption by families. This series, multiplied by a fuel price series, gives a preliminary series for the trend in cordwood expenditures—which was then adjusted to a 1929 benchmark.[55] Some partial USDA figures exist for farmer's income from sale of forest products in 1924–29, but they are both incomplete and unreasonable in trend.[56] There being no other sources we rely on the above procedure to give an estimate for cordwood expenditures. These were then added to series developed separately for other fuels, benchmarked to the BEA 1929 figure to give the final series used.

2. Other fuel. Shaw's estimates for manufactured fuels (minor group 5a) were increased to retail levels using Barger's margin data, by the procedure outlined above. The share for gasoline and lubricating oils was then excluded, utilizing detailed product output data from Shaw and Kuznets.[57]

3. Ice. Output data for census years are available from Shaw and Kuznets.[58] Ratios of these figures to the corresponding total for the food group, of which it is a part, were computed, interpolated, and applied to their food group estimates to give the intercensal total for ice.[59]

Nondurable Toys

The proportion of nondurable to all toys was computed from output data for the census years in Shaw, interpolated, and applied to the marked-up annual estimates of totals derived from Shaw and Kuznets by the general procedure.[60]

Wheel Goods, etc.

Shaw's motorcycles, bicycles, and pleasure craft categories (groups 21, 22) were marked up by margin ratios derived from Barger and figures for durable toys were added to that series.

Flowers and Seeds

Consumer purchases of flowers and seeds in 1899 were estimated from data in the 1900 Census of Agriculture, which reported $18.4 million of floriculture products (on the farms) retailing at an estimated $30 million.[61] The same markup ratio applied to the farm value of nursery products gave a combined total of $47 million at retail.[62] For 1929 the BEA total of $221 was assumed comparable with the Strauss Bean estimate for these items at farm level.[63] The 1899 ratio and the 1929 markup ratios were encouragingly similar—60.4% and 65.7%, respectively. We therefore interpolated linearly between these markup ratios and applied them to a series for flowers and seeds at farm level. The latter was derived for 1910–29 by computing receipts from the sale of nursery products and greenhouses per farm reporting in the decennial Census of Agriculture, interpolating by average cash receipts per self-employed farm worker.[64] For 1900–1910 the 1910 figure was extrapolated by the number of farms in each year times the value produced per such farm.[65]

Expenditures Abroad by U.S. Government Personnel

The primary variations in this series from year to year would have been correlated with changes in the size of the army overseas. We therefore derived decennial benchmarks for the population overseas from the Census of Population, and interpolated by the number of military personnel on active duty.[66] From 1916 to 1920, however, interpolation was by the size of the American Expeditionary Forces.[67] This series was then multiplied by a series used to extrapolate the 1929 BEA total for this item.[68] In effect this assumes that the trends in expenditure by overseas employees tracked their income trends.

Remittances in Kind

Estimated by the BEA at less than $1 million a year for 1929–35 these
are assumed at less than $1 million for 1900–1928.

A Note on Inventories

The series for consumer expenditure on commodities estimated
above rely largely on output data. But between output and consumer purchases lie inventories. Would allowance for fluctuations in
inventories of consumer commodities yield series that move differently than the ones we have estimated?

1. We simply have no data on inventory change for consumer commodities in these years. (For that matter such data are lacking today.[69])

2. But it is possible to consider some orders of magnitude. In table
9.3 we compare indices for the years since 1954, when data on in-

TABLE 9.3
Manufacturing Shipments
vs. Production, 1954–1975
(1954 = 100)

	Shipments	*Production*
1954	100	100
55	113	117
56	119	129
57	123	126
58	117	120
59	129	134
1960	132	139
61	132	134
62	142	143
63	150	153
64	160	165
1965	176	181
66	192	205
67	199	209
68	215	224
69	229	242
1970	226	239
71	239	245
72	266	272
73	306	317
74	350	390
75	352	357

ventories by stage of fabrication become available. One series measures trends in production—defined as shipments plus inventory change of finished goods. The other measures trends in shipments. The shipments index is conceptually closer to what one would wish to measure. The other series is closer to what our expenditures series does measure. Yet it is difficult to make much of the difference between the two trends shown.

Some indications of total inventory change for 1918–29 (not merely finished goods) are reported in Abramowitz.[70] These data help focus on the inventory accumulation of 1919–21 and 1923–24. Since they relate to total inventory change they do not clearly contradict our conclusions from data for 1954 onward. Particularly when it is noted that these data contrast inventories as of the end of December and sales for the year. For the major downturns in the period took place in the fall thus tending to make the December 30 inventories more out of line with sales than would annual average holdings, as in the table.

Ignoring inventory change is undesirable, but there is no basis for accurate adjustment, by commodity line, for annual average change in inventories. (The resultant bias would also appear in data from the national income accounts since 1929. For those years such basic adjustment material is lacking.) However, the importance of the error would be restricted primarily to a few commoditites in years of very sharp and peculiar inventory change.

II. SERVICES

Housing

Housing services were previously estimated on the basis of the housing stock estimates by Grebler, Blank, and Winnick, used by Kuznets, Kendrick et al.[71]

Work with the series, however, indicated it had a basic limitation.

Grebler began with Blank's estimates for residential starts. Converted into a constant-dollar series these were then translated into current dollars by a residential construction cost series.[72] Table 9.4 contrasts that cost series with (a) price trends for one-family houses, (b) the BLS rent index, and (c) the NICB rent index (which used a different sample of cities than the BLS).

The 20% decline in Grebler's residential construction cost index from 1920 to 1921 differs largely from both (a) the trivial change in his price index for one-family, owner-occupied houses and (b) marked gains in both the NICB and BLS rent indices. The cost index presumably reflects the cost of new construction. But it fails to re-

TABLE 9.4
Construction and Housing Cost Indices

Year	Residential Construction Cost Index: Housekeeping Units (Grebler)	Price Index One Family Owner Occupied Houses (Grebler)	Rent Index (BLS)	Rent Index (NICB)
1918	100.0	100.0	100.0	100.0
1919	116.3	111.5	108.2	111.5
1920	149.9	123.9	127.3	133.2
1921	120.5	122.8	146.1	146.3
1922	110.7	126.2	150.4	143.8
1923	124.1	129.9	154.1	148.9

Sources: 1. Grebler, *Capital Formation*, p. 342.
2. Ibid., p. 351.
3. U.S. Census, *Historical Statistics . . . to 1970*, p. 211.
4. NICB, *The Cost of Living in the United States* (1925), pp. 34, 62.

flect the proper and very significant influence of interest costs over the dwelling unit's useful life. Since adjusting the constant-dollar residential wealth to current dollar values should reflect the role of interest costs, we do not follow Grebler et al. in using the construction cost index.

Instead, we explicitly recognize that the trend in current-dollar residential wealth underpins estimates for both the flow of net returns from owner-occupied housing and other elements in the rental estimate. We therefore utilize a different approach. One might use a price index for owner-occupied housing and a rent index for rentals. However, present-day BEA procedures use a rent index to deflate both series. We follow their procedure to provide comparability between our 1900–28 estimates and that agency's series for 1929 onward.

Welfare

The estimates for this category in *The American Economy* are adopted, but the description of procedures given there is corrected.[73]

III. PRICE DEFLATORS: 1900–1929

Data on price trends at retail and wholesale levels are widely available, though not all have the relevance and precision required for deflation. Little information is available on procedures used by the Bureau of Economic Analysis for 1929ff. For earlier years the primary source appears to be Shaw's characteristically careful (largely whole-sale) price estimates for major groups. To arrive at the price deflators used in Appendix table III, and thereby, the deflated estimates in table II, the following procedures were adopted.

Food, Tobacco, and Alcohol

FOOD

For 1900–1913 a new price index was computed from the original BLS retail price indices for individual food items—for example, ap-ples, potatoes, butter, flour, beef, etc.[74] These price indices were weighted together by U.S. gross income from farm production, for each item, giving a price index for the entire population.[75] (For sugar, tea, and coffee the weights were the value of imports.)[76] To combine price series for the separate cuts of beef and pork into ones to which the Strauss-Bean weights could apply we used the con-sumption weights by cut shown in BLS Bulletin 699.[77]

For food prices Douglas had used expenditure weights from the 1901 cost of living survey. That survey, however, was biased toward higher-income families, whose food expenditure pattern differed largely from U.S. production totals. Our food price series will neces-sarily differ from his for that reason. And from Rees, who adopts Douglas's food index.[78] (However, the bias in the BLS meat prices that appears in Douglas's figures will also appear, though with less weight, in the present series.)[79]

For 1913–1929 the BLS retail food price index was used.[80]

TOBACCO

An index for 1912–29 was computed from the average retail price of Camel and Chesterfield brand cigarettes.[81] This index was extrapo-lated to 1900 by Shaw's wholesale price index for tobacco products.[82]

ALCOHOLIC BEVERAGES

The average retail price of whiskey, beer, and wine in the U.S. was estimated by the editor of *The American Grocer* in the Treasury De-partment *Report* for 1887. Later reports in *The American Grocer* give the same averages for 1911 and 1915.[83] (Since wholesale prices were stable through this period retail prices would have been still more stable.) These prices were therefore used for 1900. They were extrap-olated by wholesale price data from the Cincinnati Chamber of Com-merce.[84]

To convert into 1972 prices the wholesale beer price was linked to one for 1972 kindly provided by the Schoenling Brewery Company of Cincinnati. The whiskey price was linked to the average import price of Canadian whiskey.[85]

Clothing

The three components of clothing were separately deflated. (1) Shoes and clothing: the BLS retail apparel price series was used back to 1914, and Rees's apparel series thence to 1900.[86] (2) Jewelry: Shaw's jewelry series was used.[87] (3) Clothing services: a series for average annual earnings of workers in personal service was used, adjusted by Kendrick's data on productivity.[88]

Personal Care

TOILET ARTICLES

Shaw's deflator for "drug, toilet, and household preparations" was used for toilet articles, with one adjustment. For the years prior to 1910 Shaw averaged prices for opium, quinine, bicarbonate of soda, and the export price of soap.[89] The underlying BLS data (Bulletin 269, p. 130) showed that the marked 1900–1901 decline for the group index was created by the changing price of quinine. However, the price of refined glycerine, used in many toiletries, showed virtually no change over the same period. We therefore assumed that the price of toilet articles showed no 1900–1901 change.

BARBER AND BEAUTY SHOP EXPENDITURES

This series was deflated by the wage earnings index for personal service, adjusted for productivity.

Housing

The BLS price index for rental housing, extended to 1900 by Rees's rent index, was used to deflate the total.[90]

Household Operation

FURNITURE, FURNISHINGS, AND APPLIANCES

The BLS index for house furnishing was used back to 1913, while Rees's very carefully worked-out index for "home furnishings" was used for earlier years.[91]

CLEANING MATERIALS

Benchmark estimates for census years 1899–1914 were computed from Census of Manufactures data, interpolated by Shaw's price index for drugs, toilet, and household preparations.[92] For 1914 and later the BLS price index for soap was used.[93]

STATIONERY

Benchmark estimates for census years were computed from census data on the price of fine writing paper per ton, interpolated by Shaw's price index for magazines and newspapers.[94]

GAS

Rees's estimates for 1900–1914 were extrapolated by BLS figures for the price of 1,000 cubic feet of manufactured gas.[95]

The BLS does not publish gas prices for the period prior to 1935. Presumably because in these earlier years the agency did not allow for the changing ratio of natural to manufactured gas, nor did it base rates on average family consumption rather than prices of the first thousand cubic feet. Examination of the BLS data for manufactured gas, however, shows great price stability—changes of no more than 1% a year—except during World War I. That fact suggests that variations in the changing importance of manufactured and natural gas can be ignored. Another indication is what happened when the BLS suddenly increased the number of reporting cities by 25% in 1913, without linking the series.[96] The price series then rose by only 2%. (According to Rees's adjusted figures, it should have remained unchanged.) Such a pattern of change warrants our using the manufactured gas price series as an index of change for all gas.

ELECTRICITY

The price series is based on Census and Edison Electric Institute data for 1920–29 and quinquennial census data for years prior to 1920.[97] Interpolation for the other years was by the ratio to prices of manufactured gas. Ratios were computed for census years from these data and the series for gas estimated above.

When Edison first introduced his generating station he set its price to be competitive with respect to gas. Price changes thereafter reflected both the alternatives available to consumers and increasing productivity in the electrical industry. The ratio procedure reflects both. For 1900–1902 the trend in New York City prices for electricity was used, New York then being the center of the industry.[98]

WATER AND REFUSE COLLECTION

These expenditures were largely composed of the services of municipal employees. We therefore utilized King's estimates for the annual pay of municipal employees, in 1909–25, extrapolated to 1900–1908 and 1925–29, by the average annual earnings of all state and local employees.[99]

Rees's carefully detailed series for fuel prices in 1900–1914 was extrapolated to 1929 by a weighted average of prices for bituminous coal, anthracite coal, kerosene, and gas.[100]

A proxy index of phone rates was estimated by dividing operating revenue of phone companies from local calls by the number of telephones in service in 1900 and in 1920–29, with linear interpolation in 1900–1920.[101]

Annual earnings of full-time employees in domestic service.[102]

This service item was deflated by annual earnings of employees in personal service.[103]

Medical Care

EXPENDITURES ON PHYSICIANS, DENTISTS, AND OTHER PROFESSIONALS IN CURATIVE SERVICE

The annual income for self-employed physicians in 1900 has been previously computed at 29% of that for 1929.[104] And the independently derived index for earnings in the entire medical service group gave a 28% ratio.[105] We therefore, with some confidence, used an index of average annual earnings of all persons in medical service for a deflator.[106]

DRUGS AND OPHTHALMIC APPLIANCES

Shaw's price index for drugs, toilet, and household preparations.

HOSPITALS

The average daily expense per hospital patient in 1900 was approximately $1.25 a day according to data for hospitals in several cities.[107]

The daily cost per patient in 1923 is derived from the census in that year, while for 1935 it is derived from a Public Health Service report.[108] Comparing the 1900 and 1923 estimates gives a striking result: the percentage change in the average daily patient cost in hospitals for 1900 to 1923 is virtually identical with the change shown in the medical price index. We therefore use that index for deflating hospital expenditures.[109]

The group total for medical care is the implicit index given when the sum of deflated expenditures estimated above was divided into the corresponding undeflated sum.

Personal Business

BROKERAGE

A deflator was computed as the weighted average of two indices: the average commission rate for brokers and dealers, and an index of real estate prices (assuming commissions for the latter were a constant percentage of sales price).[110]

FUNERAL COSTS

A series for average cost per funeral, previously developed for estimating the expenditure series, was used as a deflator.[111]

OTHER PERSONAL BUSINESS

Annual earnings of full-time equivalent employees in finance, insurance, and real estate, adjusted for the trend in their productivity.[112]

Transport

AUTOS

Shaw's series for motor vehicle prices was used.[113]

Auto Tires, Tubes and Accessories. Shaw's series for prices of tires and tubes.[114]

AUTO REPAIRS

The deflator averages indices for materials and for labor.[115]

GASOLINE AND OIL

Retail prices of gasoline in fifty cities are available from industry sources for 1918–29.[116] Since state taxes on gasoline were not levied prior to 1919 it is possible to use Shaw's wholesale price index for manufactured fuels to extrapolate to earlier years—assuming a constancy of margin that is consistent with Barger's margin data.

TOLLS AND INSURANCE

Most of this category was for insurance. Average annual earnings in finance, real estate, and insurance were therefore used.[117]

Average annual earnings in local and intercity rail transport were used.[118]

Recreation

BOOKS

A price index was derived by averaging the price trends for two widely distributed publications whose basic format and nature changed but little over these decades—the Merriam Webster *Collegiate Dictionary* and *The World Almanac*.[119] Attempts to price the works of standard authors proved unsatisfactory: variation in taste resulted in few standard authors (e.g., Scott, Wordsworth, Dickens) being published throughout the thirty-year period by the same publisher.

MAGAZINES, NEWSPAPERS, ETC.

The index used was based on the retail prices of leading magazines published throughout the period—the *Saturday Evening Post*, the *Atlantic Monthly*, *Harpers*, *The Nation*, *North American Review*, *South Atlantic Quarterly*, and *The Outlook*.[120]

Shaw's book and magazine index is created by averaging two BLS price series—one for newsprint (1915 ff.), the other for wrapping paper (1900 ff.). The latter series reports extremely odd price behavior—for example, no 1913–15 change followed by a 60% increase in 1916. And while paper prices remain unchanged in 1920–21, newsprint prices declined nearly 20%.[121]

Even were the wholesale paper prices satisfactory, of course, they would not necessarily reflect trends in the costs of books and newspapers, which include printing, binding, and wholesale and retail distribution. We therefore prefer to rely on a sample of actual prices for publications.

TOYS, WHEEL GOODS

We follow Shaw, using his semi-durable consumption goods price series.[122]

RADIO, TV, MUSICAL INSTRUMENTS

For 1900–1923 we used Shaw's price index for musical instruments. That series, however, is unsatisfactory after 1923 because of the increasing share for radios, whose price declined sharply. We therefore established biennial benchmarks from the Census of Manufactures for the price of radios, then deflated radio expenditures by that index. Musical instrument expenditures per se were deflated by Shaw's index.[123]

RECREATION SERVICES[124]

For this group of items we used the trend of average annual earnings in personal services, adjusted for productivity.[125]

FLOWERS AND SEEDS

The index for prices received by farmers for food grains was used to extrapolate the unpublished BEA index.[126]

Education

The group was deflated by the trend of average annual earnings in private education.[127]

Religion and Welfare

RELIGION

An index of ministerial salaries was used as a deflator. Benchmarks for 1906 and 1916 are from the Census of Religious Bodies, and, for 1929, from the BEA. These were then extrapolated by the average salary of ministers as estimated by Paul Douglas and Simon Kuznets.[128]

WELFARE

An index of earnings by social workers was used. It is based on a survey by Ralph Hurlin for 1913–25.[129] That series was extrapolated by the ministerial salary index computed above.

Foreign Travel

NET FOREIGN TRAVEL

To deflate foreign travel we referred to the procedures used by Paul Dickens for estimating travel expenditures in 1900–16, and by the Bureau of Foreign and Domestic Commerce for 1919–29. (It is these data that underly the present official balance of payments estimate.)[130] Both these sources turned out to assume a constant expenditure abroad for the period they cover—Dickens taking a flat $750 per traveler, while the BFDC assumed a constant figure for each class of traveler (e.g., first class, second class, third class).[131] Moreover, the Dickens figure for 1916 was $750, while the Maffry estimate for 1919 was $783 for all travelers. There was thus no basis for inferring that expenditure per traveler changed between the two periods. Nor is it obvious what deflator would be consistent with these constant, current-dollar, series expenditures.

EXPENDITURES ABROAD BY U.S. RESIDENTS

This series was deflated by U.K. price trends for drink and tobacco, transport, and "other service."[132]

Expenditures in the U.S. by Foreigners. These expenditures were primarily for meals and transport. They were therefore deflated by an index based on the implicit deflators for food, housing, and transport.[133]

IV. DEFLATED CONSUMPTION: 1929

Because we estimate deflated consumption prior to 1929 in fuller detail than the published BEA estimates, we combine certain BEA constant-dollar series for 1929 and later. The line item numbers below are those used in table 2.5 of the *National Income and Product Accounts of the United States*, vol. 1, 1929–58 (1993).

Food and Tobacco (2), Food minus Alcohol (8), Alcohol (9 + 10), Shoes and Clothing (12 + 13), Jewelry (18), Cleaning and Accessories Service (17 + 19), Toilet Articles (21), Barber Shops (22), Housing (23), Household Furnishings (29 + 33), Cleaning (34), Stationery (35), Electricity (37), Gas (38), Water (39), Fuel, Ice (40), Phone (41), Domestic (42), Other (43), Drugs, etc. (45 + 46), Physicians & (47 + 48 + 49), Hospitals & (50 + 56), Brokerage (61), Other Pers. Bus. (60 minus 61), Autos (70 + 71 + 72), Tires & (73), Auto Repair, Gas, Tolls & (75 plus allocation from item 69), Purchased Transport (78 + 81), Books & (87 plus 88), Toys, nondurable (89), Cycles (90), Musical (91), Recreation Service (92 + 94 + 98 + 99 + 100 + 101), Flowers (93), Education (102), Religion and Welfare (106), with each main component benchmarked to underlying BEA figures for 1929. Foreign Travel (107). For Foreign Travel by U.S. Residents, Expenditures Abroad, and by Foreigners, unpublished BEA 1929 deflators were used.

· C H A P T E R   1 0 ·

STATE CONSUMPTION, 1900–1982: ESTIMATING
PROCEDURES FOR APPENDIX B

THIS CHAPTER outlines the procedures by which the state estimates were derived, for 1900, 1929, and so on. We uniformly began with estimates, by specific item, for the United States as a whole. (Chapter 9 describes how these were derived.)

Each U.S. total was distributed among the states by an allocator, then usually checked against another allocator. Had estimates been directly made for each state, they would not necessarily add to an adequate U.S. total. More important, comparisons against the per capita average for the U.S. as well as nearby states, permit some judgment as to whether a state estimate falls outside reasonable limits.

We relied as well on regression analysis to pick up outliers for examination. We routinely regressed each per capita expenditure item as a function of the quite independent state per capita income figures. All substantial outliers were examined to locate punching and similar errors.[1]

Reality is complex, however. Outliers were not per se incorrect, merely suspect. This was equally true of comparisons within regions, and over time. North and South Dakota typically had very similar averages, as North and South Carolina did. But not all items were similar, much less in every year. The introduction of novelty— whether electric power, automobiles, or TV—generated differences. So did the passage of particular laws, the inflow of migrants, etc. Thus while outliers were always questioned, changes were only made when an obvious error was located.

For example, the estimates showed Maine and New Hampshire with similar per capita food expenditures in 1900 and 1929 but not in 1982. By 1982, however New Hampshire had instituted low tax state liquor stores, patronized by residents of Massachusetts and by tourists in New England. A similar outlier was the strikingly high alcohol figure for Montana in 1900, which reflects a high estimate in its (quite reliable) source—an extensive BLS survey. (Moreover an extremely high percentage of Montana's 1900 population consisted of male miners. Few of them were immigrants from countries with low per capita alcohol consumption.)

Because the state estimates were developed over years during which the BEA revised its basic estimates, and deflators, the state benchmarks were not as regularly adjusted to the final totals in Appendix A. At the U.S. level, however, the differences are within 1%. At the state level, of course, figures would differ even less.

1900

For many items in 1900 we rely on detailed occupation data from the U.S. Census of Population—e.g., number of dentists, physicians, barbers, saloon keepers, etc. Since the value of output per worker would differ from state to state these counts were multiplied by the average nonagricultural service income per worker in each state (as estimated by Easterlin) to derive the allocator actually used.[2]

For such major items as food, clothing, furniture, and lighting we utilize the 1901 expenditure survey of 25,440 families by the U.S. Commissioner of Labor. Our individual state averages for these individual items were checked by regressing them against relevant occupation counts times average nonagricultural service income. The results were encouraging, typically being on the order of .60. The regression coefficients were also used to compute estimates for states omitted from the Commissioner's survey.

The sources listed below, with the abbreviations indicated, are cited frequently in the following section:

A   Twelfth Census, vol. V, *Agriculture*, part 1.

A2   Twelfth Census, vol. VI, *Agriculture*, part 2.

E   Richard Easterlin, "State Income Estimates," in Everett Lee, et al., *Methodological Considerations and Reference Tables*, in Simon Kuznets, Dorothy Thomas, Population Redistribution and Economic Growth in the United States, 1870–1950 (1957).

K   Simon Kuznets, *National Income and Its Composition, 1919–1938* (1941).

L   Stanley Lebergott, *Manpower in Economic Growth* (1964).

LS   Eighteenth Annual Report of the Commissioner of Labor, 1903, *Cost of Living and Retail Prices of Food* (1904).

M   Twelfth Census of the United States, vol. VII, *Manufactures*, part 1 (1902).

M2   Twelfth Census of the United States, vol. X, *Manufactures*, part IV (1902).

M3 Twelfth Census of the United States, vol. IX, *Manufactures*, part III (1902).
O   Twelfth Census of the United States, *Occupations at the Twelfth Census* (1904).
W   U.S. Census, *Wealth, Debt and Taxation* (1907).

Food: Off-Premise

For 1901 we utilize the findings of an extensive survey by the Commissioner of Labor, which gives food expenditures per family.[3] This survey of 25,440 families provides averages for thirty-three states.

The survey results appear generally reasonable. However, it is desirable to test their validity against some other source. For this purpose we use the Population Census count of persons engaged in food retailing: merchants and dealers (exc. wholesale) in groceries and produce, hucksters and peddlers, butchers, bakers, and confectioners.[4] These all typically engaged in distributing food at retail. The $\overline{R}^2$ between (*a*) food expenditures per capita and (*b*) the total for retail food distribution employment per capita, proved to be .559.[5]

The regression coefficients from the above equation were then applied to the counts of retail food employees per capita in the remaining states to estimate their per capita food expenditures. The per capita food expenditure total for each state was multiplied by its population count, these figures then being used to allocate the U.S. total for off premise food expenditures.[6]

The resultant food estimates by state were then correlated with the Easterlin estimates of income by state in 1900 as a further check.[7] The correlation, .605, suggests that the expenditure estimates are in reasonable accord with the distribution of one of their major determinants.

Meals and Beverages

A U.S. total was allocated by the number of persons in specified occupations (hotel keepers, bartenders, restaurant keepers, saloon keepers, and waiters) times the average service income per worker in the state.[8]

The U.S. total for meals and beverages was estimated as 20.17% of off-premise food plus meals and beverages. That percentage was derived from Barger's detailed study of distribution in 1899.[9] Applied to the U.S. control total for off-premise food plus meals and beverages it gave the U.S. total for meals and beverages.[10]

The percentage distribution of this allocator by state resembles

that of the off-premise food expenditure figures previously estimated. Divergences appear where historical knowledge would suggest they should appear. New York is predictably high as a center
for restaurant and cafe life. Kansas and Maine, centers of the tem-
perance movement, are proportionately very low.

Food Furnished Employees

In 1900, employees furnished food as part of their wages were
chiefly farm laborers. (The number of live-in servants in urban areas
was limited, most of the group being female domestics in the South.)
The allocator used was the product of two series. One was aggregate
expenditures on farm labor reported by farmers.[11] The other was (a)
average monthly wages without board, minus average wages with
board, divided by (b) farm wages without board.[12] This procedure implies that food constituted the equivalent of about 30% of U.S. farm
labor expenditures.) The reliability of this procedure rests on the assumption that expenditures in this period were chiefly made for two
groups of farm labor, each of which received board as a normal part of
their wages. One group consisted of farm laborers regularly hired by
the month or year. The other consisted of laborers hired largely at
harvest time, whose meals were a normal part of their wages.

Food Produced and Consumed on Farms

The value of dairy products consumed on farms was used to allocate
the U.S. total for food produced and consumed on farms by farm
operators.[13] The significant uncertainty in this allocation, of course,
turns on whether meat consumption and produce were allocated
similarly. We take as a guide the actual allocation for a set of products that had alternative sales markets about as great as those for
meat and produce, though not bread grains.

Tobacco

The number of merchants and dealers of cigars and tobacco, times
service income per worker.[14]

Alcohol

For alcohol expenditures we utilized state data from an 1896 survey
by the Commissioner of Labor that also provided the basis for the
U.S. total.[15] That source provides estimates for the count of estab-

lishments by state buying U.S. internal revenue stamps as dealers in alcoholic beverages.[16] These counts were multiplied by the capital per firm, relying on a sample of 29,258 firms in fourteen selected states.[17] Assuming that gross sales per dollar invested were similar from state to state the capital estimates served as a preliminary indicator of liquor sales in these fourteen states.[18]

For the remaining states we adopted the following procedure. An alternative indicator for the above fourteen states was the number of saloon keepers plus bartenders times Easterlin's service income per worker in the same state.[19] This and the prior allocator were then divided by population and the per capita figures correlated, giving an $\overline{R}^2$ of .898.[20] Given so close a relationship it appeared that the estimate by occupation count times service income was giving acceptable results. We therefore applied the regression coefficients to occupation-income estimates for the thirty-five states not covered by the survey to derive the allocator actually used to estimate their alcohol expenditures in 1900.

Clothing and Accessories

Clothing expenditures per capita in thirty-three states can be derived from the survey by the Commissioner of Labor.[21] The intra-regional variation shown by these figures seemed unreasonably great, and was probably a reflection of sampling variability. We therefore averaged the per capita figures within each of eight regions. These averages were then tested by correlating them with per capita expenditures given by multiplying the occupation count for two groups of merchants and dealers (clothing and men's furnishings plus dry goods, fancy goods, and notions) times the service income per worker.[22] The $\overline{R}^2$, of .829, proved encouragingly high. The regional per capita averages were therefore assumed to apply to each state within the region, multiplied by the population counts to give the general allocator for U.S. total clothing expenditures.[23]

Shoes

Merchants and dealers in boots and shoes times service income per worker.[24]

Clothing Repair and Service

The allocator for this category was estimated as the sum of six separate components. The value of product is reported in the Census of Manufactures for five of them—boots and shoes, custom work and repairing; clothing, mens, custom work and repairing; clothing, womens, dressmaking; dyeing and cleaning; and watchmaking.[25] For laundries a U.S. total for value of product was allocated by the census count of launderers and launderesses times average income per domestic servant.[26]

Jewelry

Value of product for watch, clock, and jewelry repairing.[27]

Toilet Articles

Merchants and dealers, drugs and medicines, times service income per worker.[28]

Barbershops, Beauty Parlors, and Baths

Barbers and hairdressers times service income per worker.[29]

Housing

Nonfarm. Allocated by the estimated true value of general residential property in 1900.[30]
    Farm. Allocated by the value of farm buildings in 1900.[31]
    Other Housing. Allocated by the number of hotel keepers and boarding and lodging house keepers times service income per worker.[32]

Furniture and Furnishings

The Commissioners' survey provides average family expenditure for "furniture and household utensils" in thirty-three states. To assess these data, and provide a basis for estimating the remaining states, the figures for each region were analyzed in tables 10.1, 10.2, and 10.3.

NORTH ATLANTIC

In the North Atlantic region the averages (rounded) were as follows:

TABLE 10.1

New Hampshire	$ 9
Maine	11
Connecticut	19
Pennsylvania	23
New York	24
Rhode Island	25
New Jersey	38
Massachusetts	79

The relatively low levels for New Hampshire and Maine, and the higher levels in the Mid Atlantic, are reasonably consistent with historical knowledge about levels of living in these areas. The figure for Massachusetts, however, is far out of line. Not only is it the highest figure reported for any state, it is about triple that for New York, one of the highest income and expenditure states.

We therefore adjust Massachusetts, and provide a basis for estimating Vermont, by a regression of the survey's per family expenditures on furniture and utensils against per family expenditures on upholstery work in the seven states above.[33] The assumption that such maintenance of furniture spending was related to additions to the stock of furniture and household furnishings was consistent with the $\overline{R}^2$ of .362.

NORTH CENTRAL

State averages from the survey for this region are:

TABLE 10.2

Iowa	$ 7
Missouri	15
Kansas	17
Indiana	22
Wisconsin	24
Illinois	31
Ohio	32
Minnesota	33
Michigan	36

The figure for Iowa is improbably low, being less than that for any of the ten southern states. Figures for Iowa, the Dakotas, and Nebraska were estimated by a regression of survey expenditures of furniture against those on upholstery work in the nine North Central States.[34]

SOUTH

The survey figures for the South (in Table 10.3) show that expenditures in West Virginia and Kentucky are over double those in New York and the New England States. The per capita figure for South Carolina is an improbable half that of North Carolina. Now furnishings and utensils in the South were distributed largely through country general stores, and constituted a large portion of all furniture plus furnishings expenditure. Revised figures for these states were therefore estimated from a regression of (a) per capita general stores sales (times service income per worker) against (b) furniture

TABLE 10.3

South Carolina	$11
Louisiana	18
North Carolina	21
Texas	22
Georgia	28
Virginia	29
Alabama	31
Tennessee	34
West Virginia	41
Kentucky	50

and utensil expenditures in the southern states as reported in the survey.

WEST

Survey expenditure figures for the three western states cannot be directly assessed, because the observations are so few. Instead, a scatter for all states of general store sales per family versus furniture repair expenditures per family was made. The observations for the three western states were consistent with those for most states, and fell along a similar slope. We concluded that the underlying relationships did not obviously differ between the Mountain and Pacific states, and averaged the value for the three reported states ($11, 14, 16) to estimate $13.85, for the remaining western states.

Cleaning Materials

Expenditures for soap and cleaning materials are assumed to vary as expenditures for hiring the servants who used such materials.[35]

Lighting

Of all lighting expenditure in 1900 little was for gas, and even less for electricity. The LS data on expenditures provide the best guide to the actual lighting demand, which was largely for kerosene plus candles.

Water and Refuse Collection

Expenditure by public authorities for sewer, drainage, and sanitation were used as the allocator.[36]

For Louisiana this procedure gives an extraordinarily high estimate. Since even New Orleans had no sewers, and public water supply in the state was minimal, expenditures for "sewers, drainage and other sanitation" in Louisiana undoubtedly went chiefly for state maintenance of the levees along the Mississippi.[37] A Louisiana estimate was therefore made by deducting from expenditures by all Louisiana governments the state expenditures on this category, and including only those by the parishes, cities, and other minor civil divisions.[38]

Ice and Fuel

The survey estimates of per family fuel expenditures constituted the basic source used for allocation.[39] These data, however, were tested by computing per capita expenditures from the survey data, and multiplying them by population in each state. These aggregates were then compared with ones computed by multiplying the number of coal and wood dealers in each state by nonagricultural service income per worker. The two series were closely consistent, with a single exception. The survey estimate for Louisiana was far below that indicated by the dealer figures—and in fact it was also far below the per capita survey figures for every other southern state. We therefore substituted for Louisiana the expenditure reported by the median southern state in the survey. For states not included in the survey we used median values for the states in the appropriate region.

Telegraph and Telephone

The number of telegraph and telephone operators times service income per worker.[40] We estimate that in 1900 some 80% of telephone revenue came from business and government, and 20% from consumers.[41] The state estimates are therefore very crude. They tacitly assume that states adopting the telephone more rapidly were likewise ones in which consumers also adopted it more rapidly and used it more frequently.

Domestic Service

The number of domestic servants in each state was multiplied by the average annual earnings of domestic servants as reported in a survey for the Industrial Commission.[42] For the states omitted from the survey a regression against census data for the earnings of women in the low paid confectionery industry was used to estimate the required state average earning figures.[43]

Other Household Operation

Value of product in two hand trades: (1) furniture, cabinetmaking, repairing and upholstering, and (2) bicycle and tricycle repairing.[44]

Drugs and Ophthalmic Products

Merchants and dealers of drugs and medicines times nonagricultural service income per worker.[45]

Physicians and Other Medical Services

These expenditures were allocated by multiplying the number of physicians and dentists in 1900, and the number of nurses, by weights to reflect their relative expenditure importance, and then multiplying each state count by nonagricultural service income per employee.[46] The weights represented an approximation of the expenditures on each arrived at by extrapolating Kuznets's detailed 1919 figures back by data on earnings.[47]

Hospitals

For the bulk of hospitals the Census of Benevolent Institutions reports "income from pay patients" for each hospital.[48]

To the state totals computed from this source it is necessary to add private expenditures in hospitals not covered by the census. For this purpose Polk's listing of all hospitals and sanitaria in 1900 was used.[49] For the hospitals recorded in both sources it is possible to tabulate the number of beds, total cost per year, and income from paying patients.[50] For each state the average cost per bed in such institutions was computed. This cost per bed was then applied to the number of beds in private institutions not recorded in the Census of Benevolent Institutions but recorded by Polk—giving an estimate of additional costs in private hospitals. These additional costs—largely paid by patients, but including some income from endowment, etc.—constituted the remaining portion of private expenditures for hospitals. The summation of the costs for these additional hospitals, plus the pay by patients in "benevolent" hospitals constituted the allocator used to distribute the U.S. total for private expenditures on hospitals.

Banking and Brokerage

These items of personal expenditure involve one central question currently and for historic periods: what proportion is intermediate (bought by business and government) and what represents personal business? No reliable information is available even for recent years as to those and arbitrary assumptions are required. *A foriori*, differences by state are unknown.

We estimate such expenditures by multiplying the number of bankers and brokers by nonagricultural service income per worker.[51]

Insurance

Estimates of premia received for life insurance by state were used to allocate the U.S. total.[52]

Legal Service

The number of lawyers times the nonagricultural service income per worker.[53]

Funeral Expenditures

The number of undertakers by state is multiplied by the service income per worker in 1900.[54]

Union Dues

A disproportionate amount of attention was given to this small item because it reports something of the varying interstate acceptance of unionism at a time when modernism was barely in its infancy. (Not quite 3% of the labor force was organized in 1900.[55] Wolman estimates the membership of each national union as of 1900.[56] For individual unions which in the aggregate included 91% of total union membership, we allocated membership by the relevant occupation category from the Population Census. Thus union membership of carpenters, masons, painters, and plumbers, and others in building construction was allocated by those gainfully occupied in these trades; those in the hatter's unions were allocated by hat and cap makers; those in granite and stone unions, by marble and stone workers, and so on.[57] Since dues of individual unions varied little among the states the allocation of members served to allocate the U.S. estimate for union dues and initiation fees.

Employment Agency Fees

By employment agency keepers in 1910 times nonagricultural service income per worker.[58]

Transport

Over 90% of transport expenditures by consumers in 1900 went for purchased transport, mostly within cities. The allocator used was the sum of three items: (1) gross income of street and electric railways;[59] (2) receipts of carriage and hack drivers, and livery stable keepers;[60] (3) the income of ferries and bridges in cities.[61]

Magazines and Newspapers

The value of newspaper subscriptions and sales by state is reported by the census.[62] These data are net of advertising revenues.

Books and Maps

As a proxy for purchase and use of books we use the number of librarians times nonagricultural service income per worker.[63]

Toys and Wheel Goods

The value of products of bicycle and tricycle repairing was used as an allocator, on the assumption that the flow of repairs and the flow of purchases was similarly distributed by state.[64]

Musical Instruments

The number of musicians and teachers of music, times nonagricultural service income per worker.[65]

Flowers, Seeds, and Plants

The value of products of flower and plant farms is reported by the Census of Agriculture.[66] Although most products were sold within the state, there will be some bias because of interstate shipments—e.g., from Connecticut to New York City.

Recreation Services

Personnel in each of two recreational categories times nonagricultural service income per worker was used as an allocator.

1. Personnel in billiard and poolrooms and in bowling alleys were allocated respectively by the number of billiard tables and bowling alleys licensed by the IRS in each state.[67]

2. Personnel in legitimate theaters, etc. was allocated by the number of actors, professional showmen, theatrical managers, etc.[68]

Education

Data for the various categories of schools come primarily from the Report of the Commissioner of Education.[69]

Higher Education. The income of colleges and universities from private sources was used as the allocator.[70]

Other. (a) *Secondary Education.* Tuition and fees in public secondary schools were added to total income of private secondary schools to allocate private expenditures for secondary education.[71]

(b) *Elementary Education.* The number of elementary students in private schools was multiplied by the average income per student. Lacking data specific to "private and parochial" elementary schools, we assumed their income per student equalled expenses per student in public elementary schools.[72]

(c) *Other Education.* The number of female artists, teachers of art, musicians, and teachers of music in each state was taken as an indicator of the number of persons engaged in private education (most males being engaged in the recreation industry rather than teaching). These counts were then multiplied by the nonagricultural service income per employee to give the series used for allocating the U.S. total.[73]

Religion

Expenditures on organized religion were allocated by the value of church property.[74] The tacit assumption is that aggregate expenditures for ministers, sextons, church maintenance, etc. varied among the states, as did the value of property.

Welfare

The number of religious and charity workers times per capita income by state. (Clergymen appear under a different occupational category. Since this category is not separated out in 1900 we use the 1910 distribution from the *Occupation* volume of the latter census, the growth of aggregate expenditures over the decade being mild enough to suggest the two distributions should have been broadly similar.)

Foreign Travel

Expenditures abroad would have varied among the population of the several U.S. states as a function of their incomes and their contacts abroad, usually with relatives of the country from which they came, but for business and other reasons as well. We use the value of international money orders issued, by state, to index these contacts, and thereby allocate foreign travel and expenditures abroad.[75]

1929

Sources used with some frequency in deriving these estimates are referred to in the notes below with a letter reference as follows:

C   Fifteenth Census of the United States, *Distribution*, vol. 1, *Retail Distribution*, parts 2 and 3. Commodity line sales percentages from table 15, applied to total sales for the appropriate kind of business from table 1.

O   Number of gainful workers in specified occupation, in table 4 for each state from the Fifteenth Census of the United States, vol. IV, *Occupation by State.*

S   Net sales of specified kind of business from table 1, in T.

ST   *Statistical Abstract of the United States, 1931.*

T   Fifteenth Census of the United States, *Distribution*, vol. 1, *Retail Distribution*, parts 2 and 3.

In the procedure outlined below, S refers to sales of the specified kind of retail business, while C refers to the appropriate commodity line in the particular kind of business specified. Whenever occupation data are specified—e.g., 5), 12), 22), etc.—they are multiplied by 1929 per capita personal income by state in order to reflect difference in sales per person engaged associated with differences in income levels. The line number—e.g., 2), 7), etc.—refers to the line in table 2.6 of U.S. Department of Commerce, *The National Income and Product Accounts of the United States, 1929–74.*

Total PCE) Sum of roman numeral subtotals I–XII.

2) Sum of 3) through 7).

3) Off-premise: Net sales of food group (S) plus sales of specified food items in general stores. Since the census did not analyze the sales of general stores we applied to general store sales the proportion of food items sold in "general merchandise stores with food departments." The items specified included: bakery products, bottled beverages, confectionery, delicatessen, fresh fish, fruits, groceries (6 items), meats, milk, and cream. This considerable effort was

warranted by the fact that the importance of general stores as a distribution mechanism varied markedly among the states.

4) Purchased meals: Sales of restaurants, cafeterias, and eating places (T) plus (*a*) fountain sales; (*b*) ice cream and lunches in drug stores (C,T), together with (*c*) sales of meals and beverages as reported in the 1930 *Census of Hotels*.

5) Food furnished: O—"servants, other servants, other domestic and personal service"; plus O—"soldiers, sailors, marines," the total then multiplied by per capita personal income in 1929.

6) Food . . . on farms: Farm Proprietor's Income, from U.S. Office of Business Economics, *Personal Income by States Since 1929* (1956) tables 6–61.

7) Tobacco: C—sales of cigars in cigar stores, drug stores with fountains, combination stores, grocery stores (without meat).

9) Alcohol—zero.

10) Clothing, etc.: Sum of 11), 12), 13), 16), 17), 18), 19).

11) Shoes: S—shoe stores (men's, women's, family) sales; plus C—shoe sales in department stores.

12) Shoe repair: O—shoemakers and cobblers not in factory times per capita state income.

13) Clothing and accessories: S—sales of apparel group, men's and boy's stores, women's ready-to-wear and accessory stores; plus S—sales of department stores times the percentage of such sales (C) that were misses' and women's apparel or clothing, men's and boy's; plus S—sales of dry goods stores times the proportion of such sales that were women's and misses' apparel or men's and boy's clothing.

14) Women's clothing—the above estimates of clothing and accessories times the proportion of that total for women's and misses' clothing. That proportion was calculated as the ratio of (*a*) the women's and misses' items noted in 13) above times (*b*) the total for 13).

15) Men's and boy's clothing: 13) minus 14).

16) Military: O—soldiers, sailors, and marines. Because the army and navy did not issue different allowances in different states, these counts were not adjusted for income differences by state.

17) By the sum of two components: (1) Cleaning: retail sales of cleaning and dyeing establishments from T—table 11A, headnote; plus (2) Laundering: sales of power laundries from T—table 11a.

18) Jewelry: C—sales of jewelry in jewelry stores.

19) Other: T—table 9C, repairs in general merchandise group, apparel group, and jewelry stores.

21) Toilet articles: C—sales of toilet articles plus toiletries and cos-

metics in drug, department (without food), general merchandise (without food), and variety stores.

22) Barbers: O—barbers, manicurists, hairdressers times per capita state income.

23) Sum of 24) through 27).

24) Housing—nonfarm owner: 1930 Census of Population, *Families*, p. 38: Number of nonfarm owned homes times their median value.

25) Housing—nonfarm rental: 1930 Census of Population, *Families*, p. 39: number of rented nonfarm houses times their median rental.

26) Housing—farm: 1930 Census, *Agriculture*, vol. IV, p. 59— value of farm dwellings.

27) Other: receipts for rooms in hotels (15th Census, *Census of Hotels*, 1930, tables by state). To the receipts specified as "rooms" an aliquot share of those for combined "rooms and meals" was added, using the ratio of individually specified "rooms" to those specified "meals."

28) Sum of 29) through 43).

29) Furniture: C—sales of furniture and bedding furniture stores.

30) Kitchen and other appliances: S—sales of household and appliance stores (all types) plus sales of stove and range dealers.

31) China, glassware, utensils: allocated by the sum of four component items. (1) S—sales of china and crockery stores; (2) C,S— china and kitchen utensil sales in department stores; (3) C,S—china, glass, and kitchen utensil sales in variety stores; (4) C,S—china, glass, and silverware sales in jewelry stores.

32) Other durable house furnishings: C—floor coverings sold in department stores and in furniture stores plus (S) sales of floor covering stores.

33) Semi-durables: C—sales of draperies, upholstery, curtains, and bedding, in department stores.

34) Cleaning and polishing: C—sales of "household supplies" and "other non-food products" in grocery stores without meat and in combination stores (groceries and meats).

35) C—stationery sales and school supplies in combination stores (groceries and meats), in department stores, and by stationers and engravers.

36) Sum of 37) through 40).

37) Electricity: allocated by "revenue from electric service"—average of 1927 and 1932 total domestic service sales. Census of Electrical Industries 1927, *Central Electric and Power Stations*, pp. 54–55. Census of Electrical Industries, 1932, *Central Electric and Power Stations*, pp. 38–39.

38) Gas: 1929 Census of Manufactures, vol. II, p. 758. Value of gas sales to domestic customers. The census groups data for several states with few gas companies. We split these totals by an estimate of the value of gas stoves and ranges sold in furniture stores, using the line of merchandise and store sales totals from C,S.

39) Water: for 1929 data on income from public water supply systems are available for 250 major cities from the U.S. Census, *Financial Statistics of Cities Having a Population of Over 30,000: 1929* (1932), table 11. The total for all cities in each state was computed, then adjusted to apply to all government units in each state by the ratio of public service earnings figures in these cities with 30,000 population and over in 1932 to that for all cities, towns, villages, and boroughs in 1932. The latter data are from U.S. Census, *Financial Statistics of State and Local Governments: 1932*, table 2. (For example, in 1932 income of public service enterprise in Illinois cities of 30,000 population and over came to 72.4% of earnings of all such enterprises in the state. The 1929 water supply receipts total for the twelve Illinois cities with under 30,000 population, which came to $15,956 million, was therefore raised to $22,039 million.)

40) Fuel oils and coal: this item (labeled "other fuel and ice" in the *National Income and Product Accounts, 1929–1965*, p. 44) is estimated at $1,608 million. Of that total some $1,495 was apparently purchased, the rest being farm produced and consumed.[76] Kuznets estimates that consumer expenditures, at producer level, came to $776 million for light, fuel (except gasoline and oil), and ice in 1929.[77] In effect a margin of about 50% of retail price was used by OBE. (That figure is consistent with Barger's 52% for milk dealers, and for restaurants.[78] We assume that 13.3% of the BEA figure is for ice, that being the ratio implicit in Kuznets's estimates for ice and fuel (minus gasoline and lubricants). That proportion is then used to reduce the BEA figure to give a 1929 U.S. total of $1,394 for home fuel only.

40a) Ice: the implicit BEA figure for ice expenditures (derived in 40) *supra*) was allocated by net sales of ice dealers, from S.

41) Telephone: allocated by (*a*) average number of residence telephones in 1927 and 1932 (Census of Electrical Industries 1937, *Telephones and Telegraphs*, 1937, p. 18) times (*b*) state personal income per capita.

42) Domestic Service: O—servants (other servants, other domestic and personal service) times state personal income per capita.

43) Other: T—table 9, repairs and service receipts of furniture and household group.

45) Drugs: C—sale of drugs, patent medicines, prescriptions, rubber goods, and surgical and hospital supplies in drug stores.

46) Ophthalmic: S—Sales of opticians and optometrists.

47) Physicians: number of physicians (from 0) times the mean income per physician. Income figures by region for 1929 are provided in Milton Friedman and Simon Kuznets, *Income from Independent Professional Practice* (1945), p. 510. State estimates were then derived from the regional figures by a regression of the regional average income for physicians against that for teachers, data for the latter from U.S. Office of Education, *Biennial Statistics of Education, 1928–1930*, vol. II, p. 56. (Y_{phys} = 3.384 + 1.457W_{tec}) $\bar{R}^2$ = .624.

48) Dentists: number of dentists (from O) times the mean income per dentist (from Friedman and Kuznets, ibid., p. 525, adjusted to state levels as the physicians' figures were. (Y_{den} = $ 2,967 + 1.200W_{tec}) $\bar{R}^2$ = .540.

49) Other professional: O—osteopaths, midwives, and nurses (not trained) dentists' assistants, physicians' attendants, healers, and chiropracters times state per capita income.

50) Hospitals: Trained nurses (O) times state per capita income.

51) Health Insurance—By sales of drugs as estimated above. BLS Bulletin 822, *Family Spending and Saving in Wartime*, table 31, gives data for expenditure in 1941 by income class. These indicate health and accident insurance premia by income level varied far less than did any other medical care expenditures except drugs. Since policies of lower income groups would have been cancelled during the Depression the variation would have been still less in 1929. We use drug expenditures as a guide to their allocation.

55) Sum of 56) through 62).

56) Brokerage charges: Bureau of Internal Revenue, *Statistics of Income, Individuals, 1929*, table 6, p. 73. Dividend income on stock of domestic corporations.

57–58) Services of banks and financial intermediaries—ST, p. 266, bank deposits, 1929.

59) Life insurance: The U.S. total is allocated by life insurance premia received for ordinary, group and industrial life insurance. *The Spectator*, vol CXXV (July 24, 1930), p. 39. (The data on losses incurred by state reported in this source could not be utilized: many companies included their total terminated insurance in their loss report.)

60) Legal—average income per lawyer was assumed to vary by state as did average income per physician. That series was then multiplied by number of lawyers (O), and the product used for allocation.

61) Funeral—number of undertakers by state (O) times average net sales per furniture and undertaker retail store (T—Table 1A).

62) Other personal business: sum of three items, using U.S. totals for each from the 1951 National Income supplement to allocate the 1993 BEA estimate of $165 million for this subtotal. (1) Union dues ($38m)—allocated by number of local unions in each state, using the data for each of the thirty-five major unions. Since some of the UMW locals are grouped into state combinations—e.g., Kentucky and Tennessee—they are allocated by state on the basis of the number of coal miners as given in the 1930 Census, *Occupations*, table 4 by state. These thirty-five unions had a total of 2.9 million members (as compared with the 3.6 total of the BLS for the U.S.). These data appear in BLS Bulletin 506, *Handbook of American Trade Unions, 1929 edition*. (2) Classified advertisements ($36m)—allocated by dollars of newspaper advertising, from 1929 Census, *Manufactures*, vol. II, p. 585. (3) Employment Agency Fees ($25m)—allocated by the number of employment office keepers, from 1930 Census, *Population*, vol. IV, table 4.

65–67) Cars—T: net sales of auto salesrooms plus those of used car dealers.

68) Tires, tubes—T: net sales of accessory stores with tires; batteries; plus tire shops.

69) Auto repair—1930 Census, Retail Distribution, table 9B.

70) Gas and Oil—T: net sales of filling stations.

71) Bridge, ferry: U.S. Bureau of the Census, *Financial Statistics of Cities Having a Population Over 30,000, 1929*, table 11—receipts from docks, wharves, and landings.

73) Purchased local transportation: U.S. Census of Electrical Industries: 1927, *Electric Railways, and Affiliated Motor Bus Lines 1927*. Table 72, railway operating revenues from passengers, plus table 103, electric railway and subsidiary motor bus lines, operating revenues. Where the Census report combines state figures we assume the same per capita expenditures for each state in the combined group.

77) Purchased intercity transportation: O—ticket and station agents times state per capita income.

83) Books and maps: S—sales of book stores.

84) Magazines, newspapers: 1929 Census of Manufactures, vol. II, p. 585; subscriptions and sales of newspapers, periodicals. Sheet music: C—sales of sheet music in music stores.

85) Nondurable toys and games: C—toys and games in (*a*) department stores (without food); (*b*) general merchandise (without food); (*c*) variety and 5–10¢ stores.

86) Wheel goods: S—sales of sporting goods specialty shops.

87) Radio, etc.: S—sales of radio and music stores, and of music stores without radio.

88) Radio repairs: receipts from repairs and service of radio and electrical shops, radio and musical instrument stores. 1930 Census, *Retail Distribution*, table 9C.

89) Flowers: S—sales of florists.

91) Motion pictures: O—(theatrical owners, managers, and officials, plus theater ushers) times personal income per capita by state. For New York, however, it was necessary to exclude personnel in legitimate theaters. To do so it was assumed that the ratio of motion picture owners plus ushers to population in Manhattan was the same as that in Brooklyn.

92) Legitimate theaters: O—(actors, stage hands, theater owners, theatrical and circus ushers) times income per capita.

93) Spectator sports: attendance during 1929 by major league baseball clubs. (Letter, February 22, 1978 from the National League; and *Encyclopedia of Baseball*, vol. 2, p. 240 for the American League.)

94) Clubs: O—officials of lodges, societies times per capita income.

95) Commercial participant amusements: O—(billiard room . . . keepers; keepers of pleasure resorts, attendants, pool rooms; plus laborer, recreation and amusement) times per capita income.

96) Pari-mutuel net receipts: total purses and stakes on American running tracks as reported in *World Almanac and Book of Facts for 1930*, p. 827.

97) O—(photographers, veterinary surgeons) times per capita income.

99) Higher education: Tuition receipts of public and private institutions from U.S. Office of Education, *Biennial Survey of Education, 1928–30*, pp. 374, 376.

100) Elementary and secondary schools: Number of students in private elementary and secondary schools, in U.S. Office of Education, *Biennial Survey of Education, 1928–30*, p. 788.

101) Other Education: Expenditures by private commercial schools from U.S. Office of Education, *Biennial Survey of Education, 1928–30*, p. 2 used to allocate a U.S. total for commercial and correspondence schools. The latter figure was estimated on the basis of the ratio of such fees to all "other" education expenditures in the *1951 National Income Supplement*, p. 196. The balance of the estimate for this category (from the *Supplement* for 1929–74) was allocated by the product of the number of musicians and music teachers, female times per capita income by state. (Too great a proportion of the male musicians and music teachers was engaged in commercial music production to include that group.)

102) Religion and Welfare: U.S. expenditures on religion in 1929 were estimated as 66% of expenditures for the entire 102) group, the

ratio based on detailed data for 1929 from the *1951 National Income Supplement*, p. 197.

Expenditures by churches in each state are available for the year 1926 and were used after minor adjustment. (Bureau of the Census, *Religious Bodies: 1926*, p. 312. The reported amounts were divided by the percent of churches reporting, to encompass non-reporting churches.)

The distribution is similar to that indicated by the Population Census count of clergymen in April 1930, but is believed to be more indicative of actual expenditures in 1929.

The balance of the U.S. total for this group was allocated by the number of social and welfare workers times per capita income by state.

104) Foreign travel: it was assumed that foreign travel expenditures varied among the states as did international money orders—both reflecting the extent of variation in foreign contacts. Money order data from the *Report of the Postmaster General for 1929*.

106) Expenditures in the U.S. by foreign visitors: from the *Survey of Current Business* (June 1971), p. 21. These were allocated among the states by guestroom rentals (S72, pp. 2–16ff.). Expenditures by Canadians were allocated by rentals in states along the Northern border and West Coast; of West Europeans, along the East Coast and California; from the Caribbean, Southern border, and East Coast; from Japan and other overseas countries, Hawaii, West Coast, New York, and District of Columbia.

107) Remittances to foreigners: These remittances are allocated by state as are expenditures for foreign travel by U.S. residents. We assume that states with residents who spend most in foreign travel also remit most to foreigners—by reason of descent, friendship, or business contact.

1970

U.S. government publications used frequently in the estimation are referred to by initials, as follows:

G   1972 Census of Governments, vol. 4, *Government Finances, No. 5, Compendium of Government Finances*.

H   1970 Census of Housing, vol. 1, part 1, *Housing Characteristics for States, Cities, and Counties, U.S. Summary*.

IRS   Internal Revenue Service, *Statistics of Income, 1970, Individual Income Tax Returns*.

M67   1967 Census of Manufactures, *Summary and Subject Statistics*, vol. 1.

M72   1972 Census of Manufactures, *Industry Statistics*, vol. II.

MLS   1967 Census of Business, *Retail Trade Merchandise Line Sales*,
         50 individual state reports; 1972 Census of Retail Trade,
         Merchandise Line Sales, microfiches for the individual
         states.

P   1970 Census of Population, *General Economic and Social
         Characteristics* PC(1)-C1, U.S. Summary.

P2   1970 Population Census, *Detailed Characteristics*, Individual
         State volumes.

RT1   1967 Census of Business, vol. 1, *Retail Trade, Subject Re-
         ports*.

RT2   1972 Census of Retail Trade, vol. 1, *Summary and Subject
         Statistics*.

S67   1967 Census of Business, vol. V, *Selected Services, Area Sta-
         tistics*.

S72   1972 Census of Selected Service Industries, vol. 1, *Summary
         and Subject Statistics*.

SA   *Statistical Abstract of the United States, 1971.*

SCB   *Survey of Current Business*, August 1977. (State personal in-
         come estimates).

WT67   1967 Census of Business, vol. III, *Wholesale Trade, Subject
         Reports*.

DETAILED PROCEDURES

(The numbers used—e.g., 3), 4)—refer to the row in table 2.6 for
PCE in Bureau of Economic Analysis, *The National Income and Product
Accounts of the United States, 1929–74.*)

Food and Tobacco

3) Food off-premise: (*a*) sales of groceries in grocery stores (meat,
fish, poultry, produce, frozen foods, etc.) times the ratio of total
sales of groceries to sales of groceries in grocery stores; plus (*b*) packaged alcoholic beverages. (MLS, table 1); and sales of food stores
without payroll (RT: p. 1–43, RT2: p. 1–40).

4) Meals and beverages; sales of meals, snacks, alcoholic drinks
(MLS, table 1); school lunch revenues (G: p. 48); and current fund
revenues of colleges from food services (U.S. National Center for
Educational Statistics, *Financial Statistics of Higher Education, 1969–
1970*, table 3).

5) Food furnished: sum of pay in kind to employees in private
households, hospitals, schools, nonprofit organizations, military,

military reserves (unpublished BEA, kindly provided by Edward Coleman, BEA).

6) Value of food produced and consumed on farms: (USDA, Economic Research Service, *Farm Income, State Estimates 1949–1970*, table 6, col. 3).

7) Tobacco: sales of cigars, cigarettes, and tobacco (MLS, table 1).

8) 9) minus 7).

9) The allocator was the sum of three items:

(*a*) On-premise drinks (retail stores) were computed as the average of the 1967 and 1972 merchandise line figures for alcoholic drinks (MLS).

(*b*) On-premise alcoholic drinks (hotels and motels) were from S72, pp. 2–16ff.

(*c*) Packaged liquors (MLS-1972).

Clothing

11) Shoes: sales of all footwear (MLS, table 1).

12) Shoes, cleaning and repair: (S67:p. 21 and S72:p. 34).

14) Women's clothing: sales of women's-girl's clothing excluding footwear (MLS, table 1).

15) Men's clothing: sales of men's-boy's clothing excluding footwear (MLS, table 1).

16) Military clothing: pay-in-kind to military plus military reserves (unpublished BEA).

17) Cleaning and dyeing (S67:p. 20, and S72:p. 32) and laundering (S67: pp. 18–20 and S72: pp. 31–33). The figures include repairs and alterations.

18) Jewelry: total sales of jewelry and optical goods (MLS, table 1).

19) Other: jewelry and watch repair services (S67:p. 32 and S72:p. 48).

Personal Care

21) Toilet articles: MLS sales of cosmetics for 1967; MLS sales of toiletries for 1972.

22) Barber shop and beauty services: combined revenues of both types of business (S67:p. 20 and S72:p. 33).

Housing

24) Owner occupied . . . space rent: H, table 2. Number of owner occupied housing units in urban areas times median value of such

units. Implicitly we assume that the value of housing varies between states as does imputed rent.

25) Tenant occupied . . . rent: H, table 2. Number of renter occupied units (total minus owner) in urban areas times mean contract rent. Because the inclusion of rural nonfarm units was conceptually desirable we made a tabulation of all nonfarm units from the 1970 Census 1 in 1,000 sample tapes. The results, perhaps because of greater sampling error, did not yield data that appeared preferable as an allocator. They did, however, call attention to the improbable published median rent for Pennsylvania. Discussion with census personnel, however, threw no light on that figure.

26) Rental value of farm dwellings: gross rental value of farm dwellings from USDA, Economic Research Service, *Farm Income, State Estimates, 1949–1970*, table 7.

27) Other housing: guest room rentals of hotels, motor hotels, motels (S72: pp. 2–16ff.) plus "current fund revenues, housing" of institutions of higher education (U.S. Office of Education, *Financial Statistics of Institutions of Higher Education, Current Fund Revenue and Expenditures, 1968–69*, table 3).

Household Operation

29) Furniture: percentage distributions from MLS were computed for sales of furniture-sleep equipment minus floor coverings for 1967, and for furniture and sleep equipment for 1972, and averaged.

30) Kitchen . . . appliances: for 1967 we used MLS—sales of major appliances minus sales of radio and TV. Computed by applying to MLS sales of major appliances the ratio of kitchen appliance sales to total appliance sales in department stores and radio and TV stores. (The remaining MLS appliance sales were allocated to row 87 below.) For 1972, we used the MLS breakdown of major appliances (SIC code 300).

31) China . . . : MLS—kitchenware, home furnishings.

32) Other durables . . . : MLS2—hardware, electrical supplies, and floor coverings.

33) Semidurables . . . : MLS—sales of curtains-draperies and dry goods.

34) Cleaning and polishing . . . : MLS—sales of "All other merchandise" in food stores and grocery stores for 1967. For 1972, we used sales of detergents in grocery stores. Percentage distributions were computed for the 1967 and the 1972 data and averaged.

35) Stationery . . . : MLS sales in department stores, variety stores, and drug stores.

37) Electricity: kilowatts of electric energy sold to residential consumers are reported by the Federal Power Commission for 1970. (*Statistical Abstract of the United States, 1972*, p. 512.) These were multiplied by the average of typical residential bills for the appropriate state as of January 1970 and January 1971. (Federal Power Commission, *Typical Electric Bills, December 1971*, p. xiii.) Typical bills are reported for residences consuming 250, 500, 750, and 1,000 kWh monthly. We utilized those for 500 kWh since the FPC average for most communities fell in the annual range of 5,000 to 6,000. (FPC, *Typical Electric Bills, Typical Net Monthly Bills as of January 1, 1970*, table 13.) In most states the 250 kWh bill ran about 70% of that for 500 kWh.

38) Gas: revenues from residential customers (SA, p. 505).

39) Sum of: general revenue for current charges for sewage, plus governmental utility revenue from water supply. G, tables 28, 56.

40) Fuel oil and coal: MLS—sales of household fuels-ice.

41) Telephone: Federal Communications Commission, *Statistics of Communications Common Carriers, Year ended . . . 1970*, p. 10. Number of residence phones.

42) Domestic service: payroll for private household employees (SCB).

43) Other: receipts of electrical repair shops (radio-TV, refrigerator, etc.) plus those of reupholstery, furniture repair stores (S67: p. 31 and S72: pp. 46, 47).

45–46) These medical care expenditure items were allocated by detailed estimates from HEW.[79]

47) Physicians: proprietors income received by physicians (unpublished BEA). Two alternative estimates were confirmatory, but not clearly superior. One used number of physicians times per capita state income. The second used IRS medical deductions data from individual income tax reports.

48) Dentists: proprietor's income received by dentists (unpublished BEA).

49) Other professional services: proprietor's income received in medical services, excluding physicians, surgeons, and dentists (unpublished BEA).

51) Health insurance: Health Insurance Institute, *Source Book of Health Insurance, 1972–73*. Health insurance benefits were deducted from the state figures for health insurance premiums to give the overhead figures (costs plus profits) used to allocate the U.S. BEA total. (The HEW estimates for health insurance relate to benefits, and do not therefore serve as an accurate allocator for the BEA totals, which include only the costs net of benefits.)

55) Sum of 56) through 62).

56) Brokerage charges . . . : allocated by the amount of dividends received by individuals (IRS, p. 230).

57) Bank service charges: allocated by the aggregate of demand deposits held by insured commercial banks (SA, p. 436).

58) Services furnished . . . by financial intermediaries: imputed interest of financial institutions (unpublished BEA).

59) Expense of handling life insurance: dollar value of life insurance in force (SA, p. 451).

60) Legal services proprietor's income received by lawyers (unpublished BEA).

61) Funeral . . . : receipts by funeral service businesses and crematories (S, pp. 1–21, S2: p. 34).

62) Other personal business: estimated by allocating the sum of:

(a) total receipts of labor unions in 1970 allocated by labor union membership by state—from 1972 Statistical Abstract, p. 242.

(b) employment agency fees—by receipts of private employment agencies. S72, p. 39.

(c) classified advertisements—by advertising revenues of newspapers, averaging 1967 and 1972 data. M72, vol. 2, p. 27A–34.

65) New autos: MLS, sales of "new passenger cars retail," and MLS2.

66) Net purchases of used cars: MLS, sales of "used passenger cars retail," and MLS2.

67) Other motor vehicles: sales of miscellaneous auto dealers (e.g., motorcycles, etc.) minus sales of boat dealers (RT67: pp. 1–47, 1–48; RT72: p. 46).

68) Tires, tubes . . . : sales of auto tires, batteries, accessories, MLS. Table 1 by state.

69) Repair, greasing . . . : receipts of automobile repair shops; of private parking; of leasing (without drivers), auto laundries (S, pp. 1–27 to 1–30; S2, pp. 43–47) plus receipts from public parking facilities (G: p. 49).

70) Gasoline and oil: sales of "auto fuels-lubricants," MLS, table 1 by state, and MLS2.

71) Bridge, tunnel . . . : general revenue for current charges for water transport and terminals, toll highway facilities (G: p. 49).

72) Auto insurance premiums: "direct premia written" times the complement of the "overall adjusted loss ratio" by state. These data are from Best's Executive Data Service and were kindly provided by the A. M. Best Company.

74, 75, 79) Transit systems, taxicabs, and bus: personal income originating from local and interurban passenger transit (SCB).

76, 78) Railway: ICC, *Annual Report, 1970* and ICC, *Transport Statistics in the United States, 1970.*

80) Airline: Person-nights spent by air travelers by region of origin, appears in the 1972 Census of Transportation, vol. 1, *National Travel Survey,* table 6. To exclude business travel from those figures we assume that business trips by air (table 8, ibid.) had the same region of origin as did all business trips. The regional person-night figures were allocated by state within each region by the number of people moving to another county or abroad between 1965 and 1970 (1972 SA: p. 27). The basis for this procedure was the observation that the number of trips taken by families is linked to the extent of permanent out-mobility within the prior five years, trips being frequently generated by the desire to see relatives and friends from the old home area. (Cf. John Lansing and Eva Mueller, *The Geographic Mobility of Labor,* 1967, pp. 146–47.)

81) Others: 1967 Census of Business, *Travel Agencies,* BC67-SS7, total receipts of travel agencies.

82) Sum of 83) through 97).

83) Books and maps: sales of bookstores (RT67: p. 1–59; RT72: pp. 1–61).

84) Magazines, newspapers . . . : weighted average of (1) receipts from subscriptions and sales of newspapers by state from M72, p. 27A–34 (averaging 1967–72) and (2) sales of newsdealers and newsstands (RT72, p. 35). Weighting for each series is dollar total, value of subscriptions and sales for newspapers and periodicals from M72, pp. 27A–29, 30.

85) Nondurable toys: sales of hobby toy and game shops (RT67: pp. 1–60; RT72: p. 62).

86) Wheel goods . . . : sales of sports and recreation equipment (MLS, table 1), and MLS2 plus sales of boat dealers (RT72: pp. 1–47).

87) Radio and TV receivers: sales of radio, television, and musical stores (record and instrument). Computed from MLS in 30) *supra,* and MLS2—sales of radios, TVs, and instruments.

88) Radio, TV repair: sales of radio and TV repair establishments (S72: p. 46)

89) Flowers, seeds . . . : Sales of florists (RT67: pp. 1–58; RT72: p. 60).

91) Motion picture theaters: receipts (S67: pp. 1–33; S72: p. 50).

92) Legitimate theaters . . . : receipts of theatrical producers and services (S67: pp. 1–36; S72: p. 51).

93) Spectator sports: receipts of commercial sports establishments (S67: pp. 1–36; S72: p. 53).

94) Clubs . . . : by taxable pay rolls of reporting units in SIC 869 (nonprofit member organizations). Bureau of the Census, *County Business Patterns, 1970,* U.S. Summary (1971).

95) Commercial participant amusements: receipts of "amusements and recreation services, except motion pictures" minus those of "theatrical producers" and those in "commercial sports" (S67: pp. 34–36; S72: pp. 49–53).

96) Gross distribution of stakes and purses plus revenues to states from racing. Data from *The American Racing Manual*, 1971 edition, pp. 334, 344.

97) Other: receipts of photographic studios (S67: pp. 1–20; S72: pp. 1–33); of photofinishing laboratories (S67: pp. 1–26; S72, pp. 1–40); of sporting and recreational camps (S67: pp. 1–18; S72: pp. 1–30); of pet shops (RT72: p. 65); plus expenditures for pet care. The latter is estimated by multiplying the number of veterinarians by state (from the state volumes of P2, table 170) times the average receipts per veterinarian. The latter is indexed for each state by receipts per pet shop (S72: pp. 1–65) adjusted to a national average per veterinarian equal to the average for other in category 97).

98) Sum of 99) through 101).

99) Higher education: estimated as the sum of two items.

(A) Institutions of higher learning under private control—total current funds expenditures minus sponsored research expenditures, and minus expenditures of auxiliary enterprises, from U.S. National Center for Educational Statistics, *Financial Statistics of Institutions of Higher Education, Current Funds Revenues and Expenditures, 1969–70*, table 2. These state expenditures were then reduced to exclude expenditures by in-migrant students, using the ratio of student residents to students enrolled. (U.S. National Center for Educational Statistics, *Residence and Migration of College Students, Fall 1968*, table 9.) To this subtotal there was then added an estimate for expenditures on higher education by state students attending colleges out of state. For this purpose the number of students migrating out of state (id.) were multipied by the U.S. average expenditure per student, using U.S. totals from the two sources cited above.

(B) Tuition and fees paid public colleges by the residents of each state was the sum of:

   i) tuition and fees paid to home state public colleges. Total tuition and fees collected (U.S. National Center for Educational Statistics, id.) times the percentage collected from in-state students. This percentage was computed as the number of "Students Remaining" (U.S. National Center for Educational Statistics, *Residence and Migration of College Students*, Fall 1968, p. 26) times the average in-state tuition and fee charge divided by total revenue collected from tuition and fees. [(number in-state students) × (in-state fees) + (number of out of state students) × (out of state fees)]. The data on tuition and fees for each state in 1970–71 were obtained by correspondence from the National Association of State Universities and Land Grant Colleges.

ii) tuition and fees paid to out-of-state public schools: was estimated as number migrating out (U.S. National Center of Education, *Residence and Migration*, p. 26) times the average out-of-state tuition and fee charge.

100) Elementary and secondary education: taxable payrolls, from Census, *County Business Patterns, 1970.*

101) Other education: Proprietor's income received by persons in other education (unpublished BEA).

102) Religious and welfare activities: payroll of nonprofit membership organizations (SCB).

103) Sum of 104), 105) minus 106), 107).

104) Foreign travel: data for 1972 are available on the number of person-nights spent on trips with destinations outside the U.S., classified by U.S. region of origin. (1972 Census of Transportation, vol. 1, *National Travel Survey*, p. 47.) These are related to estimates of the population by region for 1972 to establish regional rates. (U.S. Census Current Population Survey Reports, Series P-25, No. 488, "Estimates of Population of States: July 1, 1971 and 1972.") Each regional rate was applied to the population totals for each state within that region to derive estimates of foreign travel by residents of that state. These estimates were then used to allocate the BEA total for net expenditures on foreign travel. [The proportion of all person-nights spent in commercial establishments—as against those spent with friends, etc.—differs so little from region to region (ibid., p. 67) as to suggest that average expenditures per person-trip would not differ greatly by region of origin.]

105) Expenditures abroad by U.S. residents: These expenditures are by definition made in foreign countries, and hence cannot be allocated among the states. (The income from which expenditures by overseas military are made is deducted from personal income by the Bureau of Economic Analysis in making its estimates of personal income by state.)

1977

Abbreviations for frequently used sources are as follows:

G   Census of Governments, 1977, *Compendium of Government Finances*, T47.

MLS   Merchandise line statistics from microfiches for the 1977 Census of Retail Trade, table 1.

RT 77   1977 Census of Retail Trade, Geographic Area
    Statistics, Pt. I.
S77 1977   Census of Services, Geographic Area Series,
    Vol. 2, Pt. 1.
SA78, SA79, SA82   *Statistical Abstract* for the respective years.
SCB   Survey of Current Business.

2) Food and tobacco: sum of 3), 4), 5), 6), 7).

3) Food purchased for off-premise consumption: sales of groceries and packaged alcoholic beverages. MLS.

4) Purchased meals and beverages: meals, snacks, and alcoholic beverages.

5) Food furnished employees: income from employment in private households. SCB August, 1980, T3.

6) Food produced and consumed on farms: value of home consumption, from Research Service Statistical Bulletin 678, *Economic Indicators of the Farm Sector Income and Balance Sheet Statistics*, T3.

7) Tobacco products: sales of cigars, cigarettes, and tobacco. MLS.

9) Alcoholic beverages purchased for off-premise consumption: sales of packaged alcoholic beverages. MLS.

11) Clothing, accessories, and jewelry: sum of 2), 14), 15), 16), 17), 18), 19).

12) Shoes and other footwear: sales of footwear. MLS.

13) Clothing and accessories except footwear: sum of 14), 15).

14) Women's and children's clothing: sales of women's-girl's wear. MLS.

15) Men's and boy's clothing: sales of men's-boy's wear. MLS.

16) Standard clothing issued to military personnel allocated by personal income from the (federal) military. SCB, August 1980.

17) Cleaning, storage, and repair of clothing and shoes: allocated by the sum of:

(a) Laundry cleaning and garment service minus industrial launderers and minus linen supply, from S77 (SIC 721–7218–7213).

(b) Shoe repair, shoe shine, and hat repairs from S77 (SIC 725).

18) Jewelry and watches: sales of jewelry. MLS.

19) Clothing and accessories, other. These items consist watch, clock, and jewelry repairs, costume and dress rentals, and miscellaneous personal services related to clothing. Allocator is watch repairs, Census of Service Industries, 577 (SIC 763).

20) Personal care: sum of 21), 22).

21) Toilet articles and preparation: sales of health and beauty aids. MLS.

22) Barber shops, beauty parlors, baths, and health clubs: receipts of barber and beauty shops S77, (SIC 723, 4).

23) Housing: sum of 24), 25), 26), 27).

24) Owner occupied nonfarm housing: allocated by number of owned houses multiplied by state median value of house. From 1980 Census of Housing, *General Housing Characteristics*, (HC 80-1-A8) Ch. A, table 1.

25) Rent of tenant occupied nonfarm dwellings allocated by median rent multiplied by the difference between total year-round housing and owner occupied housing. 1980 Census of Housing, *General Housing Characteristics*, (HC 80-1-A8) Ch. A.

26) Rental value of farm dwellings: gross-rental value of farm dwellings for 1977. From unpublished U.S. Department of Agriculture data kindly provided by Sandra Sudderdorf.

27) Other housing: guest room rentals of hotels, motels, trailering parks, and camps (S77) (SIC 701, 3) plus one-half of college auxiliary enterprises, from National Center for Education Statistics, *Financial Statistics of Institutions of Higher Learning*.

28) Household operation: sum of 29)–35), 37)–43).

29) Furniture, including mattresses and bedsprings: sales of furniture and sleep equipment. MLS.

30) Kitchen and other household appliances: sales of household appliances plus sales of small electrical appliances. MLS.

31) China, glassware, tableware, and utensils: kitchenware and home furnishings. MLS.

32) Other durable house furnishings: floor covering plus lawn and garden equipment. MLS.

33) Semi-durable house furnishings: curtains, draperies, and dry goods. MLS.

34) Cleaning and polishing preparations . . . : Sales of detergents in groceries. MLS.

35) Stationery and writing supplies: sales of stationery in department and variety stores. MLS 77. A.

36) Household utilities: sum of 37), 38), 39), 40).

37) Electricity: residential sales of electricity. (SA 79, p. 613) multiplied by the average electric bill (Federal Power Commission, *Typical Electric Bills, Jan. 1. 1978*). Typical bills are reported for residences consuming 250, 500, 750, and 1000 kwh monthly. We used those for 750 kwh.

38) Gas: residential gas revenue, SA77, p. 619.

39) Water and other sanitary services: revenue from water supply utilities of local government G., T47.

40) Fuel oil and coal: sales of household fuels, MLS.

41) Telephone and telegraph: number of residence phones, from FCC, *Statistics of Communications Common Carriers Year Ended December 1977.*

42) Domestic Service: 1977 payroll for private household employees. SCB, Aug. 1980, table 3, p. 60.

43) Other household operations: sum of (*a*) receipts of electrical and electronic repair shops (except radio and television); (*b*) lawn mower, saw, knife and tool sharpening, and repair; (*c*) sewer and septic tank cleaning; (*d*) reupholstery and furniture repair. S77.

44) Medical care: sum of 45)–51).

45) Drug preparations and sundries: sales of drugs, MLS.

46) Ophthalmic products and orthopedic appliances: optical goods, MLS.

47) Physicians: receipts: S77, *Other Service Industries.*

48) Dentists: receipts: S77, *Other Service Industries.*

49) Other professional services. Receipts of all health services minus receipts of physicians, dentists, and hospitals: S77 *Other Service Industries.*

50) Privately controlled hospitals and sanitariums, sum of:

(a) Taxable hospitals plus nursing and personal care facilities (SIC 805 + 806).

(b) Non-taxable: hospitals plus nursing and personal care facilities (SIC 805 + 806). May include outpatient care facilities and other health and allied services (SIC 808 + other 80).

From S77, *Other Service Industries:*

51) Health insurance: premiums minus benefits, from the Health Insurance Institute, *Source Book of Health Insurance,* 1978–79, pp. 25, 30.

55) Personal Business: Sum of 56)–62).

56) Brokerage charges and investment counseling: allocated by domestic and foreign dividends received. From *1977 Statistics of Income, Individual Income Tax Returns,* p. 154.

57) Bank services charges, trust services, and safe deposit rental: demand deposits for insured commercial banks. SA78, p. 539.

58) Services furnished without payment by financial intermediaries except life insurance carriers: allocated by imputed interest from BEA, unpublished tabulation.

59) Expense of handling life insurance: total dollar value of life insurance in force. SA78, p. 554.

60) Legal services: receipts of legal service establishments. S77 (SIC 81).

61) Funeral and burial expenses: receipts of funeral service businesses and crematories, S77 (SIC 726).

62) Other personal business: estimated by allocating the sum of:

(a) Total disbursements by labor unions, from *Union Financial Statistics;*
(b) Receipts of employment agencies, from S77 (SIC 7361);
(c) Advertising of daily and Sunday newspapers from M77, pp. 27A–34.

65,66) New and used autos: cars, trucks, and other passenger transport. MLS.

67) Other motor vehicles: recreational vehicles, MLS.

68) Tire, tubes, accessories, and other parts: sales of auto tires, batteries, and parts.

69) Repair, greasing . . . receipts of auto repair shops, of private parking, of leasing (without drivers). S77 (SIC 753).

70) Gasoline and oil: auto fuels and lubricants, MLS.

71) Bridge, tunnel, ferry, and road tolls: water transportation and state highway tools, from G, p. 49.

72) Insurance premiums less claims paid: premiums written for private passenger automobiles × (100—adjusted loss ratio). From unpublished data kindly supplied by A. M. Best, Executive Data Service.

73) Purchased local transportation: annual payroll for local transportation, *County Business Patterns, 1977,* table 21, line 41.

77) Purchased intercity transportation: allocated by number or person trips to destinations in other states, from the National Travel Survey, *Travel During 1977,* table 28.

82) Recreation: sum of 83)–89), 91)–97).

83) Books and maps: sales of bookstores. RT77, vol. 2, part 1, p. 41.

84) Magazines, newspapers, and sheet music: newspaper sales and subscriptions. M77, pp. 27A–34.

85) Nondurable toys and sport supplies: sales of hobby, toy, and game shops. RT77, p. 42.

86) Wheel goods . . . sales of sporting goods. MLS.

87) Radio and television receivers, records, and musical instruments: sales of televisions and audio equipment. MLS.

88) Radio and TV repairs: receipts. S77 (SIC 7622).

89) Flowers, seeds, and potted plants: sales of florists. RT77, p. 46.

90) Admissions to specified spectator amusements: sum of 91), 92), 93).

91) Motion picture theaters: receipts. S77 (SIC 783).

92) Legitimate theaters: receipts of theatrical producers and services. S77 (SIC 7922).

93) Spectator sports: receipts of commercial sports establishments. S77 (SIC 794).

94) Clubs and fraternal organizations except insurance: expenses of civil, social, and fraternal organization, 1977 Census of Service Industries, *Miscellaneous Subjects*, T33.

95) Commercial participant amusements: receipts of "bowling and billiard and pool establishments," plus "other amusement and recreation services" minus commercial sports. S77 (SIC 793, 79 exc 792, 3 minus 794).

96) Pari-mutuel net receipts: receipts from racing. S77 (SIC 7948)

97) Other recreation: allocated by sum of:

(a) Receipts of photo studios and photo laboratories. S77 (SIC 722, SIC 7395).

(b) Gross receipts of state lotteries minus prizes. SA79, p. 297.

(c) Sales of pet shops, from RT77, vol. II, part 1, p. 47.

Pet shop sales multiplied by 3.5 in order to allow for expenditure on veterinarians.

98) Private education and research: sum of 99), 100), 101).

99) Higher education: estimated as the sum of:

(a) Institutions of higher learning under private control—tuition and fees plus private gifts plus sales of education enterprise, from U.S. National Center for Education Statistics, *Financial Statistics of Institutions of Higher Learning*.

(b) Tuition and fees paid to public colleges, same source as (a) above.

100) Elementary and secondary school: 1977 enrollment in non-public elementary and secondary schools (SA80, p. 114) multiplied by average teacher salary. U.S. National Center of Education Statistics, *Digest of Educational Statistics, 1980*, p. 58.

101) Other private education and research: receipts from correspondence schools and vocational schools plus specialized non-degree granting schools. From S77, *Other Service Industries*.

102) Religious and welfare activities: allocated by payroll of social services and religious organization. 1977 *County Business Patterns*. Table 1B, SIC 83 + SIC 866.

1982

With very minor exceptions the same procedures were used for 1982 as 1977. The 1982 Census of Retail Trade information on line of merchandise, however, was available only from census microfiches rather than printed material.

· C H A P T E R   1 1 ·

VALIDITY OF ESTIMATES

I. TIME SERIES

A

The expenditure changes shown by the present series differ from those of Kuznets and Kendrick (who adopts Kuznets's consumption figures). Four main reasons are at work.

1. Kuznets (and therefore Kendrick) adopts the Grebler-Blank-Winnick residential construction deflator, which uses a construction cost series to proxy for a rent series. Though a tolerable proxy in most years, it fails whenever great capital gains and losses occur. Since the Commerce concept for the imputed rental value of owner occupied homes is relevant here we use the BLS price index for rents, and check it by the NICB series. These rental series gives the more reasonable results we show.[1]

2. The present deflators for commodities differ from those of Kuznets for two main reasons: (*a*) we use retail price series instead of the wholesale price series Shaw and Kuznets rely on for various sectors (e.g., food, tobacco, gasoline, furniture); and (*b*) we provide some series where Shaw gives no detail (e.g., books, alcohol) and revise others (e.g., radio, musical instruments).

3. We derive individual deflators for about thirty consumer service items, whereas Kuznets ultimately relies on a single all-commodity deflator for services except rent.

4. The major quantitative difference between the aggregate series for the 1919–29 period comes in 1919–21, as Table 11.1 indicates.

Unlike the 1919–21 rise shown by Kuznets's series we estimate a marked fall, the chief reason being the use of different construction deflators (noted above in 1.). Capital losses in 1921 were of chief importance in creating that difference.

B

The basic Kuznets, and Kuznet-Kendrick series have been revised by Romer and Balke-Gordon.[2] However, these revisions are made at

TABLE 11.1
Index of Personal Consumption Expenditures
(constant dollar)

Year	Present	Kuznets[a]	Kendrick[b]
1919	100	100	100
1920	99	104	105
1921	91	109	112

Sources: [a]Cf. his *National Product Since 1869* (New York: 1946), p. 105. For rent he uses a series by Carl Snyder.
[b]John Kendrick, *Productivity Trends*, table A-IIa.

the aggregate GNP level. Since one cannot merely assume the same percentage revision for PCE as for the other GNP components they do not automatically create a better consumption series than Kuznets provided (and therefore Kendrick). More important, the analytic bases for the regressions are too dubious to warrant their use for deriving a new consumption series.

Both leading candidates rely on a novel and arbitrary economic constant. It is developed as follows.

"To impose the postwar relationship is straightforward," according to Romer.[3] Only two GNP components are needed. Given C (Commodities at producers' prices) "straightforward imposition" creates O (all other GNP components, i.e., distributive margin plus all services).[4] The model ignores all information for period 1 except C_1.

$$GNP_{t1} = C_{t1} + O_{t1}$$
$$GNP_{t2} = C_{t2} + O_{t2}$$

The procedure is simple although not explicitly articulated in all its steps:

TABLE 11.2 Romer GNP-Consumption Model

By regression:	(1) $GNP_{t2} = \gamma C_{t2}$
By substitution:	(2) $C_{t2} + O_{t2} = \gamma C_{t2}$
Combining terms:	(3) $O_{t2} = (\gamma - 1)C_{t2}$
By simple assertion:	(4) $(\gamma - 1)C_{t2} = (\gamma - 1)C_{t1}$
Therefore, by substitution:	(5) $O_{t1} = (\gamma - 1)C_{t1}$
Yielding:	(6) $GNP_{t1} = C_{t1} + O_{t1}$

GNP_{t1} is then asserted to be superior to the Kuznets-Kendrick series for 1869–1918.[5] Assertion (4) defines γ for "1909–28 and 1947–85 combined" as identical with γ for 1869–1908. Evidently Marshall's "Natura Non Facit Saltum" has become "Natura non Movet."

The entire enterprise is, however, circular. The "unquestioning acceptance of the historical data" that Romer attributes to Lucas,

Tobin, and Baily refers, if anything, to their comparison between the stability of different periods.[6] But (4) imposed the assumption that the coefficient in both periods had to be identical.[7] How could estimates that thus "impose" stability then be used to test whether stability actually changed from prewar to postwar?

Balke and Gordon in turn describe Romer's key equation as "misspecified,"[8] its .66 Durbin-Watson as unacceptable.[9] They add a second explanatory variable (construction activity) to her single variable for commodity output. But they then create their series by similarly defining an empirical coefficient from one era (1869–1908) as identical with that for another (1909–28). Since their series rests on a basic estimating equation[10] whose $\bar{R}^2$ is only .096, estimates so derived are hardly persuasive.[11] (Nor do they become more so when the period fitted is extended to 1938. By adding only ten observations their $\bar{R}^2$ rockets from .096 to .580,[12] a gain hardly confirming their assertion that "prewar/postwar ratios are robust to the choice of an alterative set of benchmark years.")[13]

C

A comparison between changes in the present figures and prior estimates by Lough and Dewhurst is given in table 11.3[14] Dewhurst used Lough's estimates, with few exceptions, to indicate trends.

TABLE 11.3
Personal Consumption Expenditures
in 1909 as a Percent of 1929:
Three Estimates

	Present	Dewhurst	Lough
Food and Tobacco	50%	42%	42%
Clothing	34	37	37
Personal Care	22	23	26
Housing	33	49	31
Household Operations	27	31	30
Medical Care	23	24	27
Personal Care	28	12[a]	n.a.
Transportation	15	19	13
Recreation	20	22	28
Education	24	33	36[b]
Religion and Welfare	29	37	33
Foreign Travel	57	54	56
Total	33	36	33

[a]Dewhurst intentionally omits various items.
[b]Lough's private education includes only tuition.

Hence the basic comparison is really with Lough. Each provides estimates for quinquennial years 1909–19, and biennial, 1919–29. We contrast the 1909–29 change as an index of major differences.

1. One of the most striking, and significant, differences between the present estimates and others is that for housing. Dewhurst's description of procedures makes little sense. Hence his difference from Lough, his primary source, as well as from the present estimates, is not meaningful.[15]

2. Two major sources account for the food and tobacco difference.[16]

(a) Lough (and therefore Dewhurst) includes $2 billion for alcohol in 1929. The BEA (and therefore the present estimate) reports $0 because it excludes illegal goods and services. Lough excluded only illegal services.[17]

(b) The USDA has revised various underlying series for farm production and farm income since the official series used by Lough were first made. For example, it now estimates farm marketings of livestock in 1910 at $1.6 billion. But Lough estimates only $1.6 billion in 1909 for consumer purchases of meat products (i.e., farm marketings plus manufacturing costs and distribution spread).[18] Presumably Lough failed to include farm slaughterings sold directly to retailers in small towns, for his data were linked to the Census of Manufactures.

3. Dewhurst explicitly omits six items of personal business, all included in the BEA benchmark for 1929.

4. Lough (and presumably Dewhurst) included only tuition rather than total expenditures for private education.

Remaining differences (e.g., clothing, personal care) are small and reflect the use of revised data (e.g., USDA), different procedures, etc.

D

Expenditure series for durable goods 1900–1929 (in current and 1982 prices) have been derived from Shaw's data by Martha Olney.[19] Our current price series had been created over a decade earlier as part of a set including services and nondurables. Otherwise I should have utilized hers, which shows (with few exceptions) similar 1900–1929 changes.[20] The present series, however (unlike hers), utilizes revised BEA 1929 benchmarks for extrapolation to 1900, and deflates to 1987 prices, as the BEA now does.

II. Budget Surveys

Budget survey estimates of consumption by income level, though widely used, lack essential accuracy and detail. Even recent official surveys reveal significant biases in reporting major consumer expenditure items. They may, in addition, have compensating biases for other expenditure items. These limitations are discussed below.

A

Standard investment theory refers to a considerable array of determinants. But even the highest quality work on consumption functions has had to rely on little more than two variables—price and income.[21] Yet consumption is about three times greater than investment, with incredibly varied components. One reason for the difference in theoretical approach has been the limitation of generally available consumption data.

Even the most recent U.S. expenditure survey sample, and the most careful, surveyed less than one-thousandth of one percent of American "consumer units."[22] Recent BLS publications classify expenditures by region, family size, and a few other variables. But the samples are too small to permit analysis of more than one variable at a time—e.g., age, but not age *and* race, or family size *and* age.

B

The surveys, however, suffer from a more serious limitation: bias. The BLS survey for 1984 understated U.S. food and clothing expenditures by $173 billion (table 11.4). Not to mention $33 billion for

TABLE 11.4
Survey as Percentage of National
Income Accounts Estimates

	1960–61	1982–83	1984	1987
Food purchased				
for home use	101	73	64	62
food away from home	105	95	86	87
Alcoholic beverages	42	47	47	45
Tobacco	72	56	69	61
Personal Care Products	144	62		70
Personal Care Service	146	93	118	70
Housekeeping Supplies	107	60		
House furnishings and equipment	93		82	78

Sources: 1960–61: H. Houthakker and L. Taylor, *Consumer Demand in the United States: Analyses and Projections* (1970), table 6.1.

1982–83: BLS Bulletin 2245, *Consumer Expenditure Survey: Diary Survey, 1982–83*, p. 5.

1984: BLS Bulletin 2354, *Consumer Expenditure Survey, 1984*, p. 6.

1987: *Monthly Labor Review* (March 1987), p. 11.

house furnishings, $28 billion for alcohol, and $46 billion for enter-tainment.[23] A $280 billion understatement for these items had to be compensated for elsewhere in the survey estimates for other expen-diture items and/or income. Survey supervisors, the central office, and even the enumerators edit the reports so that at least a rough consonance appears between the expenditure total and its equiva-lent—income (minus saving). Where was that one-third of a trillion dollars implicitly or explicitly reallocated?

The 1984 and 1987 survey collection procedures addressed such biases far more carefully than earlier surveys. But the errors remain disconcertingly large. If overall aggregates are so distorted what re-liance can be put on the underlying distributions of expenditures by income, race, region, or age?

The increased gap for food between 1960–61 and 1984 suggests one specific bias. When survey agent and family respondent reached the final spending totals in earlier surveys, and came up with an imbalance between income expenditure and saving, they usually ad-justed food—the largest subtotal—upwards to produce an accept-able balance. When the survey adopted the diary approach it may well have removed that specific bias. Doing so, however, revealed the deeper difficulty in asking family members to remember, with-out bias, thousands of purchases.[24]

C

The consumption estimates in the present study add (a) U.S. PCE series for 1900–1928 that are comparable with the BEA series for 1929 ff.; and (b) PCE estimates by item for individual states in 1900, and for selected years 1929–82. (For 1929–82 the state estimates sum to the U.S. totals in the BEA national income and product accounts.)

It is well known that the BEA and consumer expenditure survey estimates differ. We prefer the BEA estimates for three reasons.

1. The BLS relies on reports in which individual members of households try to remember expenditures in the prior year. Very few households keep records. The memory feat required even to report major expenditure items accurately is beyond the ability of most respondents.

BEA data, by contrast, rest largely on the massive Censuses of Business. Covering most or all large business (and thus a dispropor-tionate share of total purchases) and a large systematic sample of smaller ones, the censuses provide reports from firms with a strong interest in keeping accurate sales records. (Both for control of opera-tions and to conform to Federal income tax laws, state income tax laws, state sales tax regulations, etc.)

BEA, data for service items reported by regulated electric power, gas, and telephone companies (through the FPC, and DOE), the regulated insurance companies, etc. are superior to those summoned from consumer memories.

2. The Census and regulatory respondent samples are immensely greater than those of the BLS. In 1982 the Retail Census alone relied on 1.9 million reports—i.e., forty-two times as many respondents as the BLS Survey had. (The Census of Services added 3.7 million more firms.[25] Thus the sampling error would be less even if householders could remember expenditures for groceries, tobacco, haircuts, and a hundred other items as accurately as businesses record them.

3. The Census of Business totals can be checked back to the independent Census of Manufactures production data, and the U.S. Department of Agriculture data, for various items. The consumer memory reports are less consistent with these other data than are the Census of Business totals.

D

Given such distortions in the aggregates the underlying BLS distributions hardly permit solid analysis of how spending varies even by income—much less color, or region. And are even less likely to permit assessing the role of any single variable free of the impact of others. (Had the BLS detailed data been made available to scholars, that doubt might prove to apply to some but not other variables.)

Table 11.5 compares one substantial expenditure item from published BLS data with similar data from the census.[26] The census monthly rent sample was one thousand times greater than that of the BLS.[27] Can one doubt that the larger sample of census respondents yields a superior estimate for rent?

Or that implied errors in the estimates for the remaining expenditure items for New York, Philadelphia, or Los Angeles are disturbing? Even BLS estimates for average U.S. housing expenditure by income level, color, etc. are in doubt since the BLS sums such SMSA data to derive its U.S. averages?[28]

III. VALIDITY OF STATE ESTIMATES

A

The most persuasive test for the adequacy of the state PCE estimates will come as they are used in different contexts. But table 11.6 makes the obvious comparison with BEA state estimates of personal in-

TABLE 11.5
Monthly Rent
1980–81

	BLS Mean ($)	Census Median ($)	BLS as % of Census
Cleveland	197	152	130
Philadelphia	259	209	123
Detroit	210	173	121
Buffalo	167	141	118
New York City	236	202	117
Kansas City	181	165	110
Anchorage	357	338	106
Pittsburgh	174	169	103
Cincinnati	184	181	102
Baltimore	192	195	99
San Francisco	264	269	98
Chicago	208	212	98
Portland	209	213	98
St. Louis	149	153	97
Washington, D.C.	276	287	96
Boston	183	191	96
Los Angeles	252	274	92
San Diego	251	282	89
Atlanta	206	234	88
Dallas/Fort Worth	222	264	84
Houston	203	268	76
Milwaukee	136	181	75
Seattle	216	289	75
Minneapolis/St. Paul	150	243	62
Miami	152	253	60
Honolulu	251	474	53

Sources: BLS: BLS Bulletin 2267, *Consumer Expenditure Survey, 1984*, tables C1–C4 for 1980–81.

Census: U.S. Census of Housing, 1980, *General Housing Characteristics, U.S. Summary*, table 7.

come. Our new PCE estimates prove to be within reasonable hailing distance of the BEA figures for 1929–82. Moreover, the differences narrowed over time, probably because better source data (e.g., on wages) became available to the BEA.[29]

Table 11.7 offers a more precise comparison for 1982.[30] It adjusts for conceptual differences between PCE and DPI—e.g., savings, contributions to social insurance, etc. For forty-one states the PCE

TABLE 11.6
PCE ÷ Personal Income: Ratios

	1900	1929	1970	1977	1982
US	.99	.91	.80	.86	.79
ME	1.08	.89	.85	.89	.85
NH	.96	.86	.91	.93	.85
VT	.98	.89	.88	.94	.88
MA	.93	.94	.81	.83	.81
RI	.88	.89	.78	.82	.83
CT	.89	.82	.71	.75	.76
NY	.99	.92	.79	.78	.78
NJ	.93	.89	.75	.75	.77
PA	.89	.86	.77	.79	.80
OH	.96	.91	.77	.79	.81
IN	.94	.97	.80	.79	.78
IL	.94	.89	.75	.76	.78
MI	1.04	.91	.77	.77	.78
WI	1.01	.92	.75	.79	.76
MN	1.01	1.03	.77	.82	.81
IA	.91	.96	.74	.71	.75
MO	1.06	.90	.79	.83	.80
ND	.93	1.02	.79	.88	.78
SD	.93	1.01	.79	.85	.82
NE	.91	.94	.78	.80	.75
KS	.91	.94	.71	.74	.69
DE	.92	.73	.82	.84	.82
MD	.98	.85	.76	.79	.81
VA	1.14	.84	.77	.78	.73
WV	1.07	.75	.80	.79	.75
NC	1.40	.82	.77	.80	.76
SC	1.65	.85	.79	.80	.74
GA	1.18	.89	.83	.83	.79
FL	1.14	.97	.94	.96	.87
KY	1.19	.82	.87	.79	.76
TN	1.14	.93	.86	.87	.84
AL	1.27	.81	.82	.80	.74
MS	1.23	.90	.84	.79	.74
AR	1.35	.84	.83	.81	.78
LA	.99	.82	.84	.85	.79
OK	1.28	.92	.81	.81	.73
TX	1.06	.94	.84	.85	.78
MT	.75	.93	.82	.93	.87
ID	.93	.99	.82	.85	.80
WY	.72	.86	.81	.82	.72

Continued on next page

TABLE 11.6—*Continued*

	1900	1929	1970	1977	1982
CO	.98	1.05	.85	.87	.81
NM	.94	.81	.86	.89	.81
AZ	.71	.97	.88	.94	.89
UT	1.00	.97	.92	.94	.90
NV	.79	.85	1.03	1.15	1.01
WA	.94	.96	.79	.84	.77
OR	1.04	1.05	.87	.91	.86
CA	1.02	.94	.81	.85	.82
AK			.66	.68	.69
HI			.79	.97	.98

estimate in the last column comes within 10% of adjusted personal income. That is really strikingly close, for the present state estimates were derived from totally different sources than the BEA used. Over one hundred items were independently estimated on the PCE side for each state, and dozens on the income side. Estimates for Florida,

TABLE 11.7
Personal Income, Savings, Consumption in 1982, by State

	Pop (Millions)	Dispos. Pers. Inc.	Cont. to Soc. Ins.	Int. to Business	Total Savings	Adj. Income	PCE	PCE ÷ Adj. Inc.
US	231.79	2255.12	110.88	56.80	135.00	1952.44	2045.53	1.05
Maine	1.14	9.37	0.44	0.18	0.53	8.22	8.91	1.08
NH	0.95	9.63	0.44	0.22	0.59	8.39	8.94	1.07
Vermont	0.52	4.57	0.21	0.08	0.27	4.00	4.35	1.09
Mass.	5.75	61.59	2.88	1.17	4.00	53.55	57.44	1.07
RI	0.95	9.14	0.49	0.19	0.58	7.88	8.64	1.10
Conn.	3.13	37.77	1.75	0.84	2.60	32.58	33.08	1.02
NY	17.57	182.96	9.42	3.14	12.67	157.73	167.19	1.06
NJ	7.43	88.00	4.07	1.86	6.03	76.04	75.05	0.99
Penn.	11.88	116.01	5.62	2.29	6.99	101.11	103.31	1.02
Ohio	10.77	100.34	4.89	2.71	5.72	87.03	92.50	1.06
Indiana	5.48	47.95	2.33	1.28	2.82	41.52	42.73	1.03
Illinois	11.47	121.13	5.78	2.93	7.23	105.20	106.90	1.02
Michigan	9.12	86.01	3.80	2.27	4.72	75.22	76.65	1.02
Wisc.	4.75	44.33	2.10	1.06	2.63	38.54	38.93	1.01
Minn.	4.13	39.67	2.17	1.12	2.55	33.82	37.75	1.12
Iowa	2.91	26.59	1.27	0.64	1.72	22.95	23.15	1.01
Missouri	4.94	45.27	2.25	1.04	3.08	38.90	41.70	1.07

Continued on next page

TABLE 11.7—*Continued*

	Pop (Millions)	Dispos. Pers. Inc.	Cont. to Soc. Ins.	Int. to Business	Total Savings	Adj. Income	PCE	PCE ÷ Adj. Inc.
N. Dakota	0.67	6.14	0.35	0.13	0.40	5.26	5.79	1.10
S. Dakota	0.69	5.82	0.27	0.12	0.36	5.07	5.33	1.05
Nebraska	1.59	14.73	0.73	0.38	0.92	12.69	12.98	1.02
Kansas	2.41	23.72	1.16	0.57	1.53	20.46	19.56	0.96
Delaware	0.60	5.84	0.32	0.15	0.39	4.98	5.82	1.17
Maryland	4.27	44.72	2.02	1.26	2.80	38.63	42.38	1.10
DC	0.63	7.42	0.88	0.09	0.60	5.85	10.37	1.77
Virginia	5.49	53.74	2.55	1.63	3.38	46.18	45.54	0.99
W. Virginia	1.95	15.14	0.74	0.30	0.81	13.29	13.22	0.99
N.C.	6.02	47.98	2.61	1.21	2.63	41.53	41.67	1.00
S.C.	0.28	24.02	1.29	0.62	1.23	20.88	20.60	0.99
Georgia	5.65	47.18	2.50	1.36	2.75	40.57	42.76	1.05
Florida	10.47	100.35	4.11	2.65	7.28	86.31	99.31	1.15
Kentucky	3.69	29.52	1.36	0.66	1.68	25.81	25.34	0.98
Tenn	4.66	37.37	2.04	0.93	1.97	32.43	35.17	1.08
Alabama	3.94	29.77	1.53	0.75	1.49	26.00	25.27	0.97
Miss.	2.57	17.68	0.87	0.42	0.88	15.51	14.87	0.96
Arkansas	2.31	17.02	0.82	0.39	0.93	14.88	15.18	1.02
Louisiana	4.38	30.32	1.86	0.86	2.05	33.55	34.72	1.03
Oklahoma	3.22	30.14	1.55	0.74	1.70	26.15	26.06	1.00
Texas	15.33	151.79	7.69	3.75	8.12	132.23	135.91	1.03
Montana	0.81	7.05	0.38	0.17	0.41	6.09	6.78	1.11
Idaho	0.98	7.84	0.38	0.23	0.44	6.79	7.05	1.04
Wyoming	0.59	5.16	0.29	0.14	0.29	4.44	4.39	0.99
Colorado	3.07	32.45	1.57	1.12	2.05	27.70	30.57	1.10
N. Mexico	1.37	11.13	0.56	0.29	0.58	9.70	10.35	1.07
Arizona	2.89	25.51	1.31	0.84	1.46	21.90	25.80	1.18
Utah	1.57	12.02	0.71	0.45	0.61	10.24	12.26	1.20
Nevada	0.88	9.34	0.38	0.31	0.44	8.21	10.56	1.29
Wash.	4.28	44.64	2.19	1.33	2.39	38.73	38.15	0.99
Oregon	2.67	23.81	1.23	0.77	1.45	20.36	23.41	1.15
Cal.	24.70	280.81	13.80	8.73	15.52	242.75	254.64	1.05
Alaska	0.44	6.42	0.39	0.17	0.25	5.63	5.18	0.92
Hawaii	1.0	11.74	0.55	0.26	0.48	8.6	11.30	1.32

Source: See Note A at end of chapter.

Nevada, Arizona, Montana, and Hawaii differ more than 10% because of tourist items. Regressions in table 11.8 adjust for such tourist expenditures (e.g., as meals and alcohol) in these state.[31] A troublesome gap still remains for Oregon and Minnesota.

TABLE 11.8
Per Capita Expenditures
Selected Items as Functions of Per Capita Income

	Actual	Estimated
New Hampshire		
MLSBEV	487.6	512.5
ALOFPRM	287.3	151.1
JEWELRY	47.9	7.3
CLOTHING	63.4	65.8
LOCINT	8.9	129.0
SPECSP	13.2	9.9
COMPTAM	91.8	95.6
Total	1072.1	1034.2
Vermont		
MLSBEV	455.7	441.6
ALOFPRM	181.8	13.9
JEWELRY	36.3	61.8
OTHHOUS	93.9	51.1
LOCINT	99.9	79.5
SPECSP	4.0	7.2
COMPTAM	25.2	55.0
Total	1121.8	827.2
Rhode Island		
MLSBEV	463.8	483.6
ALOFPRM	134.5	142.9
JEWELRY	69.3	66.8
OTHHOUS	47.0	59.8
LOCINT	95.6	108.8
SPECSP	12.0	8.8
COMPTAM	44.3	79.0
Total	866.5	949.8
Florida		
MLSBEV	582.7	482.8
ALOFPRM	197.9	142.6
JEWELRY	99.8	66.7
OTHHOUS	102.2	59.6
LOCINT	69.4	108.3
SPECSP	23.5	8.8
COMPTAM	125.7	78.6
Total	1201.2	947.5
Montana		
MLSBEV	553.8	44.5
ALOFPRM	148.6	13.5

Continued on next page

TABLE 11.8—*Continued*

	Actual	Estimated
JEWELRY	52.0	61.6
OTHHOUS	59.2	5.9
LOCINT	115.5	108.3
SPECSP	1.5	7.2
COMPTAM	41.5	54.4
Total	972.1	853.4
Arizona		
MLSBEV	536.0	445.0
ALOFPRM	141.1	131.8
JEWELRY	77.3	62.2
OTHHOUS	54.0	51.8
LOCINT	116.3	81.9
SPECSP	11.6	7.4
COMPTAM	47.2	57.0
Total	983.5	837.1
Nevada		
MLSBEV	664.3	538.1
ALOFPRM	216.0	158.4
JEWELRY	132.7	73.4
OTHHOUS	38.7	71.1
LOCINT	557.1	146.9
SPECSP	1.9	1.9
COMPTAM	114.0	11.2
Total	3092.7	1109.0
District of Columbia		
MLSBEV	959.9	737.78
ALOFPRM	379.2	215.39
JEWELRY	89.4	97.42
OTHHOUS	226.5	112.38
LOCINT	269.6	286.24
SPECSP	14.9	18.53
COMPTAM	119.0	224.31
Total	2058.5	1692.0
Hawaii		
MLSBEV	949.9	589.11
ALOFPRM	184.0	172.96
JEWELRY	227.9	79.53
OTHHOUS	298.1	81.63
LOCINT	408.9	182.46
SPECSP	1.7	12.86
COMPTAM	85.8	139.34
Total	2156.3	1257.9

B

Skilled and massive efforts by BEA over the years surely created more reliable state income estimates than our limited effort for state PCE. But BEA procedures for the entire U.S. are not fully applied to derive the state income figures. The U.S. accounts since 1943 have been consistently improved by working back and forth between preliminary estimates for income (relying on one set of sources) and for expenditure (from another set). Any marked discrepancy between estimates of income and product alerts the estimators. They then work to reduce discrepancies to a tolerable level, adjusting components. Reasonable estimators wisely do not accept too great a "statistical discrepancy." They assume, plausibly, either (a) an error in estimation and/or (b) that their usual quantitative ratios and rules of thumb do not apply because some "new" economic or political factor has intervened. Indeed, one of the central virtues of the BEA accounts is that they thus approach estimation from both the income and the product side.

However, no such comparisons have been made when deriving the state income estimates. Corresponding estimates of product by state have not existed until recently. Thus when BEA attempted to judge the validity of its new state income estimates, it settled for testing only their variability over successive revisions, quite another matter.[32] Such revisions reflect changes within the usual ambit of estimation. But the dispersion of successive estimates can say little about their validity. Such computations are closer to reports on sampling error than the real concern, total error.

C

At the national level BEA adjusts for three items. But differential adjustment by state is not made for these items of personal income because it is not feasible.

1. *Income understatement*. BEA adjusts U.S. personal income to allow for IRS audit adjustment. That adjustment is not varied by state. Behavior, however, is not likely to conform to that assumption. IRS audits since the 1940s have shown that farmers understate their income more frequently than almost any other industry category. (*Statistics of Income* for 1981 indicate, e.g., that the entire farm sector in each of forty-two states reported a financial loss. Hardly a likely state of affairs.) Given that the ratio of farm to total personal income differs largely between states, a differential audit adjustment should be made, but is not.

Nor is it likely that profits from heroin distribution appear in the personal income estimate for Utah and Nebraska as they do in Florida or New York. Nor income from prostitution, illegal gambling, etc.

The PCE data, however, are less likely to be subject to such biases. Cadillacs are bought as readily with illegal as legal income. (Perhaps even more so.)[35] And car dealers, clothing stores, jewelers, appliance stores, and furniture stores are more likely to report sales accurately to the Census of Business (which we use to estimate PCE) than their criminal customers are to report the income they so use to the IRS (used to estimate personal income). Because the IRS generally finds net income understated, it may not be happenstance that the ratios of PCE to adjusted PI (in table 11.7) nearly all exceed 100%.

2. *Consumption by Business.* The BEA must allocate retail sales between purchases by consumers and by business. There is little information on that split. What share of automobiles, gasoline usage, lunches, hotel bills, airplane fares, etc. is really business expense, and what share consumers'? How well does each of those BEA national percentages apply to each state? Failure to differentiate percentages by state will distort BEA estimates of entrepreneurial income by state, and thereby, personal income.

There is little warrant for BEA to estimate different splits in different states. But surely, for example, business purchases bulk larger in states with a relative large defense (hence cost-plus) industry than those without. Moreover, big business purchases its computers, typewriters, and office supplies from manufacturers and wholesalers, while small business relies on retailers. Reliance on census data for Retail Trade, which underlie the BEA estimates, necessarily misses the effect of that difference.

In closing, it should be emphasized that the two sets of state figures are really extraordinarily close when a detailed comparison is made for 1982. And close even in the cruder comparison for earlier years. The limitations of the BEA estimates are, by now, limitations in the sources to which its staff is constrained. There is little question that their skilled efforts have created unusually reliable figures. Their IRS raw material, etc. is another matter. The limitations of the present series, inevitable when computing over twenty thousand estimates, will become apparent in the course of time as they are used.

IV. State Estimates: 1900

The ratio of the present estimates to the standard personal income series of Richard Easterlin appeared in table 11.6.[33]

We may also compare them (in table 11.9) with estimates Preston and Haines have recently made for annual earnings level by state, based on a regression of Lebergott's wage estimates for six occupations by state.[34]

Their annual earnings series does not weight the occupation earnings by their relative importance in each state. Their earnings will therefore have an unknown bias compared to Easterlin's. For testing the present PCE series their earnings' figures will, of course, be of limited value. For they intentionally exclude income from capital—though it is used, together with earnings, to purchase goods and services. Nor was capital income unimportant in a period when about half of all Americans earned their income from farms.

Our PCE estimates compare well with Easterlin's figures in table 11.9, being within 5% for most states.

a. For many southern states, however, the PCE figures significantly exceed the personal income figures. The Preston Haines se-

TABLE 11.9
Annual Income/Consumption
1899–1900
(3 estimates)

	Personal Consumption Expenditure	Income Easterlin	Earnings Preston-Haines
Maine	$202	$187	$281
New Hampshire	206	214	296
Vermont	187	190	265
Massachusetts	282	304	303
Rhode Island	257	293	303
Connecticut	248	278	287
New York	321	323	279
New Jersey	257	277	275
Pennsylvania	222	250	280
Ohio	212	222	262
Indiana	171	182	249
Illinois	243	260	291
Michigan	192	185	260
Wisconsin	180	179	270
Minnesota	208	207	278
Iowa	183	202	251
Missouri	199	188	259

Continued on next page

TABLE 11.9—*Continued*

	Personal Consumption Expenditure	Income Easterlin	Earnings Preston-Haines
N. Dakota	195	209	364
S. Dakota	171	183	340
Nebraska	194	212	293
Kansas	171	187	259
Delaware	201	220	237
Maryland	199	204	214
Virginia	125	110	192
W. Virginia	125	117	247
N. Carolina	101	72	153
S. Carolina	96	74	150
Georgia	102	86	141
Florida	128	112	180
Kentucky	143	120	221
Tennessee	116	101	176
Alabama	112	88	163
Mississippi	104	84	160
Arkansas	120	89	179
Louisiana	127	128	181
Oklahoma	120	114	242
Texas	146	138	217
Montana	309	415	535
Idaho	205	221	470
Wyoming	223	311	495
Colorado	313	318	388
New Mexico	140	148	307
Arizona	229	321	471
Utah	183	183	429
Nevada	311	395	529
Washington	279	296	418
Oregon	259	248	382
California	371	365	374

ries also exceeds Easterlin's service earnings series for these southern states, tending to confirm the PCE results. (The occupational data they used constitute a broader set than those used by Easterlin.)

b. For four western states the PCE estimate exceeds that for personal income by more than 10%. Part of that difference reflects imports. With local production of many consumer items just getting underway one would expect miners' incomes were used to buy jeans in San Francisco, furniture in St. Louis, recreation in New Orleans, etc.

A further element may well have been Easterlin's use of a standard rate of return on capital invested in those states. As of 1900 there should be no such fixed standard for current earnings, since sizeable capital gains from rising prices (e.g., of copper) were expected in those years. Hence to make total metal mine expected returns equal across states smaller current capital returns would have to offset the differences in expected capital gains.

· NOTE TO CHAPTER 11 ·

BRIDGE ITEMS in table 11.7 between personal income in 1982 and personal consumption expenditures were estimated as follows:

Disposable personal income: *Survey of Current Business* (Aug. 1988), p. 31. Personal contributions to social insurance: *Survey of Current Business* (Aug. 1985, table 3, lines 1, 7.

Interest paid by consumers to business: The bulk of this interest being for mortgages we used net changes in mortgage payments (*infra*) as an allocator.

The BEA U.S. savings total (*SCB*, August 1984, p. 6) consistent with the state PI figures (*SCB*, 8/85) was allocated between seven major components by changes in sector balance sheets, year-end 1981—year-end 1982. (Board of Governors, Federal Reserve System, *Balance Sheets for the U.S. Economy, 1948–87*, table 15 for households, personal trust, and nonprofit organizations.) These seven U.S. totals were then allocated among the states as indicated below.

1. Owner equity: Owner-occupied houses, assets, minus home mortgages. Allocated by state by number of owner occupiers with mortgages times the differences in median monthly owner costs between owners with mortgages and those without. (1980 Census of Housing, *Detailed Housing Characteristics, U.S. Summary*, table 15.)

2. Consumer durables: Assets minus installment and other consumer credit, allocated by the sum of consumer durable expenditures for individual durable items from the detailed PCE estimates by state.

3. Deposits and credit market instruments: Allocated by imputed interest, an unpublished component of the BEA personal income series by state.

4. Corporate equities: Allocated by dividends received by consumers, an unpublished component of the BEA personal income series by state.

5. Equity in noncorporate business: Allocated by BEA proprietors income (*SCB*, 8/85, table 3).

6. Pension fund reserves: By BEA personal contributions for social insurance (*SCB*, 8/85, table 3).

7. Life insurance reserves: Allocated by value of life insurance policies in force (*US Statistical Abstract, 1984*, p. 526).

·APPENDIXES·

PERSONAL CONSUMPTION EXPENDITURES

· A P P E N D I X A ·

U.S. ESTIMATES

TABLE A1

Personal Consumption by Type of Expenditure U.S. Aggregates, 1900–1929 (current dollars in millions)

		1	2	3	4	5	6	7	8	9	10	11
				Food, Alcohol, Tobacco						Clothing		
											Civilian	
	Pop. (millions)	Total PCE	TOTAL FOOD ALC & TOB	Pur Food, Mls (Exc Alc)	Food Furn	Food on Farm	Alcohol	Tobacco	TOTAL	Shoes	Total	Women's	Men's
1900	76.09	16393	7164	4892	97	822	955	398	2127	428	1262	500	762
1901	77.58	17785	7902	5444	89	917	1022	430	2254	485	1297	530	767
1902	79.16	19079	8653	6069	99	956	1101	428	2381	484	1385	583	802
1903	80.63	19904	8650	6059	78	911	1145	457	2596	525	1526	661	865
1904	82.17	20768	8913	6286	81	928	1169	449	2689	551	1577	689	888
1905	83.82	22208	9499	6741	86	967	1230	475	2895	593	1670	754	916
1906	85.45	23897	9958	7012	89	984	1342	531	3450	674	2059	942	1117
1907	87.01	25222	10425	7326	94	1085	1378	542	3536	684	2095	971	1124
1908	88.71	25026	10607	7563	98	1107	1303	536	3386	683	2025	951	1074
1909	90.50	27499	11921	8710	114	1196	1322	579	3820	708	2302	1095	1207
1910	92.41	29059	12786	9375	123	1269	1393	626	3828	739	2229	1077	1152
1911	93.86	29109	12079	8786	113	1129	1429	622	4142	764	2479	1216	1263
1912	95.34	31042	13001	9558	124	1224	1460	635	4368	814	2643	1316	1327
1913	97.23	32410	13309	9759	127	1247	1488	688	4597	897	2757	1393	1364
1914	99.11	33140	14001	10456	137	1258	1468	682	4277	808	2570	1317	1253
1915	100.55	32234	12745	9286	122	1275	1409	653	4173	806	2476	1272	1204
1916	101.96	37811	14672	10835	143	1448	1531	715	5457	1096	3283	1690	1593
1917	103.27	46448	19410	14386	225	2124	1812	863	6737	1346	4267	2200	2067
1918	103.21	53209	22421	15693	950	2376	2215	1187	8433	1632	5490	2837	2653
1919	104.51	59353	23923	17509	321	2476	2240	1377	9701	1864	6260	3242	3018
1920	106.46	62949	21621	17317	263	2409		1632	10854	2042	7213	3804	3409
1921	108.54	51942	15445	12315	184	1509		1437	8379	1429	5525	2966	2559
1922	110.05	55947	16015	12961	193	1493		1368	9404	1494	6408	3490	2918
1923	111.95	61890	17280	14218	208	1426		1433	10518	1705	7223	3994	3229
1924	114.11	62716	17784	14669	214	1437		1464	9453	1611	6252	3470	2782
1925	115.83	68234	19505	16087	237	1688		1493	10198	1592	6954	3880	3074
1926	117.40	71847	20885	17367	254	1727		1537	10395	1643	7042	3992	3050
1927	119.04	71997	20485	17067	248	1582		1588	10756	1655	7361	4238	3123
1928	120.51	74603	20464	17002	248	1621		1593	10910	1657	7431	4395	3036
1929	121.77	77457	21239	17688	257	1599		1695	11193	1675	7682	4662	3020

TABLE A1 (Cont'd.)

	12	13	14	15	16	17	18	19	20	21	22
		Clothing		Personal Care				Housing			
	Military	Jewelry	Cloth Serv	Total Personal Care	Toilet Articles	Barber & Beauty	TOTAL	Owner Occ	Tenant Occ	Rent of Farmhouse	Other Housing
1900	3	147	287	119	64	55	2426	1266	804	307	49
1901	3	153	316	134	74	60	2570	1331	868	319	52
1902	3	173	336	147	84	63	2617	1316	905	340	56
1903	3	178	364	157	89	68	2831	1422	1003	345	61
1904	3	179	381	160	89	71	3141	1560	1112	405	64
1905	3	214	415	187	109	78	3280	1634	1207	370	69
1906	3	260	454	201	117	84	3514	1724	1303	413	74
1907	4	270	483	222	133	89	3793	1861	1432	421	79
1908	4	193	481	218	129	89	3784	1878	1459	427	80
1909	4	264	542	241	141	100	3942	1897	1520	435	90
1910	4	276	580	256	151	105	4146	1992	1613	445	96
1911	4	273	622	271	158	113	4220	2002	1652	464	102
1912	4	278	629	278	164	114	4361	2060	1699	498	104
1913	5	281	657	286	167	119	4561	2108	1827	518	108
1914	5	219	675	286	164	122	4727	2183	1903	529	112
1915	5	202	684	313	190	123	4870	2231	1959	563	117
1916	7	308	763	381	244	137	5179	2373	2062	614	130
1917	33	300	791	452	300	152	5344	2486	2043	671	144
1918	207	263	841	551	377	174	5650	2652	2092	739	167
1919	83	548	946	604	396	208	6325	3030	2274	824	197
1920	30	495	1074	712	460	252	7498	3680	2745	835	238
1921	19	343	1063	615	346	269	8066	3884	3180	769	233
1922	14	430	1058	675	386	289	8553	4114	3445	767	227
1923	14	514	1062	743	432	311	9267	4496	3686	850	235
1924	15	486	1089	784	445	339	9944	4848	4006	854	236
1925	14	518	1120	848	477	371	10487	5132	4236	868	251
1926	13	542	1155	895	487	408	11050	5423	4479	869	279
1927	12	531	1197	969	523	446	11303	5563	4561	878	301
1928	13	547	1262	1069	573	496	11637	5734	4687	883	333
1929	12	560	1264	1116	591	525	11672	5868	4542	913	349

Continued on next page

TABLE A1 (Cont'd.)

	23	24	25	26	27	28	29	30	31	32	33	34	35	36	37
	TOTAL House. Op.	Furn, Matt	Kitchen Appl	China	Other Durable Furnish	Semi-dur House Furnish	Clean & Polish	Sta-tionery	Elec	Gas	Water	Wood, Gas & Coal	Tel & Tel	Dom Serv	Other HH Op
Household Operation															
1900	1810	172	103	147	203	80	64	17	15	72	50	399	13	419	56
1901	1891	191	118	155	207	80	73	17	17	86	52	387	17	430	61
1902	2073	207	132	166	236	86	82	18	20	97	54	420	22	476	57
1903	2254	223	132	191	246	87	87	21	22	109	59	489	26	493	69
1904	2275	229	124	193	236	86	87	21	24	120	60	472	30	514	68
1905	2395	258	144	229	253	90	107	22	26	127	65	446	34	523	71
1906	2533	306	174	258	186	113	115	23	29	134	68	466	38	546	77
1907	2788	298	171	253	297	111	132	28	34	139	72	510	51	613	79
1908	2634	246	142	196	239	98	128	31	39	146	76	509	57	645	82
1909	2891	316	157	216	300	122	141	32	45	155	80	513	62	661	91
1910	3037	336	163	239	323	140	151	37	56	164	89	506	69	682	82
1911	3116	350	174	244	314	139	157	37	66	174	93	497	77	695	99
1912	3350	391	219	255	337	153	163	36	79	185	96	546	84	709	97
1913	3566	432	207	271	361	176	165	40	89	195	99	611	94	723	103
1914	3486	418	181	262	334	170	163	41	102	208	103	579	100	719	106
1915	3430	410	196	262	322	162	185	39	110	222	107	544	104	657	110
1916	4089	539	232	334	422	224	234	58	118	241	110	694	116	648	119
1917	4945	612	315	460	526	322	282	75	129	264	117	919	133	667	124
1918	5528	688	351	409	591	421	350	76	157	290	128	1083	154	695	135
1919	6591	1060	424	476	702	458	361	95	197	341	137	1138	187	865	150
1920	8252	1152	589	625	946	564	421	114	248	389	150	1589	220	1070	175
1921	6758	872	342	391	623	410	315	85	268	433	168	1330	243	1092	186
1922	7400	945	407	392	788	462	342	87	288	446	190	1450	269	1140	194
1923	8460	1100	542	557	1016	580	372	118	332	463	208	1368	292	1301	211
1924	8456	1175	550	422	934	562	373	114	362	471	222	1330	323	1393	225
1925	9221	1201	612	557	1041	659	386	121	420	478	237	1426	371	1466	246
1926	9849	1240	676	628	1028	714	390	121	465	521	258	1588	418	1535	267
1927	9695	1224	653	529	1025	659	420	124	522	543	268	1371	459	1607	291
1928	10253	1241	625	634	1110	679	459	137	561	539	274	1578	509	1595	312
1929	10664	1192	699	628	1148	717	485	143	616	542	285	1608	569	1716	316

TABLE A1 (Cont'd.)

	38	39	40	41	42	43	44	45	46	47	48	49	50
	Medical Care						Personal Business						
	TOTAL	Drugs	Ophthal	MD, DDS, Oth Prof	Hospitals	Health Ins	TOTAL	Brokerage	Bank & Fin Serv	Life Ins	Legal Serv	Funeral	Other Bus
1900	384	103	11	253	15	2	754	103	249	100	81	185	36
1901	417	118	12	269	16	2	866	149	287	110	81	191	48
1902	451	132	14	286	17	2	916	135	316	121	85	198	61
1903	481	139	14	307	18	3	983	130	329	135	90	216	83
1904	498	139	14	323	19	3	1027	135	321	144	90	243	94
1905	552	162	17	344	25	4	1154	181	406	147	94	239	87
1906	581	167	19	361	30	4	1209	199	436	140	96	252	86
1907	643	181	23	394	42	3	1158	169	396	130	100	268	95
1908	644	168	23	414	35	4	1109	155	350	133	102	274	95
1909	679	177	26	431	41	4	1156	170	363	146	106	282	89
1910	715	189	26	435	60	5	1213	161	388	154	111	303	96
1911	752	198	27	460	61	6	1253	143	410	167	116	311	106
1912	787	207	26	485	61	8	1318	144	454	179	116	315	110
1913	828	212	31	506	69	10	1377	125	506	190	119	323	114
1914	877	208	39	543	75	12	1419	106	543	193	122	334	121
1915	965	237	50	576	87	15	1586	140	633	221	127	348	117
1916	1102	300	60	609	116	17	1912	173	868	223	137	387	124
1917	1278	364	92	655	147	20	2114	169	995	250	152	412	136
1918	1643	450	179	742	248	24	2471	163	1147	281	175	552	153
1919	1675	465	147	833	196	34	2814	302	1361	355	206	406	184
1920	1961	499	171	995	254	42	2938	349	1169	439	255	497	229
1921	1983	347	118	1256	234	28	2809	319	1134	434	302	405	215
1922	2053	386	123	1239	252	53	2905	396	1114	471	329	415	180
1923	2129	432	117	1239	280	61	3090	459	1088	568	314	496	165
1924	2258	447	122	1314	310	65	3184	472	1150	576	323	502	161
1925	2482	480	117	1455	360	70	3488	576	1196	664	360	530	162
1926	2574	486	117	1480	409	82	3397	558	1066	720	346	543	164
1927	2775	516	125	1579	449	106	3654	591	1201	762	385	551	164
1928	2923	567	122	1621	500	113	3686	712	1013	813	394	592	162
1929	3104	604	131	1692	569	108	3886	784	1048	880	402	607	165

Continued on next page

Table A1 (Cont'd.)

	51	52	53	54	55	56	57	58	59	60	61	62	63	64	65	66
		Transportation								Recreation						
	TOTAL Trans-port	Motor Veh & Wagons	Tires & Acc	Auto Rep	Gas & Oil	Auto Ins & Tolls	Purch Local	Purch Intcity	TOTAL Recr	Books & Maps	Mag & News	Nondur Toys	Dur. toys, Wheel gds	Music, Rad, TV	Flwrs & Plants	Rec Services
1900	533	57	6	*	*	2	247	220	498	64	88	37	45	80	47	137
1901	581	74	5	1	1	2	259	239	561	69	97	48	50	92	57	153
1902	601	70	4	1	1	2	255	268	631	72	109	50	49	108	65	178
1903	649	70	3	1	2	2	284	287	666	75	111	52	45	123	66	194
1904	727	81	6	2	2	2	331	303	685	78	116	55	49	109	68	210
1905	818	100	10	3	3	3	377	322	755	83	126	61	55	134	70	226
1906	919	129	15	5	5	4	414	347	803	82	134	68	58	154	69	238
1907	1013	158	20	7	9	5	430	384	860	83	144	63	72	167	79	252
1908	1062	188	26	11	10	6	435	386	770	79	115	61	49	120	83	263
1909	1121	212	33	19	14	7	452	384	889	93	154	74	60	146	90	272
1910	1291	267	47	26	28	9	486	428	915	89	153	79	63	149	93	289
1911	1383	264	54	32	42	11	533	447	963	88	153	85	70	158	87	322
1912	1581	365	75	41	54	12	584	450	1039	99	169	89	73	188	91	330
1913	1756	426	103	46	73	14	620	474	1133	116	175	98	91	208	91	354
1914	1953	449	112	54	187	16	656	479	1119	102	182	105	85	185	84	376
1915	2098	586	132	77	182	18	663	440	1158	111	182	113	87	184	85	396
1916	2696	932	209	111	248	23	703	470	1438	116	250	175	126	239	98	434
1917	3258	1065	366	161	360	29	730	547	1829	137	288	305	201	281	129	488
1918	3414	820	476	189	429	35	785	680	1836	152	314	194	140	304	152	580
1919	4321	1347	570	225	471	40	892	776	2281	196	322	225	161	528	153	696
1920	5073	1700	689	211	556	41	1028	848	2534	215	353	216	163	581	141	865
1921	4144	1165	346	173	630	37	1035	758	2225	188	370	190	119	370	103	885
1922	4889	1616	412	278	779	52	1045	707	2377	194	390	199	123	446	110	915
1923	5937	2290	506	441	793	73	1077	757	2709	204	431	253	166	553	131	971
1924	6028	2012	523	540	1084	86	1081	702	2914	227	440	238	153	664	150	1042
1925	6824	2451	734	649	1108	102	1097	683	3152	236	482	257	161	716	172	1128
1926	7231	2625	784	694	1224	108	1125	671	3441	246	496	277	179	832	176	1235
1927	6510	2064	747	706	1141	114	1120	618	3597	274	509	286	179	754	190	1405
1928	7211	2396	730	748	1482	125	1104	562	4072	287	520	314	199	945	226	1581
1929	7721	2697	648	776	1814	134	1117	535	4356	309	538	336	219	1012	221	1721

TABLE A1 (Cont'd.)

	67	68	69	70	71	72	73	74	75	76
		Education			TOTAL			Net	For Trav	Exp in US
	TOTAL	Higher Ed	Elem Ed	Other Ed & Rsrch	Religion & Welfare	Religion	Welfare	Foreign Travel	By US Res	by Aliens
1900	105	14	42	51	326	226	100	149	157	8
1901	115	15	42	60	325	225	100	162	170	8
1902	121	16	41	66	327	227	100	153	162	9
1903	135	18	48	71	337	237	100	157	166	9
1904	135	19	48	70	337	237	100	170	183	13
1905	141	20	48	75	338	238	100	191	209	18
1906	147	21	50	78	345	245	100	222	250	28
1907	159	26	50	85	362	262	100	244	280	36
1908	166	30	52	86	366	266	100	264	304	40
1909	171	31	54	88	365	265	100	286	328	42
1910	181	34	63	91	357	257	100	308	347	39
1911	193	37	65	96	377	277	100	336	378	42
1912	199	39	74	97	387	287	100	350	400	50
1913	218	42	82	105	397	297	100	356	407	51
1914	234	45	82	110	422	314	108	316	356	40
1915	243	49	85	112	446	332	114	184	209	25
1916	254	52	84	122	461	346	115	139	161	22
1917	266	53	86	130	683	366	317	96	131	35
1918	277	54	89	137	867	411	456	64	109	45
1919	329	74	96	162	647	442	205	104	161	57
1920	398	93	110	199	835	523	312	181	249	68
1921	459	116	128	220	840	574	266	185	262	77
1922	504	139	137	233	884	618	266	256	318	62
1923	531	160	146	234	929	664	265	267	340	73
1924	552	179	146	232	1014	729	285	317	396	79
1925	594	201	155	243	1038	790	248	369	454	85
1926	644	221	166	263	1088	832	256	375	487	112
1927	682	249	173	267	1147	867	280	407	523	116
1928	727	278	184	271	1180	905	275	462	586	124
1929	769	298	188	283	1247	949	298	490	632	142

*Less than $1 million.

TABLE A2

Personal Consumption by Type of Expenditure

U.S. Aggregates, 1900–1929 (1987 dollars, in millions)

		1	2	3	4	5	6	7	8	9
			Food, Alcohol, Tobacco							
	Total PCE	TOTAL FOOD ALC & TOB	Food off prem, Meals (Exc Alc)	Food Furn	Food on Farm	Alcohol	Tobacco	TOTAL Clothing	Shoes	Total Civilian
1900	248699	107793	79821	1820	7975	12871	5307	20738	6037	8845
1901	268622	115838	86246	1616	8637	13681	5658	22781	6898	9437
1902	274973	119084	88869	1674	8323	14660	5558	23191	6874	10324
1903	282827	120655	90154	1335	8061	15246	5859	25152	7344	11375
1904	291955	123948	93069	1379	8167	15649	5684	26285	7614	11865
1905	313193	132889	100302	1477	8557	16689	5864	27560	7764	12565
1906	326145	135090	100469	1471	8384	18209	6556	31290	8088	15197
1907	328213	136756	100756	1614	8870	18825	6691	31363	8122	14963
1908	326164	138444	102952	1537	8959	18378	6617	30868	8313	15165
1909	348920	149439	112926	1694	9216	18541	7061	33495	8161	16913
1910	358726	154279	115909	1757	9332	19647	7634	33871	8556	16616
1911	357208	146679	109190	1612	8341	20042	7494	36520	8886	18479
1912	370431	150976	112600	1678	8571	20477	7651	37614	8967	19231
1913	383911	156941	116921	1757	8886	20987	8390	38656	9160	19691
1914	386609	161676	122577	1853	8771	20055	8420	36437	8251	18520
1915	379164	147973	110372	1671	9006	18862	8062	35229	8038	17518
1916	410715	154119	115094	1974	9145	19185	8720	41862	10002	21094
1917	421914	157919	118412	2134	10397	17695	9280	40278	9073	22908
1918	415593	148488	108161	7543	9737	12354	10694	39450	9690	22356
1919	402384	130522	104416	2205	8919	5862	9119	35310	8045	19613
1920	388848	119317	98941	1729	8185		10462	34409	7860	19062
1921	371030	110329	92654	1593	6751		9331	34593	7452	18362
1922	407375	123085	104180	1784	7135		9985	44932	8856	25096
1923	445713	130119	110938	1869	6619		10694	48865	10007	27928
1924	455703	135884	115510	1935	6727		11712	45091	9518	24425
1925	483135	138001	116784	1985	7289		11944	48226	9212	27589
1926	503494	143738	122157	2060	7225		12296	49409	9553	28227
1927	511908	146229	124577	2080	6868		12704	51607	9388	29899
1928	531579	148085	125478	2107	7114		13387	51810	8765	30336
1929	554055	151818	128733	2154	6922		14008	53169	9165	31613

Continued on next page

TABLE A2 (Cont'd.)

	12	13	14	15	16	17	18	19	20	21	22
		Clothing		Personal Care				Housing			
	Military	Jewelry	Cloth Serv	TOTAL Personal Care	Toilet Articles	Barber & Beauty	TOTAL	Owner Occ	Tenant Occ	Rent of Farmhouse	Other Housing
1900	18	999	4838	2139	454	1686	19503	9395	6066	3410	632
1901	19	945	5482	2363	524	1838	20251	9628	6384	3583	656
1902	19	1069	4905	2421	533	1888	20983	9683	6770	3817	714
1903	19	1100	5313	2567	569	1997	21471	9871	7080	3784	735
1904	19	1086	5700	2649	587	2062	22856	10251	7430	4444	731
1905	19	1299	5913	2914	692	2222	23415	10657	8003	3975	780
1906	19	1667	6319	3118	725	2393	24646	11075	8510	4233	828
1907	24	1684	6570	3278	818	2460	25536	11525	9018	4153	841
1908	25	1366	5997	3168	735	2433	26568	11975	9459	4275	860
1909	26	1972	6423	3422	767	2655	27769	12371	10079	4302	1017
1910	25	2061	6612	3493	782	2711	28617	12703	10458	4393	1063
1911	25	2039	7090	3662	822	2840	29762	13056	10954	4600	1153
1912	25	2010	7381	3761	873	2888	30845	13434	11266	4970	1175
1913	30	1910	7864	3918	904	3014	31425	13343	11758	5140	1184
1914	31	1474	8161	3910	871	3040	32480	13777	12211	5263	1228
1915	30	1373	8270	3945	960	2985	33323	14018	12516	5519	1270
1916	38	1774	8954	4180	1050	3131	34822	14696	12985	5744	1398
1917	151	1236	6911	4112	949	3164	35608	15508	12958	5579	1564
1918	717	903	5785	4369	1198	3171	36604	16307	13078	5441	1778
1919	221	1741	5690	4512	1238	3274	37569	17160	13094	5368	1947
1920	67	1385	6035	4680	1352	3327	37603	17698	13423	4491	1992
1921	54	1014	7711	4898	1295	3603	37148	16389	13643	5412	1703
1922	47	1484	9450	5552	1642	3910	35576	14136	14291	5543	1605
1923	46	1468	9416	6014	1807	4207	40385	17918	14937	5900	1631
1924	50	1371	9727	6351	1874	4476	41949	18632	15653	6087	1578
1925	47	1593	9785	6756	1966	4790	44093	19635	16479	6311	1668
1926	44	1780	9805	7053	1954	5099	46888	21028	17659	6324	1876
1927	41	1744	10535	7582	2202	5379	48576	21867	18228	6430	2050
1928	45	1796	10867	8222	2555	5667	51106	23066	19169	6545	2325
1929	42	1839	10510	8657	2663	5993	52406	24169	19021	6713	2502

Continued on next page

TABLE A2 (Cont'd.)

	23	24	25	26	27	28	29	30	31	32	33	34	35	36	37
	TOTAL	Furn, Matt	Kitchen Appl	China	Other Durable Furnish	Semi-dur House Furnish	Clean & Polish	Sta-tionery	Elec	Gas	Water	Wood, Gas & Coal	Tel & Tel	Dom Serv	Other HH Op
						Household Operation									
1900	35439	2787	343	2316	1854	728	753	237	13	523	1486	7279	46	16178	897
1901	36778	3149	389	2612	1934	797	887	241	15	635	1510	7027	60	16538	984
1902	37626	3273	435	2771	2260	822	837	263	23	717	1548	7002	80	16702	895
1903	38949	3393	431	3022	2299	796	888	318	26	805	1666	7260	93	16884	1066
1904	39566	3484	417	2968	2281	792	911	314	31	894	1644	7497	111	17191	1033
1905	41560	3894	479	3761	2533	793	1067	329	37	946	1766	7340	126	17433	1056
1906	42533	4382	568	3892	1815	919	1120	340	46	1033	1795	7669	140	17670	1142
1907	43589	3802	542	3410	2686	815	1253	390	60	1102	1820	8393	194	17977	1145
1908	42449	3201	459	3064	2213	834	1115	418	70	1168	1917	8377	216	18220	1175
1909	45203	4194	483	3273	2740	1006	1169	416	83	1252	2014	8552	242	18515	1265
1910	46042	4100	506	3264	2950	1128	1205	485	107	1349	2250	8527	270	18788	1112
1911	46674	3760	563	3564	2840	1179	1253	488	130	1464	2328	8717	301	18784	1302
1912	48236	3807	708	3892	3021	1278	1337	486	156	1571	2395	9201	338	18757	1288
1913	50425	4682	676	3822	3208	1471	1379	543	186	1672	2318	9992	379	18731	1365
1914	48652	3608	591	3568	2902	1499	1379	563	224	1820	2290	9652	403	18773	1381
1915	48254	3524	641	3999	2670	1427	1565	536	253	1961	2368	9351	431	18135	1393
1916	50916	4516	734	3895	3132	1447	1919	532	277	2153	2414	11207	481	16788	1422
1917	52082	4637	887	3409	3340	1455	1724	546	314	2382	2540	13067	552	15881	1351
1918	49797	4505	810	2116	2919	1342	1683	536	390	2512	2688	13468	659	14882	1288
1919	50116	5415	894	2554	2754	1504	1518	589	479	2677	2313	12539	753	14888	1239
1920	51807	3925	1040	2882	3022	1461	1653	526	610	2922	2352	14443	859	14903	1209
1921	49880	3838	627	2914	2369	1943	1598	564	667	2729	2422	12425	897	15578	1309
1922	56046	4693	754	2917	3532	2082	2134	666	684	2873	2557	14547	966	16262	1377
1923	59165	5303	888	3578	4237	2314	2308	850	846	3051	2740	13565	1048	16940	1498
1924	59883	6128	924	2584	3963	2282	2328	776	923	3159	2732	13753	1160	17611	1561
1925	64896	6506	1081	3663	4512	2692	2359	775	1110	3200	2898	14845	1265	18325	1665
1926	69241	6945	1176	4603	4566	3230	2317	727	1230	3541	3057	15748	1356	18998	1748
1927	68579	7033	1146	4132	4658	3053	2582	737	1417	3722	3034	14064	1465	19694	1841
1928	73468	7171	1146	4923	5173	3061	2765	815	1564	3636	3075	16427	1624	20215	1871
1929	76199	6969	1268	4914	5400	3418	2818	844	1813	3685	3098	16612	1775	21500	1892

TABLE A2 (Cont'd.)

	38	39	40	41	42	43	44	45	46	47	48	49	50
	Medical Care						Personal Business						
	TOTAL	Drugs	Ophthal	MD, DDS, Oth Prof	Hospitals	Health Ins	TOTAL	Brokerage	Bank & Fin Serv	Life Ins	Legal Serv	Funeral	Other Bus
1900	12607	579	74	10902	1004	47	19055	8898	4882	1111	1929	1927	308
1901	13391	695	85	11502	1063	46	24378	12263	6097	1325	2077	2170	444
1902	13700	663	84	11817	1091	45	24084	11739	6330	1360	2024	2106	526
1903	14291	704	85	12315	1122	65	24675	11429	6573	1517	2143	2298	716
1904	14618	725	88	12591	1151	63	25026	11663	6286	1600	2143	2531	803
1905	15462	815	102	12996	1467	82	30454	15146	8125	1652	2238	2543	750
1906	16203	820	112	13454	1737	80	32998	16345	9088	1628	2400	2769	768
1907	17631	881	135	14204	2353	58	29547	14113	7923	1461	2381	2851	819
1908	17465	757	124	14591	1917	76	26506	12917	6491	1385	2267	2686	760
1909	17716	768	135	14585	2156	73	28852	14316	6973	1570	2409	2848	736
1910	18233	776	129	14198	3043	88	28686	13790	7191	1588	2413	2942	762
1911	18438	816	134	14416	2970	102	28052	12599	7454	1687	2522	2962	828
1912	19310	872	132	15200	2970	135	29225	12414	8401	1865	2578	3088	880
1913	20184	908	160	15636	3313	167	29992	11312	9727	2043	2705	3263	942
1914	21147	875	197	16367	3512	195	27843	9860	9521	1911	2542	3093	917
1915	22015	948	240	16678	3914	234	32009	11618	11295	2210	2702	3283	900
1916	22909	1023	246	16507	4885	249	39478	13542	15490	2398	3114	3909	1025
1917	23183	1005	306	16022	5587	264	40218	12269	17463	2475	3167	3815	1030
1918	25863	1131	541	15741	8174	275	46338	10449	22050	3022	3977	5576	1264
1919	22631	1152	438	15164	5544	334	55575	16825	25210	3660	4478	3942	1460
1920	22360	1158	483	14596	5789	333	51617	17450	19156	4065	5000	4322	1624
1921	22368	1028	420	16074	4653	193	48686	14566	18893	4056	6040	3584	1547
1922	21868	1301	498	14987	4736	346	50779	18000	17683	4168	6208	3487	1233
1923	24182	1431	466	16175	5679	430	56295	19935	18759	5462	6408	4509	1222
1924	25879	1490	488	17155	6288	458	58653	20171	20182	5703	6729	4648	1220
1925	26741	1567	459	17523	6736	455	64966	24589	20627	6385	7347	4818	1200
1926	29792	1544	447	19051	8180	570	62280	23495	18381	6990	7208	4982	1224
1927	29869	1717	498	18710	8266	678	67432	24447	21076	7545	8021	5102	1242
1928	31686	2002	517	19228	9215	724	69534	29331	17462	7893	8208	5431	1209
1929	34124	2146	560	20179	10543	695	74423	31360	18714	8800	8553	5726	1269

Continued on next page

TABLE A2 (Cont'd.)

	51	52	53	54	55	56	57	58	59	60	61	62	63	64	65	66
	TOTAL Trans-port	Motor Veh & Wagons	Tires & Acc	Auto Rep	Gas & Oil	Auto Ins & Tolls	Purch Local	Purch Intcity	TOTAL Recr	Books & Maps	Mag & News	Nondur Toys	Dur. toys, Whl. gds	Music, Rad, TV	Flwrs & Plants	Rec Services
		Transportation							Recreation							
1900	10763	265	3	3	*	19	7577	2896	6334	1072	1047	207	227	69	526	3185
1901	11607	343	3	6	6	19	8045	3185	7054	1155	1154	286	249	78	571	3583
1902	12030	327	2	9	6	19	8041	3626	7845	1206	1297	290	222	83	609	4137
1903	12904	327	2	9	10	19	8746	3792	8295	1256	1321	295	202	94	661	4466
1904	14437	417	3	19	10	19	10029	3939	8803	1306	1380	312	225	85	681	4813
1905	15980	340	4	23	17	23	11397	4177	9397	1390	1499	327	236	98	681	5167
1906	17218	378	5	34	26	27	12317	4430	9754	1373	1595	338	249	112	671	5415
1907	17594	402	6	44	44	31	12339	4728	9979	1390	1714	298	289	114	706	5469
1908	18062	477	7	69	48	38	12619	4805	9717	1323	1369	310	205	85	705	5721
1909	19414	888	21	160	72	59	13348	4866	10744	1557	1833	365	253	105	701	5930
1910	20997	1213	24	227	167	80	13996	5289	11204	1490	1821	382	268	108	696	6440
1911	22484	1264	29	281	268	98	15108	5437	11768	1474	1821	427	291	112	724	6919
1912	25019	2099	49	395	291	112	16589	5485	12248	1658	2011	439	328	144	693	6975
1913	26042	2545	68	446	313	139	16966	5565	13122	1942	2083	478	400	155	673	7391
1914	27611	3167	87	554	889	158	17327	5429	13227	1708	2166	528	397	147	615	7667
1915	28774	4467	117	813	941	189	17315	4931	13573	1859	2166	568	382	137	629	7832
1916	32561	7632	179	1172	936	242	17406	4993	15389	1942	2975	723	578	186	625	8359
1917	33362	8503	254	1604	1211	287	16271	5231	17240	2294	3427	924	908	216	565	8906
1918	27134	5973	286	1684	1249	313	12853	4777	17737	2545	3737	459	525	194	595	9681
1919	30150	8330	375	1756	1435	308	13068	4878	19568	3282	3832	518	501	280	566	10590
1920	29880	9399	408	1420	1570	277	12412	4393	19593	3010	3803	408	429	260	532	11150
1921	28405	7158	266	1220	2266	261	13113	4121	17777	1958	3986	548	334	177	600	10175
1922	35706	12219	491	2104	2643	400	13833	4016	17911	2020	4150	614	383	236	663	9844
1923	44838	18553	636	3396	3091	562	14290	4310	19501	1894	4586	718	463	263	794	10784
1924	44780	16485	777	4105	4534	662	14248	3970	20537	2107	4682	726	412	304	904	11402
1925	49656	20501	1024	4871	4352	750	14330	3828	21352	2191	5129	809	465	352	861	11546
1926	53124	23123	1078	5143	4627	794	14618	3741	22945	2101	5278	925	505	400	881	12855
1927	48481	17739	1374	5062	5534	803	14529	3440	24410	2340	5416	1049	494	354	1012	13745
1928	51704	19737	1584	5094	7063	845	14266	3116	26522	2451	5533	1197	546	441	1162	15192
1929	55428	21418	1636	5224	9064	905	14252	2929	28077	2639	5628	1291	604	475	1128	16314

TABLE A2 (Cont'd.)

	67	68	69	70	71	72	73	74	75	76
		Education			TOTAL Religion & Welfare	Religion	Welfare	Net Foreign Travel	For Trav By US Res	Exp in US by Aliens
	TOTAL	Higher Ed	Elem Ed	Other Ed & Rsrch						
1900	2999	380	1506	1113	9975	7279	2695	1355	1307	147
1901	3130	396	1462	1272	9681	7064	2617	1373	1325	144
1902	3209	417	1410	1382	9433	6890	2543	1366	1333	154
1903	3315	431	1517	1366	9164	6779	2385	1389	1352	154
1904	3469	475	1586	1408	8970	6626	2344	1328	1363	221
1905	3581	499	1580	1502	8741	6476	2265	1240	1370	305
1906	3611	507	1593	1512	8607	6415	2191	1078	1389	461
1907	3754	609	1546	1599	8213	6231	1982	972	1407	569
1908	3921	701	1605	1615	8105	6166	1939	892	1396	628
1909	4036	723	1663	1650	7928	6030	1898	902	1415	637
1910	4416	789	1930	1697	7851	5925	1925	1037	1452	567
1911	4549	842	1952	1755	7638	5865	1773	985	1456	608
1912	4814	875	2191	1748	7472	5787	1685	911	1482	697
1913	4957	887	2287	1782	7350	5736	1614	901	1489	714
1914	5046	940	2261	1846	7439	5696	1743	1141	1527	546
1915	5137	1002	2295	1840	7485	5645	1840	1449	1597	343
1916	5268	1050	2239	1979	7428	5572	1856	1782	1795	274
1917	5084	994	2130	1960	10644	5589	5056	2182	2234	352
1918	4975	954	2076	1945	12170	5632	6538	2667	2636	371
1919	5377	1202	2059	2115	8317	5783	2535	2737	2792	409
1920	5673	1325	2069	2279	9326	5850	3475	2586	2696	448
1921	5756	1446	2106	2204	8690	5911	2779	2500	2759	618
1922	5825	1596	2078	2151	7344	6103	1240	2753	2893	525
1923	6096	1803	2173	2120	7709	6495	1215	2543	2796	606
1924	6194	1986	2139	2069	8137	6852	1285	2366	2688	655
1925	6526	2183	2222	2121	9287	7066	2221	2636	2934	665
1926	6836	2319	2300	2218	9769	7469	2300	2419	2941	853
1927	7040	2533	2324	2183	9763	7375	2388	2339	2915	899
1928	7328	2758	2410	2160	9838	7543	2295	2276	2919	959
1929	7511	2893	2410	2208	10140	7713	2427	2103	2893	1084

*Less than $1 million.

	1	2	3	4	5	6	7	8	9	10
						Food				Memo:
	Total PCE	TOTAL FOOD ALC, TOB	Pur Food, Meals (Exc Alc)	Food Off Prem	Pur Meals	Furn Emp	On Farm	Tobacco	Alcohol	Food Exc Alc
1900	3268	1417	1049			24	105	70	169	
1901	3463	1493	1112			21	111	73	176	
1902	3474	1504	1123			21	105	70	185	
1903	3508	1496	1118			17	100	73	189	
1904	3553	1508	1133			17	99	69	190	
1905	3736	1585	1197			18	102	70	199	
1906	3817	1581	1176			17	98	77	213	
1907	3772	1572	1158			19	102	77	216	
1908	3677	1561	1161			17	101	75	207	
1909	3855	1651	1248			19	102	78	205	
1910	3882	1670	1254			19	101	83	213	
1911	3806	1563	1163			17	89	80	214	
1912	3885	1584	1181			18	90	80	215	
1913	3948	1614	1203			18	91	86	216	
1914	3901	1631	1237			19	88	85	202	
1915	3762	1472	1098			17	90	80	188	
1916	4061	1512	1129			19	90	86	188	
1917	4086	1529	1147			21	101	90	171	
1918	4027	1439	1048			73	94	104	120	
1919	3850	1249	999			21	85	87	56	
1920	3662	1121	929			16	77	98	0	
1921	3418	1016	854			15	62	86	0	
1922	3702	1118	947			16	65	91	0	
1923	3981	1162	991			17	59	96	0	
1924	3994	1191	1012			17	59	103	0	
1925	4171	1191	1008			17	63	103	0	
1926	4289	1224	1041			18	62	105	0	
1927	4300	1228	1047			17	58	107	0	
1928	4411	1229	1041			17	59	111	0	

Continued on next page

Table A3 (*Cont'd.*)

	11	12	13	14	15	16	18	17	20	21	22	23	24	25	26	27
			Clothing, Access, Jewelry						*Personal Care*				*Housing*			
	TOTAL CLOTH, ACCESS, JEWEL	*Shoes*	*Total Civilian*	*Civilian*		*Military*	*Jewelry*	*Cloth Serv*	*Total Personal Care*	*Toilet Articles*	*Barber & Beauty*	*TOTAL*	*Non-Farm*		*Rent of Farmhouse*	*Other Housing*
				Women	*Men*								*Owner*	*Tenant*		
1900	273	79	116			0	13	64	28	6	22	256	123	80	45	8
1901	294	89	122			0	12	71	30	7	24	261	124	82	46	8
1902	293	87	130			0	14	62	31	7	24	265	122	86	48	9
1903	312	91	141			0	14	66	32	7	25	266	122	88	47	9
1904	320	93	144			0	13	69	32	7	25	278	125	90	54	9
1905	329	93	150			0	15	71	35	8	27	279	127	95	47	9
1906	366	95	178			0	20	74	36	8	28	288	130	100	50	10
1907	360	93	172			0	19	76	38	9	28	293	132	104	48	10
1908	348	94	171			0	15	68	36	8	27	299	135	107	48	10
1909	370	90	187			0	22	71	38	8	29	307	137	111	48	11
1910	367	93	180			0	22	72	38	8	29	310	137	113	48	12
1911	389	95	197			0	22	76	39	9	30	317	139	117	49	12
1912	395	94	202			0	21	77	39	9	30	324	141	118	52	12
1913	398	94	203			0	20	81	40	9	31	323	137	121	53	12
1914	368	83	187			0	15	82	39	9	31	328	139	123	53	12
1915	350	80	174			0	14	82	39	10	30	331	139	124	55	13
1916	411	98	207			0	17	88	41	10	31	342	144	127	56	14
1917	390	88	222			1	12	67	40	9	31	345	150	125	54	15
1918	382	94	217			7	9	56	42	12	31	355	158	127	53	17
1919	338	77	188			2	17	54	43	12	31	359	164	125	51	19
1920	323	74	179			1	13	57	44	13	31	353	166	126	42	19
1921	319	69	169			0	9	71	45	12	33	342	151	126	50	16
1922	408	80	228			0	13	86	50	15	36	323	128	130	50	15
1923	436	89	249			0	13	84	54	16	38	361	160	133	53	15
1924	395	83	214			0	12	85	56	16	39	368	163	137	53	14
1925	416	80	238			0	14	84	58	17	41	381	170	142	54	14
1926	421	81	240			0	15	84	60	17	43	399	179	150	54	16
1927	434	79	251			0	15	88	64	19	45	408	184	153	54	17
1928	430	73	252			0	15	90	68	21	47	424	191	159	54	19

Continued on next page

Table A3 (Cont'd.)

	28	29	30	31	32	33	34	35	37	38	39	40	41	42
					Other House Furn				Household Operation					
	Total House. Op.	Furn, Matt	Kitchen Appl	China	Durable	Semi-dur	Clean & Polish	Stationery	Elec	Gas	Water	Fuel	Tel & Tel	Dom Serv
1900	468	37	5	30	24	10	10	3	*	7	20	96	1	213
1901	489	41	5	34	25	10	11	3	*	8	19	91	1	213
1902	488	41	5	35	29	10	11	3	*	9	20	88	1	211
1903	486	42	5	37	29	10	11	4	*	10	21	90	1	209
1904	485	42	5	36	28	10	11	4	*	11	20	91	1	209
1905	495	46	6	45	30	9	13	4	*	11	21	88	1	208
1906	499	51	7	46	21	11	13	4	1	12	21	90	2	207
1907	500	44	6	39	31	9	14	4	1	13	21	96	2	207
1908	477	36	5	35	25	9	13	5	1	13	22	94	2	205
1909	499	46	5	36	30	11	13	5	1	14	22	94	3	205
1910	500	44	5	35	32	12	13	5	1	15	24	92	3	203
1911	499	40	6	38	30	13	13	5	1	16	25	93	3	200
1912	507	40	7	41	32	13	14	5	2	16	25	97	4	197
1913	524	48	7	39	33	15	14	6	2	17	24	103	4	196
1914	489	36	6	36	29	15	14	6	2	18	23	97	4	189
1915	473	35	6	40	27	14	16	5	3	20	24	93	4	180
1916	500	44	7	38	31	14	19	5	3	21	24	110	5	165
1917	471	45	9	33	32	14	17	5	3	23	25	127	5	154
1918	480	44	8	20	28	13	16	5	4	24	26	130	6	144
1919	480	52	9	24	26	14	15	6	5	26	22	120	7	142
1920	488	37	10	27	28	14	16	5	6	27	22	136	8	140
1921	459	35	6	27	22	18	15	5	6	25	22	114	8	144
1922	498	43	7	27	32	19	19	6	6	26	23	132	9	148
1923	528	47	8	32	38	21	21	8	8	27	24	121	9	151
1924	526	54	8	23	35	20	20	7	8	28	24	121	10	154
1925	560	56	9	32	39	23	20	7	10	28	25	128	11	158
1926	591	59	10	39	39	28	20	6	10	30	26	134	12	163
1927	575	59	10	35	39	26	22	6	12	31	25	118	12	165
1928	611	60	10	41	43	25	23	7	13	30	26	136	13	168

Continued on next page

TABLE A3 (Cont'd.)

	43	44	45	46	47–49	50	56	60	61	62	64	65	66	67
	Other HH Op	Medical Care						Personal Business						
		TOTAL	Drugs	Ophthal	MD, DDS, Oth Prof	Hospitals	Health Ins	TOTAL	Brokerage	Bank & Fin Serv	Life Ins	Legal Serv	Funeral	Other Bus
1900	12	166	8	1	143	13	1	250	117	64	15	25	25	4
1901	13	173	9	1	148	14	1	314	158	79	17	27	28	6
1902	11	173	8	1	149	14	1	304	148	80	17	26	27	7
1903	13	177	9	1	153	14	1	306	142	82	19	27	28	9
1904	13	178	9	1	153	14	1	305	142	76	19	26	31	10
1905	13	184	10	1	155	18	1	363	181	97	20	27	30	9
1906	13	190	10	1	157	20	1	386	191	106	19	28	32	9
1907	13	203	10	2	163	27	1	340	162	91	17	27	33	9
1908	13	197	9	1	164	22	1	299	146	73	16	26	30	9
1909	14	196	8	1	161	24	1	319	158	77	17	27	31	8
1910	12	197	8	1	154	33	1	310	149	78	17	26	32	8
1911	14	196	9	1	154	32	1	299	134	79	18	27	32	9
1912	14	203	9	1	159	31	1	307	130	88	20	27	32	9
1913	14	208	9	2	161	34	2	308	116	100	21	28	34	10
1914	14	213	9	2	165	35	2	281	99	96	19	26	31	9
1915	14	219	9	2	166	39	2	318	116	112	22	27	33	9
1916	14	225	10	2	162	48	2	399	133	164	24	31	38	10
1917	13	224	10	3	155	54	3	389	119	169	24	31	37	10
1918	12	251	11	5	153	79	3	449	101	214	29	39	54	12
1919	12	217	11	4	145	53	3	532	161	241	35	43	38	14
1920	11	221	19	8	137	54	3	485	164	180	38	47	41	15
1921	12	206	9	4	148	43	2	449	134	174	37	56	33	14
1922	13	199	12	5	136	43	3	461	164	161	38	56	32	11
1923	13	216	13	4	144	51	4	503	178	168	49	57	40	11
1924	14	227	13	4	150	55	4	514	177	177	50	59	41	11
1925	14	231	14	4	151	58	4	561	212	178	55	63	42	10
1926	15	254	13	4	162	70	5	530	200	157	60	61	42	10
1927	15	251	14	4	157	69	6	566	205	177	63	67	43	10
1928	16	263	17	4	160	76	6	577	243	145	65	68	45	10

Continued on next page

TABLE A3 (Cont'd.)

	68	69	73	74	75	76	77	78	79
		Motor				Total	Purch Transp		
	TOTAL	Veh &	Tires	Auto	Gas &	Auto Ins			TOTAL
	Transport	Wagons	& Acc	Rep	Oil	& Tolls	Local	Intcity	Rec
1900	141	3	*	*	*	*	100	38	83
1901	150	4	*	*	*	*	104	41	91
1902	152	4	*	*	*	*	102	46	99
1903	160	4	*	*	*	*	108	47	103
1904	176	5	*	*	*	*	122	48	107
1905	191	4	*	*	*	*	136	50	112
1906	201	4	*	*	*	*	144	52	114
1907	202	5	*	1	1	*	142	54	115
1908	204	5	*	1	1	*	142	54	110
1909	215	10	*	2	1	1	147	54	119
1910	227	13	*	2	2	1	151	57	121
1911	240	13	*	3	3	1	161	58	125
1912	262	22	1	4	3	1	174	58	128
1913	268	26	1	5	3	1	174	57	135
1914	279	32	1	6	9	2	175	55	133
1915	286	44	1	8	9	2	172	49	135
1916	319	75	2	11	9	2	171	49	151
1917	323	82	2	16	12	3	158	51	167
1918	263	58	3	16	12	3	125	46	172
1919	288	80	4	17	14	3	125	47	187
1920	278	88	4	13	12	3	117	41	184
1921	262	66	2	11	21	2	121	38	164
1922	324	111	4	19	24	4	126	36	163
1923	401	166	6	30	28	5	128	38	174
1924	392	144	7	36	40	6	125	35	180
1925	429	177	9	42	38	6	124	33	184
1926	453	197	9	44	39	7	125	32	195
1927	407	149	12	43	46	7	122	29	205
1928	429	164	13	42	59	7	118	26	220

Continued on next page

TABLE A3 (Cont'd.)

	87	88	89	90	91	93	94	102	103	104	105
	Recreation							Education			
	Books & Maps	Mag & News	Nondur Toys	Whl gds, Dur Toys	Music Rad, TV	Flwrs & Plants	Rec Services	TOTAL	Higher	Elem	Other Ed & Rsrch
1900	14	14	3	3	1	7	42	39	5	20	15
1901	15	15	4	3	1	7	46	40	5	19	16
1902	15	16	4	3	1	8	52	41	5	18	17
1903	16	16	4	3	1	8	55	41	5	19	17
1904	16	17	4	3	1	8	59	42	6	19	17
1905	17	18	4	3	1	8	62	43	6	19	18
1906	16	19	4	3	1	8	63	42	6	19	18
1907	16	20	3	3	1	8	63	43	7	18	18
1908	15	15	3	2	1	8	64	44	8	18	18
1909	17	20	4	3	1	8	66	45	8	18	18
1910	16	20	4	3	1	8	70	48	9	21	18
1911	16	19	5	3	1	8	74	48	9	21	19
1912	17	21	5	3	2	7	73	50	9	23	18
1913	20	21	5	4	2	7	76	51	9	24	18
1914	17	22	5	4	1	6	77	51	9	23	19
1915	18	22	6	4	1	6	78	51	10	23	18
1916	19	29	7	6	2	6	82	52	10	22	19
1917	22	33	9	9	2	5	86	49	10	21	19
1918	25	36	4	5	2	6	94	48	9	20	19
1919	31	37	5	5	3	5	101	51	12	20	20
1920	28	36	4	4	2	5	105	53	12	19	21
1921	18	37	5	3	2	6	94	53	13	19	20
1922	18	38	6	3	2	6	89	53	15	19	20
1923	17	41	6	4	2	7	96	54	16	19	19
1924	18	41	6	4	3	8	100	54	17	19	18
1925	19	44	7	4	3	7	100	56	19	19	18
1926	18	45	8	4	3	8	109	58	20	20	19
1927	20	46	9	4	3	9	115	59	21	20	18
1928	20	46	10	5	4	10	126	61	23	20	18

Continued on next page

TABLE A3 (Cont'd.)

	106			107	108	110
	TOTAL Religion & Welfare	Religion & Welfare			Foreign Travel	
		Religion	Welfare	Net Foreign Travel	For Trav by US Res	Exp in US by Aliens
1900	131	96	35	18	17	2
1901	125	91	34	18	17	2
1902	119	87	32	17	17	2
1903	114	84	30	17	17	2
1904	109	81	29	16	17	3
1905	104	77	27	15	16	4
1906	101	75	26	13	16	5
1907	94	72	23	11	16	7
1908	91	70	22	10	16	7
1909	88	67	21	10	16	7
1910	85	64	21	11	16	6
1911	81	62	19	10	16	6
1912	78	61	18	10	16	7
1913	76	59	17	9	15	7
1914	75	57	18	12	15	6
1915	74	56	18	14	16	3
1916	73	55	18	17	18	3
1917	103	54	49	21	22	3
1918	118	55	63	26	26	4
1919	80	55	24	26	27	4
1920	88	55	33	24	25	4
1921	80	54	26	23	25	6
1922	67	55	11	25	26	5
1923	69	58	11	23	25	5
1924	71	60	11	21	24	6
1925	80	61	19	23	25	6
1926	83	64	20	21	25	7
1927	82	62	20	20	24	8
1928	82	63	19	19	24	8

*Less than 1.

TABLE A4

Personal Consumption by Type of Expenditure Per Capita, 1929–1958 (1987 = 100.0)

| | | Food, Alcohol, Tobacco | | | | | | | | | Clothing, Accessories, Jewelry | | |
| | | | | | | Food | | | | | | | |
	Total PCE	TOTAL Food, Alcohol, Tobacco	Food Off Prem, Meals (Exc. Alc.)	Food Off Prem	Pur Mls & Bev	Furn Emp	On Farm	Tobacco	Alcohol	Memo: Food Exc Alc	TOTAL Cloth, Acc, Jewel	Shoes	Total Civilian
1929	4551	1246	1056	819	237	18	57	115	0	1131	436	75	260
1930	4221	1206	1028	788	240	18	56	103	0	1102	390	65	232
1931	4036	1205	1025	772	253	17	59	103	0	1102	367	66	226
1932	3813	1120	954	706	248	16	59	91	0	1029	320	66	193
1933	3906	1084	910	721	189	16	63	95	34	955	285	59	173
1934	3745	1129	951	738	213	17	60	102	83	944	303	65	179
1935	3934	1171	991	765	226	18	55	107	106	959	324	64	197
1936	4288	1311	1121	865	256	20	56	115	131	1065	353	70	213
1937	4434	1372	1175	886	289	22	55	121	144	1108	356	74	206
1938	4276	1395	1198	908	290	21	55	121	135	1139	354	72	208
1939	4409	1428	1227	911	316	22	56	123	140	1165	373	71	226
1940	4505	1483	1280	948	332	24	55	125	143	1215	386	72	232
1941	4717	1549	1331	971	360	31	52	135	155	1259	415	77	241
1942	4662	1572	1329	951	378	47	50	146	163	1263	428	80	236
1943	4734	1598	1323	904	419	72	53	151	169	1278	461	74	252
1944	4850	1689	1396	940	456	98	49	146	171	1372	446	71	240
1945	5107	1801	1494	982	512	106	50	150	185	1465	466	77	244
1946	5511	1876	1602	1102	500	54	51	168	197	1510	490	85	259
1947	5504	1775	1522	1089	433	37	45	171	193	1411	462	76	248
1948	5544	1734	1485	1071	414	33	42	173	180	1381	456	73	248
1949	5573	1720	1477	1064	413	33	39	171	175	1374	446	73	243
1950	5764	1720	1480	1070	410	32	37	171	181	1369	448	76	244
1951	5799	1744	1494	1061	433	41	36	174	183	1388	435	66	242
1952	5883	1776	1522	1076	446	43	34	177	178	1421	447	66	255
1953	6032	1807	1561	1104	457	42	31	172	183	1452	445	65	255
1954	6080	1801	1568	1119	449	40	30	163	176	1461	440	63	252
1955	6335	1839	1611	1157	454	38	28	162	180	1498	451	67	259
1956	6412	1865	1637	1177	460	37	27	164	182	1519	453	65	263
1957	6448	1873	1646	1190	456	36	24	167	179	1526	441	63	257
1958	6444	1846	1619	1177	442	35	22	170	177	1499	436	65	253

Continued on next page

TABLE A4 (Cont'd.)

| | Clothing, Accessories, Jewelry | | | | | Personal Care | | | | Housing | | | | |
	Women's, Girls' Cloth	Men's, Boys' Cloth	Milit Cloth	Jewel	Cloth Serv	TOTAL Pers Care	Toilet Art.	Barber Beauty	TOTAL Housing	Non-Farm Owner	Non-Farm Tenant	Rent Farm House	Other Housing
1929	150	110	0	15	86	71	22	49	430	198	156	55	21
1930	136	96	0	14	79	68	19	48	420	191	156	54	20
1931	133	93	0	9	67	64	19	44	412	184	157	53	18
1932	112	81	0	7	53	57	16	40	401	176	156	52	17
1933	97	76	0	5	48	48	12	36	391	177	147	51	16
1934	100	79	0	6	52	56	16	40	409	178	163	50	18
1935	112	85	0	7	56	60	16	44	409	177	164	49	20
1936	117	96	0	7	63	64	17	48	414	177	167	48	21
1937	112	94	0	10	67	67	18	50	419	177	171	48	22
1938	117	91	0	10	64	64	18	45	422	177	175	48	22
1939	128	98	1	10	65	66	20	46	428	178	179	49	22
1940	133	99	1	11	70	67	21	46	438	182	184	49	23
1941	135	106	6	13	78	71	24	47	458	193	191	49	25
1942	137	99	15	14	83	73	26	47	473	206	195	48	24
1943	154	98	23	17	95	77	30	47	485	219	193	47	27
1944	146	94	22	16	96	79	32	47	497	234	189	46	29
1945	145	99	23	18	103	81	34	47	503	247	181	44	31
1946	151	108	7	23	116	79	32	47	540	275	187	44	34
1947	145	103	4	20	115	75	30	45	578	301	191	45	41
1948	146	102	3	20	112	73	29	43	598	319	196	46	36
1949	142	101	3	19	107	73	30	43	623	338	204	47	34
1950	140	104	4	20	104	76	33	43	655	363	210	48	34
1951	139	103	6	19	101	75	32	43	691	390	218	48	34
1952	150	105	4	21	102	79	35	45	723	416	224	49	35
1953	152	103	2	21	102	83	36	47	750	437	228	49	35
1954	150	102	1	22	101	88	37	52	772	457	230	49	36
1955	154	105	1	24	100	93	40	53	797	481	231	49	36
1956	157	106	1	24	99	98	43	56	821	503	232	49	37
1957	155	102	1	24	97	102	45	58	848	523	237	48	39
1958	155	98	1	25	93	104	46	58	872	544	243	48	38

Continued on next page

TABLE A4 (Cont'd.)

	TOTAL Household Op.	Furn	Kitch & HH Appl	China, Glass, Tablwr	Other House Furn Dur.	Other House Furn Semi-Dur.	Clean Light Paper	Writ Suppl	Electr.	Gas	Water & Sanit Svc	Fuel	Tel & Tel	Dom Svcs	Oth House Opr
1929	623	57	10	40	44	28	23	7	15	30	25	136	15	176	16
1930	573	45	9	29	38	24	22	7	16	32	27	132	15	163	16
1931	537	44	9	31	35	25	22	6	17	32	27	119	14	144	15
1932	480	34	6	31	29	23	19	4	17	31	26	113	12	122	14
1933	465	30	7	28	23	23	19	5	17	29	27	118	11	115	12
1934	495	30	9	28	25	23	22	6	18	29	30	121	11	130	13
1935	520	40	11	26	27	24	23	7	19	29	29	125	12	135	13
1936	575	48	13	30	35	30	26	7	20	30	30	134	13	143	15
1937	590	48	14	34	34	31	28	8	22	31	30	132	14	150	15
1938	552	44	12	31	32	30	27	7	23	30	30	122	13	136	16
1939	596	51	13	31	35	38	29	8	25	30	31	131	14	144	16
1940	631	55	15	33	36	40	31	9	27	32	32	139	15	150	16
1941	656	62	19	39	41	42	33	10	28	32	33	142	17	141	18
1942	641	50	11	36	37	39	35	11	29	35	33	145	19	142	19
1943	599	40	4	29	36	40	36	12	30	36	33	145	21	116	21
1944	582	35	2	27	32	39	35	14	32	37	33	142	22	109	23
1945	602	37	4	32	33	37	32	16	34	39	33	150	24	107	25
1946	712	52	19	50	48	45	38	17	38	42	35	160	26	97	44
1947	747	56	30	51	50	37	46	15	42	47	36	165	26	102	43
1948	760	56	31	53	53	39	47	14	47	50	36	163	28	99	44
1949	740	55	28	49	51	44	49	15	51	50	37	141	29	97	42
1950	798	61	35	50	56	48	54	15	57	56	37	149	30	104	44
1951	793	57	32	47	56	47	53	14	62	63	38	146	32	100	45
1952	783	60	31	44	51	47	52	15	67	66	38	140	34	91	45
1953	790	63	32	44	49	46	56	16	72	69	38	133	36	88	47
1954	792	64	33	43	46	43	57	17	78	75	38	133	37	81	47
1955	849	72	37	44	51	46	61	17	82	80	38	139	41	94	49
1956	873	74	40	41	53	46	63	16	87	86	38	137	43	97	50
1957	867	69	40	37	53	45	66	17	92	88	37	133	45	93	51
1958	870	67	38	35	51	43	67	18	95	92	35	136	46	94	51

Household Operations

Continued on next page

TABLE A4 (Cont'd.)

	Medical Care						Personal Business						
	TOTAL Medical Care	Drug Prep & Sundr	Ophth & Orthop Equipt	Profess Serv	Hosp	Health Ins	TOTAL Personal Bus	Brokerage	Bank & Finan Svcs	Life Insurance	Legal Svc	Funeral	Other Per Business
1929	280	18	5	166	86	6	613	257	155	72	71	47	10
1930	274	16	5	153	94	6	514	169	147	76	69	45	9
1931	269	15	4	145	98	6	467	119	143	80	74	44	9
1932	253	14	3	133	97	5	425	96	128	87	66	43	6
1933	235	14	3	121	92	5	469	149	112	91	67	42	7
1934	240	15	5	127	89	5	400	75	110	89	72	43	10
1935	241	16	5	125	90	5	436	91	119	97	74	43	11
1936	254	17	5	136	91	5	450	99	126	94	74	46	12
1937	261	18	6	138	93	5	455	91	133	93	75	44	18
1938	257	19	6	130	97	6	420	63	128	93	74	42	20
1939	268	20	6	136	100	7	420	54	132	95	77	41	21
1940	274	20	7	138	102	7	410	45	131	93	77	42	22
1941	283	23	8	142	102	8	406	37	136	90	79	41	24
1942	297	26	9	146	108	9	386	28	134	81	79	40	24
1943	302	30	10	139	113	10	383	41	119	79	75	42	27
1944	318	31	10	150	114	11	366	40	114	76	70	40	26
1945	322	32	11	152	114	12	374	52	119	72	67	39	24
1946	366	35	12	186	121	13	389	47	142	72	73	30	25
1947	383	33	11	196	119	23	392	38	148	81	70	32	23
1948	409	34	11	213	124	26	394	37	148	81	74	32	22
1949	416	35	11	209	131	29	384	32	144	79	76	33	21
1950	433	38	12	213	137	33	404	48	146	81	74	33	21
1951	449	41	13	217	137	41	402	41	148	81	76	34	22
1952	464	42	13	222	145	42	391	33	150	79	72	35	21
1953	479	42	14	227	151	45	395	31	156	79	71	36	21
1954	497	42	13	241	158	43	411	39	161	80	74	36	21
1955	506	44	13	238	166	46	418	38	166	85	73	36	22
1956	531	48	14	245	175	49	413	31	164	91	68	36	22
1957	551	51	13	253	182	51	417	30	162	94	71	37	23
1958	578	52	13	279	197	37	433	33	169	94	75	38	24

Continued on next page

	TOTAL Transport	Motor Veh & Wagons	New Autos	Net Used Auto	Other Motor Veh.	Tires & Acc	Auto Rep Rent & Oth	Gas & Oil	Tolls & Ins	Tolls	Auto Ins Prem	Purch Transp Local	Purch Transp Int City
1929	459	180	97	79	4	13	43	74	8	1	7	117	24
1930	388	130	62	65	3	12	35	74	9	1	8	108	19
1931	335	94	45	47	2	11	30	77	9	1	8	98	16
1932	274	60	26	33	1	9	26	70	9	1	8	87	13
1933	282	73	35	36	2	8	30	70	9	1	8	80	13
1934	309	89	44	42	3	9	32	74	9	1	8	81	15
1935	352	126	66	57	3	10	32	78	9	1	8	83	16
1936	409	161	83	74	4	11	36	84	10	1	9	87	20
1937	426	165	83	78	4	11	37	90	12	1	11	87	24
1938	362	109	48	58	3	10	35	92	11	1	10	83	22
1939	409	140	67	69	4	12	41	97	11	1	10	85	23
1940	450	165	87	74	4	14	44	102	13	1	12	88	25
1941	495	273	95	78	5	18	50	112	14	1	13	94	29
1942	379	82	4	78	0	8	35	84	11	1	10	120	40
1943	381	72	4	68	0	8	32	52	10	1	9	147	59
1944	392	64	1	63	0	9	39	53	11	1	10	157	60
1945	421	60	1	59	0	13	52	70	13	1	12	154	60
1946	574	104	54	42	8	27	89	125	17	1	16	158	54
1947	624	162	94	59	9	25	93	130	21	1	20	147	47
1948	653	195	105	80	10	23	97	136	22	1	21	137	44
1949	700	255	145	102	8	21	100	146	22	1	21	118	38
1950	755	314	189	116	9	25	102	149	27	2	25	105	35
1951	723	272	149	114	9	21	107	159	31	2	29	95	37
1952	710	253	124	122	7	22	109	169	30	2	28	89	38
1953	757	295	169	120	6	19	115	176	31	2	29	84	38
1954	751	300	159	135	6	17	113	178	32	2	31	75	35
1955	838	370	221	140	9	20	119	190	34	3	31	69	35
1956	798	315	172	134	9	22	122	198	40	3	37	67	35
1957	799	310	174	128	8	24	125	202	39	3	36	64	34
1958	755	271	128	136	7	25	126	208	37	4	33	58	31

Continued on next page

TABLE A4 (Cont'd.)

	Recreation							Education & Research					Foreign Travel		
	TOTAL Recreation	Books & Maps	Mag & News	Nondur Toys	Wheel Goods, Sp Eqpt	Music, Radio, TV	Flowers, Plants	Rec Serv	TOTAL Education & Res	Higher	Elem	Other	TOTAL Relig & Welf	TOTAL Net Foreign Travel	Foreign Travel by U.S.	Exp in U.S. by Foreign
1929	230	22	46	11	5	4	9	134	62	24	20	18	83	17	24	9
1930	219	19	44	9	4	5	8	131	63	26	21	17	87	19	25	8
1931	210	19	41	9	4	3	7	127	65	28	22	15	88	18	21	7
1932	171	12	37	8	3	3	7	102	56	26	17	13	80	176	19	5
1933	164	12	37	7	3	2	7	97	51	25	15	11	73	358	14	5
1934	174	13	39	7	3	2	6	104	51	25	16	11	69	111	15	6
1935	182	15	39	7	4	2	6	109	53	26	16	11	67	118	15	7
1936	201	17	42	8	5	3	8	119	56	27	18	12	68	133	18	7
1937	213	19	44	8	6	4	6	126	61	27	22	12	65	147	20	8
1938	202	17	42	8	6	3	8	118	63	27	24	12	69	115	17	9
1939	212	17	44	9	6	4	11	120	63	27	24	11	69	76	14	9
1940	224	17	46	9	6	5	10	130	64	29	24	11	74	4	7	6
1941	239	19	49	11	8	6	12	135	65	28	24	13	74	5	8	6
1942	252	21	52	10	7	5	9	147	69	29	24	16	77	16	5	7
1943	265	24	56	10	6	3	8	157	71	29	24	18	85	26	6	8
1944	263	28	57	10	7	2	9	151	68	29	24	15	94	55	7	10
1945	278	31	59	11	8	2	10	157	66	28	25	13	94	*	8	11
1946	325	34	64	16	15	8	10	178	66	31	22	14	96	3	13	16
1947	307	28	66	16	16	8	9	164	74	37	23	13	84	12	17	15
1948	296	27	66	18	15	7	8	155	76	39	24	14	83	23	19	13
1949	288	27	64	19	13	8	9	148	80	41	25	15	81	23	21	15
1950	292	28	64	22	14	11	9	144	81	41	25	16	79	32	23	16
1951	294	31	65	24	13	10	9	141	82	40	27	16	88	43	26	17
1952	292	29	65	24	14	11	9	140	85	41	28	17	90	56	27	18
1953	292	29	64	24	15	13	10	136	88	42	29	17	93	54	27	19
1954	291	28	64	23	16	14	10	136	90	43	30	19	92	56	31	20
1955	300	29	63	24	19	15	11	139	94	45	31	19	99	56	33	22
1956	307	30	62	25	21	15	11	143	98	47	32	19	98	55	35	23
1957	293	29	60	25	22	14	11	132	104	51	34	19	101	57	37	24
1958	284	28	58	26	23	14	10	127	108	54	34	19				24

*Less than 1

TABLE A5
Personal Consumption by Type of Expenditure Per Capita, 1959–1993 (1987 dollars)

| | | Food, Alcohol, Tobacco | | | | | | | | Cloth, Acc, Jewelry | |
| | | TOTAL Food, Alcohol, Tobacco | Food Off Prem | Pur Mls & Bev | Food Furn Emp | Food On Farm | Tobacco | Alcohol | Memo: Food Ex Alc | TOTAL Cloth, Acc, Jewel | Shoes |
	Total PCE										
1959	6658	1881	1207	446	32	20	176	179	1526	447	65
1960	6837	1866	1195	448	31	18	175	175	1516	439	64
1961	6994	1876	1196	454	31	17	177	175	1523	438	63
1962	7303	1870	1184	464	31	15	175	181	1515	448	64
1963	7578	1860	1169	472	31	14	174	182	1504	449	63
1964	7986	1894	1196	485	30	13	169	185	1540	474	67
1965	8454	1954	1245	496	31	11	171	189	1595	491	67
1966	8889	1996	1282	499	35	10	169	196	1631	519	70
1967	9162	2003	1303	485	37	10	169	195	1639	520	70
1968	9643	2062	1347	506	35	9	166	203	1694	537	73
1969	10002	2085	1371	509	34	8	162	208	1715	539	75
1970	10072	2102	1383	516	31	8	163	217	1722	525	70
1971	10581	2085	1379	507	28	8	162	220	1703	534	70
1972	11512	2126	1397	530	27	8	164	229	1733	847	74
1973	11673	2118	1363	549	27	7	172	241	1706	596	78
1974	11598	2065	1316	537	30	9	173	243	1649	582	73
1975	11838	2084	1324	550	31	8	171	244	1669	593	72
1976	12465	2161	1374	565	33	8	180	250	1731	621	74
1977	12969	2176	1383	581	32	8	172	261	1743	647	77
1978	13508	2163	1360	590	33	6	174	264	1725	691	84
1979	13828	2161	1358	593	34	6	171	270	1720	700	88
1980	13821	2141	1350	581	34	6	170	271	1700	690	87
1981	13988	2112	1326	576	35	5	171	268	1674	711	91
1982	14140	2106	1327	578	34	5	162	265	1679	705	88
1983	14793	2134	1347	592	35	4	156	265	1713	746	91
1984	15509	2153	1357	602	35	4	155	260	1738	795	95
1985	16185	2178	1381	604	36	4	152	262	1763	820	98
1986	16763	2200	1390	623	36	4	147	262	1791	876	104
1987	17239	2206	1371	651	37	3	144	256	1806	887	106
1988	17859	2230	1383	671	38	2	135	255	1840	904	107
1989	18203	2215	1373	669	38	2	133	252	1829	932	112
1990	18482	2224	1380	675	39	2	128	258	1837	918	112
1991	18403	2171	1354	659	38	2	118	241	1812	893	107
1992	18872	2136	1318	657	38	2	122	230	1784	919	108
1993	19533	2143	1318	672	38	1	115	225	1803	935	107

Continued on next page

TABLE A5 (Cont'd.)

| | Clothing, Accessories, Jewelry | | | | | Personal Care | | | Housing | | | | |
| | | | | | | | | | | Non-Farm | | Rent | |
	Women's Girls' Cloth	Men's Boys' Cloth	Milit Cloth	Jewel	Cloth Serv	TOTAL Pers Care	Toilet Art.	Barber Beauty	TOTAL Housing	Owner Occ.	Tenant Occ.	Farm House	Other Housing
1959	161	102	1	25	93	107	46	61	903	569	250	47	38
1960	160	100	1	24	89	111	50	61	930	591	255	46	38
1961	162	100	1	24	89	119	54	64	957	611	264	45	38
1962	168	102	1	25	88	126	58	68	995	638	274	43	40
1963	171	101	1	26	87	128	61	67	1027	658	284	42	42
1964	181	108	1	27	90	134	65	69	1060	680	294	41	44
1965	187	113	1	31	93	140	69	71	1105	710	307	40	47
1966	197	120	2	38	93	154	77	77	1142	736	317	40	49
1967	193	122	2	40	94	159	81	79	1180	762	327	39	53
1968	199	126	2	42	95	164	84	80	1225	791	343	38	54
1969	201	126	2	42	94	162	85	77	1278	828	358	37	56
1970	200	123	1	41	89	166	87	79	1166	704	366	39	57
1971	209	127	1	43	84	162	87	75	1352	882	378	38	54
1972	219	137	1	45	84	166	90	77	1410	923	392	36	59
1973	233	146	1	54	84	172	97	75	1466	962	407	35	62
1974	231	142	1	59	77	168	97	71	1528	1018	413	34	63
1975	238	145	1	63	74	161	93	68	1558	1041	418	33	66
1976	249	150	1	74	74	160	96	64	1590	1063	424	32	71
1977	259	157	1	80	74	167	100	67	1613	1083	427	31	72
1978	283	167	1	84	72	170	104	66	1675	1141	430	30	73
1979	292	171	1	81	68	171	107	64	1723	1190	430	29	75
1980	295	170	1	74	63	167	106	61	1754	1224	431	28	72
1981	312	173	1	75	59	162	104	58	1771	1236	440	26	69
1982	317	171	1	74	55	154	100	54	1764	1233	441	24	67
1983	338	178	1	81	58	165	103	62	1773	1235	445	23	70
1984	364	188	1	91	56	172	110	63	1805	1258	453	23	71
1985	375	193	1	97	56	178	113	65	1828	1263	470	22	72
1986	402	201	1	111	57	185	118	68	1837	1266	477	21	73
1987	404	208	1	111	58	195	123	72	1863	1284	483	20	76
1988	411	212	1	109	65	202	125	77	1884	1296	492	19	77
1989	430	216	0	105	68	208	128	80	1896	1305	497	19	76
1990	418	213	1	102	72	209	131	78	1898	1306	502	18	72
1991	413	210	1	97	65	206	130	76	1896	1309	503	18	72
1992	433	215	1	97	65	207	129	77	1899	1310	507	17	65
1993	438	220	1	102	68	208	131	77	1907	1317	508	16	66

Continued on next page

TABLE A5 (Cont'd.)

Household Operation

	TOTAL Household Oper	Furn. Matt	Kitch & HH Appl	China Glass Tblwr	Other House Furn Dur	Other House Furn Semi-Dur	Clean Polish Paper	Writ Suppl	Electr	Gas	Water & Sanit Svc	Fuel	Phone	Dom Svcs	Oth House Opr
1959	888	71	41	36	54	45	72	19	99	95	38	128	48	90	53
1960	888	69	39	34	53	44	76	19	103	97	41	120	50	89	54
1961	894	67	39	33	53	46	84	19	107	102	42	112	52	85	54
1962	926	70	40	33	56	49	91	20	112	107	44	110	54	83	56
1963	957	74	42	33	61	50	95	21	116	110	48	114	58	81	55
1964	1008	82	45	35	68	54	102	22	121	114	49	117	61	79	58
1965	1051	85	46	39	73	57	109	22	127	116	50	121	67	75	63
1966	1104	89	50	44	78	61	118	25	133	120	50	123	73	71	68
1967	1124	88	51	45	79	62	119	24	139	124	50	122	78	71	72
1968	1151	90	56	46	84	64	124	26	147	127	51	114	84	67	72
1969	1170	90	59	45	82	62	127	29	155	131	54	107	92	63	74
1970	1166	87	61	44	79	59	129	28	162	132	57	99	97	58	74
1971	1161	89	65	45	79	58	125	25	167	131	57	94	100	54	72
1972	1224	98	72	46	85	60	130	27	174	135	61	102	106	52	75
1973	1296	106	78	50	95	65	141	28	184	130	64	110	116	50	78
1974	1250	103	77	49	97	60	133	25	187	126	66	86	121	43	76
1975	1227	97	70	45	93	59	116	24	197	129	67	84	132	40	74
1976	1273	101	72	48	99	61	115	25	205	130	65	93	142	41	77
1977	1321	112	76	51	107	62	113	26	221	124	64	89	151	42	83
1978	1376	117	76	56	113	64	123	30	228	126	65	87	163	42	85
1979	1408	122	78	57	117	66	133	31	230	123	68	80	175	36	92
1980	1385	113	75	56	111	65	137	32	237	121	71	61	180	32	92
1981	1355	110	72	57	107	67	138	33	233	116	70	51	182	29	90
1982	1328	102	66	58	102	64	139	32	233	117	69	47	185	30	84
1983	1363	111	71	59	110	65	145	32	245	112	71	47	178	30	87
1984	1422	121	77	62	119	69	157	35	245	112	74	47	179	34	92
1985	1461	125	85	63	121	70	163	35	251	112	77	48	182	34	95
1986	1502	133	91	64	130	74	171	36	251	105	80	50	183	34	98
1987	1543	136	93	62	141	74	176	38	259	105	82	49	195	34	98
1988	1601	135	98	66	150	79	180	41	267	111	84	49	208	36	98
1989	1639	143	103	70	155	80	179	43	267	114	86	46	212	38	101
1990	1633	139	106	70	155	79	182	43	265	104	86	42	220	38	104
1991	1635	137	108	70	148	80	179	43	272	107	85	42	229	35	100
1992	1684	138	116	72	155	84	181	42	264	109	84	44	256	37	103
1993	1739	146	123	76	160	87	185	43	270	112	85	47	266	37	103

Continued on next page

TABLE A5 (Cont'd.)

| | Medical Care | | | | | | Personal Business | | | | | | |
	TOTAL Medical Care	Drug Prep & Sundr	Ophth & Orthop Equipt	Profess Serv	Pvt Hosp	Health Ins	TOTAL Pers Bus	Brokerage	Bank & Finan Socs	Life Ins	Legal Socs	Funeral	Other Per Business
1959	606	56	15	277	210	49	445	42	175	86	80	38	24
1960	618	60	14	281	214	49	448	36	179	92	77	38	25
1961	635	66	13	285	220	50	466	48	180	91	85	38	24
1962	679	72	15	303	236	53	460	37	180	92	87	38	26
1963	710	76	16	313	251	54	471	34	188	93	92	39	25
1964	755	78	17	339	264	57	490	38	196	100	91	38	27
1965	796	80	18	362	277	59	513	46	201	107	93	39	29
1966	826	82	19	362	303	60	532	49	207	105	100	39	31
1967	850	88	17	355	332	58	549	60	216	101	99	39	33
1968	908	96	19	364	369	62	564	57	226	105	100	41	36
1969	968	103	20	377	403	65	570	45	240	105	100	40	39
1970	1018	115	22	389	425	68	583	36	253	110	106	40	39
1971	1071	118	21	389	475	68	585	35	258	106	106	40	39
1972	1136	127	22	406	508	72	597	35	266	109	106	40	41
1973	1209	136	24	443	531	75	614	28	276	117	110	40	43
1974	1246	142	24	448	554	79	623	23	287	120	111	39	43
1975	1288	141	24	454	584	85	645	26	302	128	107	38	44
1976	1340	144	24	465	618	88	682	30	312	144	110	39	46
1977	1385	145	24	483	642	90	707	30	325	150	112	40	49
1978	1432	154	25	487	674	92	743	29	343	157	120	41	53
1979	1483	165	25	496	699	97	758	31	358	160	118	39	53
1980	1522	170	25	506	720	101	771	35	363	166	117	39	51
1981	1581	173	24	537	747	100	762	31	354	168	123	36	50
1982	1589	171	24	530	765	99	790	37	371	178	121	33	50
1983	1621	176	25	550	773	96	837	55	405	172	123	30	50
1984	1656	182	28	573	778	96	855	57	411	177	129	30	52
1985	1695	186	30	600	786	95	907	68	428	189	138	31	53
1986	1744	190	32	615	811	96	929	84	439	176	144	30	56
1987	1813	196	33	657	829	99	964	93	459	173	152	30	57
1988	1860	195	36	687	843	100	985	83	453	194	163	31	61
1989	1881	194	35	701	850	101	992	92	445	196	167	30	63
1990	1934	197	39	729	868	101	999	92	447	199	166	30	65
1991	1960	193	35	742	888	102	1017	102	439	224	159	30	63
1992	1998	186	34	766	910	103	1026	119	440	214	161	29	63
1993	2025	185	34	782	922	101	1050	148	438	211	159	30	64

TABLE A5 (Cont'd.)

| | | Autos | | | | | | | | Purch Transp | |
	TOTAL Transport	New	Net Used	Other Motor Veh.	Tires & Acc	Auto Rep Rent & Oth	Gas & Oil	Tolls	Auto Ins Prem	Local	Inter-City
1959	808	163	138	8	28	131	215	4	33	57	31
1960	816	172	130	8	29	135	218	4	34	56	30
1961	771	146	116	7	30	137	217	4	33	52	30
1962	817	180	111	9	33	142	222	5	34	50	31
1963	854	204	111	11	35	147	226	5	35	48	31
1964	883	214	107	13	37	153	235	5	36	46	35
1965	946	253	112	16	37	159	243	6	37	45	39
1966	970	250	107	20	39	165	255	6	40	44	44
1967	976	234	109	21	40	171	261	6	43	42	49
1968	1060	275	109	28	44	177	276	7	46	43	54
1969	1102	275	110	34	50	184	292	7	46	44	59
1970	1070	231	102	32	53	192	307	8	46	43	58
1971	1157	282	104	41	59	199	317	8	46	43	58
1972	1242	315	108	58	64	204	327	9	50	43	65
1973	1298	335	106	69	73	202	340	9	53	42	70
1974	1173	250	96	59	73	194	321	8	53	43	75
1975	1180	247	94	64	72	199	327	8	55	43	71
1976	1295	299	105	94	74	205	337	8	53	43	77
1977	1377	328	103	115	78	220	344	8	56	43	82
1978	1401	329	102	128	76	222	348	9	59	42	86
1979	1346	307	97	103	73	225	339	8	61	40	94
1980	1207	264	91	67	67	212	316	8	61	34	86
1981	1198	270	91	67	65	209	318	8	61	30	79
1982	1193	270	87	78	62	199	318	8	62	29	80
1983	1303	323	90	106	69	211	323	7	61	31	81
1984	1430	365	106	132	74	237	330	7	61	32	86
1985	1546	396	117	166	77	264	332	7	61	34	91
1986	1615	432	122	172	77	264	344	8	63	34	99
1987	1584	385	116	177	77	271	349	8	64	33	104
1988	1646	404	124	183	83	288	351	7	65	33	107
1989	1646	388	123	200	83	293	353	8	63	31	105
1990	1612	366	132	186	87	290	346	7	62	32	105
1991	1474	288	136	161	87	274	329	7	60	30	101
1992	1528	305	137	181	89	286	335	7	59	28	100
1993	1589	315	147	201	96	300	335	7	58	28	101

Continued on next page

Table A5 (Cont'd.)

	Recreation							Education					Foreign Travel		
	TOTAL Recreation	Books & Maps	Mag & News	Nondur Toys	Wheel Goods, Sport Eqpt	Radio TV, Music Inst	Flowers, Plants	Recr Svcs	TOTAL Educ & Res	Higher	Elem	Other	TOTAL Relig & Welf	TOTAL Net Foreign Travel	Foreign Travel by U.S.	Exp in U.S. by Foreign
1959	295	28	57	28	25	15	11	130	111	55	37	19	109	58	40	24
1960	296	29	56	28	23	15	12	133	116	57	39	20	111	58	43	24
1961	296	30	51	29	22	16	11	136	121	60	42	19	114	54	42	24
1962	311	31	56	31	22	17	13	140	126	63	44	19	116	57	45	24
1963	323	33	57	33	24	18	15	143	133	66	47	20	120	57	48	24
1964	338	39	55	35	28	21	15	146	141	72	48	20	135	57	48	27
1965	353	38	57	37	31	26	17	147	152	81	50	21	141	59	5	29
1966	387	41	64	41	38	32	19	152	165	88	52	25	148	63	53	32
1967	395	40	63	42	42	36	19	154	172	91	52	29	158	74	62	32
1968	413	40	62	45	47	39	20	161	185	96	55	34	165	70	58	33
1969	429	43	62	46	50	40	20	167	194	102	57	36	165	74	63	37
1970	445	51	64	46	50	43	20	171	203	109	57	37	173	79	70	39
1971	449	49	64	47	51	44	20	175	210	115	58	37	181	75	68	40
1972	481	45	66	52	65	49	21	182	217	119	60	38	192	73	75	43
1973	518	45	71	58	74	55	22	194	221	122	59	40	193	51	72	49
1974	536	46	72	60	73	57	23	206	213	119	57	36	183	35	65	52
1975	546	43	67	62	77	61	22	215	216	118	57	40	182	25	63	56
1976	570	38	67	66	83	66	23	227	218	119	55	44	194	18	66	62
1977	596	39	69	70	90	69	21	239	217	120	54	44	199	18	68	62
1978	633	43	75	75	95	73	25	248	225	121	58	46	219	16	69	66
1979	666	44	82	79	103	77	26	255	227	123	58	46	224	10	67	68
1980	654	45	81	76	89	77	26	260	227	124	59	43	225	4	65	74
1981	673	46	79	78	88	79	27	277	229	127	59	43	232	-16	64	98
1982	678	44	75	79	84	78	27	291	233	132	59	42	241	3	71	90
1983	720	46	75	83	84	95	27	311	239	134	60	45	253	24	80	80
1984	778	49	78	90	99	108	29	325	242	134	60	47	272	37	117	107
1985	819	48	75	93	102	125	29	346	250	135	63	52	284	51	125	105
1986	866	49	75	98	109	147	32	357	257	137	63	57	304	18	110	115
1987	921	54	77	105	116	161	35	373	264	139	64	61	313	16	122	124
1988	965	58	81	107	118	185	38	379	276	141	66	69	334	0	123	140
1989	1001	59	82	111	117	199	39	393	288	144	70	74	342	-26	118	165
1990	1034	61	84	115	113	216	39	406	294	146	69	80	360	-40	120	178
1991	1048	61	80	117	109	246	36	399	296	148	67	81	359	-66	101	182
1992	1098	64	79	120	108	276	37	414	300	149	67	84	382	-79	104	193
1993	1165	64	79	125	109	324	41	424	304	149	68	87	389	-76	113	198

Personal Income and Its Disposition, 1900–1929
($000)

Year	Personal Income	Soc. Ins. Contrib.	Tax & Nontax Payments	Disposable Personal Income	Personal Consumption Expenditures	Saving	Transfer Payments to Foreigners	Interest Paid by Consumers
	0	1	2	3	4	5	6	7
1900	17113	13	223	16877	16393	277	95	112
1	18901	14	253	18634	17785	601	104	144
2	20293	15	269	20009	19079	644	105	181
3	20807	16	287	20504	19904	316	115	169
4	21740	16	295	21429	20768	396	127	138
1905	25618	18	308	25292	22208	1054	133	208
6	26795	19	312	26464	23897	848	147	247
7	26567	21	331	26215	25222	525	177	291
8	26417	22	345	26050	25026	652	192	180
9	29574	23	362	29189	27499	1282	187	221
1910	30512	25	385	30102	29059	598	204	241
1	30636	26	394	30216	29109	635	224	248
2	32968	27	405	32536	31042	989	212	293
3	33918	31	446	33441	32410	527	207	297
4	34593	30	472	34091	33140	462	170	319
1915	34666	29	512	34125	32234	1439	150	302
6	40794	40	622	40132	37811	1806	150	365
7	50899	53	1213	49633	46448	2567	180	438
8	60361	53	1710	58598	53209	4596	268	525
9	65593	59	1908	63626	59353	2757	832	684
1920	66530	62	1778	64690	62949	313	634	794
1	55185	66	1472	53647	51942	612	450	643
2	60169	70	1740	58359	55947	1519	314	579
3	66270	73	1587	64610	61890	1726	328	666
4	67440	77	1690	65673	62716	1996	339	622
1925	73011	83	1825	71103	68234	1708	373	788
6	76591	89	1890	74612	71847	1509	361	895
7	77390	95	2055	75240	71997	1986	355	902
8	79133	101	2452	76580	74603	472	346	1159
9	84232	100	2300	81832	77457	2500	343	1532

TABLE A7

Price Indices for PCE, 1900–1929 (1987 = 100.0)

| | | | | Food, Alcohol, Tobacco | | | | Clothing | | |
| | | 1 | 2 | 3 | 4 | 5 | 6 | 7 | 8 | 9 |
	Total PCE	Total Food Alc & Tob	Pur Food, Mls Exc Alc	Food Furn	Food on Farm	Alcohol	Tobacco	TOTAL	Shoes	Total Civilian
1900	0.071	0.063	0.061	0.053	0.103	0.074	0.075	0.162	0.071	0.143
1901	0.071	0.065	0.063	0.055	0.106	0.075	0.076	0.154	0.070	0.137
1902	0.074	0.069	0.068	0.059	0.115	0.075	0.077	0.167	0.070	0.134
1903	0.075	0.068	0.067	0.058	0.113	0.075	0.078	0.170	0.071	0.134
1904	0.076	0.069	0.068	0.059	0.114	0.075	0.079	0.168	0.072	0.133
1905	0.076	0.068	0.067	0.058	0.113	0.074	0.081	0.174	0.076	0.133
1906	0.079	0.071	0.070	0.060	0.117	0.074	0.081	0.190	0.083	0.135
1907	0.082	0.073	0.073	0.058	0.122	0.073	0.081	0.191	0.084	0.140
1908	0.084	0.073	0.073	0.064	0.124	0.071	0.081	0.191	0.082	0.134
1909	0.086	0.076	0.077	0.067	0.130	0.071	0.082	0.202	0.087	0.136
1910	0.087	0.079	0.081	0.070	0.136	0.071	0.082	0.196	0.086	0.134
1911	0.090	0.079	0.080	0.070	0.135	0.071	0.083	0.202	0.086	0.134
1912	0.090	0.082	0.083	0.074	0.143	0.071	0.083	0.208	0.091	0.137
1913	0.091	0.081	0.085	0.072	0.140	0.071	0.082	0.212	0.098	0.140
1914	0.090	0.083	0.084	0.074	0.143	0.073	0.081	0.209	0.098	0.139
1915	0.097	0.081	0.094	0.073	0.142	0.075	0.081	0.207	0.100	0.141
1916	0.115	0.089	0.121	0.072	0.158	0.080	0.082	0.227	0.110	0.156
1917	0.143	0.113	0.145	0.105	0.204	0.102	0.093	0.311	0.148	0.186
1918	0.154	0.141	0.168	0.126	0.244	0.179	0.111	0.373	0.168	0.246
1919	0.179	0.174	0.175	0.146	0.278	0.382	0.151	0.442	0.232	0.319
1920	0.150	0.174	0.133	0.152	0.294		0.154	0.481	0.260	0.378
1921	0.148	0.139	0.124	0.115	0.224		0.137	0.385	0.192	0.301
1922	0.149	0.129	0.128	0.108	0.209		0.134	0.358	0.169	0.255
1923	0.147	0.133	0.127	0.111	0.215		0.125	0.374	0.170	0.259
1924	0.151	0.131	0.138	0.111	0.214		0.125	0.351	0.169	0.256
1925	0.152	0.140	0.142	0.119	0.232		0.125	0.370	0.173	0.252
1926	0.151	0.144	0.137	0.123	0.239		0.125	0.368	0.172	0.249
1927	0.150	0.140	0.135	0.119	0.230		0.125	0.370	0.176	0.246
1928	0.150	0.138	0.137	0.118	0.228		0.119	0.377	0.189	0.245
1929	0.150	0.141	0.137	0.119	0.231		0.121	0.383	0.183	0.243

Continued on next page

TABLE A7 (Cont'd.)

	12	13	14	15	16	17	18	19	20	21	22
	Clothing			Personal Care				Housing			
	Military	Jewelry	Cloth Serv.	Total Personal Care	Toilet Articles	Barber & Beauty	TOTAL	Owner Occ	Tenant Occ	Farm Rent	Other Housing
1900	0.168	0.147	0.059	0.056	0.141	0.033	0.124	0.135	0.133	0.090	0.078
1901	0.162	0.162	0.058	0.057	0.141	0.033	0.127	0.138	0.136	0.089	0.079
1902	0.158	0.162	0.069	0.061	0.158	0.033	0.125	0.136	0.134	0.089	0.078
1903	0.158	0.162	0.069	0.060	0.156	0.034	0.132	0.144	0.142	0.091	0.083
1904	0.156	0.165	0.067	0.060	0.152	0.034	0.137	0.152	0.150	0.091	0.088
1905	0.156	0.165	0.070	0.064	0.158	0.035	0.140	0.153	0.151	0.093	0.089
1906	0.159	0.156	0.072	0.064	0.161	0.035	0.143	0.156	0.153	0.098	0.089
1907	0.165	0.160	0.074	0.068	0.163	0.036	0.149	0.161	0.159	0.101	0.094
1908	0.157	0.141	0.080	0.069	0.176	0.037	0.145	0.157	0.154	0.100	0.093
1909	0.156	0.134	0.084	0.070	0.184	0.038	0.142	0.153	0.151	0.101	0.089
1910	0.158	0.134	0.088	0.073	0.193	0.039	0.145	0.157	0.154	0.101	0.090
1911	0.158	0.134	0.088	0.074	0.192	0.040	0.142	0.153	0.151	0.101	0.089
1912	0.162	0.138	0.085	0.074	0.188	0.039	0.141	0.153	0.151	0.100	0.089
1913	0.165	0.147	0.084	0.073	0.185	0.039	0.145	0.158	0.155	0.101	0.091
1914	0.163	0.149	0.083	0.073	0.188	0.040	0.146	0.158	0.156	0.101	0.091
1915	0.166	0.147	0.083	0.079	0.198	0.041	0.146	0.159	0.157	0.102	0.092
1916	0.183	0.174	0.085	0.091	0.232	0.044	0.149	0.161	0.159	0.107	0.093
1917	0.219	0.243	0.114	0.110	0.316	0.048	0.150	0.160	0.158	0.120	0.092
1918	0.289	0.291	0.145	0.126	0.315	0.055	0.154	0.163	0.160	0.136	0.094
1919	0.375	0.315	0.166	0.134	0.320	0.064	0.168	0.177	0.174	0.154	0.101
1920	0.445	0.358	0.178	0.152	0.340	0.076	0.199	0.208	0.205	0.186	0.120
1921	0.354	0.338	0.138	0.126	0.267	0.075	0.217	0.237	0.233	0.142	0.137
1922	0.300	0.290	0.112	0.122	0.235	0.074	0.240	0.291	0.241	0.138	0.141
1923	0.304	0.350	0.113	0.124	0.239	0.074	0.229	0.251	0.247	0.144	0.144
1924	0.301	0.355	0.112	0.123	0.237	0.076	0.237	0.260	0.256	0.140	0.150
1925	0.296	0.325	0.114	0.126	0.243	0.077	0.238	0.261	0.257	0.138	0.151
1926	0.293	0.305	0.118	0.127	0.249	0.080	0.236	0.258	0.254	0.137	0.149
1927	0.290	0.305	0.114	0.128	0.237	0.083	0.233	0.254	0.250	0.137	0.147
1928	0.288	0.305	0.116	0.130	0.224	0.088	0.228	0.249	0.245	0.135	0.143
1929	0.286	0.305	0.120	0.129	0.222	0.088	0.223	0.243	0.239	0.136	0.140

Continued on next page

TABLE A7 (Cont'd.)

	23	24	25	26	27	28	29	30	31	32	33	34	35	36	37
	TOTAL HH Op	Furn, Matt	Kitchen Appl	China	Other Durable Furnish	Semi-dur house furnish	Clean & Polish	Sta-tionery	Elec	Gas	Water	Wd, Fuel & Coal	Tel & Tel	Dom Serv	Other HH Op
						Household Operation									
1900	0.087	0.062	0.300	0.063	0.109	0.110	0.085	0.072	1.187	0.138	0.034	0.055	0.283	0.026	0.062
1901	0.087	0.061	0.303	0.059	0.107	0.100	0.082	0.071	1.139	0.136	0.034	0.055	0.285	0.026	0.062
1902	0.092	0.063	0.303	0.060	0.104	0.105	0.098	0.069	0.871	0.135	0.035	0.060	0.277	0.029	0.064
1903	0.095	0.066	0.306	0.063	0.107	0.109	0.098	0.066	0.833	0.135	0.035	0.067	0.279	0.029	0.065
1904	0.093	0.066	0.297	0.065	0.103	0.109	0.096	0.067	0.774	0.134	0.037	0.063	0.271	0.030	0.066
1905	0.092	0.066	0.300	0.061	0.100	0.114	0.100	0.067	0.708	0.134	0.037	0.061	0.271	0.030	0.067
1906	0.094	0.070	0.306	0.066	0.102	0.123	0.103	0.068	0.631	0.130	0.038	0.061	0.271	0.031	0.067
1907	0.100	0.078	0.315	0.074	0.111	0.136	0.105	0.072	0.569	0.126	0.040	0.061	0.263	0.034	0.069
1908	0.099	0.077	0.309	0.064	0.108	0.117	0.115	0.074	0.557	0.125	0.040	0.061	0.264	0.035	0.070
1909	0.099	0.075	0.325	0.066	0.109	0.121	0.121	0.077	0.544	0.124	0.040	0.060	0.256	0.036	0.072
1910	0.102	0.082	0.322	0.073	0.109	0.124	0.125	0.076	0.524	0.122	0.040	0.059	0.256	0.036	0.074
1911	0.102	0.093	0.309	0.068	0.111	0.118	0.125	0.076	0.509	0.119	0.040	0.057	0.248	0.037	0.076
1912	0.104	0.103	0.309	0.066	0.112	0.120	0.122	0.074	0.506	0.118	0.040	0.059	0.248	0.038	0.075
1913	0.103	0.092	0.306	0.071	0.113	0.120	0.120	0.074	0.478	0.117	0.043	0.061	0.248	0.039	0.075
1914	0.106	0.116	0.306	0.073	0.115	0.113	0.118	0.073	0.455	0.114	0.045	0.060	0.248	0.038	0.077
1915	0.104	0.116	0.306	0.066	0.121	0.114	0.118	0.073	0.435	0.113	0.045	0.058	0.241	0.031	0.079
1916	0.111	0.119	0.316	0.086	0.135	0.155	0.122	0.109	0.426	0.112	0.046	0.062	0.241	0.039	0.084
1917	0.127	0.132	0.355	0.135	0.157	0.221	0.164	0.137	0.411	0.111	0.046	0.070	0.241	0.042	0.092
1918	0.146	0.153	0.433	0.193	0.202	0.314	0.208	0.142	0.402	0.115	0.048	0.080	0.234	0.047	0.105
1919	0.170	0.196	0.474	0.186	0.255	0.305	0.238	0.161	0.411	0.127	0.059	0.091	0.248	0.058	0.121
1920	0.201	0.293	0.566	0.217	0.313	0.386	0.255	0.217	0.407	0.133	0.064	0.110	0.256	0.072	0.145
1921	0.176	0.227	0.545	0.134	0.263	0.211	0.197	0.151	0.402	0.159	0.069	0.107	0.271	0.070	0.142
1922	0.169	0.201	0.539	0.134	0.223	0.222	0.160	0.131	0.421	0.155	0.074	0.100	0.279	0.070	0.141
1923	0.180	0.207	0.610	0.156	0.240	0.251	0.161	0.139	0.392	0.152	0.076	0.101	0.279	0.077	0.144
1924	0.179	0.192	0.595	0.163	0.236	0.246	0.160	0.147	0.392	0.149	0.081	0.097	0.279	0.079	0.148
1925	0.179	0.185	0.566	0.152	0.231	0.245	0.164	0.156	0.378	0.149	0.082	0.096	0.293	0.080	0.153
1926	0.179	0.179	0.575	0.136	0.225	0.221	0.168	0.166	0.378	0.147	0.084	0.101	0.308	0.081	0.158
1927	0.179	0.174	0.570	0.128	0.220	0.216	0.163	0.168	0.368	0.146	0.088	0.097	0.313	0.082	0.158
1928	0.176	0.173	0.545	0.129	0.215	0.222	0.166	0.168	0.359	0.148	0.089	0.096	0.313	0.079	0.167
1929	0.178	0.171	0.551	0.128	0.213	0.210	0.172	0.169	0.340	0.147	0.092	0.097	0.321	0.079	0.167

	38	39	40	41	42	43	44	45	46	47	48	49	50
	Medical Care						Personal Business						
	TOTAL	Drugs	Ophthal	MD, DDS, Oth Prof	Hospitals	Health Ins	TOTAL	Brokerage	Finance	Life Ins	Legal Serv	Funeral	Other Bus
1900	0.030	0.178	0.148	0.023		0.043	0.040	0.012	0.051	0.090	0.042	0.096	0.117
1901	0.031	0.170	0.142	0.023	0.015	0.043	0.036	0.012	0.047	0.083	0.039	0.088	0.108
1902	0.032	0.199	0.166	0.024	0.016	0.045	0.038	0.012	0.050	0.089	0.042	0.094	0.116
1903	0.033	0.197	0.164	0.025	0.016	0.046	0.040	0.011	0.050	0.089	0.042	0.094	0.116
1904	0.033	0.192	0.160	0.026	0.017	0.048	0.040	0.012	0.051	0.090	0.042	0.096	0.117
1905	0.035	0.199	0.166	0.026	0.017	0.049	0.039	0.012	0.050	0.089	0.042	0.094	0.116
1906	0.035	0.204	0.170	0.027	0.017	0.050	0.037	0.012	0.048	0.086	0.040	0.091	0.112
1907	0.035	0.205	0.171	0.028	0.018	0.051	0.039	0.012	0.050	0.089	0.042	0.094	0.116
1908	0.036	0.222	0.185	0.028	0.018	0.053	0.041	0.012	0.054	0.096	0.045	0.102	0.125
1909	0.037	0.231	0.192	0.030	0.019	0.055	0.040	0.012	0.052	0.093	0.044	0.099	0.121
1910	0.038	0.243	0.202	0.031	0.020	0.057	0.042	0.012	0.054	0.097	0.046	0.103	0.126
1911	0.040	0.243	0.202	0.032	0.021	0.059	0.045	0.011	0.055	0.099	0.046	0.105	0.128
1912	0.040	0.237	0.197	0.032	0.021	0.059	0.045	0.012	0.054	0.096	0.045	0.102	0.125
1913	0.040	0.233	0.194	0.032	0.021	0.060	0.046	0.011	0.052	0.093	0.044	0.099	0.121
1914	0.041	0.238	0.198	0.033	0.021	0.061	0.051	0.011	0.057	0.101	0.048	0.108	0.132
1915	0.043	0.250	0.208	0.035	0.022	0.064	0.050	0.012	0.056	0.100	0.047	0.106	0.130
1916	0.047	0.293	0.244	0.037	0.024	0.068	0.049	0.013	0.056	0.093	0.044	0.099	0.121
1917	0.054	0.362	0.301	0.041	0.026	0.076	0.054	0.014	0.057	0.101	0.048	0.108	0.132
1918	1.000	0.398	0.331	0.047	0.030	0.087	0.055	0.016	0.052	0.093	0.044	0.099	0.121
1919	0.073	0.404	0.336	0.055	0.035	0.102	0.053	0.018	0.054	0.097	0.046	0.103	0.126
1920	1.000	0.431	0.205	0.068	0.044	0.126	0.058	0.020	0.061	0.108	0.051	0.115	0.141
1921	0.088	0.338	0.281	0.078	0.050	0.145	0.060	0.022	0.060	0.107	0.050	0.113	0.139
1922	0.093	0.297	0.247	0.083	0.053	0.153	0.059	0.022	0.063	0.113	0.053	0.119	0.146
1923	0.087	0.302	0.251	0.077	0.049	0.142	0.056	0.023	0.058	0.104	0.049	0.110	0.135
1924	0.087	0.300	0.250	0.077	0.049	0.142	0.056	0.023	0.057	0.101	0.048	0.108	0.132
1925	0.092	0.306	0.255	0.083	0.053	0.154	0.055	0.023	0.058	0.104	0.049	0.110	0.135
1926	0.086	0.315	0.262	0.078	0.050	0.144	0.055	0.024	0.058	0.103	0.048	0.109	0.134
1927	0.093	0.301	0.251	0.084	0.054	0.156	0.055	0.024	0.057	0.101	0.048	0.108	0.132
1928	0.092	0.283	0.236	0.084	0.054	0.156	0.053	0.024	0.058	0.103	0.048	0.109	0.134
1929	0.091	0.281	0.234	0.084	0.054	0.155	0.052	0.025	0.056	0.100	0.047	0.106	0.130

Continued on next page

Table A7 (Cont'd.)

	51	52	53	54	55	56	57	58	59	60	61	62	63	64	65	66
		Transportation							Recreation							
	TOTAL	Motor Veh & Wagons	Tires & Acc	Auto Rep	Gas & Oil	Auto Ins & Tolls	Purch Local	Purch Intcity	TOTAL	Books & Maps	Mag & News	Nondur Toys	Whls Gds, Dur Toys	Music, Rad, TV	Flwrs & Plants	Rec Services
1900	0.049	0.216	1.914	0.108	*	0.107	0.033	0.076	0.079	0.060	0.084	0.178	0.198	1.166	0.089	0.043
1901	0.050	0.216	1.914	0.108	0.161	0.107	0.032	0.075	0.080	0.060	0.084	0.168	0.201	1.182	0.100	0.043
1902	0.050	0.213	1.907	0.108	0.162	0.107	0.032	0.074	0.080	0.060	0.084	0.172	0.220	1.296	0.107	0.043
1903	0.050	0.214	1.895	0.108	0.198	0.107	0.032	0.076	0.080	0.060	0.084	0.176	0.222	1.306	0.100	0.043
1904	0.050	0.195	1.729	0.104	0.199	0.107	0.033	0.077	0.078	0.060	0.084	0.187	0.218	1.280	0.100	0.044
1905	0.051	0.295	2.611	0.132	0.176	0.130	0.033	0.077	0.080	0.060	0.084	0.201	0.233	1.372	0.103	0.044
1906	0.053	0.342	3.032	0.145	0.192	0.148	0.034	0.078	0.082	0.060	0.084	0.211	0.233	1.371	0.103	0.044
1907	0.057	0.394	3.489	0.160	0.204	0.160	0.035	0.081	0.086	0.060	0.084	0.197	0.249	1.464	0.112	0.046
1908	0.058	0.393	3.488	0.160	0.209	0.160	0.034	0.080	0.079	0.060	0.084	0.203	0.240	1.408	0.118	0.046
1909	0.057	0.238	1.568	0.119	0.195	0.118	0.034	0.079	0.083	0.060	0.084	0.207	0.237	1.395	0.128	0.045
1910	0.060	0.220	1.949	0.115	0.167	0.112	0.035	0.081	0.082	0.060	0.084	0.199	0.235	1.381	0.134	0.046
1911	0.060	0.209	1.849	0.114	0.157	0.112	0.035	0.082	0.082	0.060	0.084	0.203	0.240	1.413	0.120	0.047
1912	0.062	0.174	1.541	0.104	0.186	0.107	0.035	0.082	0.085	0.060	0.084	0.205	0.222	1.306	0.131	0.048
1913	0.066	0.167	1.506	0.103	0.234	0.101	0.037	0.085	0.086	0.060	0.084	0.199	0.228	1.338	0.135	0.049
1914	0.069	0.142	1.285	0.098	0.210	0.101	0.038	0.088	0.085	0.060	0.084	0.199	0.214	1.259	0.137	0.051
1915	0.071	0.131	1.128	0.095	0.193	0.095	0.038	0.089	0.085	0.060	0.084	0.242	0.228	1.340	0.135	0.052
1916	0.080	0.122	1.166	0.095	0.265	0.095	0.040	0.094	0.093	0.060	0.084	0.330	0.218	1.282	0.157	0.055
1917	0.094	0.125	1.440	0.100	0.297	0.101	0.045	0.105	0.106	0.060	0.084	0.422	0.221	1.301	0.228	0.060
1918	0.119	0.137	1.666	0.112	0.344	0.112	0.061	0.142	0.104	0.060	0.084	0.435	0.266	1.566	0.255	0.066
1919	0.136	0.162	1.521	0.128	0.328	0.130	0.068	0.159	0.117	0.060	0.093	0.529	0.321	1.887	0.270	0.078
1920	0.164	0.181	1.690	0.149	0.354	0.148	0.083	0.193	0.129	0.071	0.093	0.346	0.380	2.233	0.265	0.087
1921	0.140	0.163	1.300	0.142	0.278	0.142	0.079	0.184	0.125	0.096	0.093	0.324	0.357	2.096	0.172	0.093
1922	0.130	0.132	0.839	0.132	0.295	0.130	0.076	0.176	0.133	0.096	0.094	0.353	0.321	1.887	0.166	0.090
1923	0.125	0.123	0.795	0.130	0.257	0.130	0.075	0.176	0.139	0.108	0.094	0.328	0.358	2.106	0.165	0.091
1924	0.126	0.122	0.673	0.132	0.239	0.130	0.076	0.177	0.142	0.108	0.094	0.318	0.371	2.182	0.166	0.098
1925	0.128	0.120	0.717	0.133	0.255	0.136	0.077	0.178	0.148	0.108	0.094	0.299	0.346	2.035	0.200	0.096
1926	0.127	0.114	0.727	0.135	0.265	0.136	0.077	0.179	0.150	0.117	0.094	0.273	0.354	2.081	0.200	0.096
1927	0.124	0.116	0.544	0.139	0.206	0.142	0.077	0.180	0.147	0.117	0.094	0.262	0.363	2.131	0.188	0.102
1928	0.128	0.121	0.461	0.147	0.210	0.148	0.077	0.180	0.154	0.117	0.094	0.260	0.364	2.141	0.194	0.104
1929	0.129	0.126	0.396	0.149	0.200	0.148	0.078	0.183	0.155	0.117	0.096	0.260	0.363	2.131	0.196	0.105

Table A7 (Cont'd.)

	67	68	69	70	71	72	73	74	75	76
		Education								
	TOTAL	Higher Ed	Elem Ed	Other Ed & Rsrch	TOTAL Religion & Welfare	Religion	Welfare	Net Foreign Travel	For Trav By US Res	Exp in US by Foreig
1900	0.036	0.037	0.028	0.046	0.033	0.031	0.037	0.110	0.120	0.054
1901	0.038	0.038	0.029	0.047	0.034	0.032	0.038	0.118	0.128	0.055
1902	0.039	0.038	0.029	0.048	0.035	0.033	0.039	0.112	0.122	0.059
1903	0.042	0.042	0.032	0.052	0.037	0.035	0.042	0.113	0.123	0.058
1904	0.040	0.040	0.030	0.050	0.038	0.036	0.043	0.128	0.134	0.059
1905	0.040	0.040	0.030	0.050	0.039	0.037	0.044	0.154	0.153	0.059
1906	0.041	0.041	0.031	0.052	0.040	0.038	0.046	0.206	0.180	0.061
1907	0.043	0.043	0.032	0.053	0.044	0.042	0.050	0.251	0.199	0.063
1908	0.043	0.043	0.032	0.053	0.045	0.043	0.052	0.296	0.218	0.064
1909	0.043	0.043	0.032	0.053	0.046	0.044	0.053	0.317	0.232	0.066
1910	0.043	0.043	0.033	0.054	0.045	0.043	0.052	0.297	0.239	0.069
1911	0.044	0.044	0.033	0.055	0.049	0.047	0.056	0.341	0.260	0.069
1912	0.044	0.045	0.034	0.055	0.052	0.050	0.059	0.384	0.270	0.072
1913	0.047	0.047	0.036	0.059	0.054	0.052	0.062	0.395	0.273	0.071
1914	0.047	0.048	0.036	0.060	0.057	0.055	0.062	0.277	0.233	0.073
1915	0.048	0.049	0.037	0.061	0.060	0.059	0.062	0.127	0.131	0.073
1916	0.049	0.050	0.038	0.062	0.062	0.062	0.062	0.078	0.090	0.080
1917	0.053	0.053	0.040	0.066	0.064	0.065	0.063	0.044	0.059	0.099
1918	0.056	0.057	0.043	0.070	0.071	0.073	0.070	0.024	0.041	0.121
1919	0.062	0.062	0.047	0.077	0.078	0.076	0.081	0.038	0.058	0.139
1920	0.071	0.070	0.053	0.087	0.090	0.089	0.090	0.070	0.092	0.152
1921	0.081	0.080	0.061	0.100	0.097	0.097	0.096	0.074	0.095	0.125
1922	0.088	0.087	0.066	0.108	0.120	0.101	0.214	0.093	0.110	0.118
1923	0.089	0.089	0.067	0.110	0.121	0.102	0.218	0.105	0.122	0.121
1924	0.090	0.090	0.068	0.112	0.125	0.106	0.222	0.134	0.147	0.121
1925	0.092	0.092	0.070	0.115	0.112	0.112	0.112	0.140	0.155	0.128
1926	0.095	0.095	0.072	0.119	0.111	0.111	0.111	0.155	0.166	0.131
1927	0.098	0.098	0.074	0.122	0.117	0.118	0.117	0.174	0.179	0.131
1928	0.100	0.101	0.076	0.125	0.120	0.120	0.120	0.203	0.201	0.129
1929	0.102	0.103	0.078	0.128	0.123	0.123	0.123	0.233	0.218	0.131

*Less than 0.01.

TABLE A8

Service Expenditures, 1900–1929 Alternative Estimates

	Totals (Millions of current dollars)					Indices (1929=100.0)				
	1	2	3	4	5	6	7	8	9	10
Year	Present Estimates	Kuznets Var III	Kendrick Kuznets	Lough	Barger	Present Estimates	Kuznets Var III	Kendrick Kuznets	Lough	Barger
1900	5.6		4.7			18.4		14.0		
01	6.0		5.3			19.7		15.8		
02	6.2		5.6			20.6		16.6		
03	6.7		6.1			22.1		18.0		
04	7.2		6.3			23.7		18.7		
05	7.7		6.9			25.3		20.3		
06	8.2		7.8			27.0		23.0		
07	8.7		8.3			28.7		24.6		
08	8.8		7.9			29.1		23.3		
09	9.2		9.0	9.0		30.2		26.6	30.7	
1910	9.7		9.5			31.8		28.1		
11	10.1		9.8			33.1		28.9		
12	10.5		10.6			34.4		31.3		
13	10.9		11.2			36.1		33.0		
14	11.3		11.2	10.1		37.2		33.2	34.7	
15	11.6		11.0			38.1		32.7		
16	12.7		13.1			41.9		38.8		
17	13.7		15.3			45.1		45.2		
18	14.9		17.0			49.0		50.4		
19	16.9	16.3	18.4	15.5		55.7	48.8	54.5	53.3	
1920	19.4	20.6	22.4			63.9	61.7	66.2		
21	20.2	24.1	21.6	16.9	19.5	66.6	72.2	63.9	58.2	71.8
22	21.2	23.5	22.9		20.3	69.9	70.4	67.6		74.8
23	22.9	25.5	25.9	19.8	22.3	75.4	76.3	76.8	67.8	82.0
24	24.3	29.2	27.4		23.5	80.1	87.4	81.2		86.5
25	26.0	25.9	27.3	22.8	24.3	85.7	77.5	80.7	78.2	89.6
26	27.1	29.3	29.8		25.2	89.2	87.7	88.2		92.7
27	28.5	29.7	29.6	25.9	25.8	93.8	88.9	87.7	88.8	95.0
28	29.3	31.4	31.5		26.4	96.5	94.0	93.2		97.1
29	30.4	33.4	33.8	29.1	27.2	100.0	100.0	100.0	100.0	100.0

Sources: Col. 1 - Present estimates less services of financial intermediaries. Cols. 2 & 7 - Simon Kuznets, *Capital in the American Economy* (1961), p. 502, Col. 5. Cols. 3 & 8 - John Kendrick, *Productivity Trends in the United States* (1961). Table A-IIb. Col. 1 gives Kuznets's annual consumption totals. To these the ratio of services in consumption were applied using data from Kuznets, *Capital*, p. 561, Col. 4 and p. 565, Col. 8. Cols. 4 & 9 - William H. Lough, *High-Level Consumption* (1935), pp. 239–45, Intangible items. Cols. 5 & 10 - Harold Barger, *Outlay and Income in the United States, 1921–1938* (1942), pp. 228–29.

·APPENDIX B·

STATE ESTIMATES

State Aggregates for Personal Consumption, 1900
(in $ millions)

	Total PCE	Total Food, Tob & Alc.	Pur Food, Meals & Bev	Food Furnished	Farm Food	Alcohol	Tobacco	Total Clothing & Acc.
TOTAL U.S.	16393.0	7164.0	4892.0	97.1	822.3	954.6	397.8	2127.5
Maine	150.8	67.6	56.4	0.8	11.1	1.7	1.3	21.5
New Hampshire	91.2	36.4	29.9	0.7	4.7	2.4	0.5	13.7
Vermont	68.9	31.3	25.5	0.9	5.7	0.2	0.6	8.9
Massachusetts	847.4	235.3	197.1	2.8	6.1	23.0	19.0	116.0
Rhode Island	118.3	34.4	28.7	0.4	0.9	4.6	1.7	14.9
Connecticut	240.9	85.4	67.7	1.5	3.8	11.6	4.6	31.2
New York	2501.2	858.3	467.3	7.1	38.0	242.9	93.0	332.8
New Jersey	519.8	190.2	124.8	2.4	5.5	42.6	17.5	61.1
Pennsylvania	1496.8	581.8	433.4	5.5	38.0	58.1	66.2	188.9
Ohio	946.0	432.4	286.5	4.0	42.7	81.7	23.9	124.2
Indiana	462.3	221.1	150.8	2.5	33.3	32.6	6.2	64.6
Illinois	1257.8	524.6	338.5	5.3	45.6	112.0	28.9	157.0
Michigan	496.9	215.1	156.3	2.8	30.2	25.2	6.9	64.4
Wisconsin	399.6	180.0	127.6	2.9	24.7	24.7	4.7	53.8
Minnesota	391.1	178.2	125.6	3.6	23.7	26.0	3.6	50.2
Iowa	437.6	195.3	145.4	4.2	37.5	10.8	3.9	65.6
Missouri	662.9	313.8	239.8	2.5	42.2	30.2	10.9	88.2
North Dakota	66.6	39.6	27.9	2.8	8.6	0.8	0.5	7.1
South Dakota	73.6	40.1	28.4	1.6	7.5	3.2	0.4	9.4
Nebraska	221.1	108.4	75.2	2.0	17.8	11.8	3.9	28.0
Kansas	269.2	135.8	106.4	3.0	25.2	4.9	2.0	36.7
Delaware	39.9	17.2	13.3	0.3	1.4	0.6	2.3	4.9
Maryland	253.3	109.1	88.5	1.8	7.4	8.6	8.0	30.6
D.C.	107.8	30.5	24.4	0.1	0.1	3.9	3.4	11.7
Virginia	249.1	139.8	107.4	2.1	22.2	6.2	7.3	32.5
West Virginia	128.7	77.7	60.9	0.6	15.9	3.2	0.4	16.1
North Carolina	204.4	131.4	109.5	1.5	23.5	1.0	2.9	27.8
South Carolina	137.8	83.1	74.4	1.5	12.4	0.1	0.2	20.6
Georgia	241.7	134.7	118.0	1.9	21.2	1.6	0.4	34.4
Florida	72.5	36.6	32.3	0.5	4.8	1.1	0.3	9.0
Kentucky	328.9	193.1	138.8	1.6	33.2	8.5	16.4	40.6
Tennessee	250.5	140.1	107.1	1.2	28.1	6.8	2.2	35.8
Alabama	219.8	138.1	118.1	1.2	24.6	1.8	0.4	29.2
Mississippi	172.4	111.7	91.6	1.0	23.0	1.5	0.2	24.0
Arkansas	169.0	109.2	85.6	0.9	25.3	1.7	0.3	21.7
Louisiana	188.0	104.7	81.5	2.9	13.2	10.1	1.2	25.7
Oklahoma	123.9	89.3	77.7	1.1	13.6	2.2	0.2	12.5
Texas	477.6	271.7	206.7	3.1	55.5	15.0	1.4	56.0
Montana	80.6	37.0	16.0	1.1	3.1	13.8	1.6	8.6
Idaho	35.5	18.3	11.5	0.6	3.0	3.0	0.4	4.7
Wyoming	22.2	11.1	6.1	0.7	1.1	2.9	0.2	3.0
Colorado	181.2	69.4	40.0	1.2	5.8	15.2	6.9	21.0
New Mexico	29.2	14.1	10.8	0.5	1.4	1.9	0.1	5.1
Arizona	30.2	13.3	7.6	0.3	1.1	4.2	0.1	3.4
Utah	54.3	22.8	16.9	0.4	2.8	2.8	0.6	8.4
Nevada	14.0	6.9	3.0	0.4	0.8	2.3	0.2	1.5
Washington	154.9	65.0	38.0	1.5	5.9	13.5	5.9	19.4
Oregon	114.8	51.2	30.6	1.2	6.7	8.1	4.7	14.9
California	591.1	233.4	117.3	7.0	12.8	62.0	29.4	66.2

Continued on next page

TABLE B1 (*Cont'd.*)

	Shoes & Repair	Clothing Inc. Mil.	Jewelry	Cloth. & Acc. Sv.	Total Personal Care	Toilet Articles	Barber & Beauty
TOTAL U.S.	428.3	1262.0	147.0	286.8	119.5	64.3	55.2
Maine	6.3	11.3	1.9	2.0	0.9	0.5	0.4
New Hampshire	4.0	6.7	1.3	1.7	0.7	0.4	0.3
Vermont	1.8	5.6	0.7	0.8	0.5	0.3	0.2
Massachusetts	40.0	45.5	9.7	20.7	6.5	3.3	3.2
Rhode Island	3.7	7.0	1.5	2.6	0.9	0.5	0.4
Connecticut	9.0	14.8	2.6	4.8	1.9	1.0	0.9
New York	81.2	164.1	23.7	63.4	19.2	8.8	10.4
New Jersey	18.4	30.6	4.3	7.7	4.0	1.8	2.2
Pennsylvania	46.0	102.4	15.5	24.7	11.1	5.5	5.6
Ohio	37.2	64.2	7.4	15.2	7.8	4.0	3.8
Indiana	14.6	38.8	4.6	6.4	4.6	2.6	2.0
Illinois	39.3	74.4	10.6	32.5	11.2	5.9	5.3
Michigan	16.0	37.4	4.1	6.8	3.6	2.2	1.4
Wisconsin	12.4	31.9	3.8	5.6	2.5	1.4	1.1
Minnesota	8.4	32.4	3.3	6.0	2.6	1.5	1.1
Iowa	15.3	41.4	4.5	4.3	4.6	2.9	1.7
Missouri	13.8	57.5	6.2	10.5	5.6	3.4	2.2
North Dakota	0.5	5.9	0.4	0.3	0.6	0.4	0.2
South Dakota	1.0	7.5	0.5	0.4	0.6	0.4	0.2
Nebraska	4.3	19.7	1.9	2.0	2.2	1.4	0.8
Kansas	4.7	27.2	2.5	2.2	2.6	1.6	1.0
Delaware	0.9	3.0	0.5	0.5	0.2	0.1	0.1
Maryland	5.4	15.9	2.3	7.0	1.6	0.8	0.8
D.C.	1.5	5.0	1.8	3.4	0.9	0.5	0.4
Virginia	2.2	24.7	1.8	3.7	0.8	0.5	0.3
West Virginia	1.1	12.8	0.8	1.4	0.5	0.3	0.2
North Carolina	0.5	25.2	0.6	1.4	0.3	0.2	0.1
South Carolina	0.5	17.9	0.7	1.5	0.2	0.1	0.1
Georgia	1.0	29.5	1.2	2.6	0.5	0.3	0.2
Florida	0.4	7.1	0.5	1.0	0.3	0.2	0.1
Kentucky	3.7	29.6	2.0	5.2	1.4	0.9	0.5
Tennessee	2.0	27.8	1.8	4.1	0.8	0.5	0.3
Alabama	0.7	25.2	1.0	2.2	0.5	0.3	0.2
Mississippi	0.3	21.3	0.7	1.6	0.3	0.2	0.1
Arkansas	0.4	19.0	1.0	1.2	0.5	0.3	0.2
Louisiana	1.5	20.1	1.7	2.3	0.8	0.4	0.4
Oklahoma	0.4	11.5	0.2	0.4	0.6	0.4	0.2
Texas	2.4	44.4	3.3	5.8	2.9	1.9	1.0
Montana	1.2	5.7	0.8	0.9	0.7	0.3	0.4
Idaho	0.3	3.8	0.4	0.2	0.3	0.2	0.1
Wyoming	0.4	2.2	0.2	0.2	0.2	0.1	0.1
Colorado	3.1	12.6	2.3	3.0	1.9	1.1	0.8
New Mexico	0.1	4.6	0.2	0.2	0.2	0.1	0.1
Arizona	0.2	2.9	0.1	0.2	0.4	0.2	0.2
Utah	0.5	6.5	0.6	0.8	0.4	0.2	0.2
Nevada	0.2	1.0	0.1	0.2	0.2	0.1	0.1
Washington	3.1	12.1	2.1	2.1	1.4	0.8	0.6
Oregon	2.2	9.7	1.4	1.6	1.0	0.6	0.4
California	14.2	34.7	5.7	11.5	5.5	2.9	2.6

Continued on next page

TABLE B1 (*Cont'd.*)

	Total Housing	Non-Farm Ownd/Rntd	Farm Housing	Other Housing	Total Household Operation	Furni-ture	Clean & Polish
TOTAL U.S.	2426.0	2070.0	307.0	49.0	1810.0	172.0	64.0
Maine	23.5	18.1	4.1	0.6	16.0	0.7	0.6
New Hampshire	15.3	10.9	3.0	0.4	10.4	0.4	0.3
Vermont	9.3	5.0	3.2	0.3	8.1	0.4	0.3
Massachusetts	174.4	172.3	6.1	2.8	100.4	8.2	2.3
Rhode Island	27.7	27.8	0.8	0.4	12.8	1.0	0.4
Connecticut	41.5	36.6	4.2	0.8	26.4	1.6	0.8
New York	469.2	440.9	29.1	8.5	236.3	17.0	5.9
New Jersey	96.3	88.4	6.0	1.9	59.0	6.7	1.6
Pennsylvania	283.7	258.8	27.9	4.9	149.6	13.0	5.2
Ohio	129.3	113.1	18.9	2.1	95.6	12.9	3.4
Indiana	53.0	36.8	13.3	1.2	50.0	5.3	2.1
Illinois	179.7	157.3	21.7	3.3	139.7	13.6	4.0
Michigan	75.0	61.1	13.7	1.4	64.7	8.4	2.0
Wisconsin	59.4	44.3	13.4	1.2	44.2	4.4	1.7
Minnesota	54.4	43.7	9.5	1.1	48.7	4.8	1.5
Iowa	56.0	32.8	20.8	1.2	42.4	4.3	1.9
Missouri	87.8	73.0	12.8	1.8	64.9	4.3	2.6
North Dakota	6.9	3.2	2.2	0.3	7.0	0.5	0.3
South Dakota	7.0	2.8	2.7	0.3	7.6	0.6	0.3
Nebraska	26.7	16.7	7.9	0.7	22.0	2.0	0.9
Kansas	31.7	19.5	9.6	0.8	29.3	2.4	1.3
Delaware	6.6	5.6	0.9	0.1	4.8	0.7	0.2
Maryland	41.0	39.6	4.7	0.4	31.4	3.8	1.0
D.C.	24.7	26.4	0.1	0.3	14.0	0.6	0.2
Virginia	23.3	18.6	6.1	0.3	40.4	4.6	1.6
West Virginia	10.6	6.8	2.9	0.3	16.6	2.0	0.8
North Carolina	11.4	7.4	4.6	0.1	35.2	3.4	1.6
South Carolina	8.2	5.9	2.3	0.1	20.9	2.7	1.2
Georgia	20.8	17.8	3.9	0.3	39.4	5.4	1.9
Florida	9.3	8.7	0.9	0.1	10.6	1.2	0.4
Kentucky	30.4	23.9	7.9	0.4	34.1	4.5	1.8
Tennessee	19.8	13.9	5.4	0.4	36.7	4.1	1.7
Alabama	16.1	13.3	3.0	0.3	30.7	5.0	1.6
Mississippi	8.9	5.9	3.2	0.1	27.7	3.3	2.6
Arkansas	13.0	10.0	2.6	0.3	19.3	2.8	1.1
Louisiana	17.6	15.2	2.9	0.3	24.8	2.2	1.2
Oklahoma	5.9	2.4	1.8	0.3	11.2	1.9	0.7
Texas	48.7	37.8	8.7	1.1	60.1	5.5	2.6
Montana	10.4	4.6	0.8	0.7	8.0	0.3	0.2
Idaho	3.9	1.2	0.6	0.3	3.6	0.2	0.1
Wyoming	2.6	1.4	0.3	0.1	2.3	0.1	0.1
Colorado	28.2	18.0	1.4	1.4	15.6	0.6	0.4
New Mexico	3.0	1.9	0.3	0.1	4.2	0.3	0.2
Arizona	4.5	2.4	0.2	0.3	3.0	0.2	0.1
Utah	6.9	5.8	0.9	0.1	6.6	0.3	0.2
Nevada	1.9	0.7	0.2	0.1	1.1	0.1	0.0
Washington	23.7	18.2	1.4	0.8	13.7	0.6	0.4
Oregon	16.2	11.9	1.7	0.6	9.6	0.5	0.3
California	100.6	81.7	6.7	3.1	49.5	2.3	1.2

Continued on next page

TABLE B1 (Cont'd.)

	Electric & Gas	Water & Sanit.	Fuel & Ice	Telephone Telegraph	Domestic Service	Othr Hous Operation	Total Medical Care
TOTAL U.S.	87.0	49.8	399.0	12.8	419.0	55.8	390.0
Maine	0.8	0.2	4.1	0.1	4.1	0.5	3.3
New Hampshire	0.6	0.1	2.6	0.1	2.9	0.3	2.1
Vermont	0.5	0.0	2.1	0.0	2.1	0.2	2.0
Massachusetts	4.5	10.3	12.7	0.5	26.0	5.4	19.3
Rhode Island	0.4	0.6	2.1	0.1	3.4	0.8	2.4
Connecticut	1.3	0.9	6.0	0.2	6.4	1.2	5.3
New York	10.2	14.0	42.7	2.1	58.1	14.5	40.6
New Jersey	3.2	1.6	10.2	0.5	15.4	1.8	9.1
Pennsylvania	6.6	4.2	30.3	1.4	38.5	4.9	31.7
Ohio	5.4	2.2	18.1	1.1	20.8	2.6	25.1
Indiana	2.0	0.8	12.1	0.5	10.7	1.4	15.6
Illinois	6.6	3.6	31.5	1.5	31.4	5.0	35.1
Michigan	3.3	1.0	17.0	0.4	11.6	1.4	13.0
Wisconsin	1.8	0.7	11.3	0.3	9.2	1.3	8.6
Minnesota	2.1	0.5	12.6	0.3	10.4	1.7	7.9
Iowa	1.8	0.5	11.1	0.5	8.8	0.7	13.6
Missouri	4.0	1.5	13.5	0.5	16.7	2.2	22.4
North Dakota	0.4	0.0	1.8	0.0	1.8	0.1	1.5
South Dakota	0.5	0.0	2.3	0.0	1.5	0.1	2.1
Nebraska	1.2	0.1	6.2	0.2	4.4	0.3	7.0
Kansas	2.1	0.1	9.8	0.2	4.2	0.3	9.7
Delaware	0.2	0.1	1.1	0.0	1.0	0.1	0.9
Maryland	1.2	0.8	5.9	0.2	8.2	0.8	5.5
D.C.	0.3	0.8	1.5	0.1	5.2	0.9	2.6
Virginia	1.8	0.5	8.4	0.1	10.6	0.5	4.1
West Virginia	1.0	0.1	4.1	0.1	3.4	0.1	2.8
North Carolina	2.6	0.2	11.0	0.0	5.6	0.1	2.2
South Carolina	1.1	0.2	4.4	0.0	4.7	0.2	1.4
Georgia	1.2	0.5	12.2	0.1	6.0	0.2	4.3
Florida	0.5	0.2	2.5	0.0	2.4	0.2	1.4
Kentucky	1.4	0.4	9.5	0.1	5.6	0.4	8.2
Tennessee	1.5	0.3	7.0	0.1	10.6	0.3	6.7
Alabama	1.4	0.1	6.7	0.1	6.3	0.2	3.6
Mississippi	1.4	0.1	6.0	0.0	5.9	0.1	2.8
Arkansas	1.1	0.0	5.1	0.0	3.2	0.1	4.6
Louisiana	1.2	0.6	6.1	0.1	5.6	0.3	4.0
Oklahoma	0.7	0.0	3.1	0.0	1.5	0.0	3.7
Texas	2.8	0.4	14.8	0.2	15.0	0.5	15.9
Montana	0.4	0.1	2.0	0.1	2.4	0.1	1.9
Idaho	0.2	0.0	1.3	0.0	0.6	0.0	0.9
Wyoming	0.1	0.0	0.8	0.0	0.5	0.0	0.6
Colorado	0.7	0.2	4.4	0.2	3.7	0.7	6.0
New Mexico	0.3	0.0	1.6	0.0	0.6	0.0	0.6
Arizona	0.2	0.0	1.0	0.0	0.6	0.0	1.0
Utah	0.4	0.1	2.3	0.0	1.2	0.1	1.4
Nevada	0.1	0.0	0.3	0.0	0.3	0.0	0.4
Washington	0.6	0.1	3.3	0.2	3.4	0.8	4.0
Oregon	0.6	0.1	2.7	0.1	1.8	0.5	3.2
California	2.8	1.0	10.1	0.5	14.7	1.9	17.9

Continued on next page

TABLE B1 (Cont'd.)

	Drug & Ophthal.	Profes. Serv.	Hospitals	Total Personal Business	Legal Service	Funeral Services	Brokerage & Banks
TOTAL U.S.	114.0	253.0	21.0	746.0	81.0	185.0	344.0
Maine	1.0	2.1	0.2	5.3	0.5	1.4	2.2
New Hampshire	0.7	1.3	0.1	3.6	0.3	1.1	1.5
Vermont	0.5	1.3	0.1	3.5	0.3	0.6	1.8
Massachusetts	5.5	12.1	2.0	38.8	2.4	12.4	14.7
Rhode Island	0.9	1.3	0.2	4.4	0.2	1.5	1.5
Connecticut	1.6	3.3	0.4	12.3	0.7	3.6	5.4
New York	4.2	32.5	3.5	136.9	11.4	41.9	56.6
New Jersey	3.1	5.5	0.5	29.2	2.0	9.8	11.5
Pennsylvania	9.5	20.4	1.6	67.0	5.6	23.1	23.1
Ohio	7.4	16.4	1.1	41.1	4.7	14.5	14.1
Indiana	5.4	9.6	0.5	22.8	2.9	7.6	9.2
Illinois	10.8	22.2	2.0	68.4	7.1	16.4	34.6
Michigan	4.4	7.8	0.8	20.3	2.0	5.0	10.0
Wisconsin	2.8	5.0	0.9	20.9	1.5	2.8	13.1
Minnesota	3.0	4.6	0.4	15.9	1.8	1.7	10.0
Iowa	5.5	7.7	0.3	28.4	2.3	3.7	18.9
Missouri	7.7	13.8	0.7	28.4	3.9	4.2	15.5
North Dakota	0.8	0.7	0.1	2.2	0.4	0.1	1.4
South Dakota	1.0	1.1	0.1	3.4	0.6	0.3	2.1
Nebraska	2.8	3.9	0.2	11.8	1.6	1.4	7.5
Kansas	3.5	5.9	0.2	11.5	1.8	2.3	6.1
Delaware	0.3	0.5	0.0	1.9	0.1	0.8	0.6
Maryland	1.5	3.5	0.5	10.4	1.2	3.6	2.9
D.C.	0.8	1.7	0.2	4.3	0.9	1.3	1.2
Virginia	1.1	2.8	0.3	5.5	0.9	1.5	1.6
West Virginia	0.7	2.0	0.1	3.2	0.8	0.9	0.9
North Carolina	0.5	1.6	0.1	2.4	0.4	0.4	0.9
South Carolina	0.3	1.1	0.0	4.1	2.7	0.2	0.5
Georgia	0.9	3.2	0.2	5.2	0.9	0.5	2.1
Florida	0.4	0.9	0.1	1.7	0.3	0.3	0.8
Kentucky	2.4	5.5	0.2	10.1	1.8	2.4	3.4
Tennessee	1.4	5.0	0.1	6.9	1.4	1.3	2.8
Alabama	0.9	2.6	0.1	3.2	0.7	0.4	1.3
Mississippi	0.7	2.0	0.0	2.3	0.5	0.2	1.0
Arkansas	1.1	3.3	0.1	3.0	0.7	0.4	1.4
Louisiana	1.2	2.6	0.1	4.8	0.8	0.8	1.7
Oklahoma	1.2	2.4	0.0	3.0	0.7	0.3	1.7
Texas	5.0	10.3	0.3	14.8	3.2	1.2	7.8
Montana	0.5	1.2	0.2	4.1	0.6	0.7	2.1
Idaho	0.3	0.5	0.1	1.6	0.3	0.2	0.9
Wyoming	0.2	0.3	0.1	1.0	0.1	0.1	0.4
Colorado	2.0	3.8	0.3	13.5	1.5	2.2	8.1
New Mexico	0.2	0.4	0.1	0.9	0.2	0.1	0.4
Arizona	0.3	0.6	0.1	1.7	0.3	0.2	0.8
Utah	0.4	0.8	0.1	2.8	0.4	0.4	1.7
Nevada	0.1	0.2	0.0	0.8	0.1	0.2	0.4
Washington	1.4	2.4	0.2	9.0	1.3	1.2	5.6
Oregon	1.1	2.0	0.1	7.2	0.8	0.8	4.8
California	4.9	11.4	1.8	40.2	3.6	7.0	25.0

Continued on next page

TABLE B1 (Cont'd.)

	Life Insur.	Other Business	Total Transpor- tation	Total Recreat.	Books	News & Magaz.	Toys	Musical Instr.
TOTAL U.S.	100.0	36.0	533.0	498.0	64.0	87.9	82.0	80.0
Maine	0.9	0.3	4.0	3.9	0.8	0.9	0.6	0.6
New Hampshire	0.5	0.2	2.0	2.8	0.9	0.3	0.6	0.3
Vermont	0.6	0.2	1.3	1.9	0.6	0.2	0.4	0.3
Massachusetts	7.6	1.9	44.5	39.4	9.8	6.9	7.3	5.2
Rhode Island	1.0	0.2	5.9	4.4	0.7	0.3	1.3	0.6
Connecticut	2.1	0.6	9.7	9.7	2.3	0.8	2.3	1.3
New York	20.9	6.6	114.3	112.1	11.9	26.3	16.0	15.0
New Jersey	4.6	1.4	21.1	18.5	2.1	0.9	3.8	2.5
Pennsylvania	12.4	3.2	57.1	39.2	6.0	8.4	5.7	6.4
Ohio	6.1	2.0	31.5	31.2	3.9	5.3	4.3	5.1
Indiana	2.2	1.1	10.1	13.9	1.4	2.0	3.3	2.3
Illinois	6.8	3.3	48.4	48.4	5.5	8.1	6.6	7.9
Michigan	2.3	1.0	14.3	14.3	1.6	1.8	3.6	2.5
Wisconsin	2.3	1.0	9.6	10.5	1.9	1.6	2.3	1.6
Minnesota	1.4	0.8	10.5	13.9	1.4	1.9	2.6	1.6
Iowa	1.7	1.4	8.6	11.4	1.1	2.0	1.3	2.4
Missouri	3.3	1.4	22.6	16.2	1.0	3.9	1.4	3.3
North Dakota	0.2	0.1	1.0	1.0	0.0	0.2	0.3	0.2
South Dakota	0.2	0.2	1.3	1.6	0.1	0.3	0.2	0.3
Nebraska	0.6	0.6	5.3	6.3	0.7	1.0	0.6	1.3
Kansas	0.7	0.6	3.4	6.0	0.7	0.9	0.8	1.6
Delaware	0.3	0.1	1.2	0.9	0.1	0.1	0.1	0.2
Maryland	2.3	0.5	9.5	5.9	1.0	0.8	0.8	1.1
D.C.	0.7	0.2	6.4	5.1	0.7	0.7	1.4	0.5
Virginia	1.3	0.3	4.2	3.0	0.2	0.4	0.8	0.5
West Virginia	0.5	0.2	2.4	1.4	0.2	0.3	0.1	0.3
North Carolina	0.6	0.1	1.9	1.1	0.1	0.3	0.3	0.2
South Carolina	0.5	0.2	2.2	1.2	0.1	0.2	0.7	0.1
Georgia	1.5	0.3	5.5	2.6	0.2	0.7	0.7	0.4
Florida	0.3	0.1	1.6	1.5	0.1	0.2	0.7	0.2
Kentucky	2.1	0.5	8.0	6.0	0.3	1.0	0.7	1.0
Tennessee	1.1	0.3	5.2	3.6	0.2	1.0	0.5	0.7
Alabama	0.7	0.2	3.7	1.5	0.1	0.2	0.5	0.3
Mississippi	0.5	0.1	1.8	0.8	0.0	0.3	0.1	0.3
Arkansas	0.4	0.1	1.5	1.1	0.0	0.2	0.2	0.4
Louisiana	1.3	0.2	5.5	2.2	0.1	0.6	0.3	0.6
Oklahoma	0.1	0.1	1.5	1.1	0.0	0.2	0.1	0.3
Texas	1.7	0.7	6.9	6.9	0.2	1.4	0.8	2.3
Montana	0.4	0.2	2.0	2.9	0.4	0.4	0.2	0.4
Idaho	0.1	0.1	0.6	0.8	0.1	0.1	0.1	0.2
Wyoming	0.3	0.0	0.3	0.5	0.0	0.0	0.1	0.1
Colorado	0.9	0.7	5.4	7.7	0.9	0.9	1.9	1.2
New Mexico	0.2	0.0	0.3	0.7	0.1	0.1	0.1	0.2
Arizona	0.3	0.1	0.5	0.8	0.2	0.1	0.1	0.2
Utah	0.2	0.1	1.1	1.3	0.1	0.2	0.3	0.3
Nevada	0.1	0.0	0.2	0.4	0.0	0.1	0.0	0.1
Washington	0.3	0.4	4.7	4.4	0.3	0.4	0.9	0.9
Oregon	0.3	0.3	2.9	3.4	0.2	0.4	0.8	0.7
California	2.2	1.9	19.2	22.4	3.7	2.6	3.4	4.0

Continued on next page

TABLE B1 (Cont'd.)

	Recreat. Services	Flowers & Plants	Total Educa- tion	Higher Educa- tion	Other Educa- tion	Religion	Welfare	Foreign Travel
Total U.S.	137.0	47.0	105.0	14.0	91.0	226.0	100.0	149.0
Maine	0.6	0.4	0.9	0.1	0.8	1.9	0.8	1.0
New Hampshire	0.4	0.3	0.7	0.1	0.6	1.5	0.4	1.0
Vermont	0.3	0.1	0.3	0.0	0.4	1.3	0.3	0.7
Massachusetts	6.2	3.9	9.2	1.6	7.3	15.4	7.4	17.3
Rhode Island	0.7	0.8	1.0	0.1	0.9	2.0	0.9	2.6
Connecticut	1.7	1.3	3.3	0.8	2.3	5.4	1.5	3.9
New York	35.6	7.3	19.1	2.6	16.4	46.1	19.5	34.9
New Jersey	4.2	5.0	3.3	0.3	3.0	9.4	3.7	6.7
Pennsylvania	7.0	5.6	10.3	1.2	9.2	30.2	8.8	12.1
Ohio	9.0	3.6	6.5	0.8	5.7	13.6	5.9	4.3
Indiana	3.9	1.0	2.5	0.2	2.3	5.8	2.2	1.4
Illinois	15.5	4.8	10.7	1.4	9.2	12.3	8.9	12.7
Michigan	3.4	1.3	3.2	0.3	3.0	5.4	2.5	3.7
Wisconsin	2.4	0.7	2.2	0.1	2.2	4.8	1.2	2.2
Minnesota	5.7	0.7	2.3	0.2	2.2	4.6	2.3	2.8
Iowa	3.8	0.9	2.7	0.3	2.4	5.4	2.8	1.2
Missouri	5.5	1.1	4.0	0.4	3.7	6.7	3.0	2.2
North Dakota	0.3	0.0	0.1	0.0	0.1	0.6	0.3	0.4
South Dakota	0.7	0.0	0.2	0.0	0.3	0.7	0.5	0.5
Nebraska	2.4	0.3	1.2	0.1	1.1	2.1	1.4	0.7
Kansas	1.8	0.2	1.5	0.1	1.5	2.5	1.6	0.7
Delaware	0.2	0.2	0.1	0.0	0.2	0.6	0.2	0.3
Maryland	1.3	0.9	1.2	0.2	1.0	4.6	1.5	1.1
D.C.	0.5	1.3	0.8	0.2	0.5	1.9	0.8	1.0
Virginia	0.6	0.5	1.0	0.2	0.7	3.6	0.6	0.7
West Virginia	0.4	0.1	0.3	0.0	0.3	1.6	0.3	0.2
North Carolina	0.1	0.1	0.7	0.2	0.4	2.4	0.2	0.2
South Carolina	0.1	0.0	0.3	0.1	0.2	1.9	0.2	0.3
Georgia	0.3	0.3	0.6	0.1	0.5	3.1	0.4	0.5
Florida	0.2	0.1	0.2	0.0	0.2	0.9	0.2	0.8
Kentucky	2.4	0.6	1.4	0.2	1.1	3.6	0.7	0.5
Tennessee	0.8	0.4	1.3	0.4	0.7	2.8	0.5	0.3
Alabama	0.3	0.1	0.5	0.1	0.4	2.4	0.3	0.4
Mississippi	0.1	0.0	0.5	0.1	0.4	1.7	0.2	0.2
Arkansas	0.2	0.1	0.5	0.1	0.3	1.2	0.4	0.2
Louisiana	0.4	0.2	0.6	0.1	0.5	1.8	0.3	1.2
Oklahoma	0.5	0.0	0.3	0.0	0.3	0.6	0.4	0.0
Texas	1.9	0.3	2.1	0.2	1.9	3.7	1.5	1.2
Montana	1.4	0.1	0.3	0.0	0.3	0.4	0.7	3.6
Idaho	0.3	0.0	0.1	0.0	0.1	0.2	0.3	0.7
Wyoming	0.3	0.0	0.1	0.0	0.1	0.1	0.1	0.6
Colorado	2.3	0.5	1.0	0.1	0.9	1.5	2.0	4.9
New Mexico	0.2	0.0	0.1	0.0	0.1	0.1	0.1	0.3
Arizona	0.2	0.0	0.1	0.0	0.1	0.1	0.4	0.8
Utah	0.3	0.1	0.3	0.0	0.4	0.6	0.8	1.1
Nevada	0.2	0.0	0.0	0.0	0.0	0.1	0.1	0.3
Washington	1.8	0.1	0.8	0.1	0.7	1.2	2.4	3.6
Oregon	1.1	0.2	0.5	0.0	0.5	0.8	1.1	1.9
California	7.2	1.5	4.0	0.4	3.7	4.6	7.1	9.6

TABLE B2
State Aggregates for Personal Consumption, 1929
(in $ millions)

State	Total Consump	Total Food & Tobacco	Purchased Food	Meals & Bev.	Food Furn.	Farm Food	Tobacco
TOTAL U.S.	77457	21239	14777	2911	257	1599	1695
Maine	428	127	95	12	2	11	8
New Hampshire	276	87	70	9	1	3	5
Vermont	203	65	48	6	1	7	3
Massachusetts	3619	877	676	132	12	8	49
Rhode Island	530	135	102	18	2	1	12
Connecticut	1329	322	249	39	5	6	23
New York	12915	3180	2197	595	58	44	286
New Jersey	3253	869	697	98	13	9	52
Pennsylvania	6471	1666	1279	185	23	42	138
Ohio	4670	1213	885	150	13	64	102
Indiana	1901	506	350	64	4	48	41
Illinois	6407	1536	1050	252	20	77	138
Michigan	3450	907	646	127	9	37	87
Wisconsin	1812	530	368	68	4	56	34
Minnesota	1585	453	306	52	4	58	33
Iowa	1383	421	240	46	3	93	39
Missouri	2029	582	394	81	5	56	47
North Dakota	262	96	61	10	1	15	9
South Dakota	298	108	63	11	1	27	7
Nebraska	770	249	138	27	2	60	23
Kansas	941	295	191	35	2	47	21
Delaware	177	46	34	4	1	2	5
Maryland	1058	275	220	26	7	11	12
D.C.	662	148	100	31	6	*	12
Virginia	877	270	188	25	5	37	17
West Virginia	587	179	131	21	1	15	11
North Carolina	852	284	185	27	2	55	15
South Carolina	402	147	103	9	1	26	7
Georgia	896	283	189	29	3	51	12
Florida	727	214	153	31	3	12	15
Kentucky	843	305	205	28	2	53	17
Tennessee	914	288	185	32	2	49	21
Alabama	694	254	171	21	2	47	14
Mississippi	513	238	158	15	1	57	7
Arkansas	485	193	122	18	1	44	9
Louisiana	707	243	168	26	3	35	12
Oklahoma	988	330	200	42	2	43	43
Texas	2587	844	545	106	7	122	65
Montana	28953	104	70	12	1	6	15
Idaho	225	73	45	7	*	14	8
Wyoming	129	49	32	6	1	6	4
Colorado	675	187	128	25	1	16	16
New Mexico	140	56	36	7	*	11	2
Arizona	249	81	56	13	1	7	5
Utah	272	74	50	9	1	9	7
Nevada	66	22	16	3	*	1	2
Washington	1107	324	221	46	3	24	31
Oregon	663	195	131	27	1	15	20
California	5142	1311	835	255	17	68	136

Continued on next page

TABLE B2 (Cont'd.)

State	Other Household	Total Medical Care	Drug Prep. & Sundries	Ophthalmic Products	Physicians	Dentists
TOTAL U.S.	316	3104	604	131	959	482
Maine	2	18	4	1	5	2
New Hampshire	2	11	2	*	3	1
Vermont	1	8	2	*	2	1
Massachusetts	7	159	23	11	42	25
Rhode Island	3	19	4	1	5	3
Connecticut	10	55	9	4	13	7
New York	62	523	77	29	156	80
New Jersey	9	114	21	5	33	18
Pennsylvania	24	251	44	8	78	40
Ohio	31	171	32	9	54	27
Indiana	6	72	15	3	25	12
Illinois	23	236	44	8	72	41
Michigan	15	114	25	3	34	17
Wisconsin	14	62	12	2	18	14
Minnesota	9	62	11	2	18	12
Iowa	5	57	13	1	17	10
Missouri	9	90	19	3	32	15
North Dakota	1	9	2	*	3	2
South Dakota	1	11	3	*	3	2
Nebraska	4	32	8	1	10	6
Kansas	3	38	10	*	12	6
Delaware	1	7	1	1	2	1
Maryland	6	45	8	2	15	6
D.C.	3	35	5	3	11	4
Virginia	6	36	8	2	12	4
West Virginia	1	24	5	*	10	4
North Carolina	1	32	8	1	12	4
South Carolina	1	16	4	*	6	2
Georgia	2	39	11	2	14	5
Florida	3	29	8	1	9	4
Kentucky	2	37	9	1	15	5
Tennessee	3	37	9	1	16	5
Alabama	3	29	8	1	11	4
Mississippi	2	18	6	*	7	2
Arkansas	1	22	7	1	10	2
Louisiana	1	31	9	1	11	4
Oklahoma	3	38	12	*	14	5
Texas	7	102	35	2	33	11
Montana	1	10	3	*	3	2
Idaho	1	10	2	2	2	2
Wyoming	0	5	1	*	1	1
Colorado	2	31	6	2	10	5
New Mexico	0	5	1	*	2	1
Arizona	1	10	3	*	3	1
Utah	0	11	3	*	3	2
Nevada	0	3	1	*	1	*
Washington	4	48	10	2	12	9
Oregon	1	29	5	1	8	6
California	25	253	38	11	70	42

Continued on next page

TABLE B2 (*Cont'd.*)

State	Cleaning & Laundry	Jewelry	Other Acc's	Total Personal Care	Toilet Articles	Barber & Beauty
TOTAL U.S.	1264	560	152	1116	591	525
Maine	5	3	1	9	6	3
New Hampshire	4	1	1	4	2	2
Vermont	1	1	*	2	1	1
Massachusetts	56	17	9	55	30	25
Rhode Island	11	2	1	7	3	4
Connecticut	20	8	3	15	7	9
New York	180	149	27	184	76	108
New Jersey	63	17	4	41	17	24
Pennsylvania	73	53	14	83	45	38
Ohio	72	26	9	68	37	32
Indiana	31	10	3	30	18	12
Illinois	139	44	12	100	53	47
Michigan	23	19	8	45	23	22
Wisconsin	21	12	4	22	13	9
Minnesota	24	8	5	21	13	8
Iowa	12	9	3	18	10	8
Missouri	43	14	4	31	17	14
North Dakota	3	2	*	2	1	1
South Dakota	3	2	1	3	1	2
Nebraska	12	5	1	11	6	5
Kansas	13	8	1	15	9	6
Delaware	1	1	*	2	1	1
Maryland	15	7	2	11	5	6
D.C.	13	5	1	10	4	6
Virginia	16	5	1	8	5	3
West Virginia	11	4	1	8	5	3
North Carolina	17	5	1	12	8	3
South Carolina	5	2	*	3	2	1
Georgia	15	6	2	13	9	4
Florida	16	11	1	20	15	5
Kentucky	16	5	1	8	4	4
Tennessee	21	6	1	13	9	4
Alabama	9	2	1	10	7	3
Mississippi	7	2	*	6	4	2
Arkansas	7	2	*	6	4	2
Louisiana	13	5	1	10	6	4
Oklahoma	20	5	1	18	11	7
Texas	55	19	4	43	26	17
Montana	4	2	1	4	2	2
Idaho	4	2	*	3	2	1
Wyoming	3	1	*	2	2	1
Colorado	13	5	1	12	8	4
New Mexico	3	1	*	3	2	1
Arizona	5	1	*	6	5	1
Utah	7	2	*	3	2	2
Nevada	1	1	*	1	*	1
Washington	23	7	3	16	7	9
Oregon	13	5	2	7	3	4
California	123	37	14	94	48	46

Continued on next page

TABLE B2 (Cont'd.)

State	Total Housing	Owner-Occupied	Tenant-Occupied	Farm	Other Housing	Household Operation	Furn.
TOTAL U.S.	11672	5868	4542	913	349	10664	1192
Maine	58	32	18	7	2	62	6
New Hampshire	37	21	13	3	1	42	3
Vermont	28	15	8	6	1	31	2
Massachusetts	540	298	220	10	10	588	59
Rhode Island	78	45	31	1	1	86	10
Connecticut	215	125	78	8	3	227	25
New York	2058	874	1059	47	76	1955	194
New Jersey	652	382	244	11	14	494	53
Pennsylvania	1035	631	340	45	16	934	109
Ohio	772	446	264	46	15	640	82
Indiana	268	146	84	32	6	253	35
Illinois	1074	515	472	50	36	966	99
Michigan	584	315	219	35	14	501	56
Wisconsin	295	162	82	44	5	257	23
Minnesota	223	112	64	41	7	202	15
Iowa	213	98	50	61	4	179	12
Missouri	303	139	117	36	10	254	32
North Dakota	35	11	8	14	1	22	2
South Dakota	40	15	9	15	1	29	2
Nebraska	108	50	26	29	3	90	5
Kansas	120	57	34	27	3	101	9
Delaware	24	13	8	2	0	31	3
Maryland	155	92	49	11	2	170	17
D.C.	99	50	44	0	6	111	9
Virginia	124	58	36	27	4	124	18
West Virginia	86	43	30	10	2	69	11
North Carolina	101	43	32	24	4	92	19
South Carolina	43	17	14	11	1	46	9
Georgia	91	38	34	16	4	123	20
Florida	86	40	36	6	5	96	13
Kentucky	119	58	37	21	3	88	13
Tennessee	104	46	35	19	4	121	22
Alabama	70	33	21	14	2	84	15
Mississippi	42	16	10	15	2	45	7
Arkansas	50	20	16	12	2	41	5
Louisiana	86	35	39	9	3	79	12
Oklahoma	113	43	50	16	4	96	13
Texas	296	129	110	45	12	293	46
Montana	30	11	13	6	2	29	3
Idaho	23	9	7	6	1	30	2
Wyoming	14	5	6	2	1	13	1
Colorado	77	36	29	8	4	92	7
New Mexico	11	3	5	2	1	15	1
Arizona	25	9	12	2	2	31	4
Utah	35	18	11	4	2	36	7
Nevada	7	3	3	1	1	7	1
Washington	136	72	46	12	8	131	11
Oregon	85	46	26	9	4	80	6
California	804	398	341	33	34	576	66

Continued on next page

TABLE B2 (Cont'd.)

State	Kitchen Appliance	China & Glass	Durable Furnish.	Semi-Dur. Furnish.	Cleaning Prep.	Station- ery	Total Utilities
TOTAL U.S.	699	628	1148	717	485	143	3051
Maine	6	5	5	3	2	*	23
New Hampshire	3	4	2	2	3	*	15
Vermont	2	3	2	2	*	*	13
Massachusetts	21	38	56	35	6	7	241
Rhode Island	4	4	8	5	2	1	33
Connecticut	10	17	16	11	5	2	83
New York	94	115	241	95	71	30	554
New Jersey	33	24	40	20	5	6	196
Pennsylvania	66	67	128	60	29	11	241
Ohio	47	40	71	41	48	9	144
Indiana	16	13	30	17	18	2	75
Illinois	44	64	98	83	64	14	277
Michigan	29	27	53	28	33	16	157
Wisconsin	18	13	27	15	16	2	84
Minnesota	10	14	15	20	8	2	67
Iowa	12	10	16	11	15	1	61
Missouri	26	9	33	9	7	3	71
North Dakota	3	1	2	2	2	*	6
South Dakota	4	1	2	2	2	*	9
Nebraska	6	8	7	5	5	1	31
Kansas	14	3	10	9	4	1	27
Delaware	2	2	2	1	4	1	8
Maryland	13	8	12	15	3	3	48
D.C.	3	8	13	7	1	2	19
Virginia	8	8	7	8	2	1	37
West Virginia	6	4	7	5	4	1	17
North Carolina	6	4	8	9	3	1	25
South Carolina	3	4	3	5	2	*	10
Georgia	9	6	10	12	11	1	30
Florida	6	2	7	8	10	2	24
Kentucky	5	6	9	7	5	*	25
Tennessee	9	5	9	12	12	1	30
Alabama	7	4	7	5	6	*	23
Mississippi	3	2	2	6	2	*	14
Arkansas	5	2	3	5	1	*	13
Louisiana	3	3	7	8	9	2	14
Oklahoma	9	7	13	9	5	1	19
Texas	32	17	36	34	18	4	52
Montana	4	2	3	2	1	*	10
Idaho	5	3	2	2	4	*	8
Wyoming	1	1	1	1	2	*	3
Colorado	9	6	12	10	7	2	24
New Mexico	2	1	1	1	1	*	5
Arizona	4	2	4	3	1	*	8
Utah	6	2	5	3	*	*	11
Nevada	1	*	1	1	*	*	2
Washington	17	9	16	9	3	2	37
Oregon	8	5	11	8	4	1	21
California	51	28	80	47	20	15	106

Continued on next page

TABLE B2 (*Cont'd.*)

State	Elec-tricity	Gas	Water & San. Svc.	Fuel & Ice	Fuel	Ice	Tel & Tel	Domestic Service
TOTAL U.S.	616	542	285	1608	1394	214	569	1716
Maine	4	2	2	16	14	2	4	10
New Hampshire	3	2	1	9	8	1	3	6
Vermont	3	1	*	9	8	1	2	5
Massachusetts	31	43	16	151	127	24	32	87
Rhode Island	5	6	2	20	17	4	4	12
Connecticut	14	15	8	45	39	6	13	36
New York	84	123	34	313	228	25	104	396
New Jersey	25	44	15	111	104	7	22	87
Pennsylvania	60	39	17	125	104	21	41	159
Ohio	41	4	18	82	75	7	36	92
Indiana	18	14	4	40	39	1	14	27
Illinois	5C	57	21	150	140	9	63	138
Michigan	2ϵ	42	11	79	71	8	22	65
Wisconsin	15	14	10	45	42	2	15	32
Minnesota	13	7	6	40	38	2	13	30
Iowa	13	10	6	32	31	2	15	21
Missouri	16	14	8	33	14	19	17	38
North Dakota	2	1	1	2	2	*	1	4
South Dakota	2	1	3	3	3	1	2	4
Nebraska	6	4	8	12	11	1	8	11
Kansas	8	0	6	14	11	3	10	12
Delaware	1	1	1	5	5	*	1	8
Maryland	7	12	3	26	21	5	6	40
D.C.	2	2	1	15	11	3	7	39
Virginia	7	7	4	18	16	3	4	24
West Virginia	7	6	3	2	2	*	3	10
North Carolina	6	4	4	10	9	1	2	15
South Carolina	3	2	1	5	3	1	1	8
Georgia	6	7	5	13	11	2	2	21
Florida	10	6	2	5	3	2	2	20
Kentucky	7	1	3	14	11	4	4	11
Tennessee	7	4	4	15	13	2	3	16
Alabama	5	2	5	12	9	3	1	13
Mississippi	3	1	6	4	3	1	1	7
Arkansas	3	*	5	4	1	3	1	5
Louisiana	6	*	3	6	3	3	2	19
Oklahoma	7	*	1	11	2	9	5	13
Texas	18	1	8	25	7	17	12	37
Montana	3	*	2	5	5	*	1	3
Idaho	2	*	2	4	4	*	1	2
Wyoming	1	*	1	1	1	*	1	2
Colorado	5	1	4	14	12	2	5	10
New Mexico	2	*	1	3	2	*	*	2
Arizona	2	2	1	4	2	2	1	3
Utah	3	*	1	7	6	*	1	3
Nevada	1	*	*	1	1	*	1	1
Washington	11	5	3	19	17	2	9	15
Oregon	5	6	2	9	8	1	7	9
California	38	31	14	23	17	6	47	90

Continued on next page

TABLE B2 (Cont'd.)

State	Other Household	Total Medical Care	Drug Prep. & Sundries	Ophthalmic Products	Physicians	Dentists
TOTAL U.S.	316	3104	604	131	959	482
Maine	2	18	4	1	5	2
New Hampshire	2	11	2	*	3	1
Vermont	1	8	2	*	2	1
Massachusetts	7	159	23	11	42	25
Rhode Island	3	19	4	1	5	3
Connecticut	10	55	9	4	13	7
New York	62	523	77	29	156	80
New Jersey	9	114	21	5	33	18
Pennsylvania	24	251	44	8	78	40
Ohio	31	171	32	9	54	27
Indiana	6	72	15	3	25	12
Illinois	23	236	44	8	72	41
Michigan	15	114	25	3	34	17
Wisconsin	14	62	12	2	18	14
Minnesota	9	62	11	2	18	12
Iowa	5	57	13	1	17	10
Missouri	9	90	19	3	32	15
North Dakota	1	9	2	*	3	2
South Dakota	1	11	3	*	3	2
Nebraska	4	32	8	1	10	6
Kansas	3	38	10	*	12	6
Delaware	1	7	1	1	2	1
Maryland	6	45	8	2	15	6
D.C.	3	35	5	3	11	4
Virginia	6	36	8	2	12	4
West Virginia	1	24	5	*	10	4
North Carolina	1	32	8	1	12	4
South Carolina	1	16	4	*	6	2
Georgia	2	39	11	2	14	5
Florida	3	29	8	1	9	4
Kentucky	2	37	9	1	15	5
Tennessee	3	37	9	1	16	5
Alabama	3	29	8	1	11	4
Mississippi	2	18	6	*	7	2
Arkansas	1	22	7	1	10	2
Louisiana	1	31	9	1	11	4
Oklahoma	3	38	12	*	14	5
Texas	7	102	35	2	33	11
Montana	1	10	3	*	3	2
Idaho	1	10	2	2	2	2
Wyoming	0	5	1	*	1	1
Colorado	2	31	6	2	10	5
New Mexico	0	5	1	*	2	1
Arizona	1	10	3	*	3	1
Utah	0	11	3	*	3	2
Nevada	0	3	1	*	1	*
Washington	4	48	10	2	12	9
Oregon	1	29	5	1	8	6
California	25	253	38	11	70	42

Continued on next page

Table B2 (Cont'd.)

State	Other Prof. Services	Private Hospitals	Health Insurance	Personal Business	Brokerage Charges	Bank Chg. & Fin Ser
TOTAL U.S.	250	569	108	3886	784	1048
Maine	2	3	1	25	4	8
New Hampshire	1	3	*	16	3	5
Vermont	1	2	*	13	2	4
Massachusetts	13	41	6	237	53	75
Rhode Island	2	4	1	36	8	10
Connecticut	5	16	2	93	24	23
New York	49	121	19	888	213	309
New Jersey	10	25	4	162	35	43
Pennsylvania	27	48	7	344	80	93
Ohio	13	30	6	220	43	48
Indiana	5	8	3	78	9	15
Illinois	18	46	8	279	63	68
Michigan	9	23	4	160	33	36
Wisconsin	4	10	2	70	13	17
Minnesota	4	13	2	61	10	17
Iowa	4	8	2	53	5	16
Missouri	5	11	3	95	17	23
North Dakota	*	1	*	8	1	2
South Dakota	1	1	*	9	*	3
Nebraska	2	4	1	28	2	7
Kansas	3	5	1	41	3	8
Delaware	1	1	*	16	9	3
Maryland	3	10	2	60	15	15
D.C.	3	9	1	29	6	5
Virginia	2	5	1	39	5	9
West Virginia	1	3	1	36	5	6
North Carolina	2	4	1	41	6	7
South Carolina	1	1	1	20	1	3
Georgia	2	3	1	39	5	6
Florida	2	4	1	30	7	5
Kentucky	2	3	1	43	7	9
Tennessee	2	3	1	41	4	8
Alabama	1	2	1	26	3	5
Mississippi	1	1	1	18	1	4
Arkansas	1	1	1	20	1	4
Louisiana	2	3	1	30	4	8
Oklahoma	2	3	1	39	5	8
Texas	5	9	4	85	12	20
Montana	1	1	*	12	1	3
Idaho	1	1	*	8	*	2
Wyoming	*	1	*	5	*	1
Colorado	3	5	1	27	5	5
New Mexico	*	1	*	4	*	1
Arizona	1	1	*	8	1	2
Utah	1	1	*	11	2	3
Nevada	*	*	*	3	*	1
Washington	4	8	2	40	6	9
Oregon	3	5	1	22	2	5
California	31	56	9	221	49	66

TABLE B2 (Cont'd.)

State	Life Ins.	Legal	Funeral Expenses	Union Dues	Employment Agencies	Other Per Bus	Total Transport
TOTAL U.S.	880	402	607	126	17	22	7721
Maine	5	2	6	1	*	*	46
New Hampshire	3	1	3	1	*	*	28
Vermont	2	1	3	1	*	*	24
Massachusetts	40	19	42	5	1	1	295
Rhode Island	7	2	9	1	*	*	45
Connecticut	16	5	22	2	*	*	116
New York	167	84	85	12	4	7	876
New Jersey	36	19	24	5	1	*	272
Pennsylvania	81	20	54	13	1	2	556
Ohio	56	23	42	8	1	2	496
Indiana	20	9	19	5	*	*	216
Illinois	69	30	34	13	2	3	558
Michigan	58	11	20	3	*	1	382
Wisconsin	18	6	13	3	*	*	193
Minnesota	16	7	9	2	*	*	175
Iowa	14	6	9	3	*	*	174
Missouri	27	13	12	3	*	1	236
North Dakota	2	1	1	*	*	*	44
South Dakota	2	2	2	*	*	*	49
Nebraska	8	4	6	1	*	*	103
Kansas	15	4	8	3	*	*	143
Delaware	3	1	1	*	*	*	18
Maryland	13	7	9	2	*	*	94
D.C.	6	10	3	*	*	*	44
Virginia	11	5	7	1	*	*	95
West Virginia	7	3	10	6	*	*	69
North Carolina	11	5	12	1	*	*	105
South Carolina	6	2	7	1	*	*	50
Georgia	11	5	10	1	*	*	103
Florida	6	5	5	2	*	*	93
Kentucky	10	5	11	2	*	*	85
Tennessee	11	5	11	2	*	*	97
Alabama	9	3	6	1	*	*	81
Mississippi	5	2	5	1	*	*	64
Arkansas	5	3	5	1	*	*	66
Louisiana	7	3	6	1	*	*	79
Oklahoma	8	8	8	2	*	*	155
Texas	17	14	19	4	*	*	356
Montana	2	2	2	2	*	*	40
Idaho	2	1	2	1	*	*	31
Wyoming	1	1	1	1	*	*	19
Colorado	7	4	3	2	*	*	83
New Mexico	1	1	1	*	*	*	19
Arizona	1	1	2	1	*	*	32
Utah	3	1	2	1	*	*	33
Nevada	*	1	1	*	*	*	9
Washington	10	6	6	2	*	*	129
Oregon	6	4	3	1	*	*	77
California	41	29	30	5	2	1	568

Continued on next page

TABLE B2 (*Cont'd.*)

State	User Op. Transport	Motor Vehicles	Tires & Accessories	Parking & Repair	Gas & Oil	Tolls	Auto Insurance
TOTAL U.S.	6069	2697	648	776	1814	40	94
Maine	36	20	3	6	7	*	1
New Hampshire	23	13	1	3	6	*	*
Vermont	21	11	2	3	4	*	*
Massachusetts	210	104	26	24	53	*	3
Rhode Island	35	16	5	5	9	*	1
Connecticut	93	42	11	12	27	*	1
New York	586	272	65	78	143	20	8
New Jersey	210	92	24	35	55	1	3
Pennsylvania	393	181	49	51	104	2	6
Ohio	403	167	49	46	135	*	6
Indiana	175	76	22	22	52	*	3
Illinois	387	174	46	49	112	*	6
Michigan	323	146	30	32	111	*	5
Wisconsin	159	70	15	21	50	*	3
Minnesota	137	56	13	18	47	*	3
Iowa	144	60	15	18	49	*	3
Missouri	182	75	20	29	54	*	3
North Dakota	34	16	2	5	11	*	1
South Dakota	41	17	4	5	15	*	1
Nebraska	87	37	8	11	30	*	2
Kansas	124	51	11	15	45	*	2
Delaware	13	6	1	2	4	*	*
Maryland	63	28	7	8	17	1	1
D.C.	35	15	4	5	12	*	1
Virginia	75	34	7	9	24	*	1
West Virginia	54	24	5	7	18	*	1
North Carolina	95	37	7	11	38	*	2
South Carolina	43	18	3	5	15	1	1
Georgia	84	37	8	10	27	*	1
Florida	80	29	9	9	30	2	1
Kentucky	66	32	6	10	17	*	1
Tennessee	80	38	11	11	19	*	1
Alabama	66	30	7	9	19	*	1
Mississippi	54	27	3	7	17	*	1
Arkansas	56	26	5	7	18	*	1
Louisiana	60	27	6	7	19	*	1
Oklahoma	141	60	14	15	51	*	2
Texas	313	143	29	41	96	*	5
Montana	34	16	3	5	10	*	1
Idaho	26	13	3	4	6	*	*
Wyoming	17	8	1	3	4	*	*
Colorado	71	31	7	9	22	*	1
New Mexico	17	8	2	2	5	*	*
Arizona	30	14	3	4	8	*	*
Utah	29	14	2	4	9	*	*
Nevada	7	4	1	1	1	*	*
Washington	107	49	10	16	29	3	2
Oregon	65	30	7	9	17	1	1
California	483	207	59	62	140	7	7

Continued on next page

Table B2 (Cont'd.)

State	Purchased Local Tran.	Purchased Intercity	Total Rec	Books & Maps	Magazines & Newspapers	Non-Dur Toys
TOTAL U.S.	1117	535	4356	309	538	336
Maine	4	6	19	1	2	2
New Hampshire	1	4	12	1	1	1
Vermont	*	3	7	1	*	1
Massachusetts	74	12	197	13	30	16
Rhode Island	8	1	27	1	2	2
Connecticut	19	4	71	5	6	5
New York	235	56	932	93	172	52
New Jersey	45	17	163	3	6	14
Pennsylvania	131	32	335	18	47	36
Ohio	69	23	261	15	41	22
Indiana	27	15	93	5	9	8
Illinois	127	43	429	34	63	29
Michigan	45	14	181	10	16	15
Wisconsin	19	15	90	4	8	8
Minnesota	19	19	72	3	8	7
Iowa	9	21	62	3	7	5
Missouri	39	16	115	14	14	8
North Dakota	*	10	10	2	1	1
South Dakota	*	7	11	2	1	1
Nebraska	5	11	39	3	4	3
Kansas	3	16	47	4	4	3
Delaware	4	1	11	2	*	1
Maryland	27	4	54	2	4	5
D.C.	8	1	54	4	12	3
Virginia	11	10	36	3	3	4
West Virginia	8	7	23	1	2	3
North Carolina	3	8	31	4	3	3
South Carolina	1	6	13	1	1	2
Georgia	9	11	34	5	4	4
Florida	5	8	34	1	2	3
Kentucky	10	9	31	3	4	2
Tennessee	9	7	34	2	6	4
Alabama	7	9	26	1	3	5
Mississippi	1	9	11	*	1	2
Arkansas	2	8	16	2	1	1
Louisiana	11	8	29	2	3	4
Oklahoma	4	9	43	2	3	4
Texas	20	23	109	7	8	12
Montana	1	5	13	1	1	1
Idaho	1	3	9	1	1	1
Wyoming	1	2	5	*	*	*
Colorado	6	6	37	3	4	3
New Mexico	*	2	5	1	*	*
Arizona	*	2	11	*	1	1
Utah	2	3	15	1	1	1
Nevada	*	1	4	*	*	*
Washington	15	7	69	4	5	5
Oregon	7	4	41	3	3	3
California	66	18	383	21	23	20

Continued on next page

TABLE B2 (*Cont'd.*)

State	Wheel Goods	Radio & Mus. Inst.	Radio Repair	Flowers & Seeds	Spectator Amuse.	Movies	Theater & Opera
TOTAL U.S.	219	1012	26	221	913	720	127
Maine	1	4	*	1	5	4	*
New Hampshire	*	3	*	1	3	3	*
Vermont	*	2	*	*	2	2	*
Massachusetts	5	35	1	12	51	40	5
Rhode Island	1	8	*	2	7	7	1
Connecticut	3	18	1	5	16	14	2
New York	61	189	4	49	173	115	41
New Jersey	8	49	1	11	39	35	5
Pennsylvania	15	73	2	21	75	57	7
Ohio	7	61	2	12	53	42	5
Indiana	8	25	1	4	16	14	2
Illinois	20	88	2	21	89	66	10
Michigan	7	51	1	10	41	32	4
Wisconsin	7	26	1	5	15	13	1
Minnesota	2	17	1	4	15	14	1
Iowa	2	16	*	3	12	11	1
Missouri	3	26	1	6	24	17	2
North Dakota	*	3	*	0	1	1	*
South Dakota	*	2	*	1	2	2	*
Nebraska	1	11	*	1	8	8	1
Kansas	2	16	*	2	8	7	1
Delaware	1	3	*	1	2	2	*
Maryland	4	14	*	3	11	10	1
D.C.	3	7	*	2	10	7	1
Virginia	3	10	*	2	5	5	1
West Virginia	1	7	*	2	4	4	*
North Carolina	3	9	*	2	4	4	1
South Carolina	1	4	*	1	1	1	*
Georgia	1	7	*	2	5	4	1
Florida	3	8	*	2	7	6	1
Kentucky	1	8	*	2	5	4	1
Tennessee	3	8	*	3	4	4	1
Alabama	1	9	*	1	3	3	*
Mississippi	*	4	*	1	2	2	*
Arkansas	*	6	*	1	2	2	*
Louisiana	1	8	*	1	6	5	1
Oklahoma	2	14	*	2	9	8	1
Texas	7	31	*	5	21	18	3
Montana	1	4	*	*	3	3	*
Idaho	1	3	*	*	2	2	*
Wyoming	*	1	*	*	1	1	*
Colorado	3	8	*	2	7	6	1
New Mexico	*	1	*	*	1	1	*
Arizona	1	2	*	*	3	2	*
Utah	1	4	*	1	3	3	*
Nevada	*	1	*	*	1	1	8
Washington	6	15	1	3	17	15	2
Oregon	2	9	*	2	10	9	1
California	18	89	3	13	106	86	20

Continued on next page

TABLE B2 (*Cont'd.*)

State	Spectator Sports	Clubs	Partic. Amuse.	Pari-mutuels	Other Rec.	Total Private Educ	Higher Educ
TOTAL U.S	66	339	170	8	265	769	298
Maine	*	1	1	*	1	5	1
New Hampshire	*	1	1	*	1	5	2
Vermont	*	*	*	*	1	3	1
Massachusetts	5	17	7	*	12	51	26
Rhode Island	*	2	1	*	1	6	2
Connecticut	*	5	4	*	4	14	5
New York	18	59	22	3	54	127	56
New Jersey	*	14	6	*	11	22	6
Pennsylvania	11	21	11	*	14	70	34
Ohio	6	23	12	*	14	46	16
Indiana	*	7	4	*	6	17	8
Illinois	13	42	14	2	25	55	21
Michigan	6	10	9	*	11	31	7
Wisconsin	*	5	6	*	6	15	6
Minnesota	*	6	4	*	6	15	5
Iowa	*	4	3	*	6	18	6
Missouri	5	9	4	*	7	20	8
North Dakota	*	1	1	*	1	2	1
South Dakota	*	1	1	*	1	2	1
Nebraska	*	3	2	*	4	8	3
Kansas	*	4	2	*	4	10	4
Delaware	*	1	*	*	*	1	*
Maryland	*	3	3	1	3	10	5
D.C.	3	8	1	*	4	9	4
Virginia	*	2	2	*	1	11	6
West Virginia	*	1	1	*	1	4	1
North Carolina	*	1	1	*	1	9	5
South Carolina	*	*	*	*	*	5	2
Georgia	*	2	1	*	1	8	4
Florida	*	4	3	*	2	6	1
Kentucky	*	2	2	1	2	10	2
Tennessee	*	2	1	*	1	11	5
Alabama	*	2	1	*	1	7	3
Mississippi	*	1	*	*	1	6	2
Arkansas	*	1	1	*	1	4	1
Louisiana	*	2	1	1	1	9	2
Oklahoma	*	3	2	*	2	8	2
Texas	*	10	3	*	6	18	7
Montana	*	1	1	*	1	2	*
Idaho	*	1	*	*	1	2	*
Wyoming	*	*	*	*	*	1	*
Colorado	*	3	2	*	3	8	3
New Mexico	*	*	*	*	*	2	1
Arizona	*	1	1	*	1	1	*
Utah	*	1	1	*	1	3	1
Nevada	*	*	*	*	*	*	*
Washington	*	8	3	*	5	11	3
Oregon	*	5	2	*	3	6	2
California	*	37	19	*	35	53	15

Continued on next page

TABLE B2 (*Cont'd.*)

State	Elem Educ	Other Educ	Music Teach	Oth Priv Teach	Total Religion & Welfare	Religion	Welfare	Foreign Travel
TOTAL U.S	188	283	189	94	1247	831	417	490
Maine	2	2	1	1	6	5	1	1
New Hampshire	2	1	1	1	4	3	1	1
Vermont	1	1	1	*	3	2	1	*
Massachusetts	11	15	11	4	62	35	27	29
Rhode Island	2	2	2	1	9	6	3	3
Connecticut	3	6	3	3	24	14	10	14
New York	24	47	37	11	218	111	107	164
New Jersey	6	9	7	2	52	34	18	38
Pennsylvania	18	20	12	8	119	86	33	35
Ohio	12	18	11	7	83	52	31	15
Indiana	3	7	4	3	28	23	5	6
Illinois	11	23	18	6	95	60	36	41
Michigan	13	10	7	3	43	26	17	23
Wisconsin	4	5	3	2	25	19	6	9
Minnesota	5	5	3	1	28	19	8	4
Iowa	7	5	3	3	21	18	4	2
Missouri	5	7	4	3	32	23	8	4
North Dakota	1	1	*	1	4	4	*	1
South Dakota	1	1	*	*	5	4	*	1
Nebraska	3	3	2	1	12	10	2	2
Kansas	2	4	2	2	15	14	2	3
Delaware	*	1	*	*	3	2	1	1
Maryland	3	3	2	1	19	14	6	2
D.C.	2	3	2	1	15	6	9	2
Virginia	3	2	1	1	18	15	3	1
West Virginia	1	2	1	1	10	9	1	1
North Carolina	2	2	1	1	21	18	2	*
South Carolina	1	1	*	1	9	8	1	*
Georgia	2	3	1	1	16	14	2	*
Florida	1	3	2	2	16	14	2	2
Kentucky	4	3	1	2	15	13	2	1
Tennessee	2	4	1	3	15	13	2	1
Alabama	2	2	1	1	14	12	2	*
Mississippi	2	2	1	1	9	8	1	*
Arkansas	1	2	1	1	8	8	1	*
Louisiana	5	2	1	1	10	9	2	1
Oklahoma	2	4	2	2	13	11	2	1
Texas	4	8	5	3	35	29	5	11
Montana	1	1	1	1	3	2	1	2
Idaho	*	1	1	*	2	2	*	1
Wyoming	*	*	*	*	1	1	*	1
Colorado	2	3	2	1	9	6	3	3
New Mexico	1	*	*	*	2	1	*	1
Arizona	*	1	*	*	2	2	1	4
Utah	1	1	1	*	3	2	1	3
Nevada	*	*	*	*	*	*	*	1
Washington	2	6	4	2	12	8	4	8
Oregon	1	3	3	1	7	5	2	3
California	7	29	24	5	73	32	40	43

*Less than $1 million.

State	Total PCE	Total Food & Tob	Purch Food	Meals & Bev	Food Furn	Farm Food	Tobacco
TOTAL U.S.	63916	152911	104436	34893	2065	725	10792
Maine	2785	765	563	137	10	3	50
NH	2529	779	588	128	7	1	53
Vermont	1389	406	288	86	5	3	25
Mass	20158	4679	3294	1014	51	2	318
RI	2924	679	465	150	16	*	48
Conn	10640	2465	1760	501	29	2	171
NY	67492	15023	10142	3669	166	16	1052
NJ	25615	6145	4344	1287	72	2	436
Penn	35667	8554	5881	1858	90	26	696
Ohio	32585	7546	5083	1804	64	25	581
Indiana	15474	3590	2373	888	31	19	285
Illinois	37571	8451	5591	2121	82	23	649
Michigan	27833	6571	4507	1532	48	22	468
Wisc	12567	3164	2090	790	29	41	221
Minn	11421	2641	1761	645	27	35	177
Iowa	7920	1828	1229	425	18	30	128
Missouri	13631	3218	2138	754	47	32	248
N. Dakota	1572	360	225	92	6	12	27
S. Dakota	1647	396	251	102	5	12	27
Nebraska	4353	945	603	257	11	14	63
Kansas	6029	1372	958	283	28	10	91
Delaware	2030	505	359	98	7	1	40
Maryland	12819	3229	2274	668	48	5	233
D.C.	4111	919	534	282	25	*	82
Virginia	13297	3249	2295	630	87	26	206
W. Virginia	4243	1069	795	178	9	9	74
N. Car	12532	3348	2374	611	82	48	225
S. Car	6084	1634	1191	284	48	11	96
Georgia	12662	3101	2159	664	71	21	185
Florida	24006	6326	4188	1620	85	8	437
Kentucky	8641	2465	1826	394	44	34	159
Tenn	10396	2629	1821	484	32	32	182
Alabama	8178	2034	1513	331	41	23	119
Miss	4758	1225	916	188	26	21	70
Arkansas	4427	1159	872	177	13	16	76
Louisiana	9332	2345	1641	461	48	13	180
Oklahoma	6925	1641	1130	330	28	15	135
Texas	33383	7872	5462	1644	132	31	597
Montana	1952	539	354	138	5	9	35
Idaho	1943	497	341	116	4	9	27
Wyoming	994	248	155	73	2	3	16
Colorado	7269	1704	1109	449	27	7	115
N. Mexico	2686	690	461	164	8	4	53
Arizona	5742	1436	957	352	17	5	106
Utah	3125	664	467	151	4	4	37
Nevada	2370	629	298	298	4	1	38
Wash	10900	2611	1762	637	45	14	157
Oregon	6776	1719	1174	408	11	11	117
Cal	72774	16829	11299	4165	242	12	1138
Alaska	939	279	175	79	11	*	13
Hawaii	2839	739	400	297	18	1	31

Continued on next page

TABLE B3 (*Cont'd.*)

State	Total Cloth & Acc.	Shoes	Shoe Repair	Cloth	Women's & Ch. Cloth	Men's & Boys' Cloth	Milit.	Clean & Laund	Jewel.
TOTAL U.S.	57639	7778	305	39849	25591	14258	161	4178	4096
Maine	224	32	1	157	96	61	1	14	15
NH	185	25	1	131	84	48	*	14	11
Vermont	92	13	*	65	40	25	*	6	7
Mass	1879	238	8	1341	882	459	3	129	115
RI	282	33	1	200	133	67	2	21	16
Conn	935	114	4	662	431	230	1	63	62
NY	6543	845	37	4481	2941	1538	4	502	505
NJ	2342	304	10	1664	1092	572	6	180	140
Penn	3421	458	20	2432	1578	854	2	212	230
Ohio	2940	391	13	2029	1298	731	2	201	229
Indiana	1341	181	6	944	602	342	1	103	84
Illinois	3783	489	16	2653	1729	924	4	301	232
Michigan	2493	342	9	1747	1120	627	2	168	159
Wisc	1033	146	5	735	463	272	1	67	62
Minn	1016	127	5	748	461	287	1	52	60
Iowa	676	90	3	460	283	176	1	72	41
Missouri	1273	175	7	881	564	317	4	91	89
N. Dakota	141	20	1	102	62	40	*	8	8
S. Dakota	138	23	1	95	57	38	*	8	8
Nebraska	362	51	2	255	160	96	*	21	24
Kansas	485	70	2	332	203	129	3	39	32
Delaware	189	24	1	140	90	49	*	9	13
Maryland	1168	157	6	821	534	287	5	78	77
D.C.	360	48	2	226	149	77	2	44	29
Virginia	1215	174	6	827	526	301	11	97	80
W. Virginia	403	56	2	278	180	98	*	33	27
N. Car	1201	170	10	820	521	299	10	100	74
S. Car	573	78	5	386	242	145	6	53	36
Georgia	1230	168	7	827	536	292	7	92	98
Florida	2003	260	10	1356	893	462	5	149	157
Kentucky	654	95	4	439	276	162	5	56	45
Tenn	984	137	5	675	433	242	2	73	71
Alabama	738	103	4	503	321	182	3	54	58
Miss	414	60	2	289	183	106	1	31	27
Arkansas	381	59	2	257	163	94	2	31	26
Louisiana	876	133	5	602	377	226	3	46	71
Oklahoma	615	91	4	420	262	158	3	45	44
Texas	3135	429	19	2128	1344	785	11	236	240
Montana	155	23	1	111	66	45	*	10	8
Idaho	144	23	1	99	59	40	*	10	10
Wyoming	73	11	1	51	31	20	*	5	4
Colorado	600	81	4	411	256	155	4	46	43
N. Mexico	225	34	1	154	95	59	1	17	16
Arizona	463	66	3	316	203	114	1	30	38
Utah	251	36	2	176	107	69	*	14	18
Nevada	187	24	1	125	78	47	*	17	17
Wash	836	124	5	574	364	210	6	50	59
Oregon	511	83	4	347	216	131	*	31	36
Cal	6142	825	36	4160	2673	1485	26	429	508
Alaska	78	10	*	50	29	20	2	8	7
Hawaii	252	28	1	169	106	63	3	14	31

Continued on next page

TABLE B3 (*Cont'd.*)

State	Other Acc.	Total Pers Care	Toilet Articles	Barber & Beauty	Total Housing	Non-Farm Owned	Non-Farm Rented
TOTAL U.S.	1272	11812	6635	5177	93967	61300	25962
Maine	4	45	26	19	287	159	93
NH	1	38	21	17	272	152	93
Vermont	2	20	12	8	132	52	47
Mass	43	331	182	149	2879	1989	774
RI	9	52	30	22	435	311	112
Conn	33	178	96	82	1673	1266	363
NY	185	1028	568	462	9732	6170	3171
NJ	30	385	224	159	4440	3297	1001
Penn	67	615	346	270	4273	2884	1095
Ohio	76	619	344	275	4743	3494	982
Indiana	16	289	162	128	1801	1179	444
Illinois	81	718	416	300	5829	4118	1415
Michigan	64	526	301	225	4139	3046	875
Wisc	14	226	120	107	1852	1240	454
Minn	22	212	119	94	1826	1211	410
Iowa	6	161	85	77	1034	664	253
Missouri	24	288	155	135	1870	1217	430
N. Dakota	1	32	19	14	194	92	65
S. Dakota	2	32	18	14	188	85	59
Nebraska	9	87	47	40	545	314	152
Kansas	6	129	68	62	811	498	225
Delaware	2	35	21	14	250	165	67
Maryland	23	228	126	103	1758	1112	548
D.C.	11	58	28	30	635	414	175
Virginia	17	231	125	107	1925	1149	589
W. Virginia	6	81	46	35	528	365	118
N. Car	18	266	141	127	1270	680	407
S. Car	8	115	66	49	675	392	184
Georgia	33	244	135	109	1519	895	439
Florida	75	447	283	159	3867	2314	1121
Kentucky	11	159	91	67	1376	988	262
Tenn	20	223	122	101	1073	568	339
Alabama	11	158	87	71	973	640	226
Miss	2	90	54	36	520	278	127
Arkansas	2	100	54	47	520	285	142
Louisiana	16	176	110	64	1297	812	354
Oklahoma	7	148	82	66	915	565	263
Texas	74	705	398	307	4624	2577	1714
Montana	1	37	23	13	251	134	73
Idaho	1	39	23	16	259	142	72
Wyoming	1	18	11	7	155	79	49
Colorado	12	139	78	61	1179	711	364
N. Mexico	2	53	32	21	383	227	116
Arizona	8	123	69	54	925	566	283
Utah	6	57	34	24	474	337	101
Nevada	2	42	24	18	419	202	125
Wash	20	203	118	84	1793	1159	518
Oregon	12	126	71	56	968	565	317
Cal	175	1434	790	644	13712	9128	4105
Alaska	1	17	11	6	157	61	83
Hawaii	5	47	24	23	612	353	169

Continued on next page

TABLE B3 (Cont'd.)

State	Total HH Op	Furn	Household Applian	China & Dur.	Other Dur.	Semi-Dur Furn.	Clean & Pol.	Station
TOTAL U.S.	84714	8571	7257	3471	7901	4919	8163	2348
Maine	410	28	26	13	46	21	41	15
NH	339	25	25	12	44	18	31	10
Vermont	212	15	14	8	26	9	23	6
Mass	2465	229	180	103	237	139	155	71
RI	363	35	27	19	36	23	18	9
Conn	1386	138	105	53	118	76	127	42
NY	8031	819	571	394	570	424	733	202
NJ	3358	346	265	129	261	180	332	67
Penn	4970	482	415	190	391	262	526	149
Ohio	4416	452	370	197	434	242	421	129
Indiana	2146	209	204	78	218	115	223	76
Illinois	4834	522	421	230	477	323	389	156
Michigan	3717	387	343	136	424	207	399	103
Wisc	1693	164	150	67	195	93	148	62
Minn	1633	155	124	79	225	105	136	49
Iowa	1155	100	97	40	137	60	101	29
Missouri	1451	181	152	76	198	125	168	65
N. Dakota	234	21	22	8	33	13	22	9
S. Dakota	248	20	21	7	37	13	24	5
Nebraska	607	67	57	21	63	33	50	20
Kansas	841	74	57	32	91	51	79	22
Delaware	294	33	29	11	23	18	33	9
Maryland	1714	183	114	71	138	97	169	44
D.C.	391	50	32	19	21	19	21	12
Virginia	1923	197	166	73	162	104	161	55
W. Virginia	579	61	59	25	66	33	62	17
N. Car	1914	203	171	61	166	108	183	49
S. Car	948	98	85	29	78	50	76	31
Georgia	1852	199	180	52	171	107	141	42
Florida	3365	364	326	129	272	189	313	110
Kentucky	1086	101	90	37	116	60	138	29
Tenn	1584	150	152	51	151	93	155	41
Alabama	1334	125	124	40	115	72	123	35
Miss	744	64	71	20	64	40	61	13
Arkansas	670	61	64	19	69	37	73	12
Louisiana	1382	124	150	46	109	84	139	43
Oklahoma	1028	95	90	35	89	69	107	42
Texas	4672	430	442	184	379	293	424	135
Montana	263	24	21	11	35	15	29	4
Idaho	265	25	21	10	32	14	30	3
Wyoming	123	10	10	4	17	7	15	3
Colorado	919	101	84	41	97	56	91	26
N. Mexico	348	37	33	15	35	24	43	10
Arizona	738	80	65	28	68	48	76	22
Utah	385	49	32	15	36	27	40	10
Nevada	255	24	19	11	23	14	27	7
Wash	1423	148	114	56	145	80	129	46
Oregon	934	83	70	35	102	50	102	25
Cal	8661	950	757	430	818	548	1017	165
Alaska	130	10	11	6	19	7	16	4
Hawaii	279	24	29	16	23	24	24	11

Continued on next page

TABLE B3 (Cont'd.)

State	Total Utilities	Electric	Gas	Water & Sanit.	Fuel & Ice	Phone & Telegraph	Domestic Service	Other
TOTAL U.S.	22652	9604	5557	3068	4423	10088	4499	4845
Maine	144	41	3	7	91	43	23	10
NH	108	33	7	4	61	37	15	14
Vermont	75	25	2	4	42	19	13	5
Mass	842	225	167	46	391	285	92	134
RI	121	29	23	9	58	45	14	17
Conn	405	139	60	15	183	175	77	70
NY	2246	707	520	237	742	984	509	578
NJ	984	279	251	106	331	411	133	250
Penn	1420	476	389	212	315	654	210	271
Ohio	1252	470	460	213	80	537	161	221
Indiana	627	276	161	72	105	255	76	65
Illinois	1309	497	486	127	172	594	165	248
Michigan	981	295	373	181	114	444	124	169
Wisc	495	191	141	51	102	201	53	67
Minn	447	196	117	53	71	195	52	67
Iowa	356	154	100	34	60	144	45	48
Missouri	55	218	152	56	90	233	84	114
N. Dakota	65	35	8	5	15	28	8	5
S. Dakota	74	38	13	4	17	30	11	7
Nebraska	167	71	50	17	25	77	23	29
Kansas	234	103	70	30	26	114	39	46
Delaware	74	27	14	10	22	32	21	10
Maryland	453	176	113	63	92	208	94	144
D.C.	84	20	24	20	18	53	61	19
Virginia	544	251	76	97	108	204	132	125
W. Virginia	158	73	56	16	9	66	28	4
N. Car	524	278	37	61	137	204	150	96
S. Car	263	153	27	24	53	101	94	43
Georgia	471	231	97	69	65	203	173	113
Florida	845	557	29	122	116	344	257	216
Kentucky	288	131	79	43	35	124	58	44
Tenn	459	300	45	63	38	168	103	63
Alabama	373	215	68	37	44	136	119	71
Miss	224	135	31	15	38	78	79	29
Arkansas	186	87	40	19	36	72	46	29
Louisiana	321	193	64	30	26	155	128	84
Oklahoma	280	137	71	37	28	123	50	48
Texas	1217	659	232	188	109	535	319	313
Montana	78	35	22	7	11	30	8	10
Idaho	77	46	10	7	13	30	9	14
Wyoming	31	10	9	4	8	16	5	6
Colorado	226	76	61	65	20	112	31	53
N. Mexico	82	31	24	12	13	38	17	16
Arizona	183	103	38	26	12	77	34	56
Utah	92	31	37	16	7	50	8	24
Nevada	81	43	10	14	11	24	7	19
Wash	418	184	45	90	91	167	51	70
Oregon	286	142	31	44	63	100	30	51
Cal	1832	729	608	372	83	1097	444	603
Alaska	41	16	3	5	15	6	3	9
Hawaii	57	35	3	9	8	31	14	26

Continued on next page

TABLE B3 (Cont'd.)

State	Total Med. Care	Drug Prep	Ophthalm. & Orth.	Phys.	Dentists	Other Prof.	Priv. Hosp.	Health Insur.
TOTAL U.S.	56056	8062	1861	13975	4872	3179	19693	4414
Maine	258	29	8	69	19	16	87	31
NH	169	18	7	43	18	11	62	12
Vermont	125	11	3	30	10	8	52	12
Mass	2005	203	78	450	171	102	895	109
RI	277	37	13	71	18	15	115	8
Conn	1001	124	32	251	99	53	358	83
NY	5543	602	185	1624	581	349	1834	380
NJ	2026	241	68	607	204	112	626	164
Penn	3306	380	120	780	240	207	1370	230
Ohio	2946	395	99	722	219	156	1120	238
Indiana	1454	233	48	366	102	68	511	122
Illinois	3361	537	128	674	255	159	1235	365
Michigan	2499	412	70	477	200	138	1065	145
Wisc	1177	138	44	200	108	52	502	130
Minn	890	138	42	139	105	52	389	28
Iowa	774	103	33	185	68	66	251	77
Missouri	1270	210	46	246	90	96	475	121
N. Dakota	145	25	6	22	12	9	64	8
S. Dakota	156	30	9	30	12	12	39	25
Nebraska	415	58	17	94	38	19	139	47
Kansas	605	89	21	149	53	45	196	57
Delaware	190	20	6	43	12	8	71	30
Maryland	1159	186	34	339	99	55	376	64
D.C.	421	80	14	75	16	12	167	55
Virginia	1117	194	37	273	100	52	352	104
W. Virginia	432	51	15	103	27	23	171	44
N. Car	1083	160	33	273	94	58	349	113
S. Car	477	76	15	110	33	22	153	67
Georgia	1070	158	35	284	81	46	320	137
Florida	1707	331	65	393	139	116	491	174
Kentucky	710	103	25	185	49	35	242	68
Tenn	954	142	30	224	68	43	359	85
Alabama	743	106	20	184	52	26	310	40
Miss	414	63	12	113	29	18	134	42
Arkansas	343	62	10	85	29	15	100	39
Louisiana	723	107	19	199	62	31	248	52
Oklahoma	604	92	22	150	46	41	212	45
Texas	2907	445	74	845	207	147	918	258
Montana	166	29	9	38	17	12	43	18
Idaho	179	35	6	49	16	9	48	15
Wyoming	91	18	3	23	7	5	29	5
Colorado	669	104	26	150	59	37	256	36
N. Mexico	212	36	7	57	17	16	67	12
Arizona	464	89	13	109	40	30	163	20
Utah	269	65	11	57	28	14	80	13
Nevada	151	31	3	35	13	8	50	9
Wash	977	159	31	246	121	61	249	109
Oregon	576	87	22	151	74	41	174	29
Cal	6611	979	178	1894	684	438	2111	322
Alaska	40	13	2	12	5	2	11	4
Hawaii	193	30	7	44	27	11	57	16

Continued on next page

TABLE B3 (*Cont'd.*)

State	Total Pers Bus	Broker	Bank Service	Financial Intermed.	Life Insur.	Legal Services	Funeral Services	Other Per. Bus.
TOTAL U.S.	32124	2301	2028	11166	6964	4895	2342	2428
Maine	120	15	5	37	28	16	13	7
NH	94	9	4	34	24	9	8	5
Vermont	52	5	2	16	13	9	5	3
Mass	1077	103	59	391	201	175	74	73
RI	142	12	6	47	32	22	13	10
Conn	581	72	24	184	130	95	40	37
NY	5043	363	455	2162	702	767	241	324
NJ	1197	99	47	370	298	209	88	90
Penn	1873	153	113	620	419	225	150	188
Ohio	1620	111	80	493	388	242	142	170
Indiana	725	39	45	220	181	100	68	73
Illinois	2130	131	141	728	435	355	150	194
Michigan	1244	89	61	361	326	169	104	137
Wisc	597	46	33	193	138	85	51	52
Minn	522	30	35	177	122	73	39	45
Iowa	404	18	26	139	93	67	41	21
Missouri	782	53	55	269	164	98	73	69
N. Dakota	74	1	5	30	17	11	6	3
S. Dakota	74	2	5	28	18	11	7	2
Nebraska	230	12	17	82	50	38	21	11
Kansas	313	21	22	109	72	48	28	13
Delaware	108	18	6	36	26	9	6	6
Maryland	563	44	24	146	132	135	36	53
D.C.	239	16	14	98	43	51	11	6
Virginia	567	44	29	152	160	104	49	32
W. Virginia	199	10	12	56	43	28	27	23
N. Car	529	38	31	166	146	67	60	22
S. Car	251	12	13	81	73	34	27	11
Georgia	580	30	34	190	160	81	51	34
Florida	1066	124	60	379	207	157	86	50
Kentucky	397	23	26	125	85	67	46	28
Tenn	481	19	31	148	120	84	47	34
Alabama	344	14	22	112	106	39	22	28
Miss	204	7	15	69	47	30	25	11
Arkansas	196	8	14	71	40	26	26	11
Louisiana	445	19	30	143	109	83	39	25
Oklahoma	348	16	26	128	80	51	31	17
Texas	1626	92	124	609	362	241	119	77
Montana	89	6	6	29	19	16	8	7
Idaho	81	4	5	28	20	11	7	4
Wyoming	46	5	3	15	10	8	3	2
Colorado	324	23	19	111	78	53	19	23
N. Mexico	101	6	7	33	28	16	7	6
Arizona	220	20	12	72	55	32	15	15
Utah	128	8	7	46	34	16	8	9
Nevada	74	4	4	27	14	13	4	7
Wash	441	25	22	154	105	60	26	49
Oregon	276	18	13	90	62	47	20	26
Cal	3151	250	172	1108	702	498	151	271
Alaska	34	1	3	13	8	5	1	3
Hawaii	122	9	6	42	38	12	4	10

Continued on next page

TABLE B3 (Cont'd.)

State	Total Transp	User Operat.	New Autos	Used Autos	Other Vehicles	Tire & Acc.	Parking & Rep.
TOTAL U.S.	81396	74417	21945	5154	2667	6087	12239
Maine	380	353	98	28	15	34	45
NH	319	294	91	23	16	24	38
Vermont	176	160	50	13	6	11	16
Mass	2230	1955	600	130	35	135	350
RI	325	293	92	21	7	29	45
Conn	1207	1105	351	71	23	61	176
NY	6924	5637	1653	275	102	479	1315
NJ	2903	2570	819	135	38	186	451
Penn	4358	4011	1242	308	100	346	700
Ohio	4288	4015	1220	299	123	331	577
Indiana	2142	2019	617	159	84	144	245
Illinois	4753	4308	1411	273	110	344	689
Michigan	3677	3450	1166	226	160	237	479
Wisc	1578	1461	441	121	54	139	184
Minn	1460	1338	366	89	51	130	187
Iowa	1133	1066	306	83	40	89	141
Missouri	1990	1867	528	123	55	194	319
N. Dakota	231	217	65	18	7	25	22
S. Dakota	250	237	61	19	10	24	29
Nebraska	626	590	154	41	22	53	82
Kansas	922	869	246	68	42	74	106
Delaware	237	221	64	16	10	16	38
Maryland	1631	1494	482	87	33	99	275
D.C.	342	284	66	11	5	22	97
Virginia	1799	1612	524	129	47	109	208
W. Virginia	553	516	161	46	19	49	46
N. Car	1826	1731	539	160	66	128	250
S. Car	875	834	253	66	26	80	113
Georgia	1884	1780	522	119	68	152	318
Florida	3153	2940	876	242	138	180	540
Kentucky	1070	1005	277	95	24	96	114
Tenn	1512	1436	436	121	45	114	226
Alabama	1140	1083	342	96	38	95	158
Miss	695	663	210	51	19	70	78
Arkansas	672	638	196	57	22	53	87
Louisiana	1210	1129	357	66	31	118	152
Oklahoma	1001	943	270	65	49	92	150
Texas	4672	4388	1314	282	142	451	677
Montana	283	265	69	21	15	30	26
Idaho	292	269	65	21	21	29	32
Wyoming	155	146	33	9	6	13	15
Colorado	978	903	248	67	49	79	164
N. Mexico	410	384	103	26	18	38	48
Arizona	782	734	171	52	54	59	137
Utah	439	415	103	30	22	50	69
Nevada	298	265	58	17	16	17	48
Wash	1415	1282	275	93	86	137	189
Oregon	963	878	214	67	68	75	142
Cal	8869	8051	2087	526	417	512	1550
Alaska	107	87	19	4	8	8	13
Hawaii	285	251	33	13	7	25	82

Continued on next page

TABLE B3 (Cont'd.)

State	Gas & Oil	Tolls	Auto Ins.	Purchased Local	Purch. Intercit	Total Recreat.	Books & Maps
TOTAL U.S.	21921	652	3752	2988	3991	42713	2922
Maine	108	7	18	5	22	191	9
NH	85	3	14	5	20	211	15
Vermont	55	*	9	4	11	109	12
Mass	539	33	134	158	117	1392	84
RI	79	2	17	13	19	224	11
Conn	334	22	66	38	64	648	39
NY	1336	95	382	882	405	5340	203
NJ	716	76	150	140	193	1779	135
Penn	1090	44	182	199	148	2536	180
Ohio	1227	25	213	105	167	2194	157
Indiana	661	13	96	30	93	927	55
Illinois	1200	35	245	271	175	2655	171
Michigan	1005	5	172	74	153	1962	100
Wisc	442	1	78	45	72	721	24
Minn	437	3	76	45	76	733	28
Iowa	360	*	46	15	51	472	35
Missouri	561	1	86	50	72	851	78
N. Dakota	71	*	9	2	11	108	9
S. Dakota	84	*	11	2	11	108	9
Nebraska	210	*	28	10	26	359	80
Kansas	287	10	36	9	44	339	33
Delaware	63	5	8	5	11	149	4
Maryland	432	25	60	41	97	870	37
D.C.	73	*	10	47	11	269	5
Virginia	516	20	60	56	131	763	52
W. Virginia	163	5	26	12	25	294	21
N. Car	497	3	89	30	66	691	47
S. Car	261	4	31	7	34	335	41
Georgia	532	5	63	27	77	712	53
Florida	833	31	100	54	158	1370	44
Kentucky	347	10	42	24	40	466	24
Tenn	441	*	53	31	45	551	30
Alabama	300	5	48	17	40	460	37
Miss	205	3	27	5	28	306	29
Arkansas	194	*	29	7	28	280	29
Louisiana	328	12	64	33	47	603	29
Oklahoma	266	10	41	10	48	404	20
Texas	1291	26	206	82	202	2084	220
Montana	91	*	12	4	14	122	7
Idaho	86	*	14	3	21	127	11
Wyoming	65	*	5	2	7	62	7
Colorado	258	*	38	16	59	514	39
N. Mexico	138	*	14	8	18	193	22
Arizona	233	*	29	10	38	393	43
Utah	125	*	17	7	17	241	30
Nevada	100	*	9	16	17	270	10
Wash	396	32	74	22	111	820	65
Oregon	257	9	46	19	66	475	57
Cal	2444	61	454	272	546	4772	402
Alaska	29	1	5	4	15	71	5
Hawaii	72	6	13	10	24	183	35

Continued on next page

TABLE B3 (Cont'd.)

State	Magaz News	Non-Dur Toys	Wheel Goods	T.V. & Radio	Rad. T.V. Repair	Seeds & Plants	Spectat. Amusem.
TOTAL U.S.	4097	5498	5191	8540	1383	1798	3296
Maine	24	10	28	50	6	8	15
NH	13	23	31	37	4	8	22
Vermont	7	4	22	23	2	3	12
Mass	225	244	143	264	33	54	104
RI	27	34	21	44	5	8	17
Conn	65	130	84	148	18	30	28
NY	602	743	450	1099	129	164	583
NJ	137	382	172	394	59	64	110
Penn	304	443	223	587	71	106	153
Ohio	249	205	224	481	68	98	138
Indiana	112	70	115	253	29	47	58
Illinois	255	456	263	506	81	115	225
Michigan	191	215	305	462	53	78	145
Wisc	92	56	143	135	27	31	64
Minn	78	110	132	132	20	31	61
Iowa	61	31	52	121	21	24	31
Missouri	87	74	94	211	32	44	65
N. Dakota	10	5	16	36	3	4	5
S. Dakota	9	6	12	28	4	4	10
Nebraska	27	18	33	97	13	13	33
Kansas	26	36	46	90	15	20	19
Delaware	9	28	17	22	5	6	28
Maryland	59	243	96	165	31	32	74
D.C.	76	20	19	27	8	12	15
Virginia	57	100	88	207	29	43	51
W. Virginia	27	9	23	96	7	18	39
N. Car	67	63	85	175	30	45	43
S. Car	24	10	40	106	15	19	22
Georgia	54	89	92	168	27	45	43
Florida	111	203	234	208	66	62	167
Kentucky	39	43	43	125	16	30	46
Tenn	63	33	76	140	24	39	39
Alabama	37	20	53	145	19	30	33
Miss	13	13	31	106	12	17	23
Arkansas	19	9	34	86	12	14	29
Louisiana	42	46	82	154	28	26	50
Oklahoma	37	24	58	103	16	23	31
Texas	138	243	278	593	79	100	177
Montana	11	13	25	26	3	5	10
Idaho	10	8	29	33	4	5	8
Wyoming	3	3	11	13	3	3	4
Colorado	36	34	114	115	18	21	43
N. Mexico	9	17	27	49	6	6	17
Arizona	34	32	50	91	12	14	28
Utah	19	15	53	60	9	9	16
Nevada	11	16	20	21	5	5	12
Wash	69	70	135	171	24	26	80
Oregon	31	43	90	13	19	16	9
Cal	372	740	637	117	159	157	253
Alaska	4	4	17	2	1	1	1
Hawaii	15	10	22	5	3	11	8

Continued on next page

TABLE B3 (Cont'd.)

State	Movies	Theaters & Opera	Comm Sports	Clubs	Commer. Amusem.	Pari-mutuels	Other Recreat.
TOTAL U.S.	1629	527	1135	1465	2367	1095	5065
Maine	5	1	7	11	6	4	22
NH	5	1	15	5	9	23	24
Vermont	3	*	5	3	9	7	9
Mass	57	9	45	43	55	29	108
RI	6	1	9	6	9	28	16
Conn	24	4	2	29	25	*	49
NY	123	258	195	207	351	390	425
NJ	59	8	34	45	79	78	133
Penn	80	14	49	81	83	45	269
Ohio	71	11	58	65	126	39	342
Indiana	35	1	11	32	37	*	131
Illinois	97	39	89	93	123	105	261
Michigan	63	12	52	42	94	48	249
Wisc	27	4	8	22	41	*	112
Minn	31	5	11	26	37	*	90
Iowa	23	1	3	16	22	*	62
Missouri	40	5	20	41	45	*	80
N. Dakota	4	*	1	5	4	*	12
S. Dakota	5	*	5	5	6	*	15
Nebraska	14	1	9	9	16	5	24
Kansas	18	1	2	11	18	*	23
Delaware	3	1	21	4	5	16	10
Maryland	26	3	39	22	44	33	37
D.C.	11	5	5	59	8	*	13
Virginia	30	1	7	21	33	*	93
W. Virginia	9	*	19	11	12	24	18
N. Car	38	2	9	24	30	*	76
S. Car	16	*	3	11	16	*	34
Georgia	39	2	12	25	29	*	75
Florida	69	5	119	31	118	42	58
Kentucky	19	2	24	25	21	15	39
Tenn	19	6	4	20	36	*	62
Alabama	19	*	1	20	14	*	65
Miss	12	*	*	29	9	*	36
Arkansas	11	*	10	10	11	6	28
Louisiana	25	1	16	21	24	11	97
Oklahoma	22	*	2	16	17	*	66
Texas	103	9	24	63	89	*	145
Montana	6	*	*	6	5	*	14
Idaho	6	*	1	3	5	*	12
Wyoming	3	*	*	2	4	*	10
Colorado	26	3	13	14	30	2	50
N. Mexico	10	*	8	8	6	2	23
Arizona	16	1	11	16	17	3	54
Utah	13	*	1	6	9	*	17
Nevada	5	4	1	3	153	*	15
Wash	27	4	10	25	36	6	152
Oregon	17	1	6	11	19	2	151
Cal	222	100	135	155	360	132	1085
Alaska	4	*	1	3	2	*	26
Hawaii	12	1	6	5	14	*	46

Continued on next page

APPENDIX B: STATE ESTIMATES

TABLE B3 (Cont'd.)

State	Total Private Education	Higher Education	Element. Education	Other Education	Religion & Wel.	Foreign Travel
TOTAL U.S.	12500	6600	3223	2575	11968	4514
Maine	58	29	20	9	34	23
NH	86	48	28	10	33	20
Vermont	47	31	12	4	19	10
Mass	772	531	152	89	466	170
RI	83	52	21	11	55	27
Conn	315	150	108	57	204	100
NY	1793	1082	451	260	2137	723
NJ	412	164	144	104	389	296
Penn	917	552	242	123	806	229
Ohio	612	327	160	125	597	178
Indiana	236	123	67	46	781	84
Illinois	811	462	205	144	197	210
Michigan	425	213	138	74	491	162
Wisc	223	112	78	33	273	70
Minn	197	103	61	33	267	61
Iowa	161	106	30	25	115	45
Missouri	304	169	90	45	311	80
N. Dakota	21	11	6	4	27	9
S. Dakota	29	18	6	5	25	9
Nebraska	83	46	23	14	87	25
Kansas	98	46	25	27	90	41
Delaware	31	9	15	7	32	13
Maryland	276	152	73	51	190	87
D.C.	218	170	28	20	299	19
Virginia	234	92	83	59	214	90
W. Virginia	40	23	8	9	41	31
N. Car	142	41	34	67	204	70
S. Car	94	46	17	31	90	33
Georgia	228	121	48	59	220	66
Florida	328	135	95	98	304	116
Kentucky	115	55	34	26	119	42
Tenn	222	135	44	43	179	52
Alabama	117	60	22	35	116	43
Miss	69	35	16	18	62	25
Arkansas	42	18	6	12	53	23
Louisiana	125	34	59	32	116	46
Oklahoma	80	40	13	27	116	40
Texas	441	181	102	158	519	189
Montana	24	9	6	9	15	11
Idaho	26	8	3	15	21	17
Wyoming	9	5	1	3	8	6
Colorado	138	66	28	44	88	40
N. Mexico	36	14	10	12	25	15
Arizona	87	30	30	27	87	34
Utah	43	20	9	14	166	16
Nevada	15	5	2	8	16	16
Wash	128	43	34	51	175	91
Oregon	95	40	21	34	90	56
Cal	1255	628	282	345	943	613
Alaska	8	3	1	4	9	10
Hawaii	58	8	36	14	48	24

*Less than $1 million.

State Aggregates for Personal Consumption, 1977
(in $ millions)

State	Total PCE[a]	Total Food & Tob.	Off-Prem Cons	Pur Meals & Bev.	Food Furn.	Farm Food	Tobacco	Alcohol[b]
TOTAL U.S.	1267220	272924	182538	68564	3749	1093	16980	15640
Maine	5720	1374	963	289	18	3	102	92
NH	5393	1397	998	276	12	2	109	141
Vermont	2694	645	441	140	10	6	47	58
Mass	35334	7822	5233	1987	71	2	529	588
RI	5325	1178	787	272	11	*	108	72
Conn	19271	4132	2833	967	60	2	270	181
NY	106316	21430	14632	5266	394	27	1111	1036
NJ	44515	9912	6993	2255	104	4	557	625
Penn	65977	14505	9875	3248	382	36	963	758
Ohio	61289	13498	8873	3502	124	31	968	611
Indiana	29343	6465	4230	1676	60	25	474	29
Illinois	69958	14448	9342	3925	127	23	1032	864
Michigan	53946	11628	7673	3032	95	47	781	548
Wisc	25509	5762	3710	1570	41	54	386	271
Minn	23741	4825	3135	1269	39	57	325	292
Iowa	14471	3083	2198	651	27	56	152	157
Missouri	26900	5790	3776	1484	67	57	405	270
N. Dakota	3561	685	428	191	6	10	49	42
S. Dakota	3466	728	462	198	8	13	47	40
Nebraska	8515	1816	1201	500	18	18	79	81
Kansas	12407	2577	1735	633	31	17	161	111
Delaware	3764	840	587	182	17	1	52	57
Maryland	25168	5899	4086	1394	75	7	338	417
D.C.	6338	1122	606	408	48	*	60	161
Virginia	28069	6112	4211	1411	107	38	344	320
W. Virginia	8885	2021	1471	378	22	13	138	98
N. Car	26337	5950	3985	1359	119	77	410	352
S. Car	13005	3048	2104	680	76	18	169	154
Georgia	25837	5794	3821	1410	137	32	394	409
Florida	56039	12235	7860	3210	208	12	945	920
Kentucky	16498	3883	2599	851	47	63	323	226
Tenn	22167	4719	3150	1120	81	63	305	242
Alabama	16866	3753	2660	774	93	33	193	228
Miss	9590	2179	1556	396	61	34	132	97
Arkansas	9663	2191	1557	433	36	25	141	111
Louisiana	20173	4662	3177	1039	100	16	328	268
Oklahoma	14818	3219	2171	735	41	23	249	121
Texas	75484	16075	10792	4007	255	35	986	854
Montana	4420	1054	695	287	6	8	58	75
Idaho	4640	1067	725	271	7	7	57	65
Wyoming	2566	586	398	149	4	3	31	39
Colorado	16786	3566	2323	1062	24	11	146	210
N. Mexico	6321	1479	1019	373	13	5	67	108
Arizona	14390	3070	2001	812	28	9	220	195
Utah	7327	1325	914	345	6	5	55	57
Nevada	6175	1017	666	278	5	1	67	91
Wash	23944	5261	3542	1438	39	19	224	335
Oregon	15876	3463	2287	948	23	14	191	198
Cal	152414	31363	20726	8663	354	27	1593	2214
Alaska	3065	787	494	259	3	*	31	55
Hawaii	6777	1485	838	559	11	1	76	95

Continued on next page

TABLE B4 (*Cont'd.*)

State	Total Clothing	Shoes	Cloth Exc Shoes	Women's & Child	Men's Clothing	Std Mil Clothing	Clean, Laund & Shoe
TOTAL U.S.	102780	12211	71902	45948	25834	121	4945
Maine	428	64	300	168	132	1	17
NH	367	41	273	168	105	*	21
Vermont	158	22	115	73	42	*	6
Mass	2893	346	2100	1367	728	1	135
RI	419	43	297	195	101	*	21
Conn	1500	158	1091	718	371	1	77
NY	9175	1100	6318	4140	2161	3	492
NJ	3858	431	2784	1799	979	2	193
Penn	5715	683	4168	2683	1477	2	228
Ohio	4902	514	3543	2222	1316	2	234
Indiana	2412	280	1786	1154	628	1	113
Illinois	6316	734	4479	2886	1584	3	325
Michigan	4366	514	3122	1897	1224	1	204
Wisc	1744	209	1260	772	487	*	75
Minn	1831	194	1340	852	487	1	69
Iowa	863	103	635	386	250	*	34
Missouri	2092	259	1453	932	518	1	101
N. Dakota	285	33	210	126	84	1	14
S. Dakota	243	32	170	100	70	1	11
Nebraska	652	79	468	288	180	1	24
Kansas	954	115	679	418	261	2	40
Delaware	320	36	238	155	83	*	12
Maryland	2130	250	1529	998	528	3	110
D.C.	400	53	264	177	87	2	35
Virginia	2297	313	1612	1042	567	10	121
W. Virginia	737	100	527	329	198	*	25
N. Car	2213	288	1583	1007	575	6	112
S. Car	1076	141	772	484	287	4	44
Georgia	2309	275	1583	1017	563	4	121
Florida	4208	480	2866	1875	986	6	211
Kentucky	1320	163	927	586	340	3	58
Tenn	1829	226	1285	819	465	1	84
Alabama	1468	177	1011	647	362	2	61
Miss	813	102	579	375	203	2	36
Arkansas	766	107	535	340	194	1	32
Louisiana	1798	223	1247	795	449	2	63
Oklahoma	1226	160	836	534	301	2	61
Texas	6739	817	4536	2919	1608	11	351
Montana	316	42	227	134	93	*	12
Idaho	302	37	217	127	90	*	13
Wyoming	161	21	115	66	48	*	7
Colorado	1262	157	853	516	336	3	73
N. Mexico	491	66	328	200	128	1	21
Arizona	1097	124	748	490	256	2	47
Utah	540	71	374	226	148	*	23
Nevada	388	43	254	160	94	1	22
Wash	1731	210	1208	754	453	4	77
Oregon	1081	147	759	479	280	*	49
Cal	11596	1327	7709	4981	2712	18	595
Alaska	237	29	142	85	56	2	14
Hawaii	758	72	442	284	158	4	20

Continued on next page

TABLE B4 (Cont'd.)

State	Jewelry	Other	Total Pers Care	Toilet Articles	Barber & Beauty	Total Housing	Non Farm Owned
TOTAL U.S.	10985	2736	20740	12586	8154	179509	121336
Maine	35	11	66	43	23	738	514
NH	30	2	74	49	25	733	508
Vermont	14	1	35	22	14	382	250
Mass	243	73	565	339	226	4224	2739
RI	43	16	76	43	33	659	451
Conn	122	52	307	163	145	2901	2219
NY	1034	247	1541	945	596	12636	6796
NJ	402	52	710	436	274	6486	4600
Penn	490	151	975	588	387	7824	5580
Ohio	478	135	980	583	396	7819	5697
Indiana	213	24	421	271	150	3688	2487
Illinois	614	170	1109	717	392	9586	6471
Michigan	399	127	950	620	330	6200	4380
Wisc	166	34	450	242	208	3708	2650
Minn	165	63	359	209	150	3717	2660
Iowa	81	11	194	110	84	2220	1486
Missouri	209	70	477	284	193	3232	2217
N. Dakota	24	3	57	31	25	508	332
S. Dakota	26	3	51	30	21	472	297
Nebraska	59	20	149	80	69	1126	719
Kansas	94	25	218	125	93	1672	1120
Delaware	30	3	61	37	24	449	307
Maryland	198	43	439	257	182	3659	2554
D.C.	38	9	81	37	44	648	299
Virginia	210	35	552	351	200	4211	2836
W. Virginia	77	9	152	93	59	1225	940
N. Car	191	33	466	299	167	3469	2433
S. Car	108	7	266	197	68	1778	1227
Georgia	245	83	513	355	158	3257	2171
Florida	543	107	961	557	404	8597	5578
Kentucky	121	48	276	183	93	2205	1464
Tenn	206	27	389	224	165	2786	1912
Alabama	183	36	296	183	113	2105	1543
Miss	87	9	164	116	48	1253	893
Arkansas	89	2	170	115	55	1273	866
Louisiana	222	43	318	223	95	2750	1924
Oklahoma	153	16	236	168	69	2015	1361
Texas	838	194	1392	829	563	9949	5995
Montana	31	3	60	35	25	669	438
Idaho	34	1	75	46	28	757	515
Wyoming	16	2	35	20	15	488	332
Colorado	147	29	249	127	122	3029	2122
N. Mexico	69	6	101	60	41	970	659
Arizona	150	27	289	164	125	2506	1733
Utah	56	17	94	61	33	1165	879
Nevada	61	7	91	56	34	1083	602
Wash	182	51	340	156	184	4068	2930
Oregon	106	20	263	145	118	2551	1778
Cal	1402	560	2443	1426	1016	28197	19722
Alaska	47	4	66	50	16	490	283
Hawaii	204	17	137	84	53	1385	868

Continued on next page

APPENDIX B: STATE ESTIMATES

TABLE B4 (Cont'd.)

State	Non Farm Rented	Rent Val. of Farmhs	Other Housing	Total HH Op	Furn.	Kitchen Appl.	China	Oth Dur Furn
TOTAL U.S.	47016	4316	6841	170562	16306	12725	7134	15213
Maine	173	13	39	872	44	59	31	62
NH	183	8	34	739	53	57	37	60
Vermont	87	14	30	415	22	24	18	33
Mass	1307	14	165	4553	367	269	192	325
RI	188	2	19	709	48	42	26	43
Conn	617	12	53	2600	205	164	103	220
NY	5191	112	537	13942	1100	708	585	959
NJ	1712	22	152	6230	573	384	268	504
Penn	1843	137	264	9062	789	634	342	757
Ohio	1660	250	212	8720	788	640	326	770
Indiana	773	296	133	4144	387	327	147	395
Illinois	2431	376	308	9416	949	693	515	884
Michigan	1509	127	183	7289	667	547	266	686
Wisc	791	161	105	3358	299	271	165	318
Minn	715	232	110	2989	289	236	158	257
Iowa	436	216	82	1790	149	142	62	194
Missouri	745	143	126	3707	314	285	129	344
N. Dakota	115	38	22	481	46	42	18	48
S. Dakota	103	48	24	468	39	40	18	49
Nebraska	265	99	44	1135	117	94	39	130
Kansas	388	108	56	1777	173	163	67	187
Delaware	120	7	15	531	57	40	23	48
Maryland	977	42	87	3060	348	227	127	302
D.C.	265	*	85	677	53	32	20	36
Virginia	1100	91	184	4136	394	279	158	353
W. Virginia	215	31	39	1343	128	129	49	129
N. Car	756	141	138	4294	417	320	136	344
S. Car	355	48	149	2218	188	154	66	162
Georgia	833	89	163	4107	372	279	142	345
Florida	2436	60	523	8088	843	594	328	680
Kentucky	485	137	120	2245	223	204	73	201
Tenn	634	102	138	3226	319	265	126	266
Alabama	414	79	69	2652	259	210	93	214
Miss	236	70	55	1576	134	127	46	112
Arkansas	272	85	51	1472	137	130	44	140
Louisiana	651	47	129	2923	298	260	130	234
Oklahoma	491	83	79	2126	214	168	78	197
Texas	3365	208	382	10681	1064	869	430	911
Montana	136	57	38	539	52	62	22	56
Idaho	148	59	26	617	54	65	25	71
Wyoming	100	24	32	273	26	27	12	32
Colorado	738	53	115	2048	230	188	104	221
N. Mexico	233	31	47	751	78	73	41	71
Arizona	640	26	107	1847	203	134	92	182
Utah	209	24	53	890	106	79	42	92
Nevada	286	5	189	547	59	46	30	47
Wash	957	77	104	2603	238	256	134	309
Oregon	616	80	77	1990	206	193	87	214
Cal	7602	127	746	17539	2105	1405	901	1785
Alaska	180	*	27	384	32	34	17	30
Hawaii	334	7	176	781	53	55	49	205

Continued on next page

TABLE B4 (Cont'd.)

State	Semi-Dur Furn	Cleaning, Lighting Paper	Station-ery	Elec	Gas	Water	Fuel
TOTAL U.S.	7906	14586	3727	25209	12436	6669	11057
Maine	32	63	24	110	3	17	255
NH	32	56	18	107	15	15	155
Vermont	13	39	7	68	5	8	105
Mass	196	258	95	548	384	159	839
RI	30	27	10	87	61	23	159
Conn	101	114	53	361	148	42	487
NY	565	878	230	1931	1236	504	2005
NJ	268	352	98	830	541	142	862
Penn	388	626	190	1343	839	245	946
Ohio	384	927	205	1332	1038	298	234
Indiana	185	405	105	657	381	77	252
Illinois	521	700	196	1018	1263	418	314
Michigan	314	804	162	898	849	320	282
Wisc	152	298	63	450	322	107	247
Minn	173	224	93	431	231	96	204
Iowa	79	194	45	274	143	63	101
Missouri	176	298	110	555	353	106	208
N. Dakota	26	51	7	82	23	18	32
S. Dakota	22	44	7	85	23	17	33
Nebraska	59	53	29	169	95	43	60
Kansas	90	144	53	218	139	93	65
Delaware	23	25	10	90	26	11	68
Maryland	154	186	68	289	242	97	231
D.C.	16	5	6	189	48	26	52
Virginia	177	349	79	834	159	158	328
W. Virginia	58	171	22	221	125	25	36
N. Car	189	492	95	849	91	136	311
S. Car	91	277	58	467	59	75	126
Georgia	171	395	99	746	244	193	173
Florida	354	943	193	1713	58	300	260
Kentucky	103	325	58	226	159	90	94
Tenn	139	350	60	720	91	125	74
Alabama	109	177	65	550	146	105	114
Miss	66	148	37	362	70	47	80
Arkansas	67	129	36	275	76	57	80
Louisiana	127	320	78	453	163	77	60
Oklahoma	98	192	84	343	148	99	51
Texas	518	962	266	1746	612	547	310
Montana	29	57	21	59	42	16	16
Idaho	32	67	10	99	31	17	28
Wyoming	16	19	4	26	24	14	13
Colorado	105	136	60	210	155	163	55
N. Mexico	42	63	17	77	61	35	31
Arizona	95	172	40	350	93	97	27
Utah	56	96	28	82	79	47	13
Nevada	30	45	20	91	25	25	21
Wash	152	167	32	315	108	118	168
Oregon	97	188	23	316	75	77	129
Cal	930	1478	337	1815	1115	1027	203
Alaska	15	38	7	42	11	14	62
Hawaii	42	61	13	100	8	38	1

Continued on next page

TABLE B4 (Cont'd.)

State	Telephone Telegraph	Domestic Service	Other HH Serv	Total Med Care	Drug Prep	Ophthal	Physician	Dentist
TOTAL U.S.	21544	6082	9968	139836	14166	3231	29644	10274
Maine	104	31	37	675	60	11	103	35
NH	88	21	25	472	50	7	93	35
Vermont	43	18	11	305	29	4	39	20
Mass	566	122	233	4903	329	63	704	298
RI	93	18	44	680	57	7	120	35
Conn	339	104	157	2435	205	57	427	182
NY	1712	679	848	13642	986	300	2344	922
NJ	827	180	401	4869	451	136	980	398
Penn	1274	277	412	7865	702	171	1330	477
Ohio	1034	213	532	6845	711	160	1360	449
Indiana	540	103	186	3220	444	54	647	197
Illinois	1271	219	454	8281	641	166	1507	536
Michigan	931	164	399	6508	608	139	1201	519
Wisc	440	70	155	3028	235	45	634	234
Minn	396	68	133	2726	207	82	458	204
Iowa	221	46	78	1389	131	26	326	88
Missouri	478	115	238	3082	314	82	572	188
N. Dakota	64	11	14	430	36	5	99	23
S. Dakota	64	14	13	366	39	8	71	22
Nebraska	162	31	56	875	96	34	96	64
Kansas	243	53	88	1398	147	23	310	94
Delaware	65	30	16	404	37	13	77	28
Maryland	440	129	220	2571	257	81	580	196
D.C.	92	83	21	1159	60	17	157	37
Virginia	469	185	213	2932	319	72	616	204
W. Virginia	143	38	69	998	130	17	203	53
N. Car	506	206	204	2526	445	46	569	201
S. Car	254	131	109	1157	192	16	280	89
Georgia	503	236	210	2414	314	81	676	208
Florida	911	359	552	5964	644	200	1531	434
Kentucky	292	80	117	1802	238	34	375	99
Tenn	399	139	152	2736	304	48	559	162
Alabama	318	161	131	1839	258	39	429	128
Miss	197	105	45	928	156	20	226	59
Arkansas	181	62	60	1007	170	9	229	64
Louisiana	356	173	193	1854	277	49	489	130
Oklahoma	282	70	102	1530	215	29	340	101
Texas	1250	440	756	7709	953	301	1795	497
Montana	72	11	24	410	47	8	95	34
Idaho	82	12	24	371	57	8	99	8
Wyoming	41	6	15	222	24	3	45	17
Colorado	260	41	119	1335	165	55	350	137
N. Mexico	96	23	43	570	64	13	114	41
Arizona	214	49	101	1265	142	48	362	115
Utah	124	10	37	622	78	29	156	58
Nevada	68	8	33	533	45	13	110	38
Wash	368	67	173	2409	239	61	530	271
Oregon	231	40	116	1702	169	28	364	155
Cal	2342	611	1485	16038	1605	284	4540	1592
Alaska	23	5	54	232	21	11	66	30
Hawaii	78	19	59	423	59	20	158	67

Continued on next page

TABLE B4 (*Cont'd.*)

State	Oth Prof Services	Priv Hosp & Nurs.	Health Insur	Total Per Bus	Broker	Bank	Financial Services	Life Insur
TOTAL U.S.	9717	63439	9365	66082	3578	3167	24781	16248
Maine	39	401	27	227	18	7	81	67
NH	21	229	36	208	18	5	73	61
Vermont	16	170	27	104	10	4	33	32
Mass	291	2921	297	1799	111	68	695	411
RI	35	398	29	257	16	8	94	74
Conn	141	1280	143	1087	112	35	379	282
NY	756	7522	812	8858	443	652	3937	1365
NJ	261	2310	333	2299	160	79	739	642
Penn	356	4290	538	3465	210	148	1238	898
Ohio	347	3259	559	3018	174	110	978	861
Indiana	188	1430	261	1384	75	63	446	409
Illinois	411	4376	644	4171	221	206	1473	970
Michigan	413	3105	524	2480	130	93	750	767
Wisc	153	1466	261	1166	61	51	404	332
Minn	131	1420	224	1133	47	52	391	314
Iowa	83	600	134	775	41	38	293	227
Missouri	178	1557	192	1444	67	78	535	354
N. Dakota	12	239	16	165	4	9	73	45
S. Dakota	18	180	29	161	7	8	65	45
Nebraska	37	381	66	455	18	25	181	126
Kansas	91	661	73	624	27	35	268	176
Delaware	15	200	33	199	21	8	64	64
Maryland	122	1180	154	1086	74	35	342	320
D.C.	220	537	131	700	19	20	181	95
Virginia	369	1155	198	1313	81	49	434	400
W. Virginia	51	468	77	387	18	19	138	109
N. Car	143	889	232	1148	57	52	419	370
S. Car	67	394	117	574	27	23	202	189
Georgia	188	695	251	1265	59	60	433	394
Florida	521	2301	333	2662	253	104	940	555
Kentucky	111	810	134	796	39	44	301	209
Tenn	341	1151	170	983	47	47	355	310
Alabama	147	712	126	804	32	38	274	261
Miss	65	303	99	423	14	23	154	125
Arkansas	80	389	66	445	12	25	212	108
Louisiana	148	647	115	1014	28	51	354	272
Oklahoma	122	647	76	767	41	45	313	191
Texas	733	3033	396	3967	165	231	1609	966
Montana	21	169	36	191	9	10	77	47
Idaho	28	140	31	200	9	10	81	57
Wyoming	8	111	16	111	7	7	47	28
Colorado	95	406	126	773	35	36	291	217
N. Mexico	26	271	41	255	14	13	99	74
Arizona	80	445	74	582	38	25	178	176
Utah	35	234	32	304	13	14	130	84
Nevada	47	245	33	226	13	9	87	58
Wash	141	1033	133	1110	60	41	441	252
Oregon	99	781	105	631	30	26	245	159
Cal	1451	5791	774	7429	376	315	3118	1574
Alaska	9	82	15	199	2	6	60	34
Hawaii	76	25	17	272	13	10	92	91

Continued on next page

TABLE B4 (Cont'd.)

State	Legal Services	Funeral Services	Other Per Bus	Total Transport	User Operated	New Autos	Oth Mot Vehicles
TOTAL U.S.	9566	3504	5238	179613	164912	44407	26237
Maine	32	15	9	762	728	207	76
NH	28	14	9	782	755	192	137
Vermont	14	9	3	333	307	91	18
Mass	279	115	121	3941	3414	859	226
RI	33	16	15	572	533	137	45
Conn	144	59	74	2187	2020	534	142
NY	1444	316	700	10291	8924	2297	810
NJ	339	140	200	5294	4742	1303	365
Penn	433	235	304	8675	7777	2273	807
Ohio	375	202	317	9225	8702	2374	1339
Indiana	142	111	139	4848	4571	1265	782
Illinois	650	193	458	8928	8151	2560	907
Michigan	319	150	269	8600	7948	2270	1430
Wisc	145	71	102	3620	3171	926	430
Minn	151	81	96	3442	3088	797	594
Iowa	85	44	46	2703	2571	676	575
Missouri	163	88	159	4250	3780	1070	412
N. Dakota	16	11	7	661	603	161	165
S. Dakota	16	14	5	630	570	136	132
Nebraska	51	30	25	1431	1338	322	248
Kansas	65	31	22	2076	1968	537	391
Delaware	22	8	12	473	436	109	58
Maryland	155	90	69	3357	3104	835	351
D.C.	326	10	50	432	350	56	4
Virginia	170	122	56	3978	3727	1073	390
W. Virginia	42	31	32	1305	1188	399	131
N. Car	123	86	41	3929	3581	1128	357
S. Car	71	47	16	1858	1706	520	154
Georgia	179	75	66	3843	3620	1033	423
Florida	486	208	115	7661	7208	1962	1008
Kentucky	90	60	53	2507	2315	689	259
Tenn	112	46	66	3452	3194	1003	370
Alabama	93	63	43	2520	2371	767	294
Miss	54	34	17	1432	1302	436	104
Arkansas	43	31	15	1540	1439	452	176
Louisiana	176	68	65	2932	2577	794	307
Oklahoma	96	42	39	2370	2196	654	425
Texas	534	216	247	12258	10780	3262	1540
Montana	23	10	15	783	716	175	174
Idaho	23	10	11	899	826	190	271
Wyoming	12	5	6	515	483	98	108
Colorado	120	18	55	2688	2478	605	616
N. Mexico	33	11	12	1138	1044	265	232
Arizona	98	25	42	2397	2200	469	595
Utah	34	12	16	1175	1133	280	246
Nevada	31	7	22	980	882	187	244
Wash	142	46	127	4048	3733	719	1248
Oregon	88	23	60	2743	2684	577	907
Cal	1199	146	702	21860	21129	4492	5133
Alaska	30	4	63	369	334	58	79
Hawaii	35	7	25	920	514	134	1

Continued on next page

TABLE B4 (Cont'd.)

State	Tires	Repair	Gas & Oil	Tolls	Auto Insur	Purch Local	Purch Intercity
TOTAL U.S.	12877	25729	46934	908	7820	4759	9942
Maine	70	127	215	9	25	12	21
NH	51	94	254	5	22	12	15
Vermont	29	37	120	*	13	9	18
Mass	268	634	1078	44	305	413	114
RI	44	97	179	2	28	35	3
Conn	176	355	662	23	127	75	92
NY	622	1943	2530	121	601	875	493
NJ	369	890	1534	97	184	318	234
Penn	612	1319	2412	49	305	394	504
Ohio	627	1276	2611	30	445	96	427
Indiana	329	587	1411	15	182	52	226
Illinois	542	1303	2366	48	426	249	528
Michigan	531	1170	2216	4	327	73	580
Wisc	224	441	985	1	163	91	357
Minn	222	429	913	4	130	92	262
Iowa	189	335	704	*	93	24	108
Missouri	316	625	1188	*	169	70	399
N. Dakota	50	66	148	*	14	7	51
S. Dakota	46	58	180	*	19	7	53
Nebraska	108	207	401	*	52	16	78
Kansas	168	245	545	11	70	23	84
Delaware	38	66	141	7	19	10	27
Maryland	245	413	1057	41	164	44	209
D.C.	20	128	122	*	20	52	31
Virginia	305	491	1265	19	185	86	166
W. Virginia	94	119	402	8	36	23	94
N. Car	319	553	1085	4	135	42	307
S. Car	149	232	572	10	69	22	129
Georgia	298	590	1086	15	174	47	176
Florida	534	1192	2000	53	458	125	329
Kentucky	190	258	838	10	70	31	162
Tenn	266	474	953	*	128	54	205
Alabama	225	331	633	16	105	26	123
Miss	138	186	376	3	59	18	113
Arkansas	126	234	382	*	69	16	86
Louisiana	234	352	735	19	137	77	279
Oklahoma	198	293	524	15	86	18	156
Texas	930	1640	2892	34	482	275	1203
Montana	63	86	194	*	25	12	55
Idaho	69	85	179	*	31	7	66
Wyoming	39	53	172	*	12	9	23
Colorado	207	387	572	*	91	28	181
N. Mexico	87	118	305	*	37	23	71
Arizona	188	303	564	*	80	78	119
Utah	90	161	310	*	45	13	28
Nevada	58	116	254	*	23	57	41
Wash	297	460	807	61	141	56	258
Oregon	213	313	540	24	110	46	12
Cal	1629	3595	5097	97	1085	414	317
Alaska	28	64	81	3	22	33	2
Hawaii	8	196	145	7	23	76	329

Continued on next page

TABLE B4 (Cont'd.)

State	Total Recreat	Books & Maps	Magaz & News	Toys	Wheel Goods	TV & Radio	TV & Rad Repair	Flowers & Plants
TOTAL U.S.	86382	4074	7727	10843	13714	15737	2459	2871
Maine	366	19	43	31	89	59	8	12
NH	417	25	24	74	79	64	4	10
Vermont	168	9	17	20	33	23	3	4
Mass	2657	164	390	382	318	385	49	75
RI	487	18	57	71	46	47	79	12
Conn	1301	55	136	177	176	191	26	42
NY	8246	470	1083	1187	810	1028	182	191
NJ	3138	123	243	575	407	511	89	92
Penn	4490	196	558	791	519	731	111	158
Ohio	4027	177	453	531	560	773	112	142
Indiana	1838	76	187	186	279	451	50	74
Illinois	4785	219	449	605	605	902	156	175
Michigan	4102	180	377	529	750	673	83	120
Wisc	1637	71	174	173	359	331	43	51
Minn	1634	74	144	115	360	325	30	50
Iowa	896	46	110	85	164	191	33	42
Missouri	1704	78	148	179	264	352	49	64
N. Dakota	199	6	22	10	47	44	5	9
S. Dakota	233	6	18	21	55	47	5	7
Nebraska	538	24	50	76	100	98	22	20
Kansas	758	38	51	82	125	176	27	36
Delaware	304	12	24	59	36	54	6	8
Maryland	2063	79	114	412	315	327	50	56
D.C.	389	41	25	12	15	52	12	15
Virginia	1626	94	97	263	279	335	53	67
W. Virginia	520	16	68	26	74	114	13	31
N. Car	1501	67	127	120	270	341	49	77
S. Car	634	28	58	38	137	139	37	32
Georgia	1528	77	109	212	264	319	49	72
Florida	4087	140	278	513	781	672	121	120
Kentucky	873	34	78	89	148	186	29	50
Tenn	1306	64	141	88	242	283	49	64
Alabama	857	46	67	60	183	203	36	49
Miss	434	11	33	27	106	116	22	28
Arkansas	532	17	34	36	126	131	22	29
Louisiana	1251	40	71	100	325	276	53	47
Oklahoma	843	33	64	84	174	208	33	40
Texas	4660	209	301	555	881	1093	163	190
Montana	270	21	23	25	70	51	5	9
Idaho	271	10	23	23	75	62	10	12
Wyoming	128	4	8	5	33	33	5	6
Colorado	1231	59	73	141	255	231	35	38
N. Mexico	400	18	22	45	68	95	18	12
Arizona	870	42	72	80	157	189	26	26
Utah	467	30	33	21	116	94	18	18
Nevada	1230	17	14	35	64	63	9	11
Wash	1703	92	131	119	431	322	43	52
Oregon	998	66	66	97	219	215	33	30
Cal	11160	590	792	1576	1585	2041	285	269
Alaska	213	20	9	26	64	37	4	6
Hawaii	410	22	37	55	73	54	5	20

Continued on next page

TABLE B4 *(Cont'd.)*

State	Movies	Theater & Opera	Spec Sports	Clubs	Comm Part Amuse	Pari-mutuels	Other Recreation
TOTAL U.S.	2368	1083	1582	2226	6358	1883	13457
Maine	7	2	3	9	18	5	62
NH	6	2	18	9	30	32	39
Vermont	4	1	10	5	29	2	9
Mass	74	22	58	72	118	57	492
RI	13	3	5	12	47	7	71
Conn	30	9	29	44	67	19	301
NY	263	268	264	241	568	323	1367
NJ	66	3	33	58	200	61	677
Penn	87	31	110	157	210	114	717
Ohio	87	26	91	102	299	99	575
Indiana	44	8	16	72	82	23	290
Illinois	128	43	100	156	249	146	852
Michigan	85	23	64	80	226	86	824
Wisc	35	10	12	42	123	6	207
Minn	38	24	19	57	89	2	308
Iowa	27	4	3	28	60	4	101
Missouri	50	14	36	48	116	2	306
N. Dakota	7	1	*	12	8	1	27
S. Dakota	7	1	3	9	16	6	32
Nebraska	18	3	2	25	32	3	65
Kansas	24	4	2	34	36	3	119
Delaware	4	2	18	6	13	33	29
Maryland	40	12	44	39	91	50	434
D.C.	11	2	3	76	93	3	26
Virginia	43	7	11	37	108	16	218
W. Virginia	11	2	27	15	19	48	56
N. Car	54	7	10	37	87	12	243
S. Car	26	3	4	14	49	6	63
Georgia	48	10	16	29	78	4	239
Florida	101	36	147	72	460	196	450
Kentucky	27	5	33	15	45	58	77
Tenn	37	36	2	28	86	3	183
Alabama	27	4	8	18	38	12	106
Miss	16	2	1	10	20	1	42
Arkansas	17	2	17	12	29	29	33
Louisiana	38	6	39	15	55	68	117
Oklahoma	28	6	3	21	44	4	101
Texas	162	33	36	89	259	8	681
Montana	9	1	1	8	15	1	30
Idaho	11	1	1	11	13	1	18
Wyoming	7	*	*	6	9	*	10
Colorado	37	9	27	24	102	28	171
N. Mexico	15	2	11	14	22	17	41
Arizona	28	5	20	29	52	29	114
Utah	18	4	2	10	27	1	75
Nevada	13	23	1	6	924	1	47
Wash	44	15	27	52	97	39	240
Oregon	25	5	10	25	47	11	148
Cal	351	333	186	213	809	203	1928
Alaska	5	*	*	11	7	*	23
Hawaii	16	8	1	12	34	*	74

Continued on next page

TABLE B4 (Cont'd.)

State	Total Private Education	Higher Education	Element Education	Other Education	Total Relig & Welfare
TOTAL U.S.	24014	12120	6481	5413	24780
Maine	88	59	18	11	124
NH	130	97	21	12	74
Vermont	84	73	8	3	65
Mass	1171	831	194	146	806
RI	165	105	41	19	123
Conn	446	236	114	96	375
NY	3248	1769	928	550	3308
NJ	906	335	316	255	813
Penn	1828	917	540	371	1574
Ohio	1140	604	323	213	1116
Indiana	450	285	123	42	472
Illinois	1470	696	489	285	1448
Michigan	922	479	322	121	901
Wisc	492	247	211	34	544
Minn	472	217	117	138	614
Iowa	277	187	71	19	279
Missouri	561	319	138	105	563
N. Dakota	35	20	10	5	55
S. Dakota	57	38	12	8	57
Nebraska	152	85	41	25	188
Kansas	153	90	34	30	201
Delaware	112	37	27	48	71
Maryland	526	243	152	131	379
D.C.	310	203	31	76	419
Virginia	410	226	80	105	502
W. Virginia	95	41	14	41	102
N. Car	359	258	66	35	484
S. Car	177	105	53	19	220
Georgia	388	192	89	107	418
Florida	781	315	236	230	795
Kentucky	231	114	77	40	358
Tenn	385	221	77	87	356
Alabama	296	122	69	104	275
Miss	143	78	47	18	245
Arkansas	83	47	18	18	182
Louisiana	359	133	165	61	311
Oklahoma	207	107	16	83	278
Texas	792	381	164	246	1262
Montana	39	20	10	9	90
Idaho	38	28	6	4	53
Wyoming	25	9	5	11	22
Colorado	329	159	45	125	275
N. Mexico	74	30	23	21	92
Arizona	240	74	53	113	226
Utah	110	92	7	11	634
Nevada	35	12	8	14	46
Wash	312	128	83	101	359
Oregon	219	120	33	66	234
Cal	2562	904	698	960	2227
Alaska	32	11	7	14	56
Hawaii	98	21	51	25	107

*Less than $1 million.
[a]Excludes Foreign Travel, etc.
[b]Included in off-premise food and purchased meals and beverages.

State Aggregates for Personal Consumption, 1982
(in $ millions)

State	Total PCE	Total Food & Tob	Off-Prem Cons	Purch Mls & Bev	Food Excl Alc
U.S. (Total)	2058244	410310	269623	108805	334500
Maine	8672	2040	1456	448	1692
NH	8892	2106	1513	446	1631
Vermont	4241	875	575	228	674
Mass	57518	10957	6933	3237	9052
RI	8640	1675	1117	426	1341
Conn	33044	5941	3984	1522	4899
NY	167836	29369	19925	7601	24517
NJ	75120	14150	9870	3329	11277
Penn	103443	19411	13198	4711	16050
Ohio	92989	18765	12270	5059	15711
Indiana	42882	9214	5974	2490	7670
Illinois	107791	19375	12368	5460	15579
Michigan	77835	15797	10696	4030	13249
Wisc	39114	8453	5538	2302	6827
Minn	38205	7293	4810	1938	5871
Iowa	22873	4753	3159	1177	3846
Missouri	41956	8204	5333	2160	6713
N. Dakota	5836	1048	666	285	818
S. Dakota	5308	1046	667	277	822
Nebraska	13006	2523	1601	710	2058
Kansas	19398	3847	2473	1001	3229
Delaware	5818	1138	748	288	892
Maryland	43195	8157	5422	2065	6490
DC	11029	1431	716	579	1004
Virginia	45399	9277	6001	2295	7485
W. Virginia	13179	2927	2119	573	2452
N. Car.	41048	9408	6191	2342	7716
S. Car.	20086	4933	3329	1201	4132
Georgia	42212	9764	6526	2449	7633
Florida	99341	20941	13519	5882	16750
Kentucky	25347	5882	3943	1336	4751
Tenn	35449	7360	4948	1783	6151
Alabama	25069	5630	4022	1170	4736
Miss	14680	3440	2510	649	2890
Arkansas	15090	3302	2304	686	2714
Louisiana	34802	7495	4957	1916	6123
Oklahoma	26071	5777	3740	1498	4889
Texas	136121	28816	18550	7851	23512
Montana	6877	1519	981	430	1179
Idaho	7148	1569	1074	379	1273
Wyoming	4444	1032	668	285	802
Colorado	30930	6290	3825	1919	4998
N. Mexico	10433	2383	1563	649	1927
Arizona	26117	5278	3415	1494	4317
Utah	12330	2191	1517	538	1888
Nevada	10775	1881	1188	562	1470
Wash	39029	8188	5210	2289	6460
Oregon	23824	5013	3242	1381	3995
California	260791	48810	31215	14174	39468

Continued on next page

TABLE B5 (Cont'd.)

State	Alc in Pur Mls	Alc in Off Prem	Tobacco	Food Furn Employees	Food Farms
U.S. (Total)	17091	34410	24303	6547	1032
Maine	54	176	95	37	4
NH	64	295	120	25	2
Vermont	45	102	52	15	6
Mass	619	1236	616	163	3
RI	89	139	99	33	*
Conn	283	403	350	82	2
NY	1441	1955	1373	433	25
NJ	775	1327	780	164	4
Penn	853	1208	1146	317	40
Ohio	738	1167	1176	225	31
Indiana	310	636	597	120	35
Illinois	919	1742	1239	267	39
Michigan	669	1004	870	167	30
Wisc	594	553	435	126	54
Minn	377	627	410	99	37
Iowa	211	340	301	66	56
Missouri	284	631	525	146	43
N. Dakota	65	87	65	21	12
S. Dakota	55	87	65	22	16
Nebraska	134	165	146	41	27
Kansas	72	227	253	91	33
Delaware	43	123	82	18	2
Maryland	326	813	527	134	9
DC	114	257	87	49	*
Virginia	232	713	685	288	14
W. Virginia	46	204	189	34	14
N. Car	128	838	609	236	35
S. Car	72	391	243	147	14
Georgia	240	1314	565	207	18
Florida	888	2246	1237	284	13
Kentucky	120	475	436	133	40
Tenn	123	548	478	115	40
Alabama	77	411	297	128	15
Miss	46	228	187	77	19
Arkansas	33	267	237	53	26
Louisiana	264	602	474	135	14
Oklahoma	91	337	415	94	33
Texas	1062	2367	1923	438	56
Montana	133	130	78	17	12
Idaho	73	127	86	18	14
Wyoming	61	112	67	8	4
Colorado	367	538	440	89	16
N. Mexico	102	231	127	36	8
Arizona	256	442	297	63	7
Utah	29	164	106	22	8
Nevada	124	206	113	14	3
Wash	490	717	528	131	32
Oregon	263	467	314	52	25
California	2366	4686	2602	765	35

Continued on next page

TABLE B5 (*Cont'd.*)

State	Total Clothing	Shoes	Shoe Repair	Cloth Exc Shoes	Men's Clothing	Women's Clothing	Std Mil Cloth
U.S. (Total)	146227	19189	531	101292	35466	65670	156
Maine	679	112	1	497	222	276	1
NH	588	75	1	449	169	280	*
Vermont	260	33	1	201	82	119	*
Mass	4345	519	9	3030	1052	1973	1
RI	600	63	1	406	141	264	*
Conn	2119	264	3	1493	524	967	1
NY	12407	1629	48	8460	2991	5458	3
NJ	5429	699	13	3929	1382	2541	2
Penn	7325	916	25	5288	1813	3464	1
Ohio	6106	771	20	4290	1518	2765	1
Indiana	2763	362	11	1997	698	1296	1
Illinois	8044	1064	23	5636	1888	3735	5
Michigan	5143	686	21	3668	1246	2415	1
Wisc	2453	329	7	1748	648	1099	*
Minn	2428	290	8	1780	623	1154	*
Iowa	1458	190	3	1068	381	686	*
Missouri	2769	363	8	1929	691	1235	2
N. Dakota	397	53	2	288	103	185	1
S. Dakota	321	43	2	226	84	142	1
Nebraska	828	116	2	586	207	378	1
Kansas	1335	177	5	944	350	593	3
Delaware	446	56	1	332	117	215	1
Maryland	2968	402	14	2079	722	1353	4
DC	524	65	3	346	117	228	1
Virginia	3382	460	14	2369	782	1581	10
W. Virginia	933	132	3	659	234	424	*
N. Car.	3155	452	15	2217	763	1450	11
S. Car.	1567	216	8	1096	379	715	6
Georgia	3461	455	11	2306	780	1522	7
Florida	7141	948	24	4795	1594	3189	8
Kentucky	1770	231	5	1240	438	801	5
Tenn	2439	342	8	1708	593	1112	1
Alabama	1901	251	8	1342	469	871	3
Miss	1145	166	3	799	274	524	2
Arkansas	1055	142	5	756	268	486	1
Louisiana	2726	395	9	1789	635	1152	3
Oklahoma	2048	263	5	1419	515	903	4
Texas	11934	1628	53	7827	2706	5107	16
Montana	408	59	3	298	105	192	1
Idaho	424	61	2	308	117	191	1
Wyoming	251	36	1	180	66	114	*
Colorado	2036	283	11	1395	508	886	5
N. Mexico	713	105	3	495	175	319	2
Arizona	1797	222	7	1269	421	844	3
Utah	820	119	7	558	208	350	1
Nevada	761	101	3	499	180	318	1
Wash	2479	329	11	1707	612	1093	5
Oregon	1435	212	6	989	369	620	*
California	17368	2176	74	11727	4190	7523	23

Continued on next page

TABLE B5 (Cont'd.)

State	Cln & Laundry	Jewelry & Watch	Other Clothing	Total Pers Care	Toilet Articles	Barber
U.S. (Total)	5269	15635	4301	29696	19334	10362
Maine	15	43	15	74	43	31
NH	21	43	2	114	72	42
Vermont	10	18	*	61	39	22
Mass	155	474	154	772	471	301
RI	24	62	40	86	48	38
Conn	83	179	93	449	246	203
NY	462	1210	572	1884	1150	731
NJ	194	513	96	919	559	360
Penn	209	641	256	1367	862	505
Ohio	228	608	188	1453	924	529
Indiana	104	256	41	618	444	174
Illinois	289	793	245	1450	971	479
Michigan	192	448	136	1122	772	350
Wisc	74	238	63	661	391	270
Minn	75	212	67	599	389	210
Iowa	40	139	25	418	274	144
Missouri	105	261	100	672	444	228
N. Dakota	13	43	*	80	44	36
S. Dakota	13	33	4	75	45	30
Nebraska	24	78	24	191	104	87
Kansas	42	127	41	297	178	119
Delaware	17	38	3	74	44	30
Maryland	121	287	66	596	359	237
DC	37	53	16	104	52	52
Virginia	139	339	60	686	400	286
W. Virginia	23	111	12	171	105	66
N. Car.	127	309	38	558	364	194
S. Car.	62	168	17	287	209	78
Georgia	127	355	189	682	498	184
Florida	252	981	147	1559	990	569
Kentucky	56	185	53	373	270	103
Tenn	93	266	30	591	410	181
Alabama	60	215	30	372	247	125
Miss	35	144	3	195	143	52
Arkansas	32	117	7	223	165	58
Louisiana	79	385	73	460	333	127
Oklahoma	79	235	47	421	348	73
Texas	468	1539	399	2460	1693	767
Montana	11	39	1	105	74	31
Idaho	14	41	1	125	88	37
Wyoming	7	28	1	68	46	22
Colorado	94	210	41	458	285	173
N. Mexico	24	87	3	152	99	53
Arizona	55	210	37	440	251	189
Utah	48	85	3	125	91	34
Nevada	32	109	15	157	117	40
Wash	88	245	95	523	265	258
Oregon	44	155	34	285	162	123
California	639	2007	697	3867	2633	1234

Continued on next page

TABLE B5 (*Cont'd.*)

State	Total Housing	Owner Occup	Tenant Occup	Rental Farmhouse	Other Housing	Total HH Op
U.S. (Total)	31135	217880	76655	5039	11561	273014
Maine	1154	812	268	14	65	1222
NH	1198	853	295	9	57	1119
Vermont	577	375	128	16	46	518
Mass	7687	5080	2393	24	339	7615
RI	1183	854	310	2	43	1359
Conn	5367	4239	1116	18	109	4459
NY	21737	11358	9634	93	986	21365
NJ	11936	8711	3061	42	362	11600
Penn	14067	10657	2983	148	416	13330
Ohio	14135	10934	2731	187	368	11171
Indiana	6206	4589	1180	178	147	4785
Illinois	16252	11569	4157	196	440	14474
Michigan	10930	8230	2318	160	262	10517
Wisc	5641	3760	1304	212	178	3950
Minn	6299	4597	1160	216	157	3934
Iowa	3835	2597	621	246	90	2553
Missouri	5545	3870	1090	209	195	5936
N. Dakota	833	475	163	71	33	621
S. Dakota	773	448	139	67	33	639
Nebraska	1972	1287	383	117	54	1529
Kansas	2942	2009	568	140	84	2804
Delaware	781	583	174	7	28	875
Maryland	6787	4993	1659	58	162	6707
DC	1093	505	473	*	135	1426
Virginia	7323	5181	1734	109	312	6714
W. Virginia	1988	1558	316	37	73	1677
N. Car.	5722	4184	1106	137	230	5146
S. Car.	2870	2123	520	48	175	2958
Georgia	5506	3821	1310	100	256	7121
Florida	13472	9128	3411	89	1018	12969
Kentucky	3500	2398	711	146	110	3034
Tenn	4868	3339	968	179	227	5128
Alabama	3562	2660	613	116	89	4216
Miss	2033	1434	325	104	63	2764
Arkansas	2127	1434	386	113	73	1865
Louisiana	4799	3452	1017	96	205	6393
Oklahoma	3543	2416	707	152	123	4395
Texas	17438	11204	5053	323	777	19878
Montana	1025	671	193	56	45	814
Idaho	1224	844	201	70	35	883
Wyoming	749	503	147	25	53	590
Colorado	4972	3871	826	72	220	4228
N. Mexico	1609	1127	340	41	79	1364
Arizona	4085	3004	952	33	148	3729
Utah	2182	1700	342	46	80	1671
Nevada	1765	992	459	10	318	681
Wash	7296	5433	1586	110	187	4871
Oregon	4403	3161	996	99	109	2393
California	51111	36936	13334	286	1417	31418

Continued on next page

TABLE B5 (Cont'd.)

State	Furn & Matt	Kitch Appl	Chna, Glass Tablware	Oth Dur Furn	Semi-Dur Furnish	Station-ery	Cleaning Prep.
U.S. (Total)	21020	15177	12482	21701	12400	6600	27800
Maine	58	62	62	83	51	19	110
NH	73	69	71	98	65	26	111
Vermont	31	28	39	42	26	35	69
Mass	542	377	304	494	359	204	550
RI	63	56	52	70	43	28	61
Conn	280	200	164	300	153	125	339
NY	1553	854	858	1327	824	816	1731
NJ	739	468	460	715	441	300	1026
Penn	936	685	529	1010	587	238	1526
Ohio	832	644	484	986	507	128	1437
Indiana	384	326	255	493	231	82	646
Illinois	1026	714	645	1049	701	309	1623
Michigan	688	508	381	842	426	199	641
Wisc	344	269	257	412	241	54	576
Minn	359	271	261	396	306	124	281
Iowa	197	185	135	327	132	46	420
Missouri	405	306	234	440	263	94	503
N. Dakota	62	44	37	60	37	*	72
S. Dakota	50	37	28	89	31	2	75
Nebraska	128	107	73	190	76	5	159
Kansas	201	171	116	247	139	82	331
Delaware	65	45	34	70	40	5	86
Maryland	437	271	244	445	247	110	387
DC	56	25	35	43	24	32	57
Virginia	553	350	329	531	259	108	692
W. Virginia	129	125	88	151	75	24	283
N. Car.	613	420	276	521	283	118	795
S. Car.	353	229	148	267	148	70	271
Georgia	505	365	273	471	283	109	633
Florida	1261	958	698	1258	664	356	1548
Kentucky	353	214	147	272	153	27	507
Tenn	378	306	222	388	216	56	537
Alabama	288	221	175	280	180	51	300
Miss	182	156	100	175	113	*	208
Arkansas	165	143	98	181	106	20	254
Louisiana	425	378	235	395	228	126	671
Oklahoma	330	229	180	325	215	66	398
Texas	1636	1280	984	1678	945	523	2141
Montana	68	65	38	75	44	14	115
Idaho	63	59	41	75	49	26	134
Wyoming	36	31	27	54	25	16	83
Colorado	333	211	200	338	181	128	454
N. Mexico	104	88	80	102	71	35	170
Arizona	291	167	157	296	170	77	290
Utah	129	86	79	123	80	41	194
Nevada	87	78	59	96	59	29	146
Wash	375	255	262	431	238	128	609
Oregon	217	169	161	232	141	108	456
California	2504	1748	1585	2624	1439	1209	2913

Continued on next page

TABLE B5 *(Cont'd.)*

State	Elec	Gas	Water	Fuel Oil & Coal	Telephone Telegraph	Domestic Service	Oth Hous Operation
U.S. (Total)	47066	25567	11657	14471	35140	6541	15475
Maine	218	5	31	329	186	29	40
NH	193	33	25	244	173	17	46
Vermont	115	12	17	143	82	12	14
Mass	974	756	239	1201	1145	108	353
RI	143	127	35	222	186	14	88
Conn	797	302	106	747	667	63	211
NY	3340	2385	688	2612	2518	658	1270
NJ	1482	1120	253	1063	1654	165	630
Penn	2314	1589	350	1366	1958	223	625
Ohio	2291	1959	503	276	1496	214	639
Indiana	1165	740	160	250	647	89	271
Illinois	1929	2331	659	270	2054	185	822
Michigan	1153	1732	532	308	1566	162	489
Wisc	737	718	150	360	543	62	228
Minn	781	574	145	236	585	78	163
Iowa	693	429	130	173	375	52	109
Missouri	1057	756	173	216	749	116	384
N. Dakota	151	55	28	45	103	10	18
S. Dakota	171	58	27	45	100	14	20
Nebraska	309	232	65	67	189	24	110
Kansas	514	357	156	67	409	42	140
Delaware	138	43	18	105	131	17	36
Maryland	836	451	148	376	901	168	333
DC	75	92	35	48	169	93	25
Virginia	1476	299	282	451	744	278	362
W. Virginia	369	243	53	36	245	39	67
N. Car.	1521	189	250	347	560	193	312
S. Car.	851	109	131	145	361	100	153
Georgia	1106	498	410	191	913	223	344
Florida	3382	99	676	333	1379	334	1003
Kentucky	723	334	164	96	406	79	149
Tenn	1137	196	235	96	674	138	258
Alabama	893	286	186	136	551	135	189
Miss	545	140	74	127	386	80	109
Arkansas	449	186	90	129	254	48	88
Louisiana	926	356	142	60	739	199	392
Oklahoma	735	294	189	74	565	171	170
Texas	3672	1233	1013	394	2226	494	1444
Montana	109	96	27	19	125	12	34
Idaho	144	51	27	37	139	14	33
Wyoming	67	70	31	24	94	6	24
Colorado	576	451	281	66	612	63	218
N. Mexico	201	143	68	37	179	26	82
Arizona	747	187	181	46	521	61	204
Utah	234	192	92	37	262	16	76
Nevada	211	98	74	41	57	16	70
Wash	662	213	199	212	639	114	267
Oregon	411	140	135	145	298	59	144
California	4021	2573	1878	330	3434	1006	2096

Continued on next page

TABLE B5 (*Cont'd.*)

State	Total Med Care	Drug Prep	Ophthalmic Products	Dentist	Physician	Oth Prof Services	Priv Hosp	Health Insur
U.S. (Total)	272771	27608	4675	17370	55170	16715	133347	17866
Maine	1208	96	12	6	187	94	763	70
NH	948	99	12	67	182	51	481	62
Vermont	566	47	8	35	88	35	318	40
Mass	6303	653	96	457	1199	587	2826	397
RI	1295	99	10	66	194	97	779	62
Conn	4527	360	69	300	741	325	2425	316
NY	24042	1914	514	1318	3594	1560	13841	1488
NJ	8906	886	168	635	1651	513	4496	580
Penn	16091	1371	261	796	2466	842	9905	724
Ohio	14593	1254	219	739	2478	890	8001	1146
Indiana	5708	596	90	330	1216	357	2677	434
Illinois	16241	1304	229	810	2585	783	9152	1661
Michigan	11930	1039	155	848	1962	799	6484	694
Wisc	6007	436	90	392	1164	349	3169	422
Minn	5212	435	118	353	869	603	2256	452
Iowa	2902	285	53	190	614	240	1294	187
Missouri	6356	584	99	292	1073	375	3540	467
N. Dakota	926	63	10	42	198	50	540	29
S. Dakota	746	59	11	39	136	53	395	55
Nebraska	1874	167	37	101	377	105	898	195
Kansas	2876	277	37	159	575	178	1478	180
Delaware	723	78	14	46	136	35	386	33
Maryland	5006	545	108	310	1037	283	2516	209
DC	1827	69	21	55	244	72	1101	320
Virginia	5439	624	110	357	1180	247	2554	386
W. Virginia	2016	211	21	89	413	83	1076	154
N. Car.	4844	643	74	331	1117	206	2261	235
S. Car.	2209	316	32	154	516	141	841	195
Georgia	4311	647	113	353	1323	272	1184	301
Florida	12610	1372	301	799	3212	672	5811	342
Kentucky	3397	415	49	168	757	162	1689	184
Tenn	5067	544	68	268	1123	239	2635	228
Alabama	3340	405	57	204	824	187	1449	198
Miss	1627	263	22	107	437	113	539	125
Arkansas	1927	247	13	109	476	123	850	103
Louisiana	4157	561	84	243	1048	197	1762	253
Oklahoma	3093	387	41	194	700	206	1318	231
Texas	15718	2045	378	991	4103	845	6135	1069
Montana	878	91	14	58	179	41	444	55
Idaho	756	109	11	70	187	44	281	48
Wyoming	339	61	7	35	98	19	63	48
Colorado	3652	375	86	279	746	203	1649	301
N. Mexico	1171	145	24	80	239	56	544	88
Arizona	3321	386	69	227	724	212	1476	206
Utah	1455	177	47	109	307	70	644	96
Nevada	910	170	22	83	289	45	258	22
Wash	4899	570	91	505	1053	392	1792	397
Oregon	3052	360	27	257	713	180	1350	151
California	33913	3488	436	2761	8073	2349	14310	2068

Continued on next page

TABLE B5 (Cont'd.)

State	Total Pers Bus	Brokerag Charges	Bank Charges	Financial Services	Life Insur	Legal Services	Funeral Services	Other Per Bus
U.S. (Total)	122107	8762	9134	42909	28879	18370	5086	8967
Maine	366	6	21	138	108	58	23	14
NH	425	6	25	186	117	54	17	22
Vermont	183	4	17	71	55	26	10	3
Mass	3360	270	185	1284	710	474	125	297
RI	472	12	37	189	124	56	23	34
Conn	1953	90	91	800	503	245	79	146
NY	15797	3907	1197	4240	2204	2626	430	1055
NJ	4917	197	236	2273	1084	604	174	342
Penn	5746	227	472	2236	1445	769	259	362
Ohio	4735	144	312	1875	1386	556	303	205
Indiana	2392	43	198	993	673	214	150	144
Illinois	7282	699	590	2350	1591	1157	295	582
Michigan	4364	103	301	1701	1211	571	222	280
Wisc	2125	92	162	828	561	240	108	145
Minn	2242	125	187	827	577	294	92	150
Iowa	1357	33	138	564	384	139	85	32
Missouri	2613	147	206	1066	617	287	146	156
N. Dakota	293	5	33	116	94	28	17	5
S. Dakota	287	4	47	111	82	25	19	5
Nebraska	763	32	74	288	225	75	46	34
Kansas	1134	23	108	482	324	114	65	33
Delaware	328	13	44	95	105	38	12	25
Maryland	2204	69	103	967	572	258	86	156
DC	1641	54	51	91	215	833	18	301
Virginia	2707	62	162	1212	717	284	129	155
W. Virginia	677	9	64	262	185	69	66	29
N. Car.	2003	57	150	718	678	203	140	86
S. Car.	984	18	56	342	352	129	67	35
Georgia	2506	124	154	927	723	325	118	149
Florida	5340	270	346	2141	1093	982	214	277
Kentucky	1327	24	123	521	357	145	107	63
Tenn	1765	62	149	571	557	181	114	147
Alabama	1270	25	106	429	455	157	64	56
Miss	749	11	74	263	236	98	65	13
Arkansas	762	31	76	283	214	75	70	23
Louisiana	2197	52	166	694	546	386	96	245
Oklahoma	1484	56	155	519	392	211	83	79
Texas	7614	392	796	2359	2031	1218	330	525
Montana	311	9	34	121	85	42	15	9
Idaho	340	7	31	128	103	46	18	13
Wyoming	204	6	23	77	61	26	9	5
Colorado	1854	128	108	711	452	290	48	118
N. Mexico	450	10	43	146	145	74	20	17
Arizona	1175	50	95	392	313	212	37	78
Utah	521	26	43	165	170	81	20	23
Nevada	386	10	24	126	112	72	14	29
Wash	1893	79	123	717	484	315	51	126
Oregon	1178	46	73	482	293	178	42	67
California	14764	868	1069	4676	2939	2675	333	2019

Continued on next page

TABLE B5 (*Cont'd.*)

State	Total Transport	New Autos	Used Autos	Oth Mot Vehicles	Tires	Auto Repair	Gas & Oil	Auto Insur
U.S. (Total)	263416	53336	13551	15602	15230	37903	94125	9150
Maine	1147	251	81	82	77	149	384	37
NH	1092	276	28	113	63	143	395	10
Vermont	602	132	51	31	35	53	216	21
Mass	7029	1351	322	271	310	1064	2304	397
RI	1016	160	88	56	51	146	366	43
Conn	4040	758	172	240	203	540	1439	173
NY	17177	2870	541	707	701	2729	4387	665
NJ	9550	1817	266	333	454	1307	3138	578
Penn	12042	2500	664	425	650	1716	4245	469
Ohio	11356	2237	454	508	632	1643	5276	275
Indiana	6253	1202	323	397	334	769	2708	170
Illinois	12265	2576	535	488	660	1854	4562	453
Michigan	9372	2126	320	641	535	1322	3956	228
Wisc	5179	984	251	297	240	583	2097	102
Minn	5003	993	186	387	241	571	2041	164
Iowa	3080	662	103	196	195	369	1369	116
Missouri	5941	1122	266	251	337	902	2215	186
N. Dakota	924	237	32	72	62	93	359	23
S. Dakota	758	163	13	58	48	75	355	13
Nebraska	1806	359	100	115	106	259	739	37
Kansas	2649	623	93	142	183	329	1062	95
Delaware	728	150	40	26	42	111	266	13
Maryland	5127	1071	227	318	301	664	1987	218
DC	787	26	163	8	19	152	179	21
Virginia	6176	1290	353	253	360	761	2379	190
W. Virginia	1694	378	136	60	99	134	705	82
N. Car.	5776	1269	533	272	381	724	1887	208
S. Car.	2810	593	249	112	172	341	1193	11
Georgia	5910	1270	362	215	359	946	2367	147
Florida	14297	3100	999	1353	741	2143	4746	397
Kentucky	3597	651	357	100	227	355	1543	95
Tenn	5257	1023	453	252	286	629	1945	162
Alabama	3413	743	289	171	248	502	1166	105
Miss	1987	452	176	94	164	230	683	52
Arkansas	2232	520	216	125	149	272	755	62
Louisiana	4617	1031	176	334	290	576	1528	207
Oklahoma	3621	1031	193	291	264	453	1103	95
Texas	20298	4881	1285	1298	1368	3064	6559	660
Montana	1018	198	51	76	69	118	385	26
Idaho	1020	203	75	93	76	119	351	31
Wyoming	777	140	27	31	46	85	396	16
Colorado	4111	855	242	243	272	677	1421	128
N. Mexico	1619	330	123	96	111	194	610	10
Arizona	3653	697	195	264	238	488	1298	106
Utah	1715	309	114	127	108	276	653	34
Nevada	1752	257	60	112	81	200	561	6
Wash	4676	796	232	485	357	675	1679	126
Oregon	3071	589	131	259	227	405	1100	111
California	30851	5825	1158	2142	1955	5601	10465	1500

Continued on next page

TABLE B5 (*Cont'd.*)

State	Tolls	Pur Loc & Intcit	Total Recreat	Books & Maps	Magaz & News	Non-Dur Toys	Wheel Goods
U.S. (Total)	1306	23300	139970	8025	13843	17130	17953
Maine	3	68	527	41	61	97	93
NH	1	74	722	49	75	104	128
Vermont	1	50	326	15	28	50	41
Mass	6	1036	4695	322	1182	445	394
RI	4	89	594	23	42	72	54
Conn	5	531	2680	141	270	275	272
NY	387	4310	13130	888	2907	1119	995
NJ	34	1717	6258	238	781	593	454
Penn	46	1314	7916	350	1396	687	607
Ohio	36	445	6274	315	347	653	630
Indiana	12	369	2403	159	121	313	414
Illinois	70	1146	7669	384	1210	741	689
Michigan	13	351	6366	297	284	722	806
Wisc	6	644	2023	125	96	354	376
Minn	20	453	2396	136	75	411	448
Iowa	7	95	1109	82	88	154	212
Missouri	32	656	2370	136	132	309	285
N. Dakota	4	48	410	13	15	57	87
S. Dakota	1	44	411	15	17	59	64
Nebraska	6	89	847	46	30	155	138
Kansas	17	120	1052	82	63	149	150
Delaware	11	70	557	26	67	50	35
Maryland	2	362	4626	177	352	393	336
DC	3	164	812	64	107	43	20
Virginia	24	552	2324	197	72	361	324
W. Virginia	4	74	646	31	94	78	78
N. Car.	14	356	2088	146	107	295	266
S. Car.	3	95	1034	61	54	160	152
Georgia	39	205	2244	125	328	319	301
Florida	25	706	7347	315	581	1080	1283
Kentucky	1	191	1122	64	100	177	146
Tenn	17	412	1903	120	138	253	255
Alabama	7	118	1198	79	49	200	186
Miss	8	76	723	28	77	143	117
Arkansas	4	74	893	26	50	129	125
Louisiana	9	473	2095	87	99	383	389
Oklahoma	17	144	1507	74	14	263	268
Texas	101	913	8342	486	737	1337	1430
Montana	3	91	506	36	13	86	120
Idaho	3	52	527	23	12	86	125
Wyoming	1	47	283	10	27	47	60
Colorado	26	231	2337	130	202	332	457
N. Mexico	4	118	616	38	44	83	126
Arizona	26	327	2016	87	54	210	298
Utah	10	76	874	69	25	153	192
Nevada	7	474	1672	33	17	102	119
Wash	26	280	2474	230	98	401	527
Oregon	14	231	1493	130	31	217	284
California	182	2236	16570	1190	1015	2096	2458

Continued on next page

TABLE B5 (Cont'd.)

State	Radio & TV	Rad & TV Repair	Flowers & Plants	Movies	Theater & Opera	Spec Sports	Comm Part Amuse	Clubs
U.S. (Total)	22086	2618	5665	3134	2200	2692	11586	4438
Maine	65	7	28	9	2	8	35	13
NH	101	6	26	10	1	14	81	12
Vermont	32	2	12	6	1	2	99	5
Mass	483	58	147	93	22	98	223	113
RI	68	11	21	8	5	13	39	19
Conn	248	34	74	38	16	44	123	64
NY	1524	211	406	336	798	442	639	485
NJ	664	121	180	95	41	56	404	94
Penn	772	114	296	118	37	160	460	198
Ohio	794	123	266	108	19	106	499	176
Indiana	611	59	134	56	17	29	138	82
Illinois	1005	165	332	156	63	192	391	332
Michigan	637	81	207	92	34	72	281	152
Wisc	418	41	98	45	12	24	175	75
Minn	416	25	98	46	25	19	172	88
Iowa	206	20	77	28	2	3	87	45
Missouri	614	56	134	56	25	61	197	95
N. Dakota	144	4	13	8	0	*	12	13
S. Dakota	145	4	16	8	1	4	24	9
Nebraska	203	22	37	21	2	21	35	25
Kansas	246	18	80	28	3	6	61	35
Delaware	171	8	14	6	1	21	18	10
Maryland	564	54	123	53	10	87	165	88
DC	87	3	39	12	25	11	69	389
Virginia	515	57	153	65	6	14	210	116
W. Virginia	143	14	57	15	4	5	40	21
N. Car.	463	61	152	55	5	21	194	48
S. Car.	218	30	55	29	5	5	133	47
Georgia	436	58	142	60	12	25	184	61
Florida	978	157	249	149	37	285	1223	134
Kentucky	230	29	74	30	6	53	75	33
Tenn	378	55	102	42	63	9	225	54
Alabama	293	37	83	25	9	16	72	31
Miss	155	17	44	18	3	8	59	14
Arkansas	199	22	49	18	1	30	61	17
Louisiana	407	58	66	52	14	87	140	40
Oklahoma	354	33	90	42	9	11	100	77
Texas	1681	199	373	246	51	59	699	186
Montana	128	6	24	13	1	1	31	12
Idaho	152	8	22	13	1	1	28	10
Wyoming	59	5	18	8	0	*	23	8
Colorado	378	40	90	63	21	41	269	62
N. Mexico	119	15	34	19	2	25	43	14
Arizona	258	30	81	48	5	39	127	35
Utah	129	14	33	31	11	7	64	110
Nevada	141	13	28	19	39	2	930	14
Wash	406	41	117	68	18	42	172	87
Oregon	383	28	61	34	4	17	113	46
California	3105	334	559	512	702	393	1768	504

Continued on next page

TABLE B5 (*Cont'd.*)

State	Pari-mutuels	Other Recreat	Total Priv Educ	Higher Education	Element Education	Other Education	Total Rel & Welf
U.S. (Total)	2590	26058	41743	21993	11244	8506	47855
Maine	4	69	169	91	50	21	240
NH	26	89	334	187	103	11	187
Vermont	3	23	155	89	29	32	95
Mass	126	1173	3571	2246	539	361	1705
RI	29	193	368	220	77	35	228
Conn	217	909	1086	611	325	47	647
NY	359	2509	6394	3526	1534	1153	6034
NJ	42	2525	1345	637	469	303	1370
Penn	78	2811	3660	2156	734	496	2981
Ohio	87	2126	1463	680	474	434	2052
Indiana	*	225	686	378	186	86	990
Illinois	245	1931	2852	1596	641	523	2520
Michigan	76	2589	812	322	385	193	1713
Wisc	*	147	632	305	252	69	1085
Minn	*	392	642	288	190	253	1325
Iowa	*	99	405	241	92	27	548
Missouri	*	232	762	380	252	140	1150
N. Dakota	*	25	88	49	28	2	107
S. Dakota	8	21	77	37	32	7	122
Nebraska	32	67	219	114	66	37	316
Kansas	*	125	181	78	69	55	415
Delaware	2	124	73	20	51	15	152
Maryland	60	2164	919	442	315	196	788
DC	*	9	1121	724	88	198	655
Virginia	*	205	601	249	260	156	982
W. Virginia	44	33	98	53	20	28	228
N. Car.	*	246	889	567	134	66	978
S. Car.	*	63	288	152	92	31	232
Georgia	*	201	685	338	222	145	921
Florida	397	416	1221	532	458	361	1911
Kentucky	36	74	290	127	124	56	575
Tenn	*	184	617	333	161	110	708
Alabama	*	97	294	119	112	111	480
Miss	*	33	182	51	113	61	381
Arkansas	68	92	87	54	10	19	381
Louisiana	92	147	444	151	254	108	617
Oklahoma	*	133	328	179	58	101	354
Texas	*	738	1486	802	325	377	2524
Montana	*	20	42	20	14	9	145
Idaho	*	22	73	28	41	8	103
Wyoming	*	11	18	*	9	24	65
Colorado	31	192	332	130	112	165	556
N. Mexico	7	40	81	18	59	25	179
Arizona	36	680	216	48	101	169	510
Utah	*	42	94	53	18	21	719
Nevada	1	119	18	1	8	25	110
Wash	44	202	391	174	134	127	849
Oregon	19	88	268	117	91	98	502
California	421	1347	4468	2230	1168	1349	5093

*Less than $1 million.

TABLE B6
Ratios of State
Personal Consumption to Personal Income* 1900 to 1982

State	1900			1929			1970			1977			1982		
	PCE	PI	PCE/PI	PCE	PI	PCE/PI	PCE	PI	PCE/PI	PCE	PI	PCE/PI	PCE	PI	PCE/PI
U.S. TOTAL	$16,393	$15,427	1.06	$77,457	$84,872	0.91	$639,916	$803,092	0.80	$1,267,220	$1,457,622	0.87	$2,058,244	$2,661,135	0.77
ME	151	130	1.16	428	479	0.89	2785	3282	0.85	5720	6368	0.90	8672	10870	0.80
NH	91	88	1.03	276	319	0.87	2529	2789	0.91	5393	5689	0.95	8892	10983	0.81
VT	69	65	1.06	203	227	0.89	1389	1570	0.88	2694	2830	0.95	4241	5264	0.81
MA	847	853	0.99	3619	3823	0.95	20158	24742	0.81	35334	41876	0.84	57518	73318	0.78
RI	118	126	0.94	530	595	0.89	2924	3727	0.78	5325	6382	0.83	8640	10624	0.81
CT	241	252	0.96	1329	1626	0.82	10640	14897	0.71	19271	25244	0.76	33044	45205	0.73
NY	2501	2348	1.07	12915	13971	0.92	67492	85643	0.79	106316	134524	0.79	167836	224594	0.75
NJ	520	522	1.00	3253	3646	0.89	25615	33970	0.75	44515	58835	0.76	75120	102663	0.73
PA	1497	1576	0.95	6471	7487	0.86	35667	46353	0.77	65977	82889	0.80	92989	135718	0.76
OH	946	923	1.02	4670	5095	0.92	32585	42321	0.77	61289	76410	0.80	103443	117878	0.79
IN	462	458	1.01	1901	1958	0.97	15474	19405	0.80	29343	37113	0.79	42882	56678	0.76
IL	1258	1254	1.00	6407	7188	0.89	37571	50163	0.75	69958	91088	0.77	107791	141972	0.76
MI	497	448	1.11	3450	3769	0.92	27833	33918	0.77	53946	69397	0.78	77835	101169	0.77
WI	400	370	1.08	1812	1972	0.92	12567	16673	0.75	25509	31871	0.80	39114	52532	0.74
MN	391	363	1.08	1585	1541	1.03	11421	14817	0.77	23741	28629	0.83	38205	47732	0.80
IA	438	451	0.97	1383	1429	0.97	7920	10714	0.74	14471	20314	0.71	22873	31458	0.73
MO	663	584	1.14	2029	2242	0.90	13631	17335	0.79	26900	32067	0.84	41956	53398	0.79
ND	67	67	1.00	262	257	1.02	1572	1987	0.79	3561	3987	0.89	5836	7046	0.83
SD	74	74	1.00	298	294	1.01	1647	2092	0.79	3466	4016	0.86	5308	6585	0.81
NE	221	226	0.98	770	815	0.94	4353	5567	0.78	8515	10505	0.81	13006	17538	0.74
KS	269	275	0.98	941	997	0.94	6029	8495	0.71	12407	16593	0.75	19398	28566	0.68
DE	40	41	0.98	177	242	0.73	2030	2469	0.82	3764	4440	0.85	5818	7102	0.82
MD	253	242	1.05	1058	1235	0.86	12819	16959	0.76	25168	31467	0.80	43195	54460	0.79
VA	249	204	1.22	877	1045	0.84	13297	17266	0.77	28069	35733	0.79	45399	63648	0.71
WV	129	112	1.15	587	783	0.75	4243	5308	0.80	8885	11137	0.80	13179	17612	0.75
NC	204	136	1.50	852	1037	0.82	12532	16372	0.77	26337	32848	0.80	41048	55868	0.73

SC	138	78	1.77	402	470	0.86	6084	7707	0.79	13005	16268	0.80	20086	28101	0.71
GA	242	191	1.27	896	1002	0.89	12662	15245	0.83	25837	31080	0.83	42212	55746	0.76
FL	73	59	1.24	727	746	0.97	24006	25665	0.94	56039	57741	0.97	99341	118496	0.84
KY	329	258	1.28	843	1024	0.82	8641	9971	0.87	16498	20719	0.80	25347	34059	0.74
TN	251	204	1.23	914	984	0.93	10396	12159	0.86	22167	25277	0.88	35449	42775	0.83
AL	220	161	1.37	694	851	0.82	8178	9999	0.82	16866	21047	0.80	25069	34795	0.72
MS	172	130	1.32	513	569	0.90	4758	5667	0.84	9590	12202	0.79	14680	20565	0.71
AR	169	117	1.44	485	574	0.84	4427	5333	0.83	9663	11937	0.81	15090	19896	0.76
LA	188	177	1.06	707	857	0.82	9332	11083	0.84	20173	23727	0.85	34802	44921	0.77
OK	124	90	1.38	988	1072	0.92	6925	8541	0.81	14818	18098	0.82	26071	36628	0.71
TX	478	421	1.14	2587	2743	0.94	33383	39598	0.84	75484	88578	0.85	136121	179135	0.76
MT	81	101	0.80	290	310	0.94	1952	2379	0.82	4420	4744	0.93	6877	8113	0.85
ID	36	36	1.00	225	227	0.99	1943	2364	0.82	4620	5377	0.86	7148	9062	0.79
WY	22	29	0.76	129	150	0.86	994	1225	0.81	2566	3112	0.82	4444	7235	0.61
CO	181	171	1.06	675	639	1.06	7269	8589	0.85	16786	19134	0.88	30930	38848	0.80
NM	29	29	1.00	140	172	0.81	2686	3124	0.86	6321	6986	0.90	10433	13010	0.80
AZ	30	40	0.75	249	257	0.97	5742	6548	0.88	14390	15047	0.96	26117	29695	0.88
UT	54	51	1.06	272	280	0.97	3125	3411	0.92	7327	7682	0.95	12330	14158	0.87
NV	14	17	0.82	66	78	0.85	2370	2293	1.03	6175	5294	1.17	10775	10932	0.99
WA	155	153	1.01	1107	1149	0.96	10900	13810	0.79	23944	28060	0.85	39029	51380	0.76
OR	115	103	1.12	663	633	1.05	6776	7762	0.87	15876	17124	0.93	23824	28265	0.84
CA	591	542	1.09	5142	5431	0.95	72774	90070	0.81	152414	175754	0.87	25618	327746	0.80
DC							4111	3964	1.04	6338	6805	0.93	10439	9201	1.20
AK							939	1414	0.66	3065	4842	0.63	5213	7732	0.67
HI							2839	3576	0.79	6777	7426	0.91	11394	11721	0.97

*Personal consumption and income in $ millions.

TABLE B7
Adjusted State Personal Income, Savings, Consumption: 1982*
Ratios of PCE to Adjusted Income

State	Pop	Income	Cont. to Soc. Ins.	Tax	Int. to Business	Total Savings	Adj. Income	PCE	PCE/ Adj. Inc.
U.S.	231.786	2663.494	110.88	409.3	56.8	135	1951.514	2045.5	1.048
Maine	1.136	10.902	0.439	1.595	0.177	0.527	8.164	8.9	1.092
NH	0.948	10.985	0.436	1.543	0.222	0.586	8.199	8.9	1.091
Vermont	0.520	5.267	0.206	0.778	0.081	0.274	3.928	4.3	1.106
Mass	5.750	73.243	2.875	11.758	1.167	3.999	53.444	57.4	1.075
RI	0.953	10.624	0.49	1.637	0.191	0.582	7.723	8.6	1.118
Conn	3.126	45.221	1.749	7.324	0.837	2.602	32.709	33.1	1.011
NY	17.567	224.631	9.424	41.062	3.140	12.666	158.338	167.2	1.056
NJ	7.427	102.666	4.071	16.511	1.855	6.035	74.195	75.1	1.012
Penn	11.879	135.749	5.623	20.202	2.287	6.992	100.645	103.3	1.026
Ohio	10.772	117.927	4.887	17.095	2.707	5.719	87.519	92.5	1.057
Indiana	5.482	56.708	2.333	8.096	1.280	2.816	42.183	42.7	1.013
Illinois	11.466	142.131	5.777	22.041	2.927	7.225	104.161	106.9	1.026
Michigan	9.116	101.203	3.796	16.351	2.273	4.723	74.060	76.7	1.035
Wisc	4.745	52.551	2.104	8.147	1.057	2.630	38.613	38.9	1.008
Minn	4.133	47.736	2.169	7.401	1.124	2.554	34.487	37.7	1.094
Iowa	2.906	31.476	1.272	4.765	0.643	1.719	23.077	23.2	1.003
Missouri	4.942	53.413	2.248	7.263	1.039	3.079	39.784	41.7	1.048
N. Dakota	0.672	7.046	0.345	1.086	0.126	0.405	5.084	5.8	1.138
S. Dakota	0.694	6.59	0.27	0.893	0.116	0.360	4.952	5.3	1.077
Nebraska	1.589	17.548	0.727	2.495	0.383	0.924	13.019	13.0	0.997
Kansas	2.408	28.584	1.155	4.117	0.574	1.527	21.211	19.6	0.922
Delaware	0.600	7.098	0.323	1.138	0.148	0.386	5.103	5.8	1.141
Maryland	4.270	54.491	2.023	8.627	1.263	2.802	39.776	42.4	1.065
Virginia	5.485	63.704	2.553	9.209	1.626	3.384	46.931	45.5	0.970
W. Virginia	1.961	17.621	0.741	2.741	0.301	0.809	13.029	13.2	1.015
N. Car.	6.019	55.872	2.61	7.906	1.206	2.627	41.523	41.7	1.003
S. Car.	3.227	28.041	1.291	3.909	0.620	1.229	20.991	20.6	0.982
Georgia	5.648	55.803	2.503	7.976	1.356	2.754	41.213	42.8	1.037
Florida	10.466	118.57	4.109	16.676	2.650	7.278	87.857	99.3	1.130
Kentucky	3.692	34.089	1.363	4.772	0.662	1.681	25.611	25.3	0.989
Tenn	4.656	42.871	2.043	5.916	0.928	1.974	32.010	35.2	1.099
Alabama	3.941	34.822	1.525	4.660	0.749	1.492	26.396	25.3	0.957
Miss	2.569	20.551	0.867	2.830	0.424	0.880	15.550	14.9	0.956
Arkansas	2.307	19.9	0.815	2.549	0.391	0.929	15.217	15.2	0.997
Louisiana	4.383	44.925	1.857	7.351	0.857	2.049	32.811	34.7	1.058
Oklahoma	3.226	36.704	1.553	5.827	0.740	1.698	26.887	26.1	0.969
Texas	15.329	179.679	7.694	28.149	3.752	8.119	131.965	135.9	1.030
Montana	0.805	8.113	0.378	1.311	0.167	0.409	5.848	6.8	1.159
Idaho	0.977	9.07	0.377	1.187	0.233	0.440	6.833	7.0	1.031
Wyoming	0.590	7.325	0.292	1.454	0.141	0.286	4.655	4.4	0.950
Colorado	3.071	38.857	1.574	5.806	1.123	2.052	28.301	30.6	1.080
N. Mexico	1.367	13.027	0.564	2.111	0.292	0.578	9.483	10.3	1.091
Arizona	2.892	29.751	1.311	4.396	0.844	1.457	21.743	25.8	1.186
Utah	1.571	14.048	0.712	2.082	0.454	0.614	10.186	12.3	1.204
Nevada	0.876	10.958	0.381	1.675	0.313	0.437	8.152	10.6	1.295
Wash	4.276	51.41	2.187	7.768	1.333	2.389	37.733	38.1	1.011
Oregon	2.668	28.275	1.225	4.138	0.770	1.453	20.689	23.4	1.131
Cal	24.697	328.035	13.8	48.474	8.735	15.524	241.503	254.6	1.054
DC	0.626	9.242	0.88	1.706	0.093	0.601	5.962	10.4	1.740
Alaska	0.444	7.771	0.386	2.919	0.166	0.245	4.055	5.2	1.278
Hawaii	0.997	11.736	0.547	1.879	0.257	0.479	8.574	11.3	1.321

*Income and other dollar aggregates in billions.

· N O T E S ·

Preface

1. George Santayana, *The Life of Reason, Reason in Religion* (New York: 1905), p. 182.

Chapter One

1. Arthur Okun, *Equality and Economic Efficiency* (Washington: 1975), reports "gaping disparities in economic well being" (p. 1). These are measured as deriving from "differences in income" (p. 40). Such "income rewards" are received for "productive contributions" (p. 42).

2. Cf. *American Economic Review* (May 1989).

3. Georg Simmel, *The Philosophy of Money* (London: 1900, reprint 1978), p. 373.

4. *Congressional Record* (Aug. 27, 1913), pp. 3807, 3819.

5. *New York Times* (Feb. 4, 1990).

6. Quoted by Richard Lester, *Economics of Labor* (New York: 1964), p. 340. As Lester notes (p. 332), "The sharp upward trend in nonwage benefits commenced in World War II. . . . In mid-1942 the National War Labor Board imposed definite limits on wage increases . . . but no such restraints were placed on reasonable contributions to employee benefit programs . . . as a result employer contributions to private pensions and other benefit programs rose."

7. *The National Income and Product Accounts of the U.S. 1929–82* (Washington: 1986), p. 49.

8. As though it were a simple matter of fact, an admiring biographer observes that "after what was for him a poor year [Richard Burton] put one million dollars into that fabled Swiss bank account." Melvyn Bragg, *Richard Burton: A Life, 1925–1984* (Boston: 1988), p. 123.

9. *New York Times* (June 28, 1992), p. H16. Only a court suit over plagiarism led to the discovery of data usually held in corporate records.

10. AP story in *Middletown Press* (Jan. 13, 1989), p. 18. The Foundation made grants of $45,400 and spent $70,200 in administrative expenses.

11. *New York Times* (July 8, 1992).

12. BLS Bulletin 2267, *Consumer Expenditure Survey: Interview Survey, 1984* (Washington: 1986), table 3. The BLS reports they had $11,724 in total expenditures; $1,797 in money income after taxes, receipt of food stamps, etc., plus about $300 in gifts.

13. "Survey of Consumer Finances, 1983," *Federal Reserve Bulletin* (Sept. 1984), pp. 686–88.

A small group of entrepreneurs reported low or negative incomes for the year, presumably the 7% who owned property and/or businesses. But removing them from the expenditure reports would make little change in the expenditure average for those with incomes of $5,000 and less. (The same group presumably brought the mean financial asset total to $3,254 as compared with the median of $513.)

14. Amartya Sen, *Poverty and Famines* (Oxford: 1981), p. 1. Sen refers (p. 2 n) to Nozick's "well-known exploration of the 'entitlement theory' of justice."

15. *New York Times* (Aug. 30, 1992), p. 14.

16. Smolensk Archive, quoted Hiroaki Kuromiya, *Stalin's Industrial Revolution* (Cambridge: 1988), p. 244.

17. Ivan Szelenyi, *Urban Inequalities Under State Socialism* (London: 1983), pp. 53, 56, 57, 69. Szelenyi's category for "tertiary educated people who might appear in equivalent Anglo-American classifications as 'salaried, professional, and scientific'" is "intellectual." We here label it "professional." The data came from his survey of Pecs and Szeged.

18. Nien Cheng, *Life and Death in Shanghai* (London: 1986), p. 517.

19. Ibid., p. 525.

20. James Angresano, *Comparative Economics* (Englewood Cliffs: 1992), p. 438.

Chapter Two

1. Peter Temin, *Did Monetary Forces Cause The Great Depression?* (New York: 1978). Temin's later *Lessons From the Great Depression* (Cambridge, Mass.: 1989) deepens our insight into the 1929–39 experience but does not expand or contradict his earlier views.

2. Tables 3.4 and 3.5 specify the detailed changes.

3. Temin utilizes the consumption series of Williamson and Swanson. They slightly revised Kuznets's figures, which included only two service items—rent and all other. We also estimate specific distribution margins for each of fifty-plus goods, whereas Kuznets estimated margins for three broad groups.

4. We use a 4% cut off to omit trivial changes, particularly those within the error of estimate. But do not stipulate 4% as a "statistically significant" cutoff level. However, the Appendix tables demonstrate that including all groups yields the same conclusions.

5. Stanley Lebergott, *Manpower in Economic Growth* (New York: 1964), p. 523.

6. Cf. the classic discussion in H. S. Houthakker and L. D. Taylor, *Consumer Demand in the United States: Analyses and Projections* (Cambridge, Mass.: 1970), pp. 9–24.

7. Senator Carter Glass, *An Adventure in Constructive Finance* (Garden City 1927), pp. 208–9 proudly described how "a solid Democratic vote against

insuring with government funds individual bank deposits" had won the day against "a solid Republican vote" when the FRB was established. Of course, in 1929 both Roosevelt and Hoover were opposed.

8. U.S. Census, *Historical Statistics . . . to 1970* (Washington: 1975), 2:1019.

9. William Shaw, *Value of Commodity Product Since 1969* (New York: 1947), p. 76.

10. U.S. Census, *Historical Statistics . . . 1970*, p. 693.

<h2 style="text-align:center">CHAPTER THREE</h2>

1. William E. Leuchtenburg, in John A. Garraty, *Interpreting American History* (New York: 1970), p. II–171.

2. Arthur Schlesinger, *The Crisis of the Old Order, 1919–1933* (Boston: 1957), p. 135.

3. John M. Dobson, *A History of American Enterprise* (Englewood Cliffs, N.J.: 1988), pp. 248–49.

4. Albert Niemi, *U.S. Economic History* (Chicago: 1986), p. 384.

5. Harold Faulkner, *American Economic History* (New York: 1960), p. 642.

6. Richard B. DuBoff, *Accumulation and Power: An Economic History of the United States* (Armonk, N.Y.: 1989), pp. 84–86.

7. Simon Kuznets, *National Income and Its Composition, 1919–1938* (New York: 1941), p. 218. Even if it had fallen, why would farmers and investors (who received the rest of the national income) abstain from toothbrushes and radios?

8. This, of course, is no Marxist analysis. For Marx, workers are always "exploited" under capitalism, with underconsumption and crisis following.

9. The unemployment rate is from Stanley Lebergott, *Manpower in Economic Growth*, p. 512. In multiple papers, Romer has applied a simple damping coefficient to the above unemployment series. Having based that coefficient on relationships between statistical series for 1960–80 they necessarily ignore the changes in the structure of the economy, and hence its elasticities, that occurred between the world of Coolidge and Hoover and that of Kennedy-Johnson-Nixon. A similar tactic used by Romer & Balke-Gordon for GNP is discussed below on pp. 125ff.

10. Of course in recent decades reliance on NBER dating has made this outcome inevitable by definition. However, the data underlying the classification are broadly consistent.

<h2 style="text-align:center">CHAPTER FOUR</h2>

1. The BEA income estimates for 1970 rest on even better sources than those for 1929. Items in group I rely chiefly on the Census of Business. Sources for group II were more varied, including other censuses. But they show declines quite as persistently. It is, therefore, not a decline in data quality, or grand change in sources, that can explain the change from 1929 to 1970.

2. Some nonsignificant ones arise from changes in type of source material—e.g., 1900 to 1929. Others probably report errors of estimate.

CHAPTER FIVE

1. Michael Voslensky, *Nomenklatura* (Garden City: 1984), pp. 94–95, 182–83, 202–4 is the source for USSR estimates and quotations except as indicated. Cf. also Alec Nove, "The Class Structure of the Soviet Union Revisited," *Soviet Studies* (July 1983). Cf. also Bohdan Harasymiw, *Political Elite Recruitment in the Soviet Union* (New York: 1984), p. 184 for an estimate of the Nomenklatura.

Voslensky's 1.5% is an estimate of "the privileged," who collect the battery of extra privileges. It is adopted by Christian Morrison, "Income Distribution in East European and Western Countries," *Journal of Comparative Economics* (June 1984), p. 126, and by Trevor Buck and John Cole, *Modern Soviet Economic Performance* (New York: 1987), p. 45.

Abram Bergson, "Income Inequality Under Soviet Socialism," *Journal of Economic Literature* (Sept. 1984), p. 1085 surmises that "perhaps 1%" of all wage and salary workers earned over 450 rubles per month "from all sources."

Alistair McAuley, *Economic Welfare in the Soviet Union* (Madison: 1979), p. 67 quotes Matthews as estimating 250,000 with official earnings on their primary job of 450 rubles per month (i.e., 5,400 per year) in 1970–72.

2. Internal Revenue Service, *Individual Income Tax Returns 1985* (Washington: 1987), table 1.1.

3. Voslensky, *Nomenklatura*. His book was published in 1984. U.S. data are for 1985 where possible, or are believed similar to those for that year.

4. McAuley, *Welfare*, p. 295. The marginal rate is 13% after an exemption of 70 rubles per month.

5. IRS, *Statistics of Income, 1985*, table 2.1.

6. Ibid.

7. David Shipler, *Russia, Broken Idols, Solemn Dreams* (New York: 1983), p. 247. Shipler instances large families with pensions so small they lacked food, etc. Yet their neighbors, even officials, felt it no concern of theirs.

8. *Wall Street Journal* (March 24, 1989), p. A8.

9. Voslensky, *Nomenklatura*, pp. 182, 183.

10. Matthews quoted in Bergson, "Inequality," p. 1059.

11. Cf. Morrison, "Income," p. 125.

12. Aron Katsenelinboigen, *Studies in Soviet Economic Planning* (White Plains: 1978), p. 179. During the late 1960s and 1975, when crop failures appeared, these prices went even higher: "They were one and a half to two times higher than the official limit prices" (ibid.)—i.e., up to six times official prices.

13. Kushnirsky quoted in Trevor Buck and John Cole, *Modern Soviet Economic Performance* (New York: 1987), p. 87.

14. Ibid.

15. *Time* (April 10, 1989), p. 82.

16. North Atlantic Treaty Organization, *Economic Aspects of Life in the USSR* (Brussels: 1975), p. 144.

17. *Time* (April 10, 1989), p. 51.

18. Katsenelinboigen, *Planning*, p. 193.

19. Andrei Kuteinikov, "Soviet Society—Much more Unequal than U.S." *Wall Street Journal* (Jan. 26, 1990).

20. The foreign currency store ratio for clothes is a similar "official" judgment. Only foreigners, in principle, have access to such stores.

21. We are not dealing with the "housing subsidy" to all those renting state housing but only the differential to the elite group.

22. Dennis O'Hearn, "The Consumer Second Economy: Size and Effects," *Soviet Studies* (April 1980), p. 225.

23. F.J.M. Feldbrugge, "Government and the Shadow Economy in the Soviet Union," *Soviet Studies* (Oct. 1984). The latter two cases fell under the category of "ten years in prison or the death sentence."

24. Mink, quoted in Morrison, "Income," p. 125.

25. *Voprosy Ekonomikii* quoted in Horst Herlemann, *Quality of Life in the Soviet Union* (Boulder, Colo: 1987), p. 60; and the head of the Department of Registration and Allocation of Living Space in Henry Morton, "Who Gets What, When, and How? Housing in the Soviet Union," *Soviet Studies* (April 1980), p. 241.

26. Henry Morton in Horst Herlemann, *Quality of Life*, p. 95.

27. Katsenelinboigen, *Planning*, p. 179. Joint Economic Committee, *Consumption in the U.S.S.R.: An International Comparison* (Washington: 1981), p. 77. A Soviet source quoted by the JEC reports 187 rubles—40% higher—for an apartment with 45 square meters, including bath and kitchen facilities.

28. Personal income for the average industrial worker's family averaged 3,000 rubles in 1974 (Alastair McAuley, *Economic Welfare*, p. 40). Sarkisyan is quoted as estimating rents in the late 60s consuming 4 to 5% of the urban family budget, inclusive of community services (p. 289)—which comes to about 135 rubles.

29. Dushanbe in 1962: Alfred Di Maio, *Soviet Urban Housing* (New York: 1974), p. 131. Moscow: David Shipler, *Russia* (New York: 1983), p. 175.

30. A Western diplomat is recently quoted as saying that "the cost of renovating a Soviet apartment to our standards is $100,000, if you can find one." *Time* (April 10, 1989), p. 84. Given a 10% interest rate that would mean some $8,000 as the annual rental value. If everything were bought at the official exchange rate of $1.60 the ruble rent would thus be 5,000. The Nomenklatura advantage would fall somewhere between this 5,000 figure and the 600 one we actually use. The JEC comparison is not likely to allow adequately for quality differences.

31. Murray Feshbach in 97th Cong., 2nd Sess., Joint Economic Committee, *Soviet Economy in the 1980s* (Washington: Dec. 1982), part 2, pp. 219–20.

32. Shipler, *Russia*, pp. 216–22.

33. Morrison, "Income," p. 125.

34. *Wall Street Journal* (Aug. 1987), p. 1. Cf. Mark Field, "Medical Care in the Soviet Union," in Horst Herlemann, *Quality of Life*, pp. 70–71.

35. *Time* (April 10, 1989), p. 82.

36. Their average medical deduction is 6.8 times as great as that taken by

those in the $20,000 to $30,000 AGI category. IRS, *1975*, table 2.1. It would still greater if one allowed for the fact that the rich tend to be older and have fewer children remaining in the family.

Medical expenditures reported by the median BLS family are, of course, lower than those taken by persons who deduct. BLS families spent $889 in 1984, while the corresponding income group reported $1,598 as their deduction. Given the high likelihood that those with high medical expenditures will deductions, the figures are tolerably comparable.

37. Marshall Goldman, *USSR in Crisis* (New York: 1983), p. 104.

38. Bergson, "Income," p. 1059.

39. Fedor Burlatsky, *Kruschev and the First Russian Spring* (New York, 1988), p. 198.

40. Joint Economic Committee, *Consumption*, pp. 54, 60.

41. Arkady Shevchenko, *Breaking With Moscow* (New York: 1985), p. 232. It cost $2,000 in American dollars and $13–$14,000 in rubles. Midlevel diplomats in Moscow then earned 2,400 to 2,500 rubles per year.

Since the market for new cars adjusts via black market price adjustment and competition for used cars, the waiting period for the average buyer—not the most law-abiding buyer—may be shorter. For Poland in the 1980s the average wait ran between three to six months. Cf. W. Charemza, M. Granicki, and R. E. Quandt, "Modelling Parallel Markets in Centrally Planned Economies," *European Economic Review* (1988), 32:876.

42. *Time* (April 10, 1989), p. 51.

43. North Atlantic Treaty Organization, *Economic Aspects of Life in the USSR*, p. 55.

44. Cf. *inter alia*, Shipler, pp. 194–97.

45. Voslensky, *Nomenklatura*, p. 182.

46. Morton, "Who Gets What," p. 248.

47. Goldman, *USSR*, p. 104.

48. Morrison, *Income*, p. 126.

49. Matthews makes no specific calculation, but proposes a factor of 50% or 100% as "not unreasonable." (Mervyn Matthews, "Top Incomes in the U.S.S.R.," in North Atlantic Treaty Organization, Economic Aspects, p. 148.) Buck and Cole "accept Morison's judgment based on Soviet and Polish experience" of "up to 100% on top of official incomes" (Buck and Cole, *Performance*, p. 45). These measures do not reckon with the considerable advantages of sheer availability in housing, housing repair, medical care, foreign travel, etc.

50. The careful attention to advantage across the consumption spectrum is noteworthy. More ordinary members of the nomenklatura achieved such gains by regularized blat. Those higher up were explicitly designated, in Burlatsky's joke. The "head of the Central Committee Administration of Affairs decides . . . who was eligible for . . . a salary, special rations, a flat, a dacha, a car, a special telephone and so on" (Burlatsky, *Kruschev*, p. 198).

Yeltsin noted that even as a candidate member of the Politburo his "domestic staff consisted of three cooks, three waitresses, a housemaid, and a gardener, with his own team of assistant gardeners . . . the dacha had its own cinema, and every Friday, Saturday and Sunday a projectionist would arrive complete with a selection of films." His car, driver and guard were available 24 hours a day. His Kremlin ration of generally unobtainable products was "paid for at half its nominal price." His access to otherwise unobtainable quality medical care, schools for his children, luxury housing, are also itemized. Boris Yeltsin, *Against the Grain: An Autobiography* (New York, 1950), pp. 158–59.

51. John Maynard Keynes, *The Economic Consequences of the Peace* (New York: 1920), p. 20.

52. The *Federal Reserve Bulletin* (March 1986, pp. 166, 168, and Sept. 1984, p. 68) indicates that the upper 2% of the nation's families had a net worth 13.13 times their annual income, as compared to a 5.08 ratio for all families. We applied the ratio of 2.5846 times 7.72 to infer their saving rate. The 7.72 is the sum of personal savings in 1960–82 divided by personal income for the same period, from BEA, *National Income and Product Accounts of the United States*, vol. 2, 1958–88, table 2.1. Mean income for the households over $100,000 was computed from U.S. Internal Revenue Service, *Individual Tax Returns, 1983* (Washington, 1985), tables 1.1, 1.4.

53. An interest rate of 2.2% is estimated by Henry Morton in U.S. Joint Economic Committee, *Soviet Economy in a Time of Change* (Washington: 1979), p. 787. Cf. Bergson, "Income Inequality Under Soviet Socialism," *Journal of Economic Literature* (Sept. 1984), p. 1089.

54. Savings rates from Gur Ofer and Joyce Pickersgill, "Soviet Household Saving," *Quarterly Journal of Economics* (Aug. 1980), p. 133.

55. Throughout we have compared household incomes and spending in the U.S. with official salaries and earnings in the USSR.

56. We have not adjusted the U.S. figures for unreported consumption. Only if the differential adjustment by income level were greater than that for the USSR would that matter here. And that seems highly unlikely.

57. Nien Heng, *Life and Death*, p. 517.

CHAPTER SIX

1. John Maynard Keynes, *The General Theory of Employment, International Money* (New York: 1936), p. 114.

2. E.g., "liquidity preference," which helped to determine interest rates, and "animal spirits," which helped determine investment.

Keynes later wrote that "my theory does not require my so-called psychological law as a premise. What the theory shows is that if the psychological law is *not* fulfilled, then we have a condition of complete instability." But that condition, he added, is not "characteristic of the actual state of affairs." Donald Moggridge, ed., *The Collected Writings of John Maynard Keynes* (London: 1973), XIV:276.

3. Joseph Schumpeter, *History of Economic Analysis* (New York: 1954), p. 1059 called it a type of pseudo-psychology.

4. He, of course, dealt with both income and consumption in "wage units"—i.e., each divided by the price of one day of "ordinary" [i.e., un-

skilled] "labour." That division would not affect the price/quantity changes considered here.

5. Henri Theil, *Principles of Econometrics* (New York: 1971), p. 327.

6. Herman Wold and Lars Jureen, *Demand Analyses* (New York: 1953), p. 81.

7. U.S. Commissioner of Labor, *Eighteenth Annual Report, Cost of Living and Retail Prices of Food* (Washington: 1904), p. 367.

8. U.S. Bureau of Labor Statistics, Bulletin 822, *Family Spending and Saving in Wartime* (Washington: 1945), table 73.

9. Bulletin 822, table 35.

10. U.S. Bureau of Labor Statistics, Bulletin 2267 (Washington: 1986), table 3.

11. U.S. Bureau of Labor Statistics, Bulletin 2354, *Consumer Expenditure Survey, 1987* (Washington: 1990), table 2.

12. Data computed from Horst Mendershausen, *Changes in Income Distribution During the Great Depression* (New York: 1946), averaging distributions in each region and weighting regions by the population census counts.

CHAPTER SEVEN

1. Michael Mussa, *A Study in Macroeconomics* (Amsterdam: 1976), pp. 34, 33.

2. Kenneth Arrow in Robin Hogarth and Melvin Reder, *Rational Choice* (Chicago: 1987), p. 204.

3. *General Theory*, p. 108.

4. Though put forward earlier by Houthakker, its most elegant development is in H. S. Houthakker and L. Taylor, *Consumer Demand in the United States* (Cambridge, Mass.: 1970), chap. 1.

5. G. Becker and G. Stigler, "De Gustibus Non Est Disputandum," *American Economic Review* (March 1977).

6. Franklin Fisher, *Disequilibrium Foundations of Equilibrium Economics* (Cambridge, Mass.: 1983), p. 123. "It is preferable, however, to think of the objective function as fixed, with the household's past consumption activities changing the constraints under which it operates by fixing more and more of the arguments of its utility function, as it were."

7. Richard Cyert and Morris De Groot, *Bayesian Analysis and Uncertainty in Economic Theory* (Totowa, N.J.: 1987), p. 127.

8. The penumbra of elements that surround money prices is well known: speed of delivery, credit terms, ability to return for full credit, etc. The non-monetary components omitted by the (universally used) money income measure are also well known: imputed value of owned housing, value of food stamps, medical subsidy, etc. As for cost, Buchanan has indicated why it is, in principle, unknowable. Cf. his introduction to James Buchanan, *L.S.E. Essays on Cost* (London: 1973).

9. Angus Deaton and John Muellbauer, *Economics and Consumer Behavior* (Cambridge, 1980). Arthur Lewbel, "A Unified Approach to Incorporating Demographic or Other Effects into Demand Systems," *Review of Economic*

Studies (1985). R.A. Pollak and T. Wales, "Demographic Variables in Demand Analysis," *Econometrica* (Nov. 1981), 49: 1533–59. R. Barnes and R. Gillingham, "Demographic Effects in Demand Analysis . . . ," *Review of Economics and Statistics*, 66:591–601 (1984).

Advanced statistical ingenuity, and considerable data pooling, were needed to enable the latter scholars to estimate the 110 parameters necessary merely for computing expenditure and price elasticities of four expenditure items, in five family-size groups.

10. Missing factors and interaction terms developed by measuring "tastes" may be a larger issue for psychological and sociological inquiries. Moreover, we do not propose to weight, in advance, say, education and income to get a measure of status. Each variable should have a chance to reveal its importance for a particular demand.

11. Few (completed) periods of unemployment are lengthy despite the incentives of extended periods of insurance.

12. Gary Becker, *The Economic Approach to Human Behavior* (Chicago: 1976), p. 140.

13. Studies of single variables often come up with the same result. For example, a ratio of consumer durable to nondurable prices yields "the wrong sign" in Michael Darby, "Postwar U.S. Consumption, Consumer Expenditures and Saving," *American Economic Review* (May 1975), p. 221. Cf. Mayer, ibid., p. 223.

14. An impressive analysis by Kokoski, Cardiff, and Moulton provides the first published report to give real insight into the adequacy of CPI data for interarea comparability. ("Interarea Price Indicies for Consumer Goods and Services: An Hedonic Approach using CPI data" BLS Working Paper 256, July 1994.)

Its estimates for food at home show 42 cities and regional centers in the continental U.S. with indices between 93 and 107, most within an even narrower band. But scrutiny of the other items, as well as the details for food, suggests the underlying CPI data require more work.

For example, the indices for "entertainment" expenditure show Los Angeles and San Diego less than 8% above the national average—but San Francisco, improbably, 67% greater. New automobiles, like auto parts, run within 4% of the national average in cities from Boston down the seaboard through Baltimore. The index for new cars in Washington, DC, are also within 4%, but its auto parts are reported as 80% of the average. (Even food items, at the more detailed level, raise questions. Thus New York City prices are within 12% of the overall average for cereals, fats and oils, fish and other items, but are estimated as 27% higher for "other prepared foods" (chiefly canned soups, and spices). Arbitragers with some trucks would have a field day if reality conformed to these estimates.

The housing data are not compared with those of the decennial Census, nor (as in Follain's hedonic indices) the Annual Housing Survey.

This working paper, as the earlier one by Primont and Kokoski, reflects an extremely high level of theoretical sophistication, and an enormous effort in data analysis. Its revelation of the quality of BLS price data, even if indirect, marks a welcome break with the past. One hopes so masterful a study portends continuing work of such quality on the BLS price data.

15. The stereotypes remain an efficient opening gambit in the remaining ninety-nine out of one hundred encounters.

16. The 1900 Census data do not report families by number of children, and we substitute as an approximation the total family size.

17. Collinearity prevents using both percent of the population that was foreign born and the percent alien.

18. Paul Baker and Michael Little, eds., *Man in the Andes, A Multidisciplinary Study of High-Altitude Quechau* (Stroudsburg: 1976), p. 330.

19. A recent expert analysis simply includes "region" as a "control" for cultural and environmental factors affecting consumption patterns." Panos Tsakloglov, "Estimation and Comparison of Two Simple Models of Equivalence Scales for the Cost of Children," *Economic Journal* (March 1991), p. 349.

20. The reason for including "region" is rarely specified. We assume it is somehow intended to mark tastes, mores, lifestyle, etc.

21. The District of Columbia, Alaska, and Hawaii are omitted from the regression.

22. Other NOAA measures available by state are collinear with these measures, or proved to have no relationship with a variety of expenditure items. Since nothing in economic theory makes a case for any of these measures we omit further comment on them.

CHAPTER EIGHT

1. Data from the *U.S. Statistical Abstract, 1991* (Washington: 1991), pp. 220, 224. Specifically, number of days multiplied by the number of degrees below freezing (32°F). We combined unpublished figures for each of three thousand counties, kindly provided by the Department of Energy, into estimates by state. Each county in a state was given equal weight. Tests for California showed that population weighting had little effect on the correlations.

2. The 1890 Census reports interest rates by state.

3. 1900 Census, *Supplementary Analysis* (1906), p. 436 and 1930 Census of Population, *Families* (1933), p. 13 give size distributions for native and foreign-born families.

4. We have no separate estimate for this item in 1900. The 1929 regression included four variables: percent of population aged 0–4, 5–14, 65 +, and 5 to 9 as a percent of 5–14. The $\bar{R}^2$ was .77.

5. The variables included were those used for 1900 plus percent foreign born, black, Hispanic, and degree days. The $\bar{R}^2$ was .32.

6. For example, Jerome Bentley et al., *Final Report, The Cost of Children: A Household Expenditures Approach* (Mathtech, Oct. 1981). Bentley et al. provide estimates for white families living in the Northeast and North Central Regions (in tables 7-B1) based on the BLS survey. They suggest that in families with children aged 6 or less, food spending for the children averaged from 20% of that for their parents (at the $30,000 expenditure level) to 40% (at the $10,000 level).

7. BLS, Bulletin 2246, *Consumer Expenditure Survey: Interview Data, 1982–83*, table 5. "Per capita food at home" for husband-wife families averaged $524 per adult. Families with "oldest child under 5" averaged 1.5 more persons, but spent only $344 more for food at home.

8. To be exact, 48%. Cf. 1980 Census of Population, *General Population Characteristics, U.S. Summary*, table 56, which reports 17.7 million families having "own children under 6 only." For this latter group the BLS reports an average family size of 3.5 individuals.

CHAPTER NINE

1. Cf. the author's *The American Economy, Income, Wealth and Want* (Princeton: 1976), pp. 326–76 for estimates and methodology except as covered below.

2. 1977 Census of Retail Trade, *Subject Statistics* (Washington: 1978), vol. I, pp. 1–35 and 3–49 can be used to derive this estimate. The census got returns from all firms with over three employees, and sampled the smaller.

3. 1977 Census of Service Industries, *Subject Statistics* (Washington: 1981), vol. I, pp. 1–39, A–1.

4. 1980 Census of Housing, *General Housing Characteristics, United States Summary* (Washington: 1983), pp. C–1, E–4.

5. William Shaw, *Value of Commodity Product Since 1869* (New York: 1947). The key tables used are tables 1-1 and 1-2.

6. Kuznets does not provide such detail in his later work. But totals—e.g., in his *Value of Product Since 1869* (New York: 1946)—for perishables, nondurables, and durables do reflect key revisions that Shaw made in the underlying detail.

7. Harold Barger, *Distribution's Place in the American Economy Since 1869* (New York: 1955). Since the present estimates were first completed and sent to the NS7 in 1981 Martha Olney similarly derived figures for consumer durables in her *Buy Now Pay Later* (Chapel Hill: 1991).

8. Ibid., p. 92.

9. Table B-5, pp. 132–39.

10. Comparable Shaw figures for the decennial census dates appear in Barger, pp. 131, 130.

11. Shaw's annual figures for 1900–1919 appear in his table 1-1. His 1920–29 data appear in table 1-2. Since these series frequently differ in level a 1919 ratio link was usually required to provide a continuous comparable series. The markup percentages varied by small amounts for some categories, larger for others. Thus the markup over producers' value for shoes was 33.25 for 1899; 35.02 for 1909; 35.77 for 1919; and 35.96 for 1929. For household furniture, it ran 38.31, 38.86, 44.53, and 46.78, respectively.

12. Shaw, *Value Product*, pp. 70–71, summing manufactured plus nonmanufactured food.

13. Frederick Strauss and Louis Bean, *Gross Farm Income and Indices of Farm Production and Prices in the United States, 1869–1937*, U.S. Department of Agriculture, *Technical Bulletin No. 703* (Washington: 1940), p. 28. We sum the

series for staple foodstuffs, fruits, dairy products, chickens, eggs, meat animals, and export of live cattle.

14. Exports from *Historical Statistics . . . to 1970*, p. 889. These were reduced by the distribution percentage given by Shaw, *Value Product*, p. 271.

15. The ratio of materials to value of product in food manufacturing is available for census years in Fifteenth Census, *Manufactures, Vol. II* (Washington: 1933), p. 36. Ratios were interpolated for intervening years, then applied to the export values. The implicit materials figures were then reduced by Shaw's distribution percentage for exports of manufactured food.

16. U.S. Department of Agriculture, *Agricultural Economic Report No. 138, Food, Consumption, Prices, Expenditures* (Washington: 1956), p. 177.

17. Food consumed at retail consists of unprocessed foods consumed directly plus those bought by factories, value added in food factories, and the distributive margin on both unprocessed and processed food.

18. In 1929 value added in food manufacturing came to $3.4 billion—compared to $18.0 for food bought at retail. Excluding the manufacture of animal feed would, of course, make the true ratio still lower.

19. For the quinquennial years 1899–1919 the ratios run: 16.7, 15.6, 15.4, 16.4, and 14.9. For the biennial years 1921–29 the ratios were 19.6, 20.5, 19.2, 19.1, and 21.3. Computed from the 1920 Census, *Manufactures, 1919* (Washington: 1923), XI, pp. 26ff., and 1930 Census, *Manufactures, 1929* (Washington: 1933), II, pp. 41–42, data adjusted for comparability with those for earlier years. However, they reflect the data imbedded in the census figures and, therefore, in Shaw's estimates.

20. Thus the trend is based on a margin estimate of 58.8% of retail value in 1900 and 58% in 1929, using USDA farmer's share data. Barger's margins for restaurants run from 59.6 (1899) to 62.0 (1929). (For bars and liquor stores in 1899 the figures were 55.2% and 46.0%, respectively.) Harold Barger, *Distribution's Place in the American Economy Since 1869* (New York: 1935), p. 92. What is relevant here is the trend in margin, since the present estimates are benchmarked to the BEA 1929 figure. The trend is quite consistent with that shown for this sector by Barger.

21. U.S. Department of Agriculture, *Agricultural Economics Report, No. 138* (Washington: 1968), p. 163.

22. Employment figures from the author's *Manpower in Economic Growth*, p. 515. Because the USDA estimates of farm population for these early years are based on an average of methods, none particularly precise, they do not clearly measure change in the farm consumption group more reliably.

23. Armed Forces: Census, *Historical Statistics . . . to 1970* (Washington: 1975), p. 1141. Domestic Services: *Manpower in Economic Growth*, p. 515. Population: *Historical Statistics . . . to 1970*, p. 8 data for resident population, to which armed forces overseas 1917–19 were added. On average, the typical armed forces member was provided with as much food from the U.S. as the average U.S. adult, allowing for differences in age composition, inventory accumulation, waste, and losses in shipment.

24. War Department, *Annual Reports, 1917* (Washington: 1918), vol. 1, p.

258. A subsistence total is given on p. 318 and the size of the army in the War Department, *Annual Reports, 1918* (Washington: 1919), vol. 1, p. 11.

25. *Annual Reports, 1919* (Washington: 1920), p. 754 gives a subsistence series totaling $630 million. This is adjusted down to $592 million because of an accounting change that included forage after November 2. The adjustment was made by deducting "raw materials"—i.e., fuel—from the combined fuel and forage category in November and December, then dividing by animal stocks, estimated by using data from page 752. The fiscal 1919 average size of the army was derived from data in 1918 *Reports*, p. 11, and 1919, pp. 496–97.

26. 1900 Census, *Manufactures*, Part 1 (Washington, 1902), vol. VII, pp. 281, 285, summing the value for the distilled alcohol, vinous alcohol, and malt liquor industries.

27. Commissioner of Labor, Twelfth Annual Report, *Economic Aspects of the Liquor Problem* (Washington: 1898), p. 50.

28. The return on capital thus estimated for 1896, $90 million, was increased to $109 billion for 1899 by the percentage change inferred from the decennial rate of change in investment in liquor manufacturing. (1900 Census, *Manufactures*, vol. VII, part 1, p. 10.)

29. The number of entrepreneurs and full-time equivalent employees for 1896 is given in Commissioner of Labor, *Twelfth Report*, p. 51. That number for 1896 was extrapolated to 1899 by the percentage change inferred from linear interpolation of the number of saloon keepers in 1890 and 1900. (1900 Census, *Occupations at the Twelfth Census* [Washington: 1904], p. 1.) The median earnings of bartenders in 1901 are computed from data in the Commissioner of Labor, *Eighteenth Annual Report* (Washington: 1904), p. 264.

30. U.S. Census, *Historical Statistics . . . to 1970*, p. 1108.

31. Commissioner of Labor, *Twelfth Annual Report*, p. 62. U.S. Census, Wealth, *Debt and Taxation* (Washington: 1907), p. 979.

32. Commissioner of Labor, *Twelfth Annual Report*, p. 44.

33. Barger, *Distribution's Place*, p. 92.

34. Ibid., pp. 128 (note a), 184. The Massachusetts survey was conducted by the unit that Carrol Wright had left a few years earlier to conduct the 1896 survey as Commissioner of Labor.

35. Gallons consumed: *Statistical Abstract of the United States, 1922* (Washington: 1923), p. 697.
Prices: Clark Warburton, *The Economic Results of Prohibition* (New York: 1932), p. 112, whiskey and lager beer. The 1900 Census, *Manufactures*, vol. 9, p. 599 indicates lager "had almost entirely superseded . . . ale and porter" by 1900. The fiscal year data as reported were adjusted to calendar years. Barrels were taken as equal to thirty-one gallons. The 1918–19 change was estimated from food prices by the proportion of 1917–18 change in retail food prices to that of alcohol prices.

36. Using data from his table II-1.

37. His group figures, in tables I-1 and I-2 were adjusted for comparability at 1919, as in part 1 above.

38. Data for stamps sold from *Historical Statistics . . . to 1970*, pp. 804–5. Price data from Shaw, *Value Product*, table IV-1.

39. Implicitly this assumed that the trend for the combination of three groups—newspapers, magazines, and stationery—reflects that for the first two groups.

40. Shaw, *Value Product*, p. 34.

41. For transportation cost we use the ratio implicit in Barger's tables, pp. 130–31, and for distributive margin, his p. 92 ratio.

42. Forest Service Circular 181, Albert Pierson, *Consumption of Firewood in the United States* (Washington: Sept. 1910), p. 3.

43. 1910 Census, *Manufactures, 1909* (Washington: 1913), VIII, p. 373.

44. 18th Annual Report of the Commissioner of Labor, 1903, *Cost of Living and Retail Prices of Food* (Washington: 1904), p. 508 reports data by region. To adjust for the nonrandom sample taken by the Commission we weight the regions by the number gainfully occupied in each, using data from 1900 Census, *Occupations at the Twelfth Census* (Washington: 1904), p. cxliv. The urban family count is estimated at 68% of the U.S. total, 69% being the proportion in 1910, and slightly more in 1920. *Historical Statistics . . . to 1970*, p. 43.

45. Shaw, p. 263, estimates the household share in coal consumption for 1919 at 12% (using the 1923 percentage); 13% for 1915; and the same 13% for years prior to 1915. However, the urbanization trend, and the shift to coal away from wood, would not be adequately picked up by this constant ratio, which he terms an "obviously crude estimate."

46. Pierson, *Consumption of Wood*.

47. Cf. *The American Economy*, pp. 273–74.

48. 1910 Census, *Agriculture, 1909 and 1910* (Washington: 1913), p. 729.

49. The substantial volume of lumber used for farm repairs would have been bought from sawmills, leaving only the portion exchanged directly for such lumber to be included.

50. Cf. A. E. Goldenweiser, "The Farmer's Income," *American Economic Review* (March 1916), p. 43.

51. Commissioner of Labor, *Cost of Living*, p. 370.

52. Total wood: Interpolations of Forest Service decennial data appear in Sam Schurr and Bruce Netschert, *Energy in the American Economy, 1850–1975* (Baltimore: 1960), p. 492. We interpolate for intercensal years.

53. 1910 Census, *Manufactures, 1909*, VIII, p. 373.

54. 1920 Census, *Manufactures, 1909* (Washington: 1923), X, p. 798.

55. The fuel price series is that of Albert Rees for 1900–1914 (his *Real Wages in Manufacturing, 1890–1914* [New York: 1961], p. 110).

For 1915–29 the Rees index was extrapolated by a weighted average of the price indices for anthracite and bituminous, Shaw's data indicating consumption of each by households. (Price data from *Historical Statistics . . . to 1970*, p. 214. Shaw's consumption data from ibid., p. 262.)

A 1929 benchmark was estimated by dividing the Pierson cordwood total consumption figure into Barger's estimate of firewood at producers' prices, (Barger's producer's price total from ibid., p. 130). The latter was then raised to retail levels, assuming a one-third markup. Barger estimates 31.9% of retail cost as the margin for coal and lumber stores (ibid., p. 92).

56. Quoted by Strauss and Bean, *Gross Farm Income*. This series shows little change for 1924–28, then a decline of 40 + % from 1928 to 1929.

57. Shaw, *Value Product*, p. 112; Kuznets, Value of Product, p. 82. These census year percentages were then interpolated for intercensal years.

58. Shaw, *Value Product*, p. 110; Kuznets, Value of Product, p. 80.

59. Annual food series from Shaw, tables 1-1 and 1-2.

60. To mark the trend in the proportion of durables we used output data for billiard tables, etc., sleds, pocket knives, firearms, and cameras.

61. 1900 Census, *Agriculture*, part 2 (Washington: 1903), p. 774.

62. Nursery product total from ibid., p. 783.

63. Strauss and Bean, *Gross Farm Income*, p. 14.

64. Data from the *1900 Census, Agriculture* (Washington: 1902), vol. VI, part 2, pp. 780–83; *1920 Census, Agriculture* (Washington: 1922), vol. V, pp. 884, 886; *1930 Census, Agriculture* (Washington: 1923), vol. II, part 1, p. 110. Cash receipts from Census, *Historical Statistics . . . to 1970*, p. 483, and self-employed farmers from *Manpower in Economic Growth*, p. 515.

65. Seed farms in 1900 and 1910 from the *1910 Census of Agriculture* (Washington: 1923), vol. V, other years linearly interpolated. Cash receipts per such farm extrapolated by the average for all farms.

66. Population abroad, Military personnel: *Historical Statistics . . . to 1970*, pp. 8, 1141.

67. Monthly estimates of the AEF are taken from Leonard Ayers, *The War With Germany* (Washington: 1919), p. 15.

68. Earnings data from *Manpower in Economic Growth*, p. 254.

69. The relevant data relate to commodity lines, whereas even the most detailed inventory figures available annually relate to combinations of finished and unfinished goods. Moreover, the data should cover accumulation at all levels of manufacturing (or agriculture), wholesaling, and retailing.

70. Moses Abramowitz, *Inventories and Business Cycles* (New York: 1950), table 114.

71. Leo Grebler et al., *Capital Formation in Residential Real Estate* (New York: 1956). The prior estimates appear in the author's *The American Economy: Income, Wealth and Want* (Princeton: 1976), pp. 342–44.

72. Grebler, *Capital Formation*, p. 342.

73. Lebergott, *The American Economy*, pp. 372–74. The 1929 total was extrapolated by the sum of two component series. (1) Gifts, except those to the Red Cross were estimated for 1929 as the BEA total minus the Jenkins estimate for the Red Cross. That figure was extrapolated to 1924 by gifts to identical community chests, and back to 1913 by benevolences to Protestant denominations. (2) Red Cross contributions for 1924–29, and for the years 1917–18, when they were massively important were estimated from Jenkins. The series were added, then used to extrapolate the BEA figure back to 1917. The 1917 figures were extrapolated to earlier years by procedures outlined in *The American Economy*.

74. U.S. Bureau of Labor, Bulletin No. 77, *Retail Prices of Food, 1890–1902* (Washington: 1908), pp. 181–332, and Bulletin No. 184, U.S. Bureau of Labor Statistics, *Retail Prices of Food, 1907 to June 1915* (Washington: 1916), pp. 14–15.

75. Production data from Strauss and Bean, *Gross Farm Income*, pp. 36–119. The weight for vegetables and fruit was used for the potato price series.

76. Census, *Historical Statistics . . . to 1970*, p. 901.

77. BLS Bulletin 691, *Changes in Cost of Living in Large Cities in the United States, 1913–1941* (Washington: 1941), p. 17. These weights derive from the 1918 cost of living survey. We omitted the price series for salt beef since both the 1901 and the 1918 cost of living surveys showed only trivial expenditures for such beef.

78. Albert Rees, *Real Wages in Manufacturing, 1890–1914* (New York: 1961), p. 74.

79. The BLS prices for 1907–11 were not collected concurrently but only in a single retrospective survey. (BLS Bulletin 105, *Retail Prices 1890 to 1911* [Washington: 1912] part 2, p. 6.) They show (in consequence?) an unreasonable stability for both pork and beef prices. For example, they indicate that retail pork prices rose about 20% from 1908 to 1910. Yet packers paid 60% more for hogs. (BLS Bulletin 77 and Strauss/Bean, p. 119.) The BLS data actually report constant or declining prices for bacon in some stores in Chicago and Omaha. But it is improbable that the packers cartel did not pass along the 60% rise in hog prices. And it is almost equally improbable that local meat markets absorbed such an increase, not passing it along to the consumer.

80. Census, *Historical Statistics . . . to 1970*, p. 211.

81. Price data reported in William Nicholls, *Price Policies in the Cigarette Industry* (Nashville: 1951), pp. 46, 80.

82. Shaw, *Value Product*, pp. 290–91.

83. *Quarterly Report*, Chief, Bureau of Statistics, Treasury Department, *Imports, Exports, Immigration and Navigation of the United States . . . 1886* (Washington: 1887), pp. 393–95, and Clark Warburton, *The Economic Results of Prohibition* (New York: 1933), p. 112.

84. Data from the Cincinnati Chamber of Commerce *Annual Reports* appear in Warburton, *The Economic Results of Prohibition*. Ale, lager beer and porter prices were averaged, and that series combined with a whisky price series. The weights used to combine them were the values of manufactured products in 1914. (Product data from Fourteenth Census, *Manufactures*, p. 165.)

85. U.S. Census, *Statistical Abstract, 1974* (Washington: 1973), p. 421.

86. *Historical Statistics . . . to 1970*, p. 211; Rees, *Real Wages*, p. 74.

87. Shaw, *Value Product*, pp. 292–93.

88. *Manpower*, p. 526; John Kendrick, *Productivity Trends in the United States* (Princeton: 1961), pp. 506–61.

89. Shaw, *Value Product*, p. 296.

90. *Historical Statistics . . . to 1970*, p. 211; Rees, *Real Wages*, p. 74. Separate deflation of the farm housing component has not been attempted in previous work, whether by Kuznets, Kendrick, etc. The underlying BAE estimates are not presented in sufficient detail to determine the price series initially used to compute repairs, insurance, taxes on farm housing, or the relevant weights for these and for interest.

91. *Historical Statistics . . . to 1970*, p. 211; Rees, *Real Wages*, p. 74.

92. U.S. Census, *Manufactures, 1914* (Washington: 1918–19), vol. 2, p. 593.

93. BLS Bulletin 493, *Wholesale Prices 1913 to 1928* (Washington: 1929), p. 212, averaging the Cincinnati and Philadelphia price indices.

94. *Manufactures*, vol. 2, p. 616; U.S. Census, *Manufactures, 1914* (Washington: 1933), vol. 2, p. 547; Shaw, *Value Product*, pp. 290–91.

95. Rees, *Real Wages*, p. 107, U.S. Bureau of Labor Statistics, Bulletin 495, *Retail Prices, 1890 to 1929* (Washington: 1929), p. 208.

96. *BLS Bulletin 628, Changes in Retail Prices of Gas, 1923–36* (Washington: 1937), p. 49; Rees, *Real Wages*, p. 106.

97. *Historical Statistics . . . to 1970*, p. 827.

98. Fred L. Collins, *Consolidated Gas Co. of N.Y.: A History* (New York: 1934).

99. Willford I. King, *The National Income and Its Purchasing Power* (New York: 1930), p. 365; and *Manpower*, p. 526. The sector being one with low productivity change, no adjustment was made for productivity change.

100. Rees, *Real Wages*, p. 110. Prices for 1915–29 for coal are from *Historical Statistics*, p. 214; for gas, from BLS Bulletin 495, *Retail Prices, 1890–1929*, p. 208; and for kerosene from BLS Bulletin 493, *Wholesale Prices, 1913–1928*, p. 140. Expenditure weights are available for 1890, 1918, and 1935–39 from Rees, *Real Wages*, p. 111, and BLS Bulletin 699, *Changes in Cost of Living 1913–14*, p. 99. They were interpolated for intervening years.

101. *Historical Statistics . . . to 1970*, pp. 783, 785, 786.

102. *Manpower*, Appendix table A-18.

103. Earnings from *Manpower*, p. 526, with productivity adjustment.

104. *The American Economy*, p. 358.

105. Ibid.

106. *Manpower in Economic Growth*, table A-18, adjusted for productivity change. The 1921–22 estimates in that source were, however, adjusted since subsequent study of the BLS data that underly the Kuznets's estimates show a bias because of a change in the number of reporting hospitals.

107. Data for Boston, New York, Philadelphia, and Washington hospitals appear in 55th Cong. 2nd Sess. H.R. 776, Joint Select Committee to Investigate the Charities and Reformatory Institutions in the District of Columbia, *Report*, part 2 (Washington: 1898), p. 61. The figure for the Pennsylvania hospital in 1893—$1.36—was somewhat above that for about 1898 in the above report—$1.17. Cf. J. S. Billings and H. M. Hurd, *Hospitals, Dispensaries, and Nursing* (New York: 1894), p. 61.

108. U.S. Bureau of the Census, *Hospitals and Dispensaries, 1923* (Washington: 1925). Data for general and special hospitals (except Federal) are reported on pages 8 and 19. Adjusting for the different number of hospitals reporting and expenditures leads to a daily expenditure average of $2.92 per bed. Assuming 85% bed usage gives a figure of $3.34 per patient day.

Public Health Report No. 154, *Business Census of Hospitals, 1935* (Washington: 1939), pp. 13, 22 provides data on the average daily census and income for nonprofit plus proprietary general and special hospitals.

109. The bed-patient usage ratio in 1935 is near 90% for Federal mental

hospitals 85% for TB hospitals. But it was 61% for nonprofit hospitals, and a mere 45% for proprietary hospitals. We infer that the 1935 patient day cost ($5.42) was as high as it was because of the depression impact on utilization of existing facilities. It is therefore ignored for making the 1923–29 estimates.

110. Raymond Goldsmith, *A Study of Savings in the United States* (Princeton: 1955), vol. 1, pp. 527, 625. The weights were Goldsmith's estimates of total commissions paid by individuals to each group, from ibid., pp. 529, 625.

111. This series was benchmarked to 1900 and 1929 average expenditure per funeral figures, the derivation of which is described on pages 362–63 of *The American Economy*.

112. *Manpower*, p. 527, and Kendrick, *Productivity Trends*, pp. 506, 610.

113. Shaw, *Value Product*, pp. 292–93.

114. Ibid., pp. 290–91.

115. For materials, Shaw's auto price series was used. For labor average annual earnings in retail trade were used adjusted for productivity (*Manpower*, p. 526). (The BEA includes auto repair earnings with those of retail trade until 1948. For that year it estimates wages and salaries per full-time equivalent employee as the same in each sector.) The weights used were for the figures for wages and cost of materials in automobile repairing. Fourteenth Census, vol. VIII, *Manufactures*, p. 156.

116. American Petroleum Institute, *Petroleum Facts and Figures*, Centennial Edition, 1959 (New York: 1959), p. 379.

117. *Manpower*, p. 527. These were adjusted for productivity trends.

118. Ibid., p. 525. These were adjusted for productivity trends. The weights for combining these were gainful workers in (1) electric and street railways plus livery stables and (2) in steam railroad passenger service. (U.S. Census, Population, 1910 *Occupation Statistics* [Washington: 1914], pp. 412–14.) The passenger component of railroad employment was estimated at 24.6%, using revenue data from *Historical Statistics . . . to 1970*, pp. 730, 733.

119. Prices for the dictionary were kindly provided by Crawford Lincoln of the Merriam Company, while the (paperbound) Almanac prices were taken from its cover or masthead page.

120. The prices were generally an average of those for the January and July issues of each year as reprinted on the cover or masthead page.

121. BLS Bulletin 493, *Wholesale Prices, 1913 to 1928*, p. 208.

122. For the years after the bicycle craze had moderated—i.e., after about 1903—the share of cycles (which were classed as "durables") in the total was less than 10%.

123. The average value per radio receiver was computed for census years, as was that for upright pianos and upright players. The ratio of one average value to the other was then applied to Shaw's price index (for musical instruments) to give census date benchmarks. These were then interpolated by Shaw's price index to give a radio price series. *1929 Census of Manufactures II*, pp. 1128, 1330.

124. Including radio repairs, admissions to spectator amusements, clubs, commercial participation amusements, other.

125. Earnings from *Manpower in Economic Growth*, p. 526. Productivity from Kendrick, *Productivity Trends*, pp. 506, 610, averaging his trade, finance, and service.

126. U.S.D.A. Agriculture Handbook No. 118, *Major Statistical Series*, vol. 1, *Agricultural Prices and Parity* (Washington: 1957), p. 17. The 1900–10 extrapolation was by the average price of barley and oats. BLS Bulletin 269, *Wholesale Prices 1890–1919* (Washington: 1920), p. 30.

127. *Manpower in Economic Growth*, p. 527.

128. *Census of Religious Bodies: 1916* (Washington: 1919), p. 94. Paul Douglas, *Real Wages in the United States 1890–1926* (Boston: 1930), p. 386. Simon Kuznets, *National Income and Its Composition, 1919–1938* (New York: 1941), pp. 762, 765.

129. Ralph Hurlin, *Social Work Salaries* (New York: 1926), p. 6.

130. Paul Dickens, *The Transition Period in American International Financing: 1897 to 1914* (June 1933). Unpublished ms. in George Washington University Library. U.S. Bureau of Foreign and Domestic Commerce, *Economic Series No. 4, Overseas Travel and Travel Expenditures in the Balance of International Payments of the United States, 1919–1938*, by August Maffry (Washington: 1939).

131. Cf. Dickens, *Transition Period*, p. 274 and Maffry, *Economic Series No. 4*, pp. 61, 62.

132. C. H. Feinstein, *National Income, Expenditure and Outlay of the United Kingdom, 1855–1965* (Cambridge: 1972), table 62. The weights were 25, 25, 50. The resultant series was then converted by the exchange rate.

133. Food was weighted 50%; each of the others, 25%.

CHAPTER TEN

1. Census disclosure rules created a persistent problem for recent years. These suppress publication of data for detailed 3- or 4-digit industries that are rare in a given state. Usually one can utilize a relevant ratio from a related state and the somewhat broader SIC category. Thus for 1977 the average receipts per establishment in SIC 794, commercial sports, for the 3 establishments in Mississippi was assumed to equal that for the 4 establishments in Alabama, that figure then adjusted by the ratio of the receipts per establishment of each state for the larger SIC 79 group, "other amusement and recreation services." Since the choice of state and SIC group had to be made individually for each year, and each item, no program could be written. Obvious errors in the choice of state or SIC group for comparison had to be discovered through the regression printouts.

2. Richard Easterlin in Simon Kuznets and Dorothy Thomas, *Population Redistribution and Economic Growth*, the first volume of which is: Everett Lee, Ann Miller, Carol Brainerd, and Richard Easterlin, *Methodological Considerations and Reference Tables* (Philadelphia, 1957), pp. 717 ff.

Easterlin relied chiefly on earnings per worker shown in the Censuses of Manufacturers, Mines, Electrical Industries (telephones, power stations, etc.). He also used ICC reports on railways, and the construction trades data then reported by the Census of Manufacturers. For the remaining industries

Easterlin used differentials for manufacturing. The overall upper limit of the error for nonagricultural service income per worker in "most states" is judged to be 10%. (Ibid., pp. 721–23.)

3. LS, p. 367.

4. O, table 32.

5. The per capita adjustment was made to prevent heteroscedasticity. Data for twenty-five states were used: because the samples in eight states included two hundred or fewer families we omit them from the estimate.

6. This total is derived as part of the estimate for Meals and Beverages (*infra*).

7. E, p. 753.

8. O, table 32; E, p. 754.

9. Harold Barger, *Distribution's Place in the American Economy Since 1869* (1955), pp. 92, 131–33. His input into the distribution system is allocated to type of store, then adjusted upward for distributive spread, and the result gives total food sold by type of store. We use the resultant estimate for restaurants plus bars as a percentage of total food sales at retail.

10. The Commissioner's survey item for "food" is assumed to cover only off-premise food. Comparison of the "food" average for 25,440 families—$319.92 (p. 367) with that of $326.90 for 2,567 "normal" families, with itemized food such as fresh beef, salt beef, on through vinegar and pickles (p. 497), suggests that no meals were included. A residual "other food" item comes to only $21 per family.

11. A—table 11.

12. U.S. Bureau of Agricultural Economics, *Farm Wage Rates, Farm Employment and Related Data* (Jan. 1943), pp. 16, 17, 22, 23.

13. A—table 43.

14. O—table 32 and E—p. 754.

15. U.S. Commissioner of Labor, Twelfth Annual Report, 1897, *Economic Aspects of the Liquor Problem* (1898).

16. Ibid. p. 46. We used counts for "dealers and rectifiers." These include all retail and wholesale dealers—not merely the saloons and dealers specializing in alcohol but grocery stores, hotels, billiard parlors, and others with special tax stamps. Cf. pp. 112ff.

17. Ibid., pp. 110–11. Because the survey canvassed only "representative internal-revenue collection districts" in these states these figures were only used to compute averages per establishment, then raised to state totals using the establishment counts from p. 46.

18. The Commissioner's canvass for California provides capital data only for San Francisco and Los Angeles, and for New York State it omits New York City. For California a rural component was therefore estimated by multiplying capital per establishment in San Francisco and Los Angeles by the ratio of capital per establishment (*a*) in rural Ohio to (*b*) that for Cincinnati. A New York City component was estimated by computing a similar ratio of capital per establishment for Chicago to rural Illinois and applying it to the rural New York ratio. The resultant capital per establishment ratios were then weighted by the number of saloon keepers and bartenders in each area

to give state averages. These were then multiplied by the total liquor establishment count from the Commissioner's *Report* (p. 46).

19. O, table 32; E, p. 754.

20. The per capita adjustment was made to preclude heteroscedasticity dominating the results. The correlation included only thirteen states, New York being excluded because linearity could not be assumed to apply to its data as well.

21. LS, pp. 366–67.

22. State averages were computed, then averaged as the LS figures were averaged. Because only a single mountain state was surveyed the mountain and pacific regions were combined.

23. The survey figures for the District of Columbia were used, because it was basically a city. Using a regional average substantially affected by rural expenditures would yield too low a figure.

For New York the survey cannot reflect its major role as a regional and national center. We therefore use the New York occupation count times the service income figure in the regression above, and the regression coefficients, to estimate per capita clothing expenditures for New York.

24. O, table 32 and E, p. 754.

25. M, table 4.

26. O, table 32. The U.S. value of product total had been derived previously. (Cf. Lebergott, *The American Economy*, p. 341.) The servant income figures are derived in the section on domestic service (*infra*).

27. M, table 4.

28. Ibid.

29. Ibid.

30. W—p. 17.

31. Ibid., p. 12.

32. O—table 32.

33. Number of upholsterers from O-table 32, times service income per worker divided by number of families, P2, p. 605.

34. Sources and procedure were the same as those used above for the North Atlantic States.

35. The number of launderers and laundresses, laundry work, hand (female only), plus servants, housekeepers, and stewards was used, from O—T32. These state totals were then multiplied by the average wage per servant, derived below in connection with the estimate for domestic service.

36. W, pp. 976–77.

37. The lack of New Orleans sewers as late as 1902 is indicated by the lack of expenditures on sewers as late as 1902. (Bulletin of the U.S. Department of Labor [Sept. 1901], p. 925.)

38. W, p. 985.

39. LS, pp. 366–67.

40. O—table 32.

41. Lebergott, *The American Economy*, p. 354.

42. Servants (defined as for cleaning materials, *supra*) from O—table 32.

Earnings from U.S. Industrial Commission, *Report*, vol. XIV (1901), p. 748. The quality of these earnings data is discussed in L, pp. 502–4.

43. Confectionery earnings are from M—pp. 164–65. For certain Mountain and East South Central states such data were unavailable and an average was based on data for states from the region reporting in the survey.

44. M—table 4. Though other repair industries are reported in the census, they sold primarily to business.

45. O—table 32, E, p. 756.

46. Occupation counts from O—table 32 and service income from E—p. 756.

47. K, pp. 762, 763, 766 gives data enabling us to estimate curative wages and salaries plus income of curative entrepreneurs (i.e., approximately gross income) divided by the number of curative entrepreneurs. This average was run back by average income per employee in professional service, from L, p. 526. Wages and salaries per curative employee in 1919 were similarly computed (K, pp. 762, 765) and run back by earnings per full-time employee in medical service (L, p. 527).

48. Census, *Benevolent Institutions, 1904* (1905), table 2.

49. *Polk Medical Register of the United States and Canada, 1900.*

50. From this comparison we exclude hospitals with over two hundred beds, those being largely the state institutions for the insane and the aged.

51. O—table 32 and E, p. 756.

52. The Spectator Company, *The Insurance Yearbook, 1900–1901, Life and Miscellaneous*, pp. 389–90. An approximate check was made by computing the number of insurance agents (using ratios from the 1900 Census of (*a*) insurance agents to (*b*) insurance plus real estate agents, times the 1900 Census total for the latter combined group) times nonagricultural service income per worker. The results were similar for most densely settled states. For the plains states it was clear that formal agent representation understated insurance premia and, presumably, cost of operation.

53. O— table 32; E, p. 756.

54. O—table 32 and E—p. 754.

55. This estimate is derived by the author in Lance Davis et al., *American Economic Growth: An Economist's History of the United States* (1972), p. 220.

56. Leo Wolman, *Ebb and Flow in Trade Unionism* (1936), Appendix table 1.

57. O—table 32.

58. Thirteenth Census, 1910, vol. IV, *Population*, table II. E, p. 756.

59. Census, *Street and Electric Railways, 1907*, pp. 120, 201. The data used relate to 1902. For the omitted states the number of persons occupied as street railway employees (O—table 32) was multiplied by the gross income/occupied ratio for other states within the region.

60. The number of such persons engaged is from O—table 32. Average receipts per person engaged were taken as identical with those per person employed in street and electric railways.

61. These are itemized in "Statistics of Cities" in U.S. Department of Labor, Bulletin 36 (Sept. 1901), table XVIII.

62. M3, pp. 1056–57.

63. O—table 32; E, p. 756.

64. Product data from M—table 4.

65. O—table 32, E—p. 756.

66. A2, p. 781: "value of products not fed to livestock."

67. *Annual Report of the Secretary of the Treasury on the State of the Finances, 1900*, pp. 600–602. The U.S. personnel total was estimated by multiplying the 1900 Census count of actors (O—p. xxiii) by the ratio in 1910, of actors to the sum of billiard and poolroom keepers (13,859) plus bowling alleys, dance halls, etc. keepers (2,902). (1910 Census of Population, pp. 428, 430.)

68. O—table 32.

69. Annual reports of the Department of the Interior, *Report of the Commissioner of Education*, vol. 2 (1902).

70. Ibid., p. 1632. "total income colleges and universities" minus state, municipal, and Federal appropriations. Expenditures from endowment are included in the BEA personal consumption figures as well as tuition and fees.

71. Tuition and fees from ibid., pp. 1929–30. Income of private schools was estimated as the number of students enrolled in such schools times income per student, ibid., p. 1931 (number of secondary students) and pp. 1942–43 (private expenditures for high schools).

72. Ibid., pp. 1530–31 gives the number of elementary students in private and parochial schools. The income per student is estimated as the "expenditure for all purposes except loans and bonds" divided by the number of students in such schools. Ibid., pp. 1530–33.

73. Number engaged from O—table 33, and income from E, p. 756.

74. Bureau of the Census, *Religious Bodies: 1906*, part 1, p. 521. We averaged the figures for 1890 and 1906.

75. *Annual Reports of the Post Office Department for 1900* (1900), p. 986.

76. Cf. Shaw's estimates in *Survey of Current Business* (June 1944).

77. Simon Kuznets, *Commodity Flow and Capital Formation* (1938), pp. 82, 136.

78. Harold Barger, *Distribution's Place in the American Economy Since 1869* (1955), p. 92.

79. DHEW (SSA) 75-11906, Barbara Cooper, Nancy Worthington, and Paula Piro, *Personal Health Care Expenditures by State* (1975), vol. II, table 18 gives figures on private expenditures for fiscal year 1969 on drugs and sundries, eyeglasses and appliances. We use these to allocate the relevant BEA totals. These estimates take advantage of unpublished IRS data, special surveys by the American Optometric Association, etc.

CHAPTER ELEVEN

1. Maurice Scott has derived a nonresidential GNP series from Kendrick's GNP series. He did so by deducting (a) Kuznets's consumers' outlay on rent, from Scott's constant-dollar series, and (b) from his current-dollar series, the constant-dollar series multiplied by the BLS index of rents. (Maurice Fitzgerald Scott, *A New View of Economic Growth* [Oxford: 1989], pp.

529–31.) Because Kendrick implicitly adopted the Grebler deflator to create his current-dollar series this change produces an incomparability between Scott's current- and constant-dollar series.

2. *Inter alia*: Nathan Balke and Robert Gordon, "The Estimation of Prewar Gross National Product Methodology and New Evidence," *J. Political Economy* (Feb. 1989), pp. 38–92, and Christina Romer, "The Prewar Business Cycle Reconsidered," *J. Political Economy* (Feb. 1989), pp. 1–37.

3. Christina Romer, "Prewar," p. 21. Romer has similarly noted that "to impose the postwar relationship is straightforward" for creating unemployment series as well. Cf. her "Spurious Volatility in Historical Unemployment Data," *J. of Political Economy* (Feb. 1986), p. 30.

4. Each variable is utilized in percentage deviations from trend. We abstract from the fuller model in Romer (1988) and (1989), to focus on the key parameter. Balke and Gordon advance the analysis, as noted below, but nonetheless adopt the model's key element.

5. Romer truncates the entire sequence to:

By regression: (1) $GNP_{t2} = f(\gamma C_{t2})$
By assertion: (7) $\gamma C_{t2} = \gamma C_{t1}$
By regression: (8) $GNP_1 = f(\gamma C_{t1})$

6. Romer's "Is the Stabilization of the Postwar Economy a Figment of the Data?" (1984 ms. nl, 2) described "unquestioning acceptance of the historical data," citing Lucas, Tobin, and Baily.

7. "Imposing the postwar model of the relationship between the actual and constructed series may yield a more accurate estimate." "To impose the postwar relationship is straightforward." "I impose that U1 = UA in each Census year." (Romer, "Spurious Volatility," p. 30.)

8. "Misspecified" (p. 71). "Unlike Romer, we do not include the postwar years in the sample period of our regression. The question under discussion, after all, is whether the prewar and postwar periods are different. The last thing we would want to do is to answer the question in advance by assuming that the prewar and the postwar periods exhibit the same structure" (p. 68). Their model appears on pages 42–46.

9. Romer, "Prewar Business," p. 20 finds .66 "not surprising," but for estimation corrects by the Cochrane-Orcutt procedure.

10. Table 6. We refer to the "components method" equation, on which their new GNP series rests (table 10). They emphasize "the superiority of the components method" as yielding "more precise parameter estimates" than the "indicators method" (pp. 40, 43). We therefore comment only on correlations from the former.

11. Balke-Gordon, "Estimation," tables 6, 10.

Following her approach they first used commodity output as the only explanatory variable, also getting a very low D-W (of .501—for a shorter period than Romer). Including two additional variables, they increased the D-W to 1.869. Adding these variables "markedly improves the fit of the equations and eliminates positive serial correlation in the residuals." "Almost all" of the improvement in fit and serial correlation compared to "Romer's results is contributed by construction output." Their third variable, transportation and communication activity, contributes little (p. 71).

12. P. 69. They understandably rely on data for 1909–38, not 1909–28. Yet two of their three explanatory variables are not even significant at the 1 percent level. In their "alternative deflators" equation the correlation also rises spectacularly—from − .060 to .705—when the period is extended (p. 76).

13. P. 57n. Their implicit theory for estimating O_{t1} largely accounts for their very low R^2 (.096), and the sensitivity of the coefficients when ten depression-year observations are added. Contributing to all this is the fact that the same construction materials series appears in two of their three explanatory variables. For materials constitute about half of all "construction activity" and are also included in "commodity output."

14. William Lough, *High Level Consumption* (New York: 1935), Appendix A. J. Frederic Dewhurst and Associates, *America's Needs and Resources* (New York: 1947), Appendix 6, and (New York: 1955), Appendix 4-4.

15. His procedure is described as follows: "From 1909 to 1927, Barger linked to Shaw, and Lough linked to Barger-Shaw." But neither Barger nor Shaw provided any data on "rent and imputed rent" for that period.

16. Little difference for tobacco appears.

17. Lough, *High Level*, p. 261.

18. USDA, Agriculture Handbook No. 118, *Major Statistical Series of the USDA, Gross and Net Farm Income* (Washington: 1957) vol. 3, p. 34, or *Historical Statistics . . . to 1970*, p. 485, and Lough, *High Level*, pp. 236, 249.

19. Macro consumption measures have indeed been investigated since the days of Henry Shultz and Frederic Waugh. The comprehensive and pioneering work of Houthakker and Taylor in the 1970s develops far more sophisticated analyses than, e.g., Wold and Jureen, and Ferber and Verdoorn, but still had to rely on only price and income variables. Almost two decades later cogent and elegant analyses by Deaton do the same. In time series analysis collinearity is so great that it is almost impossible to partition the contribution by slow moving changes in other critical variables.

20. Martha Olney, *Buy Now, Pay Later* (Chapel Hill, 1991).

21. For appliances, the sole major exception, she reports a 30% lower 1900 benchmark level.

22. U.S. Bureau of Labor Statistics, *Consumer Expenditure Survey: Integrated Survey Data, 1984–1986* (Washington: 1989). Bulletin 2333, p. 6.

23. BLS Bulletin 2354, *Consumer Expenditure Survey, 1984* (Washington: 1990) p. 6.

24. The introduction of a daily diary record for food items plus many clothing and house furnishing items 1980ff. is not associated with improved coverage, as table 1 indicates.

25. Census data from Miss Pam Palmer of the Business Division. The BLS sample count appears in BLS Bulletin 2246, *Consumer Expenditure Survey, 1982–83* (Washington: 1986), p. 137.

26. That the two may be reasonably compared is indicated by a study of

the BLS chief economist, who used census data to measure bias in the BLS rent index. Cf. Jack Triplett in Paul Earl, *Analysis of Inflation* (Lexington: 1975), p. 47.

27. Both agencies use the same census definition for the geographic boundaries of the SMSAs. And the near identity of mean and median in 10 SMSAs suggests that bias, not conceptual difference, explains the startling differences for Cleveland, Philadelphia, Seattle, Miami, etc.

28. Years ago I had access to some city totals from the BLS. They showed, e.g., that for entire major cities no expenditures for electric light bulbs were reported. If such city item totals were available for scholarly analysis one might be able to be more specific about the adequacy of the individual items that constitute the basis on which the BLS region and U.S. totals for those and other figures rest.

29. The 1900 income estimates, by Easterlin, had to rely on much thinner source data. Major differences in 1900 for Montana and Arizona probably reflect his assumption that the average rate of return to U.S. capital was identical with that for mineral reserves. That assumption was critical only in states with major reserves, such as Montana and Arizona.

However, reserves were held for current income plus expected capital gains—not merely income. Copper markets for electrical motors, distribution lines, telephone lines, etc. were expanding in the first flush of the electrical revolution. Thus, expected capital gains were no trivial portion of total return to capital. If capital markets were functioning reasonably well, therefore, the returns to mining investments could not have paid both the usual rate of return in the form of current income and also been supplemented by expected capital gains.

30. Derived in Chapter Note A. Comparisons are made using the BEA accounts prior to the 1993 revisions. Thus, e.g., PCE of 2045 has been revised to 2059.

31. These are (in table 11.8): MLSBEV—meals plus beverages, ALOFPRM—alcohol, off-premise, JEWELRY—jewelry, CLOTHING—clothing, LOCINT—intercity transport, local (i.e., taxis, etc.), SPECSP—spectator sports, COMPTAM—commercial amusements

Hawaii, Florida, and Nevada have very high figures for (1) meals and beverages; (2) other housing (i.e., hotels, motels); (3) jewelry; and (4) local transport (i.e., taxis). Arizona, the District of Columbia, and Oregon also had high expenditures for (1), while the District of Columbia, Vermont, and Utah did for (2).

Selective purchases by out of state residents boosted purchases of liquor in New Hampshire and the District of Columbia; and commercial spectator amusements in Vermont, Florida, Rhode Island (race tracks), and Nevada (casinos).

32. Cf. "Evaluation of State Personal Income Estimates," *Survey of Current Business* (Dec. 1990). The BEA did not compare the personal income estimates with its new GDP by state (SCB, May 1988). The conceptual difference is so substantial that comparison would offer little insight.

33. (*Supra*) Richard Easterlin, "State Income Estimates," in Everett S. Lee,

Ann Miller, Carol Brainerd, and Richard Easterlin, *Population Redistribution and Economic Growth, United States, 1870–1950, Methodological Considerations and Reference Tables* (Philadelphia: 1957), p. 753.

34. Samuel H. Preston and Michael R. Haines, *Fatal Years* (Princeton: 1991), pp. 224–25. Preston and Haines compare their earnings figures with Easterlin's personal income series, instead of his more comparable "service income."

35. In 1982 the IRS had not yet tried to prevent auto dealers from taking payment in briefcases full of large bills.

· BIBLIOGRAPHY ·

Abramowitz, Moses. *Inventories and Business Cycles* (New York: 1950).

American Economic Review (May 1989).

American Petroleum Institute. *Petroleum Facts and Figures*, Centennial Edition (New York: 1959).

Angresano, James. *Comparative Economics* (Englewood Cliffs, N.J.: 1992).

Arrow, Kenneth, in Robin Hogarth and Melvin Reder, *Rational Choice* (Chicago: 1987).

Ayers, Leonard. *The War With Germany* (Washington: 1919).

Baker, Paul, and Michael Little, eds., *Man in the Andes, A Multidisciplinary Study of High-Altitude Quechau* (Stroudsburg: 1976).

Balke, Nathan, and Robert Gordon. "The Estimation of Prewar Gross National Product Methodology and New Evidence." *J. Political Economy* (Feb. 1989).

Barger, Harold. *Distribution's Place in the American Economy Since 1869* (New York: 1955).

Barnes, R. and R. Gillingham. "Demographic Effects in Demand Analysis . . . ," *Review of Economics and Statistics* (Nov. 1984).

Becker, Gary. *The Economic Approach to Human Behavior* (Chicago: 1976).

Becker, G., and G. Stigler. "De Gustibus Non Est Disputandum." *American Economic Review* (March 1977).

Bergson, Abram. "Income Inequality Under Soviet Socialism." *Journal of Economic Literature* (Sept. 1984).

Billings, J. S., and H. M. Hurd. *Hospitals, Dispensaries and Nursing* (New York: 1894).

Bragg, Melvyn. *Richard Burton: A Life, 1925–1984* (Boston: 1988).

Buchanan, James. *L.S.E. Essays on Cost* (London: 1973).

Buck, Trevor, and John Cole. *Modern Soviet Economic Performance* (New York: 1987).

U.S. Census. *Census of Religious Bodies: 1916* (Washington: 1919).

U.S. Census. *Historical Statistics . . . to 1970.* (Washington: 1975).

Charemza, W., M. Granicki, and R. E. Quandt. "Modelling Parallel Markets in Centrally Planned Economies." *European Economic Review* (April 1988).

Cheng, Nien. *Life and Death in Shanghai* (London: 1986).

Collins, Fred L. *Consolidated Gas Co. of N.Y.: A History* (New York: 1934).

U.S. Commissioner of Labor, *Eighteenth Annual Report* (1904).

U.S. Commissioner of Labor, Twelfth Annual Report, *Economic Aspects of the Liquor Problem* (Washington: 1898).

Congressional Record (Aug. 27, 1913).

Cyert, Richard, and Morris De Groot. *Bayesian Analysis and Uncertainty in Economic Theory* (Totowa, N.J.: 1987).

Darby, Michael. "Postwar U.S. Consumption, Consumer Expenditures and Saving." *American Economic Review* (May 1975).

Deaton, Angus, and John Muellbauer. *Economics and Consumer Behavior* (Cambridge, 1980).

Dewhurst, J. Frederic, and Associates. *America's Needs and Resources* (New York: 1947 and 1955).

Di Maio, Alfred. *Soviet Urban Housing* (New York: 1974).

Dickens, Paul. *The Transition Period in American International Financing: 1897 to 1914* (June 1933) (unpublished ms.) in George Washington University Library.

Dobson, John M. *A History of American Enterprise* (Englewood Cliffs, N.J.: 1988).

Douglas, Paul. *Real Wages in the United States 1890–1926* (Boston: 1930).

DuBoff, Richard B. *Accumulation and Power: An Economic History of the United States* (Armonk, N.Y.: 1989).

Faulkner, Harold. *American Economic History* (New York: 1960).

Federal Reserve Bulletin. "Survey of Consumer Finances, 1983" (Sept. 1984).

Feinstein, C. H. *National Income, Expenditure and Outlay of the United Kingdom, 1855–1965* (Cambridge: 1972).

Feldbrugge, F.J.M. "Government and the Shadow Economy in the Soviet Union." *Soviet Studies* (Oct. 1984).

Feshbach, Murray, in 97th Cong., 2nd Sess., Joint Economic Committee. *Soviet Economy in the 1980s* (Washington: Dec. 1982).

Field, Mark. "Medical Care in the Soviet Union," in Horst Herlemann, *Quality of Life* (1987).

U.S. Census, Fifteenth Census. *Manufactures, Vol. II* (Washington: 1933).

Fisher, Franklin. *Disequilibrium Foundations of Equilibrium Economics* (Cambridge, Mass.: 1983).

Glass, Senator Carter. *An Adventure in Constructive Finance* (Garden City, N.Y.: 1927).

Goldenweiser, A. E. "The Farmer's Income." *American Economic Review* (March 1916), pp. 42–48.

Goldman, Marshall. *USSR in Crisis* (New York: 1983).

Goldsmith, Raymond. *A Study of Savings in the United States* (Princeton: 1955), I.

Grebler, Leo, et al. *Capital Formation in Residential Real Estate* (New York: 1956).

Harasymiw, Bohdan. *Political Elite Recruitment in the Soviet Union* (New York: 1984).

Herlemann, Horst. *Quality of Life in the Soviet Union* (Boulder, Colo: 1987).

Houthakker, H. S., and L. Taylor. *Consumer Demand in the United States: Analyses and Projections* (Cambridge, Mass.: 1970).

Hurlin, Ralph. *Social Work Salaries* (New York: 1926).

Internal Revenue Service. *Individual Income Tax Returns 1985* (Washington: 1987).

U.S. Joint Economic Committee. *Consumption in the U.S.S.R.: An International Comparison* (Washington: 1981).

Katsenelinboigen, Aron. *Studies in Soviet Economic Planning* (White Plains, N.Y.: 1978).

Kendrick, John. *Productivity Trends in the United States* (Princeton: 1961).

Keynes, John Maynard. *The Economic Consequences of the Peace* (New York: 1920).

———. *The General Theory of Employment, Interest and Money* (New York: 1936).

King, Willford I. *The National Income and Its Purchasing Power* (New York: 1930).

Kokoski, M., P. Cardiff, and B. Moulton. *Interarea Price Indices for Consumer Goods and Services.* BLS Working Paper 256 (July 1994).

Kuromiya, Hiroaki. *Stalin's Industrial Revolution* (Cambridge: 1988).

Kuteinkov, Andrei. "Soviet Society—Much More Unequal than U.S." *Wall Street Journal* (Jan. 26, 1990).

Kuznets, Simon. *National Income and Its Composition, 1919–1938* (New York: 1941).

———. *Value of Product Since 1869* (New York: 1946).

Lebergott, Stanley. *Manpower in Economic Growth* (New York: 1964).

———. *The American Economy: Income, Wealth and Want* (Princeton: 1976).

Lester, Richard. *Economics of Labor* (New York: 1964).

Leuchtenburg, William E., in John A. Garraty, *Interpreting American History* (New York: 1970).

Lewbel, Arthur. "A Unified Approach . . . to Demand Systems." *Review of Economic Studies* (1985).

Lough, William. *High Level Consumption* (New York: 1935).

Maffry, August. U.S. Bureau of Foreign and Domestic Commerce, *Economic Series No. 4, Overseas Travel and Travel Expenditures in the Balance of International Payments of the United States, 1919–1938* (Washington: 1939).

Matthews, Mervyn. "Top Incomes in the U.S.S.R.," in North Atlantic Treaty Organization, *Economic Aspects of Life in the U.S.S.R.* (Brussels: 1975).

McAuley, Alistair. *Economic Welfare in the Soviet Union* (Madison: 1979).

Mendershausen, Horst. *Changes in Income Distribution During the Great Depression* (New York: 1946).

Moggridge, Donald, ed. *The Collected Writings of John Maynard Keynes* (London: 1973).

Morrison, Christian. "Income Distribution in East European and Western Countries." *Journal of Comparative Economics* (June 1984).

Morton, Henry, in Horst Herlemann, *Quality of Life* (1987).

———, in U.S. Joint Economic Committee, *Soviet Economy in a Time of Change* (Washington: 1979).

———. "Who Gets What, When and How? Housing in the Soviet Union." *Soviet Studies* (April 1980), pp. 121–44.

Mussa, Michael. *A Study in Macroeconomics* (Amsterdam: 1976).

New York Times (Feb. 4, 1990).

Nicholls, William. *Price Policies in the Cigarette Industry* (Nashville: 1951).

Niemi, Albert. *U.S. Economic History* (Chicago: 1986).

North Atlantic Treaty Organization. *Economic Aspects of Life in the U.S.S.R.* (Brussels: 1975).

Nove, Alec. "The Class Structure of the Soviet Union Revisited." *Soviet Studies* (July 1983).

O'Hearn, Dennis. "The Consumer Second Economy: Size and Effects." *Soviet Studies* (April 1980).

Ofer, Gur, and Joyce Pickersgill. "Soviet Household Saving." *Quarterly Journal of Economics* (Aug. 1980), pp. 121–44.

Okun, Arthur. *Equality and Economic Efficiency* (Washington: 1975).

Olney, Martha. *Buy Now Pay Later* (Chapel Hill: 1991).

Pierson Albert. *Consumption of Firewood in the United States* (Washington: Sept. 1910). Forest Service Circular 181.

Pollak, R. A., and T. Wales. "Demographic Variables in Demand Analysis." *Econometrica* (Nov. 1981).

Primont, Diane, and Mary Kokosi. *Differences in Food Prices Across U.S. Cities.* BLS Working Paper 209 (Jan. 1991).

Public Health Report No. 154. *Business Census of Hospitals, 1935* (Washington: 1939).

Quarterly Report, Chief, Bureau of Statistics, Treasury Department. *Imports, Exports, Immigration and Navigation of the United States . . . 1886* (Washington: 1887).

Rees, Albert. *Real Wages in Manufacturing, 1890–1914* (New York: 1961).

Romer, Christina. "World War I and the Postwar Depression: A Reinterpretation based on alternative estimates of GNP." *Journal of Monetary Economics* (July 1988).

———. "The Prewar Business Cycle Reconsidered." *Journal of Political Economy* (Feb. 1989).

———. "Spurious Volatility in Historical Unemployment Data." *Journal of Political Economy* (Feb. 1986).

Santayana, George. *The Life of Reason, Reason in Religion* (New York: 1905).

Schlesinger, Arthur. *The Crisis of the Old Order, 1919–1933* (Boston: 1957).

Schumpeter, Joseph. *History of Economic Analysis* (New York: 1954).

Schurr, Sam, and Bruce Netschert. *Energy in the American Economy, 1850–1975* (Baltimore: 1960).

Scott, Maurice Fitzgerald. *A New View of Economic Growth* (Oxford: 1989).

Sen, Amartya. *Poverty and Famines* (Oxford: 1981).

Shaw, William. *Value of Commodity Product Since 1869* (New York: 1947).

Shevchenko, Arkady. *Breaking With Moscow* (New York: 1985).

Shipler, David. *Russia, Broken Idols, Solemn Dreams* (New York: 1983).

Simmel, Georg. *The Philosophy of Money* (London: 1900, reprint 1978).

Strauss, Frederick, and Louis Bean. "Evaluation of State Personal Income Estimates" *Gross Farm Income and Indices of Farm Production and Prices in the United States, 1869–1937*, Agriculture, Technical Bulletin 703.

Szelenyi, Ivan. *Urban Inequalities Under State Socialism* (London: 1983).

Temin, Peter. *Did Monetary Forces Cause The Great Depression?* (New York: 1978).

————. *Lessons From the Great Depression* (Cambridge, Mass.: 1989).

Theil, Henri. *Principles of Econometrics* (New York: 1971).

Time (April 10, 1989).

Triplett, Jack, in Paul Earl, *Analysis of Inflation* (Lexington: 1975), pp. 19–83.

Tsakloglou, Panos. "Estimation and Comparison of Two Simple Models of Equivalence Scales for the Cost of Children." *Economic Journal* (March 1991), pp. 343–57.

U.S. Bureau of Economic Analysis. *National Income and Product Accounts of the United States Vol. 1, 1929–58* (Washington: 1993). *Vol. 2, 1959–88* (Washington: 1992).

————. *The National Income and Product Accounts of the United States, 1929–82* (Washington: 1986).

U.S. BLS Bulletin 77. *Retail Prices of Food, 1890–1902* (Washington: 1908).

U.S. BLS Bulletin 105. *Retail Prices 1890 to 1911* (Washington: 1912).

U.S. BLS Bulletin 184, U.S. Bureau of Labor Statistics. *Retail Prices of Food, 1907 to June 1915* (Washington: 1916).

U.S. BLS Bulletin 269. *Wholesale Prices 1890–1919* (Washington: 1920).

U.S. BLS Bulletin 493. *Wholesale Prices 1913 to 1928* (Washington: 1929).

U.S. BLS Bulletin 495. *Retail Prices, 1890 to 1929* (Washington: 1929).

U.S. BLS Bulletin 628. *Changes in Retail Prices of Gas, 1923–36* (Washington: 1937).

U.S. BLS Bulletin 691. *Changes in Cost of Living in Large Cities in the United States, 1913–1941* (Washington: 1941).

U.S. BLS Bulletin 822. *Family Spending and Saving in Wartime* (Washington: 1945).

U.S. BLS Bulletin 2246. *Consumer Expenditure Survey, 1982–83* (Washington: 1986).

U.S. BLS Bulletin 2267. *Consumer Expenditure Survey: Interview Survey, 1984* (Washington: 1986).

U.S. BLS Bulletin 2333. *Consumer Expenditure Survey: Integrated Survey Data, 1984–1986* (Washington: 1989).

U.S. BLS Bulletin 2354. *Consumer Expenditure Survey, 1984* (Washington: 1990).

U.S. Commissioner of Labor, Eighteenth Annual Report, 1903. *Cost of Living and Retail Prices of Food* (Washington: 1904).

U.S. Department of Agriculture. *Agricultural Economic Report No. 138, Food, Consumption, Prices, Expenditures* (Washington: 1956).

U.S.D.A. Agriculture Handbook No. 118. *Major Statistical Series*, vol. 1, *Agricultural Prices and Parity* (Washington: 1957).

USDA, Agriculture Handbook No. 118. *Major Statistical Series of the USDA, Gross and Net Farm Income* (Washington: 1957).

1900 Census. *Agriculture*, part 2 (Washington: 1903).

1900 Census. *Manufactures*, part 1 (Washington: 1902).

1900 Census. *Occupations at the Twelfth Census* (Washington: 1904).

1910 Census. *Agriculture, 1909 and 1910* (Washington: 1913).

1910 Census. *Manufactures, 1909* (Washington: 1913).

1920 Census. *Agriculture* (Washington: 1922).

1920 Census. *Manufactures, 1909* (Washington: 1923).

1920 Census. *Manufactures, 1919* (Washington: 1923).

1930 Census. *Agriculture* (Washington: 1923).

1930 Census. *Manufactures, 1929* (Washington: 1933).

1980 Census of Housing. *General Housing Characteristics, United States Summary* (Washington: 1983).

U.S. Census. *Hospitals and Dispensaries, 1923* (Washington: 1925).

U.S. Census. *Manufactures, 1914* (Washington: 1918–1919).

U.S. Census. *Population, 1910, Occupation Statistics* (Washington: 1914).

U.S. Census. *Statistical Abstract, 1922* (Washington: 1923).

U.S. Census. *Statistical Abstract, 1974* (Washington: 1975).

U.S. Census. *Wealth, Debt and Taxation* (Washington: 1907).

U.S. Census. *Manufactures, 1914* (Washington: 1933).

U.S. Congress, 55th Cong., 2nd Sess. H.R. 776, Joint Select Committee to Investigate the Charities and Reformatory Institutions in the District of Columbia. *Report*, part 2 (Washington: 1898).

Voslensky, Michael. *Nomenklatura* (Garden City, N.Y.: 1984).

Wall Street Journal (March 24, 1989).

———. (Aug. 1987).

War Department. *Annual Reports, 1917* (Washington: 1918).

———. *Annual Reports, 1918* (Washington: 1919).

Warburton, Clark. *The Economic Results of Prohibition* (New York: 1932).

Wold, Herman, and Lars Jureen. *Demand Analyses* (New York: 1953).

The American Racing Manual, 1971 edition.

Richard Easterlin, "State Income Estimates," in Everett S. Lee, Ann Miller, Carol Brainerd, and Richard Easterlin, *Population Redistribution and Economic Growth, United States, 1870–1950, Methodological Considerations and Reference Tables* (Philadelphia: 1957).

Encyclopedia of Baseball.

Friedman, Milton, and Kuznets, Simon. *Income from Independent Professional Practice* (New York, 1945).

Health Insurance Institute, *Source Book of Health Insurance*, 1978–79.

The Spectator, Vol. CXXV (July 24, 1930).

U.S. Bureau of Economic Analysis, *Survey of Current Business*, August 1977–August 1980.

U.S. Bureau of Labor Statistics. Bulletin 506, *Handbook of American Trade Unions*, 1929.

U.S. Bureau of Internal Revenue, *Statistics of Income, Individuals, 1929.*

U.S. Internal Revenue Service, *Statistics of Income, 1970, Individual Income Tax Returns.*

———, *Statistics of Income, 1977, Individual Income Tax Returns.*

USDA, Economic Research Service, *Farm Income, State Estimates 1949–1970.*

———, Statistical Bulletin 678, *Economic Indicators of the Farm Sector Income and Balance Sheet Statistics.*

Federal Communications Commission, *Statistics of Communications Common Carriers*, Year Ended 1970.

——, *Statistics of Communications Common Carriers*, Year Ended December 1977.

U.S. Federal Power Commission, *Typical Electric Bills*, Jan. 1, 1978.

U.S. National Center for Education Statistics, *Digest of Educational Statistics, 1980.*

——, *Financial Statistics of Higher Education, 1969–1970.*

——, *Residence and Migration of College Students, Fall 1968.*

——, *Financial Statistics of Institutions of Higher Education, Current Funds Revenues and Expenditures, 1969–70.*

U.S. Office of Education. Biennial Survey of Education, 1928–30.

U.S. Census, 1900, *Agriculture, Part I* (Washington, 1903).

U.S. Census, 1930, *Distribution Vol. 1, Retail Distribution by States.*

——, *Occupations by States.*

——, *Census of Electrical Industries, 1937.*

U.S. Census. *Census of Electrical Industries, 1927.*

——, *Central Electric Light and Power Stations.*

——, *Electric Railways and Affiliated Motor Bus Lines 1927.*

——, *Current Population Survey Reports, Series P-25, No. 488,* "Estimates of (Population of States: July 1, 1971 and 1972)."

——, *Financial Statistics of Cities having a Population of Over 36,000, 1929*

——, *County Business Patterns, 1977.*

——, *Religious Bodies, 1906.*

——, *Statistical Abstract, 1931.*

——, *Statistical Abstract of the United States, 1971.*

——, *Statistical Abstract of the United States, 1972.*

1967 Census of Business, *Retail Trade Merchandise Line Sales,* 50 Individual State Reports.

——, Vol. 1, *Retail Trade, Subject Reports.*

——, Vol. V. *Selected Services, Area Statistics.*

——, Vol. III, *Wholesale Trade, Subject Reports.*

Census of Governments, 1977, *Compendium of Government Finances.*

Census of Manufactures, 1967, *Summary and Subject Statistics, Vol. 1.*

1970 Census of Housing, Vol. 1, Part 1, *Housing Characteristics for States, Cities and Counties,* U.S. Summary.

1970 Census of Population, *General Economic and Social Characteristics* PC(1)-C1, U.S. Summary.

——, *Detailed Characteristics,* Individual State volumes.

1972 Census of Governments, Vol. 4, *Government Finances,* No. 5, *Compendium of Government Finances.*

1972 Census of Manufactures, *Industry Statistics,* Vol. II.

1972 Census of Retail Trade, Merchandise Line Sales, microfiches for the individual states.

——, Vol. 1, *Summary and Subject Statistics.*

1972 Census of Selected Service Industries, Vol. 1, *Summary and Subject Statistics.*

1972 Census of Transportation, Vol. 1, *National Travel Survey.*

1977 Census: Retail Trade, *Merchandise Line Statistics from Microfiches.*
———, *Subject Statistics*, Vol. 1.
1977 Census of Services, *Geographic Area Series.*
1980 Census of Housing, *General Housing Characteristics, (HC 80-1-A8).*
U.S. Postmaster General, Report for 1929.
World Almanac and Book of Facts for 1930.

· I N D E X ·

DATE DUE